Pagan Consent Culture

Edited by Christine Hoff Kraemer

and Yvonne Aburrow

Amanda
Lee
morris

2019

Pagan Consent Culture

Building Communities of
Empathy and Autonomy

Edited by Christine Hoff Kraemer
and Yvonne Aburrow

Hubbardston, Massachusetts

Asphodel Press
12 Simonds Hill Road
Hubbardston, MA 01452

Pagan Consent Culture:
Building Communities of Empathy and Autonomy
© 2015 Christine Hoff Kraemer and Yvonne Aburrow
978-1-938197-17-8

Printed in cooperation with
Lulu Enterprises, Inc.
860 Aviation Parkway, Suite 300
Morrisville, NC 27560

Contents

(handwritten annotation): Put on teor website & link up read & use?

"The only consent that matters is the kind given freely and enthusiastically."

Introduction

Christine Hoff Kraemer, with Yvonne Aburrow

> *The world we envision is one in which genuine pleasure is celebrated—not feared, controlled, or commodified. Where the only consent that matters is the kind given freely and enthusiastically. Where each person's body, regardless of gender, is theirs to do with whatever pleases them—and to keep safe from whatever doesn't. It's a world that's much harder to reach than it is to see, but that's not stopping us from trying...*
>
> *– Margaret Cho, Yes Means Yes!, p. 8*

Empathy. Autonomy. Relationship.

This anthology is part of a collective effort to dream a radical new culture into being. In this culture, respect for individual autonomy—referred to in this collection as "sovereignty," "wildness," "self-possession," and by other names—is one of the principles that bind us into community.

To some, putting "individual autonomy" and "community" together in the same breath seems almost nonsensical. Wasn't individualism the force behind colonialism, the drive to expand national territories no matter who was displaced, enslaved, or slaughtered in the process? Isn't the principle of autonomy invoked by those claiming that abusive online speech is protected under the First Amendment? Doesn't the quest for individual autonomy necessarily undermine community, make us unable to tolerate to the limits posed by committed relationships, and weaken our willingness to make necessary compromises?

There is truth to this view. In all our communities, the desires of the individual and those of the group are often in tension. Yet there is a power here that calls to Pagans of many traditions: the possibility of finding that paradoxical place where the push and pull between individual and community ultimately serve both. There, the emotional awareness and other-orientedness required for empathy can balance with a passion for self-knowledge and self-expression. There, we find a mystery, also called here by many names: Presence. Goddess. Grace. Love.

With humility and hope, we offer these essays as guides to building Pagan cultures of empathy and autonomy, freedom and connection: in other words, Pagan consent culture.

Pagan Consent Culture and How to Use This Book

In a consent culture, the individual is considered to be the best judge of their own wants and needs. Seeking clear consent to social interactions, especially those involving touch or sexual contact, is the expected norm. Because each adult is fully in charge of their own body and mind, it is a violation to try to force them into an activity against their will, or to forcibly prevent them from engaging in an activity they desire (so long as that activity does not do harm). In a consent culture, children are prepared for adulthood through being given as much autonomy as is appropriate for their age and maturity level, but they remain their parents' legal and moral responsibility until they reach their community's age of consent or age of majority.

Pagan consent culture grounds the concept of consent in contemporary Pagan values, stories, and practices, which vary from tradition to tradition. Contemporary Paganism is an umbrella term for a variety of associated religious paths that often include devotion to multiple deities (including goddesses as well as gods), a belief that divinity is present in the material world, connections to pre-Christian and/or indigenous religions, an emphasis on ritual practice, and trust in personal (especially bodily) experience as a source of divine knowledge. In this collection, Pagans present the foundations for consent culture in their traditions: a Druid explores the concept of sovereignty; Wiccans analyze "The Charge of the Goddess"; a Heathen explicates medieval Icelandic lore; a modern Polytheist draws on philosophies of difference. No two of these approaches will create identical practices, and with the enormous diversity of the Pagan community, there is no reason that they should. In exploring their traditions' approaches to autonomy and empathy, however, these writers discover a surprising amount of common ground.

When collecting essays for this anthology, we imagined our reading audience copying off single essays (perhaps the ones that relate to their specific tradition or practice) and presenting them for group discussion. Because we knew that these essays would need to stand alone, basic information about what consent culture is and how it works appears in many of the included chapters. As we expect that most readers will not read the collection straight through, we see this repetition as a feature and a strength.

Our Goals for This Book

We didn't coin the term "consent culture"—far from it. Wonderful work around consent, sexual ethics, and touch is happening in feminist and sexual minority communities right now. In many ways, we're just trying to amplify the signal, as well as connect these ideas more clearly with Pagan practices and attitudes. For a secular introduction to sexual ethics and consent culture that includes a wide variety of perspectives, we recommend the collection *Yes Means Yes! Visions of Female Sexual Power & A World Without Rape* (2008), edited by Jaclyn Friedman and Jessica Valenti.

In addition to wanting to be part of this ongoing work, though, we also felt called to speak out after prominent Wiccan teacher Kenny Klein was arrested for possession of child pornography in March 2014. Pagan reactions to the news, especially online, highlighted to both of us the contrast between sex-positive Pagan ideals and the real state of Pagan community. There is a tendency among Pagans to think that we are immune to the problems of the wider society—because Pagans are exceptionally ethical; or because high priestesses are very wise and intuitive and filter out rapists and abusers from our midst; or because our counterculture status has bound us together into a family, and we would never hurt each other. These stories are myths, and not the sacred kind. We are aware of too many cases of sexual harassment, rape, and domestic violence in the Pagan community to believe that these are true. We are no different in this regard than the wider society in which we find ourselves immersed.

We also recognize that our community shares our society's wider pattern of silencing victims, a pattern that is cleverly satirized by blogger Simone Webb. In Webb's "Parable of the Rats on the Boat," perpetrators of sexual harassment, rape, and abuse are portrayed as rats infesting a ship. When the people who are bitten by the rats attempt to speak up about the problem, however, they are told by others not to *rock the boat* by trying to get rid of the rats—stability and calm are considered more important than dealing with the problem. The boat, perhaps, is weakly built; out of fear that it will capsize, passengers urge each other to avoid or ignore the rats, or they deny their deadly impact on the group ("I know there's the whole plague problem, but...") while playing up their better qualities ("really they can be quite cute and fluffy sometimes!"). As the complicit, rat-bitten passenger tells her fellow sailors, "Let's just live with the rats, m'kay? I mean, what can we really *do* about them?"[1]

This tale is an allegory, of course. Not everyone who commits a boundary violation is a hardwired predator who deserves to be compared to a plague-ridden rat, and our solutions need to be much more complex than simply "find the rats and toss them off the boat." But the parable highlights how communities sometimes tolerate destructive behaviors that threaten the very structure of the group. It shows that fear of community collapse can influence people to silence whistleblowers or even blame crimes on their victims ("You should have known better than to go below-decks!").

Though the rats of the parable are perhaps better understood as behaviors rather than people, Webb's point stands. We have to speak out—our ship has rats, and the situation is intolerable. We will not condone silence.

---

[1] Simone Webb, "The Parable of the Rats on the Boat," *Her Sins Were Scarlet, but Her Blog Was Red* February 21, 2013. Available at http://blogwasred.wordpress.com/2013/02/21/the-parable-of-the-rats-on-the-boat/.

Creating a culture that condemns boundary violations and celebrates individual autonomy is not an easy task, so let's begin simply: with the defining of terms.

Defining Rape Culture

Consent to touch—particularly sexual touch—is extremely fraught in our culture. We live in what's often called *rape culture*—a culture in which we consider widespread sexual violence to be inevitable, and in which we dismiss many smaller, daily boundary violations as a normal part of social life. Rape culture often includes highly gendered beliefs about sex. These beliefs usually include the idea that women do not naturally like sex, while men are naturally sexually aggressive and desire sex all the time. (People on both the far left and far right sometimes hold these views—these are points that radical feminist and men's rights literature tend to agree on.)

Sadly, many men are still socialized to believe that a "nice girl" always refuses sex, and that it is a man's role to convince or persuade her. In this context, a weak or uncertain refusal may be taken as a demonstration that the girl is not "easy"—often considered a valuable trait—and silence and passivity during sex are seen as normal. In a culture where many people find it difficult or embarrassing to discuss sex at all, the initiators of sexual touch rarely seek a clear "yes," while the recipients are unprepared to say either "yes" or "no." This situation easily lends itself to non-malicious sexual violations, particularly the kind where the person initiating sexual touch believes the touch is desired, while the recipient is actually uncomfortable, embarrassed, or frightened.

Analyses of rape culture tend to focus on relations between men and women, but in reality, the situation is much more complicated. We live in a web of unequal power relationships based on gender, race, class, gender identity, and other characteristics. Around these relationships, we have both explicit and unspoken social rules about who can touch others without permission, exploit their vulnerabilities, or even commit violent acts on others' bodies. These socially permitted violations can include date or marital rape, mandatory unpaid overtime or sweatshop working conditions, hate crimes committed against minorities, laws criminalizing consensual sex acts between adults, and more. Those who commit boundary violations within the "rules" will often be protected when their communities assign the blame for the act for the victim.

Victim blaming sounds something like this:

- "No wonder that happened..."
- "Look at the clothes she was wearing..."
- "His kind don't belong in that part of town..."
- "He shouldn't have flaunted that boyfriend of his in public..."

What is implied in these remarks is that violating social norms naturally attracts violence. Of course, for women and minorities, simply being out in the "wrong place" in public can be seen as violating social norms. Violence and the threat of violence are used to keep social hierarchy in place. These inequalities can make it very difficult to secure enthusiastic consent to many kinds of interactions, especially ones involving touch or sexuality.

Facing the reality of violence in our communities can be overwhelming. As practitioners of body-positive religious traditions, however, we must be careful that our grief and fear don't cause us to mirror the destructive sexual delusions of mainstream culture. Mainstream culture believes that desire is dangerous; that adolescents are asexual unless sexualized by adults; that women are doomed to be sexual victims; and that preventing assault is the responsibility of potential victims, not perpetrators. People may embrace such beliefs because they want to prevent sexual assault and abuse, but these sex-negative attitudes are also part of rape culture.

We need to change the sex- and body-hating conditions that encourage boundary violations and that allow others to overlook signs of abuse. At the same time, we need to avoid utterly demonizing those who commit sexual violations by acknowledging that problematic behaviors are rife in our communities—some persisting as a result of ignorance and lack of understanding, some as a result of genuine malice. For those who act in ignorance, we need procedures for making amends and restoring justice to our communities. And for those who are beyond our help, we need to be prepared to call the police and send predators to prison, for the good of all. This effort requires a strong redefinition of consent.

Defining Consent

Consent is permission to engage in an activity, or to be acted upon. Consent is not the absence of a "no"; it is the presence of a "yes."[2]

Although we are particularly concerned with sexual ethics and consent issues around touch, as we explained above, consent issues are ultimately about autonomy and empathy in all areas of life, not just the sexual.

According to ethicist Morten Ebbe Juul Nielsen, consent draws its moral force from the idea that individual freedom and autonomy is a basic human right.[3] Consent cannot be given to acts that destroy that autonomy. This means that if consent is given to an act that temporarily compromises autonomy—such as consenting to anesthesia for a medical procedure—it must ultimately increase that person's autonomy to be justifiable.

Nielsen gives the following four principles for evaluating whether consent is valid:

+ Consent must be *informed*, with both parties fully understanding the activities they are agreeing to perform and their risks;
+ Consent must be *wholehearted and intentional* ("enthusiastic"), not being used as a bargaining chip;

---

[2] Some portions of this section draw materials from Christine Hoff Kraemer, *Eros and Touch from a Pagan Perspective: Divided for Love's Sake* (New York: Routledge, 2014), 28-38.

[3] Morten Ebbe Juul Nielsen, "Safe, Sane, and Consensual—Consent and the Ethics of BDSM," *The International Journal of Applied Philosophy* 24:2 (2010): 265-288.

- Consent must be *voluntary*, not compromised by the threat of force or harm;
- Consenting individuals must be *competent* (not intoxicated, under extreme emotional duress, underage, etc.)

These principles draw some firm lines around what a consensual act is. Suppose we use sexual negotiations as our example. Using these principles, we know that if a person agrees to have oral sex, but then suddenly finds their partner penetrating them without any further check-in, that act is not consensual. We know that if a person has sex solely because their partner has threatened to break up if they don't, that act is not consensual. We know that any sex that occurs under force or threat of force is not consensual, and that sex with someone who is drunk or underage isn't consensual either.

These principles, however, also reveal that consent can have grey areas. For example: How "informed" is "informed"? When we sign an informed consent agreement before surgery or cancer treatment, how many of us have the medical knowledge to fully understand the procedures? If we are negotiating sex, do we need to know our partner's complete life story to feel informed about the risks, or is a quick conversation about STD status enough? What constitutes "informed consent" depends a great deal on context and the existing level of trust between participants. To make sure that all parties are operating with similar expectations, communities need to explicitly discuss what it means to be informed.

Although consent should be "wholehearted and intentional" to be valid, in the messiness of life, people often have mixed feelings about emotionally weighted decisions. It is important to remember that giving consent is an ongoing process, and we have the right to grant or withdraw it on a moment to moment basis. When trying out a new sexual activity with a partner, it is reasonable to say, "I'm not sure— let's try it, and then I'll know if I like it." A process approach to consent may also be taken with initiations, where the candidate is often asked to enter the ritual without fully knowing its contents, but retains the right to stop the ritual at any time (and may be asked repeatedly if they want to stop). Tentative consent may not *always* be a reason to halt an activity, but it is always a good reason to pause, check in, and then proceed with care.

If we are witnesses to a questionably consensual act, evaluating it using Nielsen's four principles for consent can help us decide whether or not to intervene. The more invalid the consent according to Nielsen's principles, the more our moral obligation to speak up, physically interfere with what's happening, or involve the authorities.

[handwritten note in margin: use this as a guide post]

Respecting No, Respecting Yes

Consent culture education tends to focus heavily on learning to honor others' boundaries—in other words, to respect their "no" and to create a community in which saying "no" is consistently respected. Part of supporting adults' autonomy, however, means we have to also have to honor their enthusiastic consent, even if we think they're making poor decisions. Attempts to invalidate individuals' autonomy are rampant in our culture:

[handwritten note in margin: we have to honor their enthusiastic consent]

- "You don't really love that friend of yours, you're just trying to get in with the cool crowd."
- "You don't really want to smoke marijuana, you're just giving in to peer pressure."
- "You don't really believe in this Pagan business, you're just rebelling against your parents."
- "You're not really bisexual/gay/lesbian/transgender, you're just going through a phase."
- "You don't really want kinky sex, you've just been brainwashed by the patriarchy."

The problem is that, for some people at some times, these statements may have a grain of truth. Our decisions are always influenced—and sometimes deliberately manipulated—by our friends, our families, our culture, the media we watch, and by people in our communities who may or may not care about our well-being. Consent culture requires a delicate balance between expressing appropriate concern for our loved ones while also supporting their personal freedom. Respecting a "yes" doesn't mean we can't talk to our loved ones about our concerns, but it does mean we need to refrain from second-guessing their experience or claiming they're mistaken about what they want. Sometimes the most difficult part of consent culture isn't accepting someone else's "no," but standing by nervously as a loved one joyfully embraces a risky "yes."

Pagan-Specific Challenges in Creating Consent Culture

On the level of philosophy and principles, Pagans of various traditions find a great deal of overlap in their thinking about consent. When it comes to creating concrete policies, however, the diversity of Pagan traditions makes any attempt to create pan-Pagan guidelines challenging.

Some of this difficulty stems from differences in practice. For example, some witchcraft and magical traditions use silence and secrecy as part of an initiatory container that furthers spiritual transformation.[4] A total revelation of the contents of an initiation can lessen its impact (many candidates for initiation very much want to avoid "spoilers"!). However, if the initiation involves any taboo activities, allowing the candidate to enter the ritual entirely ignorant does not constitute informed consent.

Many such groups today attempt to walk a middle path: candidates are informed of the types of activities that may be involved without being fully informed of the details. Others approach the issue by emphasizing the importance of a strong initiator/candidate relationship: if both parties want the initiation to be as much of a surprise as possible, then the initiator must understand the candidate well enough to know how they are likely to react to the ritual. The candidate, in turn, knowingly gives consent to an unknown

---

[4] For specifics on how magical secrecy and silence can support peak spiritual experiences and facilitate spiritual change, see John Michael Greer, *Inside a Magickal Lodge* (St. Paul, MN: Llewellyn Publications, 1998).

experience—but one that they know is shaped by the initiator's judgment.[5]

In this latter context, the candidate's informed consent is not based on details about the ritual, but on their knowledge of the initiator's character and competence. To allow another person to make judgments on one's behalf requires a great deal of trust; the arrangement can easily become exploitative if the power imbalance between initiator and candidate is large, or if the potential for exploitation is not openly discussed. In groups where initiator and candidate function as peers in other areas of life, however, this approach to informed consent can work well. Especially in traditions where initiations are customized to the candidate, a ritual that reflects the initiator's knowledge of and intimacy with the candidate can be a profoundly meaningful gift.

Groups that use secrecy and silence as spiritual tools must be vigilant against those who attempt to use these tools abusively or exploitatively. Any policies that are developed about what kinds of secrecy and silence are appropriate must reflect an experiential understanding of how the tools work and the group's goals in using them, as well as a commitment to group members' well-being. Groups that work this way may find themselves spending a great deal of time and thought on the relationship between magical silence and consent.

For groups that do not use these tools, however, the issue is moot; in fact, Pagans who do not work with magical secrecy may see no positive purpose for the tool at all. When the issue of consent and magical silence comes up in pan-Pagan groups, other Pagans may apply half-appropriate understandings of therapeutic confidentiality or government secrecy. Without a common understanding of how secrecy and magical silence might work in a spiritually healthy way,

---

[5] Some groups may also require that the candidate have a sponsor who comes from another group. This gives the candidate a trusted advocate and confidante with whom they can speak if any issues arise.

Pagans may find themselves talking past each other, using the same words but assigning them either subtly or wildly different definitions.

This mismatch of contexts and definitions complicates one of the hottest-button issues in Pagan consent culture: whether it is ever ethical for a teacher to have sex with a student. Coming from a mainstream culture in which teacher-student romantic relationships (even between adults) are a violation of professional ethics, many Pagans apply the same thinking to Pagan situations: there is a power differential, so the relationship is unethical; end of story. In practice, however, definitions of "teacher" and "student" in Pagan traditions vary, as does the size and nature of the power differential between them. Here are some definitions of "teacher" in various Pagan traditions:

A teacher oversees mixed-age groups of a dozen or more students in a workshop or classroom setting, for which they are paid tuition. The teacher enjoys a professional status that sets them apart from their students. They may be responsible for evaluating their students and making decisions about the students' advancement in the program or path.

A teacher directs a small group such as a coven or grove over which they have ultimate decision-making authority, particularly over the advancement of the students into positions of power in the group. The students are generally younger than the teacher. No money changes hands.

A teacher is one of the organizers for a non-hierarchical, mixed-age group in which they hold primary responsibility for providing ritual structure and organization. Decisions about the direction of the group are made collectively; initiations, if any are offered, are designed collaboratively by the group as a gift to each individual. Participants are encouraged to take turns providing content.

A teacher is an experienced practitioner of a Pagan tradition who is training and initiating a peer from a different tradition. The two have a pre-existing relationship as friends and colleagues. The student wants to learn the tradition of the teacher so that they will be able to function as working partners.

Multiple-role relationships—in other words, relationships in which two people function in multiple roles, such as friend/friend, service provider/customer, or teacher/student—are always complex. Each set of roles that is active in the relationship presents a different set of obligations and expectations, and these can easily come into conflict. Adding a sexual component to a pre-existing relationship is always risky. This is particularly true when the relationship already contains a power differential. If all sexual relationships with power differentials were inherently unethical and harmful, however, hardly any sexual relationships would exist—the classic example of a relationship with a power differential is a heterosexual marriage!

When Pagans discuss issues such as the role of sexuality in teaching relationships, in order to make progress, they must be specific about the kind of relationship they mean and its context. Because Pagan traditions vary significantly, this need to carefully define terms and context will apply to many discussions about ethics and consent.

Sexual Ethics beyond Consent

Ethics around touch and sex are a special area of concern for sex-positive Pagans. Unfortunately, many people's vocabulary around sex and consent is limited: either an act is "rape"—and the perpetrator a rapist; or it is "not rape"—and there is no perpetrator at all.

In actuality, unethical and questionably ethical sex acts fall into more than two categories. Our communities need a range of responses to problematic sexual behaviors. If we want to respect each other's autonomy, especially in the area of sexuality, we will need to expand our vocabulary around sexual ethics. Here are a few key terms:

- *Non-consensual touch*: Not all non-consensual touch is "rape," a term that has weighty legal and emotional implications. (In both the US and UK, rape is legally defined by the nonconsensual penetration of the vagina or the anus with any object.) All non-consensual touch, however, involves the violation of boundaries. We can use the terms "non-consensual touch," "boundary violation," or "sexual misconduct" to talk about problematic behaviors that may not qualify as rape, sexual assault, or sexual abuse. Non-consensual sexual touch that takes place repeatedly, especially in an exploitative and/or emotionally abusive relationship, may be referred to as "sexual abuse"; a single act of coerced sexual contact is often referred to as "sexual assault."[6]

* *Exploitation*: This term refers to relationships in which one party's vulnerability is being taken advantage of, but there is no force or threat of force. The relationship is consensual, yet still may be unethical. For example, some women enjoy doing sex work of various kinds and find it personally empowering. Sex work is rarely a woman's first-choice career, however: it is usually chosen because it is lucrative, because there is a great deal of demand for it, and often because the woman in question has few other reasonable options. Because of these pressures, some women may continue to do sex work even if the job puts their health at risk or becomes unpleasant or humiliating. For a situation of this kind to be non-exploitative, participants need what Nielsen calls "a robust exit strategy"—in other words, a way out that doesn't involve major hardship. Similarly, sexual relationships where there is a large difference in power (from social status, financial status, etc.) can be ethically problematic because of the potential for exploitation, whether deliberate or accidental: the person with fewer opportunities and less power may stay in an unhappy relationship because to leave puts them at risk of being uninsured or homeless.

[handwritten margin notes: "consensual but unethical", "teachers and students", "yes!"]

* *Manipulation:* This term refers to relationships in which one party is deliberately influencing the other toward behaviors

---

[6] Different sources give slightly different definitions of these terms; the definitions given here represent our impressions of how these terms are being used to characterize acts of varying severity.

or attitudes that they may not otherwise find appealing. In contrast to persuasion, manipulation is indirect and may involve the use of half-truths or outright deception in order to influence the other party's behavior. In other words, it is a subtle, persistent assault on that person's autonomy. Sex in a manipulative relationship may be consensual, but the relationship is unethical because it is based on dishonesty and disrespect.

+ *Harassment:* This term refers to annoying, intimidating, or otherwise unwelcome behaviors that persist even after the recipient has requested that they stop. Harassing actions are sometimes accompanied by pressuring comments or attempts to shame the recipient into accepting what is offered. For example, once someone has turned down offers of physical affection, continuing to offer hugs and kisses or calling that person rude or teasing names because they won't accept them constitutes harassment.

These terms can help widen our range of responses to problems in our communities. Too often, communities respond to complaints against a member either by trying to silence the accusers or by vilifying and ejecting the accused. Rarely is either of these an adequate response (without careful investigation). Most situations are complex: a violation has occurred. Was it a misunderstanding? Or deliberate? Is the accused of poor intent, or do they need education or therapy? What new boundaries need to be set to prevent further harm? How can the problem and its solution be talked out using language that is descriptive, specific, and not unnecessarily triggering?

One of the reasons that Pagans struggle so much with harassment, exploitation, and sexual misconduct in our communities is that often, the perpetrator of these actions is beloved. An insecure but talented leader may give inspiration and support to many members of their community while badly damaging others with unethical (but perfectly legal) sexual behavior. The better able we are to identify and condemn these behaviors without utterly demonizing the perpetrator, the better we will be able to confront them, hold them responsible, and support the healing of all affected while preventing further harm.

When community members fear that a loved one who has done something legal but wrong will be character-assassinated and driven out of community, they may rush to that person's defense rather than supporting them in taking responsibility for their actions. If we are able to talk frankly and accurately about community members' sexual misconduct—rather than immediately employing labels like "rapist" and "abuser," regardless of the nature of the offense—we may struggle less with community tendencies to silence victims and deny violations.

Having a range of words and ethical concepts to draw from also helps us realize when a line has been crossed. If we find ourselves correctly using the words "rape," "sexual assault," or "sexual abuse," it is likely time to get professional help or call the police. (For more specific guidelines on when to involve the authorities, see Cat Chapin-Bishop's essay in this collection.)

Book Summary

We have divided this anthology into three parts. In *Developing Pagan Philosophies of Consent*, the reader will find both tradition-specific and personal approaches to consent-based ethics. These essays show how Pagan lore and liturgy shape our writers' understandings of consent, as well as how their ideals translate into real-world practice. Writers also tackle complex issues such as consent in a power differential, the ethics of sexual initiation, negotiating rape culture in traditional myths, and understanding sexual relationships with the gods.

Section Two, *Responding to Abuse and Assault*, focuses on the narratives and needs of survivors. In addition to personal narratives of abuse and healing, writers examine the kinds of situations that can hide abuse, as well as the circumstances under which whistleblowers may be disbelieved or ignored. These essays outline policies to help prevent sexual abuse and assault and to effectively respond to it when it occurs, as well as considering how abuse survivors might be better accommodated in community.

Finally, in *Building Communities of Autonomy and Empathy*, our writers provide resources for teaching and practicing consent culture. These essays include reflections on consent culture parenting, curricula and exercises for children and adults, practices for sacralizing pleasurable touch in both groups and on an everyday basis, ethical approaches to teaching sacred sexuality and sex magick, and more.

Despite the considerable length of this book, we know that these resources are only a beginning. To deepen our understanding of consent culture, however, more of us need to be living in it. May this anthology support Pagans in making communities of freedom and connection a reality.

SEPTEMBER, 2015

Part I:
Developing Pagan Philosophies of Consent

Culture of Consent, Culture of Sovereignty
A Recipe from a Druid's Perspective
John Beckett

Pagans are in a position of great opportunity and of great difficulty. On one hand, we have rejected the Abrahamic idea that sex is sinful and that the body is a source of shame. We celebrate the pleasures of sex, the joy of touch, and the beauty of the human body. Yes, sex is necessary to continue our species, but it also helps us deepen our intimate relationships, and beyond that it's just plain fun. We are in a unique position to show the mainstream culture a better, healthier, more reasonable, and more responsible approach to sexuality and sexual relationships.

On the other hand, the Pagan community is just as susceptible to predators and general sexual misconduct as any other segment of Western society. We may have some lofty ideals around sexuality, but we have no moral high ground from which to insist that our way is objectively better.

We have made good progress in building a sex-positive and body-positive religious movement, but we cannot claim it is truly better until we also build a community where everyone feels safe and is safe. To do that, we must build a culture of consent. And there can be no culture of consent without a culture of sovereignty.

Sovereignty

Modern Druidry is inspired by the ancient Druids, but we know very little about them. Since the Druid Revival began in the eighteenth century, modern Druids have built our practices around Nature and our connections to the natural world, and around the preservation and promotion of Celtic culture. Druid ideas about consent and sovereignty flow from those two sources.

On the Hill of Tara in Ireland is the Lia Fáil, a single standing stone perhaps four feet tall. It is said that when the true king of Ireland touches it, the stone cries out. The land chooses the king. The land is not a mere thing to be possessed; it is an entity of its own, represented by the concept of sovereignty and the Goddess of Sovereignty.

Sovereignty is not ownership—the king did not own the land. The divine right of kings was not developed until the early modern Christian era as a rationalization for powerful men to hold on to absolute power.

Rather, sovereignty is the right to rule and the obligation to rule rightly. If the king ruled wisely and justly, the land and the people would prosper. If the king ruled poorly, Sovereignty would withdraw her blessing, the land would go barren, the people would suffer, and the king would be removed. The Lia Fáil reminds us that the right to choose the ruler rightfully belonged to the land itself.

Personal Sovereignty

The land has sovereignty. So does each and every person. You have both the inherent right to rule your life and the obligation to rule it rightly. So does everyone else. No one owns your body, your heart, your mind, or your soul. Neither do you own anyone else's. We all possess the inherent sovereignty to rule our own bodies and our own lives.

There are a few practical exceptions. There is *regency*—sovereignty held by parents and others for those who are incapable of making their own decisions. We understand that a four-year-old doesn't have the knowledge and maturity to choose which medical care to accept and which to refuse. We understand that a six-year-old doesn't know what he needs to study in school. If we are wise, we understand that some day we may be incapacitated, and we designate someone we trust to make medical and other decisions for us.

There is *delegation*. As adults, we give some of our sovereignty to governments—the rule of law promotes orderly and ethical interactions within society. We give some to employers—some necessary for the efficient running of a business, and some not. Many of our current political debates center around how much delegation is proper, how much should be mandatory, and how much should be voluntary. Those debates are outside the scope of this article, but ultimately they concern sovereignty—the right to rule and the obligation to rule rightly.

Stolen Sovereignty

Sovereignty is hard work. Having someone try to tell us what to do may immediately get our backs up, but when we're negotiating with each other as equals, deciding something as trivial as what to have for dinner can take longer than cooking the dinner itself. "What do you want?" "I don't know, what do you want?" "I don't care." "Whatever."

Try to decide a more serious question and the work gets both harder and more subtle. Each option has costs and benefits, advantages and disadvantages. What unexpected and unintended consequences may come from your choices? What options are you overlooking that might be better than what you're considering?

Choosing between red and blue is hard enough—picking from the whole spectrum of colors is nearly impossible. It is no surprise that many people make decisions based on impulse and habit and then look for reasons to justify them.

It is also no surprise that there are plenty of people willing to exploit this automatic behavior for their own ends. Our sovereignty has been swindled from us by the sorcerers of marketing, who convince us that happiness will only be found by buying what they're selling. While there is nothing inherently wrong with advertising, modern advertisers don't simply tell you they have something you might need. First they sell you the idea that you can't be happy unless you look and live a certain way, that you "should" be young and rich and thin, forever. Then it's easy for them to sell you things that create the illusion of youth, wealth, and attractiveness.

Think of the politicians and their sorcerer-consultants who try to keep us in a state of fear and outrage, promising us prosperity if we give them our money and our votes, but warning of disaster if the other party wins the election. Sovereignty may be our inherent right, but if we aren't constantly mindful, it can be stolen or swindled away.

The Cultural Effects of Stolen Sovereignty

Lose your sovereignty often enough and you forget you ever had it. You start thinking that's the way things are supposed to be: decisions are made for you, because others are so much better qualified to decide (and because making informed, rational decisions is hard work). Or worse, you start believing the propaganda: our problems are all *their* fault; those in power have our best interests at heart; certain groups are entitled to better things than others.

Maybe you start to think you are one of those people who are entitled to power or success. Or maybe you learn a bit of malevolent sorcery and figure out how to persuade people to give you what you want, whether they want to or not. The fact that they don't really want to cooperate doesn't occur to you or simply isn't important. Respecting their sovereignty means little—getting what you want means everything.

When Bill Clinton, President of the United States, was asked why he had a sexual affair with Monica Lewinsky, a 22-year-old intern, he said, "Because I could."

There can be no culture of consent without a culture of sovereignty.

Sexuality: Biology and Sociology

Humans have an evolutionary instinct to have sex and lots of it. There are many possible reasons why: the need to produce many children to compensate for those who die before reaching reproductive age, creating strong pair-bondings, or reducing tension. The precise mixture of reasons is beyond the scope of this essay—what's important here is that most of us experience a hard-wired, biological urge to have sex.

At the same time, having sex brings complications, the production of children being only the most obvious. There are issues of relationships and commitments, jealousy and possessiveness, and the desire of men to both spread their genes and ensure that any children they care for will be their own biological offspring. It is no wonder virtually every society ever known has created extensive rules around who can have sex, who they have sex with, and under what circumstances.

Whether we operate within our culture's rules or whether our instincts push us to ignore them, responding to our instincts is socially risky. Sexual activity is not called "intimate relations" for nothing. Initiating a sexual encounter carries the risk of offering offense or being rejected—and so does responding to the offer.

These social risks have led to complex mating rituals full of signaling, hinting, vague responses, and plausible deniability. Combine this with the gender roles taught by the mainstream culture that expect men to be sexually aggressive and women to be "pure," and you have a recipe for confusion and misunderstanding even among people who mean well.

Worse, not everyone means well.

Boundaries and Predators

Pagans have long argued in favor of sexual freedom and against arbitrary rules concerning sexual behavior. But sexual freedom doesn't mean having more sex. Sexual freedom means the freedom to choose whether or not to have sex, every time. It also means the freedom from requests that are obviously unwanted and therefore harassing.

We understand—both intuitively and from observation—that children cannot freely choose to have sex. Even if their bodies are capable of sexual activity, they do not yet fully comprehend the biological and social risks involved, and so cannot fully consent. Most of us understand this and are morally repulsed by the idea of having sex with children, even with those children who look like adults. Our concern for their well-being and our respect for their sovereignty outweigh any desire we may have to have sex with them.

(As an aside, while children having sex is a bad idea, criminalizing non-coercive sexual activity between children of comparable age is worse—punishment does not protect their well-being.)

Predators are people who don't care about consent, or at least, they are people whose desire to have sex overrules their respect for others' sovereignty. In the case of adults having sex with children and adolescents below the age of consent, our mainstream society has drawn clear boundaries, boundaries almost all Pagans enthusiastically support.

Boundaries are necessary wherever differences in age, experience, and power make full consent difficult. An employer has considerable power over an employee, including the power to terminate employment, and with it, the employee's livelihood. If an employer makes sexual advances toward an employee, the employee may not feel they have the power to say no.

Does that mean employees are never capable of giving a free and valid yes? A casual look at office romances—some of which actually last—shows that's not the case. And so, unlike having sex with children, having sex with a subordinate is not a crime. But it is risky, which is why many employers discourage office romances (and some actively prohibit them). Exploiting a subordinate employee sexually can lead to severe civil penalties.

Predators also include those who take advantage of our vague mating rituals to pressure or force others into sexual activities they may not want. Our mainstream culture has been unable to weed out these predators. A culture of consent cannot eliminate them either, but a culture where explicitly seeking consent is the norm makes predators more visible and thus easier to isolate... and that provides a disincentive for such behavior from all but sociopaths.

A Culture of Consent

A culture of consent keeps the Pagan concepts that sex is natural, right, and good, and that the human body is beautiful and wondrous in all its many forms. It adds one and only one qualification, but that qualification is an absolute requirement: *each person must give their consent, and that consent must be free, clear, informed, and unambiguous.*

Building a Culture of Sovereignty

How do we build a culture of consent? How do we build a culture of sovereignty, which affirms every person's right to control their own body? How do we celebrate sexuality, touch, and our bodies while ensuring no one feels pressured to do anything they don't enthusiastically want to do?

We must begin by valuing sovereignty over sexual activity. Unless our commitment to the right of each and every person to choose when, where, how, and with whom to have sex exceeds our desire to have them as a sexual partner, we cannot create a culture of consent.

Let's not talk about how consensual sex is more enthusiastic and therefore better (though I certainly believe it is). Having better sex is a by-product of respecting sovereignty, not the primary goal. And while we can understand that we wouldn't want to be forced or coerced into sex, let's be wary of "I won't do it to you, because I wouldn't want you to do it to me." That line of thinking can easily creep into "I'd like you to do that to me, so I'll do it to you." Every person has the right to control their own body, and it is our obligation to respect that right. Our total commitment to everyone's sovereignty is the only foundation solid enough to support a culture of consent.

From that commitment to sovereignty, we build a culture that recognizes and accepts our differences. Most of the Pagan community understands that people have a wide variety of sexual orientations. We're not so good at understanding people have an equally wide variety of sexual desires: not just what kind of person they want to have sex with, but when, how often, and under what conditions. If we honor the sovereignty of potential partners, we will respect their individual desires as much as we respect their orientation.

We need to build a culture where it's expected to ask. If we respect sovereignty and we respect differences, we will realize that no matter what hints and intimations we think we see, we must make sure. That can only happen by asking and then waiting for an affirmative response.

We can teach this—and learn it ourselves—by teaching children how to seek consent to touch from the earliest age. An open hand is an invitation for a handshake; an open arm is an invitation for a hug.

Both can be emphasized with an inquisitive look. You don't proceed until you get a response. If you don't get a response, you've got your response—don't touch. Learning consent to touch leads to learning consent for sex.

A question expects an answer, so we need to build a culture where it's okay to say yes. So much of our honest miscommunication is caused by judgmental morality from a bygone era. People are afraid to say yes even when they want sex, out of fear they will be condemned for being promiscuous—or humiliated for being desperate. We cannot respect the right of individuals to control their bodies and their sexuality unless we also respect the choices they make. Unless someone is making choices that are clearly dangerous (e.g. unprotected sex with strangers), a culture of sovereignty and consent requires us to refrain from passing judgment on the choices other adults make, even if we would wish their choices were different.

We need to build a culture where it's okay to say no. But more than that, we need to build a culture where "no" is the last word. It's okay to ask—it's not okay to ask "why not?" Not just because that's a subtle (or not so subtle) way to pressure the other person to change their mind, but because it implies that in the absence of a "valid" reason, the answer should be yes—and ideas about what is "valid" vary widely.

I'm a straight man. If a gay man asks me to have sex with him, it's easy for me say "I'm straight—I'm not interested in sex with you." But if a woman asks me to have sex with her, do I tell her, "Yes, I'm physically attracted to you, but you strike me as someone I wouldn't enjoy being around otherwise, and if I have sex with you once, you may make demands on me I don't want to have to deal with, so I don't think it's worth it"? I may not even be able to articulate that thought to myself, much less to someone else! But if I can simply say "no thanks" and have that answer be gracefully accepted, I can be happy that someone thought I was an attractive bed partner, and she can move on to looking for someone who will be a good match for her.

If we build a culture where it's expected to ask, it follows that we must build a culture where it's okay to ask. But we must also build a culture where asking repeatedly or trivially isn't okay. Sex isn't a trivial thing—it's an act of trust where we make ourselves vulnerable in hopes of making a connection, perhaps a brief physical connection, or perhaps one that's deeply spiritual. Asking someone for sex in a situation where there is no reasonable expectation that sex might be desired isn't honest. At best, it's trolling—randomly throwing a fishing line into the water in the hope that something bites. At worst, it's harassment.

The Long Road Forward

This proposal is nothing less than an attempt to rewrite mating rituals that are at least as old the modern era and likely much, much older. The process will not be easy, and it will not happen overnight. But the old rituals and the culture they support no longer serve the needs of many people. Too many don't feel safe because too many aren't safe.

We need a culture of consent. We need a culture of sovereignty, a culture that respects the inherent right of every person to control their body and to make their own decisions in a free and uncoerced manner.

If Pagans can add respect for sovereignty to our sex-positive and body-positive culture, we can lead the way.

John Beckett grew up in Tennessee with the woods right outside his back door. Wandering through them gave him a sense of connection to Nature and to a certain Forest God. John is a Druid in the Order of Bards, Ovates and Druids, the Coordinating Officer of the Denton Covenant of Unitarian Universalist Pagans, and a former Vice President of CUUPS Continental. His blog *Under the Ancient Oaks* is part of the Pagan Channel of the multifaith website Patheos.com. John has been writing, speaking, teaching, and leading public rituals for the past twelve years. He lives in the Dallas/Fort Worth area and earns his keep as an engineer.

Thelema and Consent

Brandy Williams

How I Became a Feminist Thelemite

I got into Thelema because I was interested in sex.

I was active in a feminist group in my youth, in what we called "second-wave feminism." The movement lost me when it went in a sex-negative direction. At that time, discussion focused largely on the right to say no, on stopping exploitation, on the ways in which the consent of women to sex had been presumed, subverted, and taken away. Some analysts went so far as to suggest that sex between women and men could never be consensual in a system where men had so much power over women.

As a teenager just beginning to feel my way into my body, I looked for images of women who were naked, sensual, inviting contact. I decorated my home with collages made from Playboy images. This scandalized my feminist friends, who earnestly lectured me on the ways in which I was inviting my own exploitation. Feminism left me no clear path to saying *yes*. So I left the group and struck out on my own.

As a magician, I quickly discovered that Thelemic writings celebrate sex. In Thelema, I encountered the opposite problem to the one that had chased me out of the feminist movement. Thelemic analysts had not begun to do their initial work in social justice education, and there was no feminist awareness among the Thelemites I encountered. Aleister Crowley's writings present a high barrier to a person committed to social justice. I'd hit a passage where he'd say the most outrageous things about women and black people and democracy and end up throwing the book against the wall. Finally I gave up, cleared my library of Crowley's works, and went on searching.

Thelema isn't the only sex-positive magical system. In my late teens, I was deeply moved by the words in Doreen Valiente's *The Charge of the Goddess*: "all acts of love and pleasure are my rituals." I took an initiation in Witchcraft, and I am still a practicing Witch today. The group that initiated me was sex-positive, but in a way that wasn't particularly comfortable for me. As a young woman exploring her sexuality, I was treated as fair game for the men in the group, many of them substantially older, and I fended off quite a few advances. The women were high priestesses in the circle, but outside circle they wielded no real power and did not act to protect me. There were no feminists here, and no discussion of women's power.

As I moved onto the national Pagan scene, I continued to scandalize the communities I encountered with my social and magical behavior. I wrote a book about sex magic; I gave classes in sex magic; I wore tight clothing and lots of jewelry and showed up at events with more than one partner. It was always a cause for comment, whether supportive and appreciative or salacious and disapproving.

Eventually I came back around to Thelema. Of all the communities I traversed, this was the one where my open sexuality met with the most overt approval. I could wear tight clothes and walk into a room with the swagger that signaled *I say yes*. In Thelemic circles, this was greeted not with disapproval or predation but with respectful appreciation. When I showed up at a party with *three* men in tow, the Thelemic hostess gave me a grin and a thumbs-up.

Encouraged, I turned my efforts toward articulating feminism in a Thelemic context. This turned out to be an easier project than I had initially feared. Many Thelemites have no problem identifying as feminist, and many more understand the word better when we talk about it for a while. Mind you, the Thelemic groups I know are still in their infancy in addressing social justice—we've got a lot of ground to cover—but the feminist discussions have made a good start.

The fundamental structure of Thelema supports feminism and social justice. Thelemic philosophy and religion are expressed in texts, policies, and community.

Aleister Crowley's Writings

A quick note about Aleister Crowley. Most people who aren't Thelemites know him as the "wickedest man in the world," a brilliant but somewhat twisted Edwardian magician, an arrogant and overbearing personality who delighted in shocking the people around him. Those of us who are Thelemites know Aleister Crowley as a man with a towering intellect, a prolific writer, and a talented ritualist, as well as an arrogant and overbearing personality who delighted in shocking the people around him. We all struggle with this mixed legacy while benefitting from his work.

Book of the Law

The word *Thelema* predates its use by Aleister Crowley, but it has come to be primarily associated with his life work. Thelema is articulated in the *Liber Al vel Legis*, commonly known as *The Book of the Law*, a revealed work dictated to Crowley by the entity Aiwass. Each reader is enjoined to interpret the book for ourselves. For that reason, Thelemites by and large don't explain it, but instead quote it. (References list the chapter, then the line: AL I.39 means *Liber Al vel Legis*, Chapter I, line 39.)

Chapter I defines Thelema and the law of freedom. "The word of the Law is Thelema" (AL I:39). (The book gives the word "Thelema" in Greek.) Line 40 goes on, "Who calls us Thelemites will do no wrong," and later gives the law itself: "Do what thou wilt shall be the whole of the Law" (AL I:40). The book also addresses who benefits from this call to freedom: "The law is for all" (AL I:39). The law does not just apply to men, but also applies to women. "Every man and every woman is a star" (AL I:3).

The discussion of consent in Thelema could actually stop here and be done. Every human being is invited to take advantage of the law of freedom, and in particular to freely reject or accept any relationship with any other human being. In another way, the law of freedom is only half of the discussion. Crowley's understanding of the Law of Thelema paired the phrase "Do what thou wilt shall be the whole of the Law" with "Love is the law, love under will" (AL I.57). The book mentions "love" many times in many aspects. In the context of consent, this phrase is helpful: "O man! refuse not thy wife, if she will! O lover, if thou wilt, depart! There is no bond that can unite the divided but love..." (AL I.41).

This points to a specific concern with relationships. Chapter III specifically addresses women's sexual freedom. "Let her be loud and adulterous! Let her be covered with jewels, and rich garments, and let her be shameless before all men!" (AL III:44).

As written in the *Book of the Law*, the law of Thelema explicitly grants women and men alike the right to say no and the right to say yes, to sexuality in particular and to any act in general.

Liber Oz

Consent and sexuality are addressed again in Crowley's *Liber LXXVII*, also known as *Oz* and *The Rights of Man*. The language of this piece is problematic as it was written in the false male generic, using "man" to mean "human." In his commentary on *Oz*, the U.S. Grand Master General Sabazius removes doubt about whether women are included in the declaration of rights: "*Liber Oz* applies to all men and women."[1]

Liber Oz calls out examples of the activities which "man" has a right to do: to live, work, play, rest, die; to drink, dwell, and move; to speak, write, draw, and dress. In discussing the right to love, *Liber Oz* states, "Man has the right to love as he will."

If we extrapolate the "Rights of Man" to include the "Rights of Woman," we can say:

- Woman has the right to say yes to sex.
- Woman has the right to say no to sex.

Consent is not given categorically or permanently, but moment by moment in context. Consent can be withdrawn and cannot be forced. Importantly, consent can be given, and where consent is given, "no other shall say nay" (AL I.43).

---

[1] Sabazius (2001). "Observations on *Liber OZ*." http://hermetic.com/sabazius/ozgloss.htm.

Gnostic Mass

Liber XV, the Gnostic Mass, is performed by numerous Ordo Templi Orientis groups around the world. It is a complicated, powerful, and beautiful ritual, and it can best be understood by participating as a congregant or as one of the officers, priest, priestess, deacon, or child ("child" being a ritual role usually filled by an adult).

In the ritual, the priest seats the priestess on an elevated altar, then draws a curtain. The priest makes an oration and the priestess responds. The ritual specifies: "During this speech the PRIESTESS must have divested herself completely of her robe." The priest responds again, then the deacon makes an oration. The ritual specifies: "The PRIEST parts the veil with his lance. During the previous speeches the PRIESTESS has, if necessary, as in savage countries, resumed her robe."

When the priest pulls back the curtain, the priestess might either be clothed or naked. The sight of a naked woman sitting on an altar was shocking when Thelemic priestesses first performed it, and it continues to be shocking today, where nude women nearly everywhere in the world are framed as promiscuous, victims, or works of art, but almost never as holy.

The ritual requires the priestess to speak while naked, but also provides for her privacy during the speech. The ritual leaves open the question of whether the priestess will remain naked. The rights of the priestess here are addressed both in the ritual and in organizational policy.

O.T.O. Policies

There are many Thelemic groups worldwide. I am a member of Ordo Templi Orientis, an international organization with grand lodges in numerous countries worldwide. O.T.O. as a fraternity incorporates the activities of a formerly separate religious organization, Ecclesia Gnostica Catholica. O.T.O. bodies sponsor the Gnostic Mass, but the ritual itself is performed by E.G.C. clergy. The E.G.C. policy manual specifies that the Priestess may choose to re-robe when the veil parts, and local officers or community standards may require her to re-robe, but no one can require her to remain unclothed in public.

I have experienced the ritual both as an officer of the O.T.O. and as an officer of the Mass. As a former master of a local body in the U.S., I asked priestesses to re-robe when we rented a hall in a conservative location and when there were minors present in the congregation. I felt that I was protecting the body from any possible legal challenge. Through conversations with priestesses, I gradually shifted my concern to protecting the right of the priestess to make the decision. I moved the performance of the Mass to a more secure location and left it solely up to the priestess to make her own choice.

As a priestess, I decide whether to re-robe after reviewing who is in the congregation. I am profoundly grateful that the policy ensures I am never required to be nude and that the decision is mine alone.

The concern for women's choice, freedom, and safety is specifically addressed in the O.T.O. harassment policy published in 2004. The policy discusses what constitutes sexual harassment and the legal and moral responsibilities of O.T.O. officers and members to address this. It includes a detailed description of the procedure to file a complaint with the O.T.O., including alternatives if the immediate officers are not receptive or are involved in the complaint.[2]

This policy was re-emphasized in 2012:

> All members—women and men—who find themselves victims of non-consensual sexual conduct, are urged to report the incident to the master of their local body as soon as possible. If, for some reason, reporting to the local master is

---

[2] Paul Hume and Sabazius (2004). "Sexual Harassment: Approaches to a Reported Problem by Paul R. Hume, President-Emeritus, U.S. Electoral College & Sabazius, U.S. National Grand Master General." *Agape, The Official Organ of the U.S. Grand Lodge of Ordo Templi Orientis.* Volume V, Number 3&4, October 1, 2003 EV & February 1, 2004. http://lib.oto-usa.org/agape/agape.5.3-4.pdf.

out of the question, or has no effect, then the incident should be reported directly to the U.S.G.L. Ombudsman.[3]

Thelemic Community

In America, as in the world, we live in rape culture. One in three women is raped in her lifetime, and men routinely assault women, as well as transgender people and other men, with little or no consequence. In Western culture, overtly sexual women, especially women who appear naked in public, are subject to shaming, and register as sexually available to every man—"fair game." In this savage country, it is not surprising that a philosophy and practice that encourages women's overt expression of sexuality and displays a naked woman in public would seem unsafe.

Women are harassed on the streets; we are harassed in our own homes; and women do in fact complain of sexual harassment in Thelemic groups. The complaints don't come in an endless stream— the severity and frequency of incidents compared to a decade ago are way down—but still the complaints come in. Some incidents are egregious. Some may be a misunderstanding. Some are clearly described and openly raised as issues. Some are never mentioned except in back channels, often years after the fact.[4]

In Western culture, women are advised to dress modestly and to avoid situations which put us at risk; the responsibility falls on the woman to avoid violence. Feminist and other voices challenge the dominant culture to put the responsibility back on men to refrain from violence and harassment, but these voices have not yet succeeded in making this cultural shift.

The policy of O.T.O. encourages the offended party to report and puts the responsibility for the actions squarely on the offender. The

---

[3] Sabazius (2012). "From The Grand Master, Non-Consensual Sexual Conduct." *Agape, The Official Organ of the U.S. Grand Lodge of Ordo Templi Orientis.* Volume XIII, Number 3, Fall 2012 EV.

[4] Hume and Sabazius (2004).

policy states, "It is unconscionable to take advantage of our rituals, the initiations, the Mass, or other rituals mounted by local Bodies, to impose on another; it is beneath contempt to intrude on another magician's inner work in this manner."[5]

In his essay on *Liber Oz*, Sabazius emphasizes that the rights of man do not include the right to impose one's own will on someone else. He says clearly, "...while one may possess the right to 'to love as he will,' it may not be the will of the object of that love to participate. *Liber Oz* does not justify rape."[6]

As Thelemic community exists within rape culture, it is not surprising that harassment occurs within Thelemic groups. Harassment occurs everywhere. However, O.T.O. policy and Thelemic philosophy and religion expressly condemn this. It can take some time for those new to Thelema, women and men both, to understand that women and men can express free sexuality and still not be sexually available to everyone else in the room. The socialization that women are not targets proceeds on both a conscious and a subtle level. We are all working toward the day when this is true both in Thelemic community and in the larger culture.

The consent policy intends to create safe space for women in Thelemic community. To this end, connection with other Thelemic women is vital. When I entered Thelemic community, I was welcomed by women in both the local and the national community. As I have continued to work in O.T.O., the women around me have held women-only discussions, organized events centered on women's contributions, and explicitly acted to protect women entering our communities who were already involved in abusive relationships. Where I come from, if you're going to harass a woman, you're going to have to get through me and my sisters.

The support of male allies is always helpful in Western culture, and Thelemic community also benefits from the work of male allies.

---

[5] Ibid.

[6] Sabazius (2001).

This is especially critical where there are fewer women, or where those women are less bonded or less aware of social justice issues. If you're going to harass a woman, you're going to have to face our brothers, too. Even if you are a Thelemite yourself.

If you read through the harassment policy, the rules are clear: unless explicitly invited, keep your hands off. But what about your eyes? In Western culture, women's appearance is linked to sexuality, and men are not only permitted but actively expected to look at women and have sexual responses to them. In rape culture, men's gaze precedes violence and is the first level of the male claim to access women's sexuality with or without our consent.

I've written about the experience of being a priestess in a savage country. I am uncomfortable remaining unrobed in a congregation in which there are men who overtly express their desire to see a priestess naked. This comment commonly evokes two responses among other priestesses. Some priestesses struggle with the chilling effect of unwanted male desire, although many are reluctant to discuss this publicly. Others quote *The Book of the Law*, "Let her be loud and adulterous! Let her be covered with jewels, and rich garments, and let her be shameless before all men!" (AL III:44). These women suggest that the priestess should take a stance that the male gaze does not matter, and that priestesses should remain unrobed as an expression of power and encouragement for other women.

This is an important point. In male-dominated culture, which describes America in general and Pagan and Thelemic community as specific cases, women police other women to remain within cultural bounds. Thelemic women report that they have experienced body shaming from other Thelemic women. There is also a tendency on the part of lovers and friends to excuse the behavior of the men they're involved with, even when it makes other women uncomfortable. Feminism can draw attention to the ways in which women fail to support each other, but feminism in itself doesn't necessarily guarantee sisterhood, and the feminist movement still isn't all that comfortable with the sexual choices women make. However, the willingness to engage in discussion about feminism can begin to address some of these issues in community. Here as in many places, there is a great deal of work to do, but there is a community willingness to do it.

In my youth, Thelema offered me a way to see myself as the agent of my own sexuality. In my adult life, Thelema has gifted me a ritual which gives me the opportunity to explore nudity as a form of power. Feminism taught me how to see power structures and connect with other women, a lens which has been helpful in participating in Thelemic community. The law of Thelema provides me a lifetime foundation for drawing boundaries, as feminism taught me to do, and for allowing the melting of boundaries which sexuality exemplifies. As a feminist Thelemite priestess, I can say no, and I can say yes; and Thelema celebrates women who say yes.

Bibliography

Crowley, Aleister. *Liber Al vel Legis, the Book of the Law.*
    Website: http://lib.oto-usa.org/libri/liber0220.html

Crowley, Aleister. *Liber Oz.*
    Website: http://lib.oto-usa.org/libri/liber0077.html

Crowley, Aleister. *Liber XV, O.T.O. Ecclesiæ Gnosticæ Catholicæ Canon Missæ.* Website: http://lib.oto-usa.org/libri/liber0015.html

Hume, Paul and Sabazius (2004). "Sexual Harassment: Approaches to a Reported Problem by Paul R. Hume, President-Emeritus, U.S. Electoral College & Sabazius, U.S. National Grand Master General." *Agape, The Official Organ of the U.S. Grand Lodge of Ordo Templi Orientis.* Volume V, Number 3&4, October 1, 2003 EV & February 1, 2004.
    Website: http://lib.oto-usa.org/agape/agape.5.3-4.pdf

Sabazius (2001). "Observations on *Liber OZ*." Website:
    http://hermetic.com/sabazius/ozgloss.htm

Sabazius (2012). "From The Grand Master, Non-Consensual Sexual Conduct." *Agape, The Official Organ of the U.S. Grand Lodge of Ordo Templi Orientis.* Volume XIII, Number 3, Fall 2012 EV.

Valiente, Doreen (nd). "The Charge of the Goddess." Website: http://www.doreenvaliente.com/Doreen-Valiente-Poetry-11.php

Brandy Williams is a member of Ordo Templi Orientis and an ordained priestess of Ecclesia Gnostica Catholica. She is also a Golden Dawn magician, an initiated Witch, and a Pagan priestess. All these traditions connect through her practice of theurgy, the work of the gods. She is an internationally known writer and lecturer on esoteric topics and has taught in the Pagan and Ceremonial communities for the past three decades. Her first book *Ecstatic Ritual: Practical Sex Magic* was republished by Immanion Press in 2008. *Practical Magic for Beginners: Techniques and Rituals to Focus Magical Energy* (Llewellyn, 2005) brings magic into immediate use in daily life. She also edited the 2008 Immanion Press anthology *Women's Voices in Magic.* Her latest book *The Woman Magician* (Llewellyn, 2011) reshapes Western Traditional Magic for the needs of women and publishes the rituals of the sororal order Sisters of Seshat.

Consent within Heathenry

Sophia Sheree Martinez

My fellow feminist Heathens and I have spoken, and we have shared the stories that empower us and teach us about consent and boundaries. Luckily, there are many within our tradition.

Historically, Heathen women have had it good compared to women in other contemporaneous cultures and civilizations, both in terms of their roles in society and in their power to shape their own destinies. Throughout our history and in our stories, both women and goddesses have had the rights to consent to their marriages, own land, become warriors, and even have active sex lives.

The tale of how Freya obtained her beloved necklace, Brisingamen, is almost always mentioned when we talk about consent and/or "slut shaming." The story is from the *Sörla þáttr*, written by Christian priests in 14th century Iceland. Freya sees four dwarves making a beautiful necklace, and offers them gold and silver for it. They decline, and tell her that they will exchange it instead for a night each with her. She accepts their offer, and leaves four days later with her lovely necklace named Brisingamen.[1]

Because Freya is seen as a strong female figure (also being a goddess of war), we do not dare question her consent to such deeds. Freya's actions are encouraging for women who have been told that it is wrong to have an active sex life or more than one partner, and for anyone working in the sex industry. She teaches that it is okay for women to say "yes" when they mean "yes," under any circumstance they feel comfortable doing so.

Another tale of Freya that is relevant to discussions of consent is from the "Thrymskvitha" poem of the *Codex Regius* manuscript from Iceland (a source from which a portion of the *Poetic Edda* is derived). It was written around the year 900 CE by an unknown author. The

---

[1] Kershaw, N. "The Tháttr of Sörli." In *Stories and Ballads of the Far Past.* Cambridge: Cambridge University Press, 1921.

story starts with a giant, Thrym, stealing Thor's hammer. Loki then borrows Freya's falcon cloak to retrieve the hammer from the land of the giants. Thrym says he will only return the hammer if the gods give him Freya to be his wife. When Loki returns from speaking with Thrym, he informs Thor of Thrym's demand to marry Freya. Thor and Loki go to Freya, and Loki says to Thor:

> "Bind on Freya the bridal veil,
> For we two must haste to the giants' home."[2]

Neither Loki nor Thor ask for Freya's permission. They don't even tell her of the details of the situation directly. Instead, they merely find her and make the decision in front of her, without seeking her consent. To this awkward situation, Freya replies:

> Wrathful was Freyja, and fiercely she snorted,
> And the dwelling great of the gods was shaken,
> And burst was the mighty Brisings' necklace:
> "Most lustful indeed should I look to all
> If I journeyed with thee to the giants' home."[3]

Freya is not doing Loki and Thor any favors. A council is held, and it is proposed by Heimdall that Thor go down in a wedding dress himself. Thor follows Heimdall's plan and gets his hammer back by disguising himself as Freya.

There are many layers in this story dealing with consent and personal boundaries. In the beginning, Freya is happy to help Loki try to get Thor's hammer back by lending to him her falcon cloak; this is obviously not asking too much. One way to interpret this aspect of the story could be "Give someone an inch, and they'll take a mile." Loki returns with a mindset that is completely inconsiderate towards Freya's right to have a say in the plan—or, perhaps he assumes that she has helped them thus far and should be willing to marry Thrym too.

---

[2] Bellows, Henry Adams. "Thrymskvitha." In *The Poetic Edda*. New York: American-Scandinavian Foundation, 1923.

[3] Ibid.

Thor seems to go along with Loki's plan without question, but Freya is so upset at his presumption that her necklace, Brisingamen, shatters off her neck and makes the realm of the gods shake.

In this story, contrary to the *Sörla þáttr*, Freya's sexuality seems more reserved. She gives the sense that she doesn't want to appear lustful or desperate. The story is empowering because it shows that women can take a stand and say "No!" when their boundaries are crossed. It demonstrates that it is acceptable to be upset when your consent is taken for granted. Those that respect you will cease doing so.

For many, a precondition to consent is negotiation. A good example of negotiating consent is the story of how Skadi chose a mate. Two parts of the complete story can be found in the *Prose Edda* by Snorri Sturluson, written in 1220:

> Now giant Thjazi's daughter Skadi took helmet, coat-of-mail and a complete outfit of weapons and went to [the home of the gods] to avenge her father. The [gods], however, offered her compensation and damages, and first that she should choose a husband from amongst the [gods] and choose him by his feet without seeing any more of him. Then she saw a very beautiful pair of feet and said: "I choose this one; there's not much that's ugly about Baldr!" but that was Njord of Noatun.
>
> A further condition was that the [gods] should make her laugh—which she thought would be impossible. When Loki, however, by his tricks succeeded in doing this their reconciliation was complete. We are told that Odin (further) compensated her by taking Thjazi's eyes and throwing them up into the sky, making of them two stars. [4]

Skadi goes to the home of the Aesir feeling very upset that her father has been killed. To the benefit of everyone involved, she is able to negotiate a compensation that she agrees is fair. She chooses a

---

[4] "Skaldskaparmál." In *The Prose Edda: Tales from Norse Mythology*. Dover ed. Mineola, N.Y.: Dover Publications, 2006.

husband from among the gods by their feet, although she doesn't choose Baldr as she had anticipated. The story continues:

> Njord has a wife called Skadi, daughter of the giant Thjazi. Skadi wanted to have the homestead her father had had, on some mountains in the place called Thrymheim, (Stone home) but Njord wanted to be near the sea. They came to an agreement that they should be nine nights in Thrymheim and then another nine at Noatun. When Njord came back to Noatun from the mountain, however, he said this:

> "Mountains I loathed, no longer than nine nights did I stay there, the howling of wolves seemed ugly to me compared with the whooping of swans."

Then Skadi said this:

> "I could not sleep by the shore of the sea for the noise of the mew that awakened me, the bird that flew each dawn from the deep."

Then Skadi went up the mountain and lived in Thrymheim, and she goes about a great deal on skis and with her bow and arrow shoots wild animals. She is called Snow-shoe-goddess, or Snow-shoe-divinity. As it is said:

> "Thrymheim's the name of Thjazi's place, that giant of monstrous frame; his daughter wed with one of the gods. Skadi, now, the fair of face, lives there in her sire's old home."[5]

Skadi and Njord try their best to make their marriage work by taking turns in each other's homelands. They soon realize that the needs of neither of them are being met, making them cranky and exhausted. Realizing that in order to be happy, they have little choice

---

[5] "Gylfaganning." In *The Prose Edda: Tales from Norse Mythology*. Dover ed. Mineola, N.Y.: Dover Publications, 2006.

other than to part, so that is what they do. Skadi returns to Thrymheim, and Njord to Noatun. The marriage didn't work out, but they don't make a big deal out of it, and they keep living their lives. In fact, they are so confident and comfortable with who they are, it seems they have little problem coming to that conclusion.

This story is encouraging for people who struggle with any form of dependency on their significant others, and for anyone stuck in an unfulfilling relationship. It is all right at any time to decide that a situation isn't right for you, even if the timing is bad or the marriage is recent.

So what happens when consent is completely taken for granted and a boundary is violated? Answers to this question can be found in the *Volsunga* saga. The Volsungs are a bloodline said to have descended from Odin. One of the most famous heroes in Heathen lore, the warrior Sigurd, belongs to this family. The young Sigurd's first victory is against a giant, Fafnar. Afterward, he travels until he comes to a hill with a bright glow on top. He approaches it and enters the fort at the peak. There, he sees a sleeping warrior, and he takes off the warrior's helmet to discover it is a Valkyrie, Brynhild. Because of her magic, she knows who Sigurd is right away. She offers to teach him the magic of the Runes along with wisdom in many other matters. After the two talk for a long time, it is agreed:

> "No one is wiser than you," said Sigurd, "and I swear it is you I shall marry, and we are ideally suited."
>
> "I should wish to marry you," [Brynhild] answered, "even though I might have the choice of all men there are." And this they swore, each to the other.[6]

The next time Sigurd and Brynhild meet, Sigurd has gained much fame as a great warrior and the most honorable of men. Although Brynhild is still in love with Sigurd, she can also tell the future, and she foretells that Sigurd will one day marry a woman named Gudrun:

---

[6] Finch, R. G. "22." In *The Saga of the Volsungs*, 40. London: Nelson, 1965.

"I shall muster the troops," replied Brynhild, "and you will marry Gudrun, [King] Gjuki's daughter."

"No king's daughter shall ensnare me," replied Sigurd. "I'm not in two minds about this, and I swear by the gods that I either marry you or no one at all."

She spoke the same to Sigurd [who] thanked her for what she had said and [gave] her a gold [ring]. Then they repeated their vows, and [he] went off to his men and he prospered for a time.[7]

So far, this seems to be the ideal relationship. This couple meets by a stroke of fate, and they feel perfect for one another. Brynhild talks to Sigurd about her worries, and he reassures her about his feelings. Everything seems to be resolved, and they repeat their vows to eventually marry. This all changes when Gudrun comes to ask Brynhild to interpret a dream:

"I dreamed," said Gudrun, "that a good number of us left our quarters, and we saw a great stag. It was far superior to other deer. Its hair was golden. We all wanted to capture that deer, but I alone managed it. The deer seemed to me more precious than anything else. Then you shot the deer down at my feet. At this, my grief was so great that I could not bear it. Then you gave me a wolf cub. It spattered me with my brother's blood."

"I'll interpret it just as it will come to pass," Brynhild answered. "Sigurd, whom I chose as my husband, will come to you. Grimhild will give him drugged mead. This will bring great sorrow to us all. You will marry and soon lose him. Then you will marry King Atli. You will lose your brothers and then kill Atli."

---

[7] Finch, R. G. "25." In *The Saga of the Volsungs*, 43-44. London: Nelson, 1965.

"To know these things overwhelms me with grief," answered Gudrun.[8]

Brynhild and Gudrun were both aware of what the future held, so why don't they do anything to stop it? They are both aware that they will be at the mercy of the consequences of magic and politics.

Brynhild knows that Gudrun's mother, Grimhild, will give Sigurd the magical mead that will make him forget Brynhild. This happens when Sigurd goes to King Gjuki's hall, seeking to build further fame as a warrior by building strong alliances. After Sigurd has forgotten Brynhild, Grimhild convinces Gjuki to offer Gudrun marriage to Sigurd. Gudrun is used as a political pawn to set their alliance with Sigurd in stone, and it is heavily implied she has little say or control over that decision.

Over two years go by, and the future foreseen by Brynhild and Gudrun happens; Sigurd and Gudrun are married. But in this never-ending soap opera, Gudrun's brother, Gunnar, also needs to get married, and so Grimhild suggests he marry Brynhild. Sigurd, having forgotten about Brynhild, agrees to accompany Gunnar in going to ask Brynhild and her family's permission:

> They now prepared for their journey. Then they rode over hill and dale to King Budli. They put forward their proposal. He received it favorably, provided she did not refuse, saying she was so proud that she would only marry a man of her choice. Then they rode to Hlymdalir. Heimar gave them a hearty welcome. Gunnar explained their business. Heimar said that hers was the decision as to whom she should marry. Then he said her hall was a short way away off and gave his opinion that she would only marry the man who rode through the burning fire that surrounded her hall. [9]

---

[8] Finch, R. G. "27." In *The Saga of the Volsungs*, 46. London: Nelson, 1965.
[9] Finch, R. G. "29." In *The Saga of the Volsungs*, 48. London: Nelson, 1965.

This passage is important on many levels. It is one example of men acknowledging and respecting a woman's right to choose her own husband (other examples can be found throughout the sagas). The story also shows that it is alright to be picky and to set our standards high. Maybe we don't have to make our suitors jump through a literal fire, but we don't have to settle for less than we desire. Finally, it is important to compare Brynhild's situation to Gudrun's situation. Gudrun's decision to marry is made for her, although she loves Sigurd.

Although Brynhild's right to choose her own husband has been acknowledged, her fate is manipulated by Grimhild's magic once again. She teaches Gunnar and Sigurd how to exchange appearances, and Sigurd rides through the flames on his horse, in Gunnar's body. He stays there for three nights and shares a bed with Brynhild. Sigurd was the only one ever capable of riding through the flames, which Brynhild knows; she is therefore perplexed as to how someone else could have come through. Regardless, she must keep her oath to marry the man who rode through the flame, so she agrees to marry Gunnar. After the wedding celebration, Grimhild's spell wears off of Sigurd, who then remembers all of the vows he had previously made to Brynhild. He keeps his feelings a secret.

There is an overload of violations here. People lie about who they really are to get what they want, and magic is used to aid in that manipulation. This should be taken as a warning to those doing magical work for love: make sure you are not non-consensually interfering with any pre-existing situations. Thinking with an honest heart makes it easier to avoid dramatic situations.

While bathing in the Rhine together, bad feelings arise between Brynhild and Gudrun. They come into conflict over an armband given to Brynhild by Sigurd, then taken away when Sigurd was disguised as Gunnar, and later given to Gudrun. Gudrun shows Brynhild the armband as proof, and Brynhild is made aware of the magic done against her by Grimhild. The situation over the armband makes Brynhild incredibly depressed; she stops speaking and stays in bed all day.

One day, Gunnar comes to visit Brynhild, and she confronts him. She tells him she knows the truth about everything, that she is bitter because Sigurd is not her husband, and that she will get vengeance on Grimhild. Her depression is so great that it becomes contagious to the people living in that land.

Sigurd comes to comfort Brynhild after she has been sleeping for seven days. He acknowledges the vows he had once made and how he was tricked by Grimhild so that he became unable even to remember Brynhild's name. He even offers to leave Gudrun to marry her again, but her depression turns into hate for Sigurd. Sigurd prophesies that neither of them has long to live.

Brynhild begins to arrange for Sigurd's assassination with her husband Gunnar, who is torn between his oaths to Sigurd and his love for Brynhild. Ultimately, his love outweighs his word. Gunnar puts the task on his youngest brother, Guttorm, who sneaks into Sigurd's room and stabs him while he sleeps, then dies himself from a returned death-blow dealt by Sigurd. Brynhild's reaction to Sigurd's death, although plotted by her, is very grim. She laughs as she revels in Gudrun's pain, then announces that she is going to end her own life. At her request, she is burnt with Sigurd on his funeral pyre so she can accompany him in the afterlife.

The message of this story is that when consent is ignored and boundaries are violated, especially repeatedly, there are negative consequences. The consequences range in intensity, and affect both the violated and the violator. In romantic relationships, friendships, families, and greater communities, identifying boundaries and respecting them is important. There will always be people who take it upon themselves to be the "Grimhild" of a situation, and they will create chaos that is hard to recover from. It is worth identifying those people and taking necessary steps towards a fitting resolution.

Honor and reputation are important concepts within Heathenry. We are our deeds, and when we follow through with our agreements and uphold our oaths and vows, we are considered honorable. Maintaining peace is desirable, and those who take responsibility for their actions and attempt to make amends for their actions are much more forgivable than those unwilling to learn from their mistakes. If there has been a violation or dishonorable action, it should not be ignored.

Experience with my kindred has taught me that having an agreed-upon protocol for conflict resolution within communities is necessary. Coming together and talking about goals and missions as a group is also important and allows everyone to be on the same page. Consent can only be achieved through clear communication of desires and expectations. It must be both given and received in order for healthy relationships to flourish.

Sophia Sheree Martinez has been a Heathen for 12 years. She is a member of Golden Gate Kindred (GGK) in the Bay Area, and of Heathens United Against Racism (HUAR), an international organization that seeks to eliminate bigotry within Heathenry. Sophia's specialties are in community building and Rune magic. As a Gythja for many events within GGK, she is always seeking to hear the needs of the community and to provide attendees with a safe place, free from discrimination and other violations. Sophia's personal goals include building larger networks of Heathens and other Pagans who recognize the struggles of the oppressed in our communities and who want to participate in making necessary changes so that our practice does not fall into the hands of the selfish and power-hungry.

Matriarchy & Consent Culture in a Feminist Pagan Community
Yeshe Rabbit

"Okay."
"I guess."
"Um, sure?"

How can we know when a "yes" is an authentic "yes"? At what point is "yes" just another way of saying, "I guess so, since it seems like that's what I should say?" At what point is "yes, I guess so" informed by other input and structures of power that converge at a particularly sexualized moment?

A culture of consent is not merely one in which permission is given for a sexual act at the moment of the act. Permission given without other contextual commitments to shared power being present is actually not consent—it is surrender. Surrender and consent are two different things. Surrender implies that pressure from circumstances or people "got someone to say yes." Consent isn't about "getting someone to say yes." It's about a clear, holistic commitment to empowered participation among all the parties in a given dynamic, a dynamic that may or may not involve any sexual act. Consent implies a lot more than just an answer of "yes" to sex.

In fact, by the time there is even the possibility of discussion and agreement between two or more people who wish to have sex of any sort, a hundred minor negotiations have already occurred, negotiations in which both parties may or may not have had the opportunity to give consent to a power dynamic that was already establishing itself. For example, how did the people meet? What is their relationship to power within their group or social circle, individually and as a couple/group? Who calls the shots most often in the dynamic, and why do they do that? Is it an agreed-upon trust between the parties or is it because one person dominates in word, social standing, intellect, or willpower?

Look at the moments where power is enacted that even might occur on a normal date. Who picked the place where dinner or another meal was shared—was it selected with all parties' dietary needs in mind? Does it have suitable options for both or all parties? Who selected the entertainment for the date, and was it sensitive to the needs of both parties? Who drove, or how was transportation worked out? Is anyone in the situation at a disadvantage due to needing a ride, or challenges with train or bus schedules? During the conversation on the date, who did more of the talking? Was the discussion balanced, with both/all parties having the opportunity to listen as well as to share, or was one person the center of attention most of the time? Why is that? These and other factors can create a power differential that will make the difference between enthusiastic consent and a tepid surrender to a sexual encounter.

In a culture of consent, decisions that will affect the collective as well as each individual involved are made with the invited input of all concerned, as well as the demonstrated desire and practical effort to meet as many stated needs of both the collective and each individual as possible. This applies whether or not the outcome is sexually motivated, whether the collective includes two people or twenty, whether the individuals are skillful in negotiation, and whether or not there is existing precedent.

Authentic, enthusiastic consent means taking time and expending considerable effort to get it right. It means lots of discussion and negotiation. It means seeing each situation as unique, not merely according to prototypes or previous examples. It also means taking previous examples into account, not misguidedly trying to reinvent the wheel each time a decision must be made. A culture of consent requires contemplation of a great deal of data, many optional-but-honored levels of participation, a diverse set of viewpoints, and free will invitation to excellence. It is not enough to be content with mandatory minimum levels of representation or collaboration. In short, a culture of consent requires investment in each unique overlapping and diverging reality present, with discernment toward the good of all.

In most matters involving legal consent in the US, the idea of consent is defined by complicity rather than enthusiasm. This means that, from the start, the law is seeking the bare minimum of consent to justify the occurrence of a sexual act. In rape cases today, the onus is still on the victim to prove that they resisted and fought the attacker; the court does not try to discern whether the accused wrongly acted without a clear agreement. While consent actually should mean that there is agreement of an affirmative and determinable nature, in our patriarchal legal system, consent is usually treated as the absence of refusal. This is because in patriarchal power systems, like those expressed in the government and legal spaces of every country on this planet, the disempowered must impress upon the empowered their right to exist, to be selective, and to have their needs and ways of knowing treated as equal.

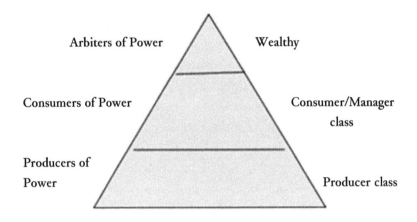

In patriarchy, power is concentrated in the smallest, top tier of a pyramid-like structure. That pyramid is most often stratified according to possession of financial resources, white skin, and an able, male body. Those at the top, the arbiters of power, use the labor, efforts, bodies, and lives of the bottom tier of the pyramid—the producers of power—to create goods, services, the potential for prestige, and media. These are sold to the consumers of power, thereby ensuring their position of financial superiority. This pyramidal structure also determines how skin color, sex, gender, and other factors are perceived in a stratified way. Anyone who wants justice must go before the arbiters of power, just as anyone who wants anything must go before the arbiters of power, and seek it. The arbiters of power are "the deciders," in the words of George W. Bush.

The arbiters of power then decide, based on flexible, highly ambiguous rules they have chosen for themselves, to adjudicate the matter at hand, whether it is a court case, a new law, property rights, or human rights.

In this model, it is visually clear that the producers actually hold the majority of power. However, the violence and culture of fear wielded by the wealthy arbiters of power (due to the forceful application of exponentially larger resources) has over generations shaped the way in which the producers of power think and act. For example, although females in the United States are the only ones capable of bearing babies at this time, and therefore ought to be the only ones deciding whether or not they will produce babies, centuries of violent and fear-based indoctrination have ensured that males actually get to make those choices for us in our governmental spaces. This is why abortion legislation remains such a thriving debate in the male-dominated space of Congress, a place where only people who can afford to run for seats are given a voice—regardless of whether they are qualified to offer an opinion or whether they bear the burden of their own choices in any way.

In a patriarchal system, obfuscation, violence, and fear establish and continually reassign authority to those concentrated in the top tier of the power pyramid. Authority is central, financial, dominance-based, and phallic, reaching the pyramid point. One might argue that some form of condensation of power is required for there to be accountability to group goals or objectives, and that power therefore must follow this kind of model in order for ventures to be effective. However, authoritative power is still available in non-patriarchal modes of power sharing. In a matriarchal approach to power-sharing, authoritative power is employed as an earned function and feature of the structure of consent culture. It begins within each individual as personal responsibility and is then shared more widely as responsibility for one's own part in transparent, balanced, voluntary circles. These circles overlap and interact around a common center of a goal or project.

In the example below, we see a power model in which there is still leadership and a central authority tasked with making sure that an outcome or goal is achieved, but this authority is balanced by individual and group input and participation.

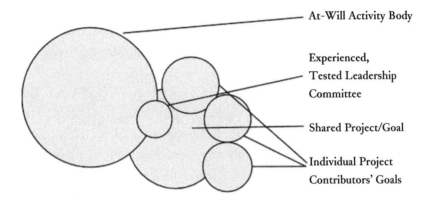

At-Will Activity Body

Experienced, Tested Leadership Committee

Shared Project/Goal

Individual Project Contributors' Goals

This graphic represents an at-will body of voluntary participants flowing together toward a shared project or goal. From the overlap between people who desire the goal and are willing to perform the duties of achieving the goal, a leadership team emerges who can see the project's overall trajectory. This team helps the group move from vision to action to accomplishment. In addition to the shared goal, the individual participants might also attach particular personal goals to the project. These personal goals are intended to help them grow and benefit as individuals along with the collective as a whole.

In this model, authoritative power shifts from person to person. In accord with how their skills fit with what is happening, different individuals emerge from the collective and take up leadership at different times. All resources and materials are sourced from the activity body as a whole, with individuals contributing greater or lesser shares according to their abilities and means. Yet in the end, the project will benefit the entirety of the activity body, with certain individuals possibly getting even more benefit because they took on more work, made more significant investments, or attached additional goals to the project. At no point is the entire project placed before anyone for permission or resources. At no point is an arbiter of power needed to bless or bestow the project with favor. At no point does the project require anyone to do what they don't want to do. This is a way in which an objective can be reached with all participants being enthusiastically involved, as opposed to being grudgingly or merely willing to be involved. This model holds empowerment and enthusiastic, informed consent from individuals and the whole as being central to its goals.

Living in a patriarchal power system, we fear power. We fear the exercise of power over us in violent or demeaning ways, as well as fearing expressing our own power (which may lead to retribution). Under this system, we are hardly ever capable of enthusiastic consent when it comes to the exercise of power because our relationship to power itself is so skewed. In this way, we are frequently faced with difficult choices about priorities. Rent or medical care? Food or child care so you can go to work? Speak up and stand in your truth or remain silent under the veil of social acceptance?

When we Pagans enter into spiritual relationships under a patriarchal system of power-over, in the effort to find the power we have been craving in the mundane world, we are susceptible to creating power schemes that replicate the imbalanced dynamics to which we are accustomed. Therefore, roles such as High Priest/ess, Elder, or other charismatic personality end up holding that pyramid point of power. They become the arbiters of power, with others around them desiring their time, energy, attention, and favor.

Under these conditions, the desire to impress the arbiter(s) of power has become such an ingrained survival behavior that both the consumers and producers of power are likely to court the arbiter(s) of power—perhaps thoughtlessly, perhaps consciously—as a means to an end. The result? The consumers/producers of power are in a vulnerable position regarding anything the arbiter of power might ask of them, including but not limited to sexual favors. Thus, their choice to go forward with any agreement, informed by this power dynamic, cannot be authentically consensual. The context of existing power in the situation prevents it from being so.

Similarly, if tactics of religious mind control have been employed in a hierarchical teacher/student relationship, the imbalance of power prevents any sexual or other favors from being contextually consensual. Thus, the lure of "mysteries" and other psychic and psychological phenomena need to be thoroughly investigated, and explicit information about the nature of these sought, before any kind of consent to participate can be authentically granted. Even then, there is still an imbalance of power for at least a period of time, where one person is in the know and another is not.

And yet, there are ways in which a mystery that is truly a mystery of universal proportions can reveal itself where there is a student and a guide, with one learning and one in the know. With a consensual context—including agreed-upon, clearly-stated intentions, demonstrations of trustworthy behavior over time, and a healthy system of checks and balances in a space where power is shared or rotates—a trust can take root that will form a ladder up which the student may climb to get a closer view of the mysteries. The guide's role is to steady the ladder, but not force the student to climb nor keep the student from climbing.

The mysteries that reveal themselves in these kinds of situations are truly the essence of a human, spiritual life. They are mysteries that we might learn alone or from one another even outside of a formal setting: mysteries of birth, illness and healing, and death; relationship with the Earth, with one another, and with deities and non-physical entities; the subtlety of energy; relationship with the body, mind, and soul(s). In certain situations, the exploration of sexual mysteries may be appropriate. When these universal mysteries arise within an overarching and specifically consensual, trusting context, where power is not imbalanced or skewed in favor of one party or another, they can be fruitful catalysts for deliberate growth. In contrast, if they are misdirected by the ego of either party into an imbalanced power dynamic, they can stunt growth.

In a contextually non-consensual situation, sexual activities as part of a student/teacher dynamic are among the most dangerous methods for exploration of the mysteries. Most community covens and groups will not want to explore this approach, while small groups where a couple, more than one couple, or a triad are the only participants in an equal or equitable setting may find it works well. Sexual exploration can also work among dedicants of a particular deity in lateral standing, or in a specifically-negotiated kink-centric context. There are ways for tantra to be done correctly and ways for it to be done improperly. The right way includes a foundation of contextual consent for all revelation of mysteries or other psychic or psychological phenomena, with a core of trust built between equals over time. The wrong way involves a great distraction from revelatory mysteries with what amounts to mentalist sleight-of-hand or the seduction of guru worship. These can actively damage an individual's ability to uncover any mysteries at all, or in fact enshroud them further from view.

In my own life, the test case for the practice of matriarchal contextual consensuality in non-sexual community activities is Come As You Are Coven in the Bay Area. I was one of the individuals at the origin point of this Coven. In all, there were six of us who started the Coven together: three white women, a Black woman, and two women of mixed race. From the beginning, our commitment to creating safe, welcoming, consensual space for magic was paramount to our project. We embraced the working model that is outlined in the circular graphic above, and over the first several years of our growth, we found ourselves stable with nearly that exact configuration. Over time, however, we grew in size, and in order to continue to diversify power, we had to be willing to allow, collectively, some uncomfortable power condensation points to rise, be recognized, and be dispersed into new circles and projects. In other words, we learned to "let it breathe." This progression of a rise-and-split paradigm regarding how power is balanced in the organization has given us new waves of creativity in how we provide our service to the community year after year.

For example, when CAYA Coven first came into being, its primary mission was to provide Goddess Full Moon circles for women.

However, quickly we reached a condensation point where several men wanted to also participate in collaborative ventures with us, as well as receiving support for their own ventures and offering their support to the women's ventures. We had some members who would consent to practicing in mixed-gender spaces and some who would not, preferring single-gender spaces. Within the first year, three new circles were born: the Women's and Men's Full Moons and collaborative Sabbats. These three circles stabilized over the next three years. However, a time then came when these rituals were no longer serving the widest possible range of stated needs. At that time, we began to include new circles, such as our Goddess Sabbats, which are clothing-optional, non-sexual rituals for women, as well as our Survivors' circles for those who had been victims of abuse. We also found new ways that we might be of service beyond rituals, such as gathering donations for local charities and volunteering at larger community events, like Beach Clean-Up Day. Our most recent endeavors include deity affinity groups, which are engaged in building bodies of literary, ritual, scholarly, and artistic work for the deities to which they are dedicated, and our new Rainbow Moon circle, which serves individuals all along the gender spectrum.

The matriarchal model is proliferative, with multiple points of entry, layers where authority is appropriately exercised by trusted individuals, and many levels of voluntary participation. In CAYA Coven, all members are considered matriarchs, including men. We use this term because we embrace an approach to power that is not biologically-deterministic, but conceptual, diverse, responsive, accountable, consensual, and circular in nature, as opposed to the patriarchal pyramid of power, which is inherently non-consensual.

From the CAYA statement on Governance:

> CAYA Coven follows a matriarchal philosophy of governance. In CAYA, we define patriarchy as the power-over, tiered, pyramid-shaped model that is often seen in modern business and social environments, where success and growth are predicated upon a sense of lack of resources and competition for limited possible returns. We define

matriarchy as a circular, power-from-within system that allows for multiple overlapping needs to be addressed and strengths to be shared simultaneously without competition for resources or top position. Our Coven is open to all, and all members who share these principles are charged with upholding the matriarchal nature of our philosophy and work, regardless of gender or sex.

Turning the energetic tide away from patriarchy and creating a more equitable balance of power by practicing and teaching matriarchy is one way in which CAYA Coven demonstrates a commitment to feminism and humanism, as well as employing a sustainable, life-affirming, organic power model that is found in communities worldwide.

The matriarchal model of Pagan community that CAYA exemplifies is not without its challenges. For example, interfacing with patriarchal institutions such as banks proves difficult. Without a top-down approach to power, there are projects that are proposed, gain support, but then falter due to individuals' lack of accountability or personal responsibility. There are times when a more authoritative stance than usual must be taken, as in cases when a member has breached trust by acting out of turn with physical violence, sexual impropriety, or failure to maintain requisite self-care or community service activities. These are times that test our collective and individual discernment. "That was tough. I had to really hold a hard line there. Am I still able to participate in this model? Does this model still work? Did we wait too long to make that hard decision? Did we not wait long enough?" We are aware that there is no "one right way" to do consensual community, but there are, and must be, many right ways to do consensual community. We have chosen matriarchy as ours.

No culture is without its challenges, and the matriarchal, consensual model that CAYA continues to employ serves us better than any other we have seen. We have found, collectively and individually, that more needs are served, more people's ways of being taken into consideration, and more honest conversation happens under this model than other models we have experienced. Every time we experience a challenge, it also gives us an opportunity to grow, to look for organic, sustainable solutions, and to become more trusting of one another in the process. None of this has anything to do with sex. It has to do with creating the kind of environment where consensual participation and empowerment provide the foundation for all of our activities. Once we have grown accustomed to these standards and ways of being accountable, personally and in community, we tend to manifest new levels of personal and community responsibility in other areas of our lives as well, including our sexual and relationship choices.

The road to building a truly consensual society is still long before us, and parts of it have not been built yet. Other parts must be deconstructed and the materials discarded or repurposed. The current system of power that is present in nearly every facet of modern life does not support enthusiastic consent. It rather prevents it from being a reality. We are often forced to compete and settle for what we can get rather than getting to choose what would make us feel safe and happy. This suffering is the reality for many in the Pagan community and outside of it. It is the result of rape culture, in which power-over is the root and return of all endeavors, even non-sexual ones.

It is the goal of CAYA Coven and other, similar small Pagan covens, societies, and groups to provide an antidote to rape culture. It is imperative that we do so, as a continuous war is being waged upon women and upon those who do not conform to strict, conservative gender codes. By embracing models of cultural creation that are fluid, circular, and responsive rather than static, rigid, or projective, and by structuring our circles and communities with a commitment to providing consensuality, safety, and diversity in all of our procedures from the ground up, we have an opportunity to not only help eliminate sexual predation in our community, but to change our community's relationship to power entirely. When these healthier structures of power prove successful, with the commitment, participation, and accountability of all, our entire society has the chance to create the kind of consent culture that will ultimately prove better for all beings.

Resources for Further Study

Noble, Vicki. *The Double Goddess: Women Sharing Power*. Rochester, NY: Bear & Company, 2003.

Goettner-Abendroth, Heidi. *Societies of Peace: Matriarchies Past, Present, and Future*. Toronto, Ontario: Inanna Publications, 2009.

Yeshe Rabbit serves the Divine as an Oracle, Ritualist, and Initiator. Her store, The Sacred Well, serves the material needs of esoteric practitioners, ecstatic wanderers, and all those drawn to the mystical arts in the sunny San Francisco Bay Area. Her coven, Come As You Are Coven, is an eclectic, drop-in coven open to all. She offers handfasting/wedding services, personal ritual consultations, Right Livelihood Intuitive coaching, and Intuitive Tarot readings through her shop and online. She is the author of the Way of the Rabbit blog (www.wayoftherabbit.com), a Priestess in the Oakland Temple of Aphrodite, and the host of Tea & Chanting Sangha.

Wicca and Consent

Yvonne Aburrow

> *And ye shall be free from slavery; and as a sign that ye be really free, ye shall be naked in your rites; and ye shall dance, sing, feast, make music and love, all in My praise. For Mine is the ecstasy of the spirit, and Mine also is joy on earth; for My law is love unto all beings.*
>
> – Doreen Valiente, *The Charge of the Goddess*

Wicca is an ecstatic religion where sexuality is celebrated and regarded as sacred. Wiccans seek authenticity and integrity, magic and mystery. Sacred touch and sacred sexuality are part of the mysteries of Wicca. These are part of the human experience and therefore sacred. That which is sacred must be entered into freely, and consent is a vital part of the process.

How do we ground our understanding of consent in the ethics of Wicca? How do we practice consent in the circle and in the coven? What are the points in Wiccan liturgy where consent is sought from the participants? And how does Wiccan mythology and theology support consensual practices?

Wiccan Mythology

As a polytheist Wiccan, I have the whole of Pagan mythology to draw upon in order to gain insights about consent, but let's look specifically at Wiccan mythology.

Wiccan mythology largely focuses on the Moon Goddess and the Horned God, sometimes referred to as the Lord of Death and Resurrection. The stories about the Moon Goddess and the Horned God generally focus on their archetypal qualities rather than their human qualities. We do not learn much in the way of biographical details, and they are archetypes rather than fully rounded characters. In the various stories associated with them, however, they are often given a choice of actions.

The Wiccan *Legend of the Descent of the Goddess,* for example, appears to be based on the story of Inanna and Ereshkigal. In the story of Inanna's descent to the underworld, no reason is given for her descent to the underworld, but she embarks on her journey deliberately, and she prepares by taking the seven divine powers with her:

> From the great heaven the goddess set her mind on the great below [...] She has taken the seven divine powers. She has collected the divine powers and grasped them in her hand. She has come on her way with all the good divine powers. She has put a turban, headgear for the open country, on her head. She has taken a wig for her forehead. She has hung small lapis-lazuli beads around her neck. [1]

At each gate of the underworld, one of the powers is taken away by the guardians, each of whom also commands her silence—a metaphorical act of binding. Inanna arrives in the underworld vulnerable and naked. There, she is turned into a corpse by Ereshkigal and her judges, then rescued by her allies according to the instructions the goddess left before her descent. Inanna then returns to the surface with new knowledge and power. Many people have interpreted this legend as a shamanic ordeal or an initiation; others have related it to BDSM, where practices of physical ordeal and psychological vulnerability can bring about powerful shamanic experiences.

The Legend of the Descent of the Goddess emphasizes choice and intentionality even more than the Descent of Inanna. Here, the reason given for the Goddess' descent to the Underworld is that "she would solve all mysteries, even the mystery of Death, and so she journeyed to the nether lands." [2]

---

[1] J. A. Black, G. Cunningham, E. Fluckiger-Hawker, E. Robson, and G. Zólyomi, "Inanna's Descent to the nether world: translation," *The Electronic Text Corpus of Sumerian Literature* (Oxford: 1998-). Available at http://etcsl.orinst.ox.ac.uk/section1/tr141.htm.

[2] Ceisiwr Serith, "*The Legend of the Descent of the Goddess,*" 2006, 2013. Available at http://www.ceisiwrserith.com/wicca/legendofthedescent.htm.

While the Goddess is in the Underworld, she is offered a choice: she can receive Death's cold hand on her heart and stay in the underworld, or be scourged. She refuses Death's plea to remain with him, and instead verbally gives her consent to scourging. Through her choice, the mystery of love triumphs over the mystery of death. Ceisiwr Serith writes:

> The Goddess submits to fate. "It is fate; better so." The God explains how death is the way things must be. "'Tis age and fate, against which I am helpless." The meaning of the Legend might almost be considered to be that we must submit to the way things are.
>
> But the Goddess shows a way out. She is herself the very personification of fate, and yet by her bold actions and her sacred presence she points to a way to escape fate. For part of fate, if is considered properly, is not merely death but also rebirth.[3]

Choice is a key factor in this myth. The Goddess' actions demonstrate a path of freedom even within the seemingly intractable laws of life and death. The decision to descend, and the choices she makes in the underworld, are entirely her own.

The Ethics of Wicca

If you ask most people what the ethics of Wicca are, they will tell you about the Wiccan Rede, "An it harm none, do what thou wilt" (If it harms no-one, do your true will). They may also mention that the Rede is akin to the Golden Rule which appears in every religious tradition, with slight variations. Some have criticised the Wiccan Rede, pointing out that nearly every action results in some harm to another being. But hardly anyone has noticed that if you turn the Rede around, what it is actually implying is that since it is impossible not to do

---

[3] Ibid.

harm, it is also impossible to do whatever you want.[4] The ethical implication is that we should think before we act and consider the possible outcomes of every action. The Rede also implies that even the smallest action can have consequences. To do something to someone else without their consent, however overtly friendly or apparently trivial the offence may be, can harm that person by violating their autonomy and integrity.

In another important piece of Wiccan liturgy, *The Charge of the Goddess,* the listener is enjoined to cultivate eight virtues: *beauty and strength, power and compassion, honour and humility, mirth and reverence.* Brought together in balance, these virtues require the practitioners of Wicca to act with integrity. Those with strength should use it gracefully. With power comes the responsibility to act compassionately. Guarding your own honour should always be paired with having the humility to know when you have done something wrong. Laughter should not violate another person's boundaries (by laughing at something they feel vulnerable about, for example).

Further, the Charge states that the Goddess does not demand sacrifice, and that Her love is poured out upon the Earth. I think the text is referring to literal sacrifice, and I interpret it as an injunction against the sacrifice of living beings. Elsewhere in Wiccan liturgy, we are told "To suffer is to learn," but this suffering is never interpreted as a sacrifice. These statements together suggest that a loving and generous Goddess may challenge us, but she does not demand that we consent to things that will hurt us beyond what we can bear. Instead, we are meant to give of ourselves freely. The Charge also states that "ye shall be free from slavery," which suggests that Wiccans should be autonomous and not enslaved by anyone or anything. That implies that we should be able to give our informed consent without feeling pressured into doing so.

Finally, *The Charge of the Goddess* states that "all acts of love and pleasure are My rituals" (the rituals of the Goddess). For something to

---

[4] I am indebted to Dee Weardale for this insight.

be an act of love and pleasure, it has to be pleasurable for all parties involved. Consent (*enthusiastic* consent) is a prerequisite for pleasure. For many Wiccans, this line above all emphasizes the religious importance of consent practices.

Initiation

During the Wiccan initiation ceremony, the candidate states that they are taking the oath, and by implication, undergoing the initiation, of their own free will and accord. As the contents of the initiation ceremony are secret, the candidate cannot specifically consent to them in advance, so they are given a number of opportunities in the ritual to call the whole thing off.

It is of course possible for a curious candidate to find the text of the initiation ceremony fairly easily on the internet, but most people choose not to, preferring it to be a surprise. Many people find it reassuring that every other Wiccan has undergone the initiatory ordeal.

I have never experienced a situation where a candidate for initiation chose to call the whole thing off, but I trust that if they did, the whole process would stop immediately. There are a few counter-cultural aspects of the initiation ceremony which some candidates might find difficult (kissing, nudity, binding, and scourging). These are seen as a test of the candidate's resolve to become a witch, as well as potentially transformative.

Kissing

Kissing is an expression of intimacy and trust. Kissing another person on the lips affirms their utterances as sacred and honours their breath. In the words of the liturgy for the Fivefold Kiss, "Blessed be thy lips, that shall utter the sacred names."

I think Wiccans need to spend more time discussing what hugging and kissing and other ritual expressions of affection mean so that everyone can give their consent in a meaningful way, rather than feeling vaguely pressured to go along with it. Not everyone is comfortable with being hugged; not everyone is comfortable with being kissed. The only people I kiss are my immediate family, my partner, very close friends, and my coven. When offering a hug to another person, I usually "telegraph" that a hug is on offer (by opening my arms in a hugging gesture), so they can decline if they want to.

Kissing someone who wants to be kissed is a beautiful experience, an affirmation of their sacredness. Why would we want to spoil it by kissing someone who has not given their enthusiastic consent?

Ritual Nudity

The value of ritual nudity is that it promotes intimacy and trust. Gerald Gardner claimed that it made magical energy flow more freely—and if the magic is based on sublimated *eros*, then this makes sense. In my experience, part of the magic of Wicca is that whilst erotic elements are present, they are not acted upon, but used symbolically to create the energy for the circle and the magic. Precisely because ritual nudity is uncomfortable and transgressive, it is also a powerful means of transcending everyday reality, and acts as a signifier that the participants have entered sacred time and sacred space. It is 'a sign that ye be really free' because all the social markers conferred by clothing (gender, status, power) are removed, and we are left in our natural state.

However, many people find ritual nudity uncomfortable, especially in front of people they do not know very well. For some people, the discomfort does not lessen over time. These people might benefit from a discussion about why we practice ritual nudity and what they find uncomfortable about it.

Most covens maintain a high level of trust between the participants because they get to know each other very well through months and years of working together. But when there is a guest in the circle, some people may feel uncomfortable with being naked in front of them. Sometimes practices that are intended to make people more comfortable can actually make them less comfortable. For example, I once worked with a group who had the women go into one room to undress and the men go into another. This separation of the sexes made me uncomfortable because it implied that there was something sexual about ritual nudity. As I have attended naturist events, where a sexual response to nudity is discouraged, I am able to dissociate nudity from the sexual. Others may find it more difficult, and may need to discuss it. I think this is one of the reasons we refer to ritual nudity as "going skyclad"—to help create this separation in people's minds.

In rape culture, nudity and scanty clothing are often seen as *de facto* consent to intercourse. The fact that Wiccans can be naked together and not end up having an orgy is sometimes a surprise to outsiders. However, Wiccan circles don't turn into orgies, and neither do naturist events: partly because nudity becomes unremarkable, and partly because it is dissociated from sexuality.

Binding

During a Wiccan initiation, the candidate is prepared for initiation by binding them. This is done in order to partially restrict blood flow and create an altered state, as well as to create a feeling of vulnerability and receptivity on the part of the candidate. In my experience, it also keeps energy within the body. Again, the candidate is given the opportunity to halt the ritual.

Binding needs to be done with care and thought. The idea is to impose a certain amount of sensory deprivation by restricting the breathing and movement of the hands. Doing it too tightly, however, may pinch nerves in the wrists. It is also a good idea to use a quick-release knot. It is important that the binding does not get any tighter.

In order to consent to being bound, a person must completely trust the person binding them. They must trust that the other person will not harm them while they are bound. Hence it is necessary to evoke such trust in the candidate for initiation by being a trustworthy person with a strong sense of boundaries.

Scourging

The practice of scourging is also difficult for many people, as they tend to see it as "mortification of the flesh" or as a "punishment." In fact, it is a way of stimulating the production of endorphins, which can lead to ecstatic altered states, and it is usually performed lightly. But again, there needs to be discussion around how people consent to this practice, and what its function in ritual actually is. Once people understand more about its symbolism, the biochemistry involved, and its function in ritual, they are usually much happier about it being a part of Wiccan ritual.

The practice of scourging is perhaps not as widespread as it once was, except perhaps in the initiation ritual, and even there it is not done so as to hurt. There have even been suggestions that it was all invented by Gerald Gardner because he was into BDSM. However, it is clear that sexuality and spirituality have always been closely associated, and that some people derive pleasure from pain; hence also there has been a link between BDSM and the sacred. Pain makes you feel intensely in your body, aware of every nerve, every sinew. In a spiritual tradition where the connection between mind, body, and spirit is of paramount importance, therefore, anything that connects body and spirit more closely is a valued part of the tradition.

The experience of pain is not the only thing evoked by the practice of scourging or the practice of BDSM. In any situation where you abdicate control, power relations come into play. In BDSM, the power relations obtaining in the world are often deliberately subverted. In the Craft, all must submit to the scourge, and all must use the scourge, so there is never an imbalance of power. As the Wiccan *Book of Shadows* notes:

> In other religions the postulant kneels while the priest/ess towers above him/her, but in the Art Magical we are taught to be humble... [5]

There are various ideas about how to frame the use of the scourge mythologically. One is that the scourge is of Hecate, because it

---

[5] Gerald Brosseau Gardner (1949), *The Initiation: First Degree* [online]. Available at http://www.sacred-texts.com/pag/gbos/gbos03.htm.

confronts the parts of the psyche hitherto considered unacceptable. Another is that it is of the higher self, to strip away the ego-bound consciousness (after all, you can't be very egocentric when you're bound and being scourged). In the initiation ceremony, it is a shamanic ordeal, such as is used by traditional societies.

The physical aspect of scourging heats the lower chakras to stimulate the *kundalini*. Safety is an important consideration here. Scourging is not something you should do casually—it takes practice and thought. When the main part of the thong has been laid on, the rest of the tail travels faster and hurts more on impact. Even someone who is trying to scourge softly can cause pain in this way. Another useful technique is to "pull" the blow, as you do with punches in stage fighting. This is done by flicking the wrist up on impact.

The experience of scourging is mutual (though not in the initiation ritual, where the experience of the postulant being scourged by the initiator is balanced by the initiator kneeling before the postulant). The other person scourges you, then you scourge them. It creates intimacy and a sense of trust.

Scourging and other practices of controlled, intense sensation are also used in BDSM, which experiments with the psychosomatic effects of pain and the boundaries of trust. These practices can be quite powerful. Within the shamanic BDSM scene, people sometimes report out-of-body experiences and other states of ecstasy or self-transformation. In BDSM, negotiation and consent are an integral part of the practice. All activities are carefully negotiated in advance, and all participants have a safeword that they can call to end any activity immediately. These practices help participants explore their boundaries in an atmosphere of safety and trust.

Consent in Coven Life

One of the aims of a Wiccan coven is to create an atmosphere of "perfect love and perfect trust." All the members of the coven have been through the same initiation ritual, which is designed to be a transformative experience; they do ritual together naked; and they usually socialise and share their joys and sorrows with each other. All these practices promote love and trust. A high degree of mutual empathy arises, often referred to as the "group mind" or "egregore." In this atmosphere, it is hoped that people will wish to avoid harming each other. However, with that degree of openness, we also become very vulnerable to each other, and so it is possible to get hurt. Yet the joy of being so open with other human beings generally outweighs the risk. People should be aware of group dynamics, though, and mindful of the possibility of hurting other coven members in such an intimate atmosphere.

Once a person is initiated into Wicca, however, they are often assumed to have consented to all the other things that happen in circle, such as ritual kissing (for example, it is customary to kiss other coven members on the lips to welcome them into the circle). I am not alone in finding these assumptions problematic. One Wiccan initiate I spoke with commented that they would find these aspects of Wicca difficult in a non-ritual context, but as they were happening in a sacred context, they were happy with them. Another Wiccan initiate seemed uncomfortable kissing other coven members on the lips, despite the sacred context.

When people are in an altered state in ritual, they are less likely to say no to things they do not really want to do. This may be partly because they do not want to disrupt the flow of the ritual, but also because they are in a dreamy and otherworldly state of mind where they are less likely to react negatively. But if something uncomfortable occurs in a ritual where participants feel subtly compelled to cooperate, it leaves a bad feeling behind that can erode the trust of the group. This might not involve touching, hugging, or kissing—it could consist of feeling obliged to partake of alcohol, for example. It is always a good idea to discuss rituals beforehand and make sure everyone is comfortable with them. The group should also discuss any requirements for accessibility, such as for people with a disability or pregnant women, who may find dancing or standing for long periods difficult.

Sacred Sexuality

The Great Rite, carried out with a beloved partner, is a beautiful ritual. The participants both have a deity invoked upon them, and while they make love, the deities are also making love. The ritual is a celebration and a fusion of divine and human sexual love. While it is happening, one feels both human and divine, and senses the movement of cosmic forces. The Great Rite may be performed by any initiate, though monogamous Wiccans prefer to reserve it for their partner. There is also a symbolic version: the consecration of a chalice with an athame.

It is fairly well-known that the Wiccan third degree initiation may involve the Great Rite. It does not have to be the version involving sexual intercourse, and whether it does or not is a matter for the initiator and the candidate. However, there is a power difference between the initiator and the candidate, in that the initiator has something to bestow. There is a general view among Gardnerian and Alexandrian Wiccans that doing the Great Rite "in true" (with sexual intercourse) is somehow better than doing it "in token" (symbolically or with energy exchange). Even the phrases used to describe the two options give greater weight to the sexual version of the Great Rite. But in actual fact, doing it symbolically or energetically may be more powerful and meaningful than doing it with sexual intercourse. If the circumstances of a sexual Great Rite may involve trying to become sexually aroused with someone the candidate does not know well, or a need to focus on the mechanics of the sex, then a symbolic Great Rite may actually help the candidate focus more completely on the movement of energy. Of course, this problem is greatly reduced if you do the sexual version of the Great Rite with your partner or with a close friend.

Most Wiccans approach the third degree and the Great Rite with delicacy and tact. Even so, care needs to be taken to prevent either the candidate or the initiator from feeling pressured into doing the sexual version of the Great Rite. A proper discussion needs to be had between the candidate and the initiator over several occasions during the months before the ritual.

Larger Groups

In larger gatherings of Wiccans, "perfect love and perfect trust" does not necessarily apply, because different groups may have different values and people will feel more vulnerable in a group of acquaintances. Consequently, they are likely to be less open and trusting. Nevertheless, there are some powerful triggers at large Wiccan gatherings which make people want to let down their guard —the pleasure of meeting with other witches, all the cues being present that tell us that we are in a safe space, and the general atmosphere of bonhomie. It is a good idea for organisers of large gatherings to have a safeguarding procedure and an anti-harassment policy, together with a designated group of people who can be contacted if the policy is violated. The organisers must commit to acting decisively if the policy is violated.

Changing Practices

What should people do if they have an issue with Wiccan ritual practices such as kissing, nudity, binding, and scourging? What if they are uncomfortable with something, but would like to overcome their discomfort? What if they are so uncomfortable with something that they cannot overcome their discomfort? Can some people opt out of the practice while others continue with it?

I think that with any practice, even uncontroversial ones like sweeping the circle with a broom, each person should explore and discuss its meaning and function in some depth.

- What does it mean to you?
- What does it mean to the rest of the coven?
- What are its symbolic purpose and/or ritual function in the coven/lineage/tradition?
- Does it require everyone to participate in it or be focused on it while it is happening?
- How does the energy change after it has happened?
- How does it make you feel?
- If you are uncomfortable with it, why?
- If you are comfortable with it, why?

- Is your discomfort with it because of ethical concerns? Can the practice be modified to address these?
- Is your discomfort with it because of personal history? Can the practice be modified to remove the trigger(s) that are making you uncomfortable?
- If you feel the need to change it or replace it with something else, can you find something else that performs the same function in the ritual?

Many people see these practices as core aspects of Wicca; others do not. Some covens omit nudity and others omit scourging from their practice. Some omit both. It is possible to find covens which have a set of practices that you are comfortable with; but then you might miss out on something that will challenge you and make you grow.

The bottom line here is that negotiation and discussion and exploration are key parts of the decision-making process. No-one should feel pressured, and everyone should be able to give informed and meaningful consent.

Conclusion

Wicca has a number of counter-cultural practices, in the sense that they go against prevailing norms, and that the practices mean something different in Wicca than what they mean in mainstream culture. Accordingly, considerable attention needs to be paid to issues of consent in Wicca. Consent is required for kissing, nudity, hugs, binding, scourging, and the sexual version of the Great Rite.

Fortunately, there are already built-in safeguards in the liturgy to offer choices and opportunities to give meaningful consent (or to opt out). However, we need to examine our practices and be sure that they are consistent with giving informed and enthusiastic consent. Discussing issues of consent and promoting consent culture with your group and with other experienced witches is a good beginning. Beyond that, we need to develop a positive consent culture that celebrates enthusiastic consent and removes any sense of obligation to comply with social norms around accepting unwanted intimacy, whether they come from Pagan culture or mainstream culture.

Yvonne Aburrow has been a Pagan since 1985 and a Wiccan since 1991. She has a MA in Contemporary Religions and Spiritualities from Bath Spa University and is the author of eight books, including *All Acts of Love and Pleasure: Inclusive Wicca* (Avalonia Books, 2014).

The Anderson Faery Tradition and Sexual Initiation: An Interview with Traci

Helix

A note from the interviewer:

Both Traci and I are initiates of the Anderson Faery tradition, an American witchcraft tradition founded in the mid twentieth century by Victor and Cora Anderson.[1] For the purposes of this interview I wanted mainly to unpack Traci's point of view, but by the end of our talk, we were enjoying ourselves so much that the interview became more of a conversation. Although Traci insists she can speak only for herself, I hope this piece provides a good example of how a Faery initiate might understand respect for sovereignty in the practice of sexual initiation.

HELIX: Tell me a bit about the Anderson Faery tradition of witchcraft. How is it different from other forms of witchcraft, like Wicca or Reclaiming?

TRACI: Well, from what I understand of traditional Wicca—I haven't trained or been initiated in that tradition—it can be gender [polarity]-based, and Faery isn't. It's a queer tradition, if anything. It's certainly gender-fluid. It's not fertility-based; it's an ecstatic tradition. As far as Reclaiming—it's very similar to Reclaiming, but Faery's not as community-focused. Reclaiming is very outward-facing; it's about sharing power, and it's really concerned with unity, with the state of our country politically, et cetera. But Faery is focused on the individual, on the development of the witch herself. It's not that Faery witches are not interested in community, but the tradition doesn't have community as a main emphasis.

---

[1] Some who trace their lineage to the Andersons use the spelling "Feri".

HELIX: What does it mean for Faery to be ecstatic as opposed to fertility-based?

TRACI: When I say those words, what I mean is that it's about raising energy for ecstasy, as opposed to some concept of life force springing from gendered sexuality, where procreation is the driver behind magic or the world in general. That goes back to Faery being non-gendered or other-gendered or queer or—well, it's just *Other*. It's not built around a system of male and female. The energy of the universe, life force, is not necessarily about procreation. Ecstasy is for pleasure; it's the experience of life.

HELIX: Before we sat down here, we were talking about how the essence of the Faery current is a kind of wildness. Can you say more about that?

TRACI: I feel that I can't speak for the Faery tradition; I can only speak for my personal experience as a Faery witch. Faery is a lineage that seeks to develop the witch as an individual, and then whatever that individual puts her hand to *is* the tradition. So I can really only speak for me.

Faery is a lineage that passes life force. Its current is amoral and wild. There's no ethical code to life force, it's just energy occurring. Ethics are something built by human-persons. But life force itself is beyond those things, beyond any ethical code.

HELIX: It sounds like you're describing the natural world.

TRACI: We like to say in witchcraft that nature is red in tooth and claw. The universe is chaos, and we're bringing order to it. So when I say "amoral," I mean something outside of our human community's decisions about what ethical codes are, what our moral obligations to each other are.

Those are human-centric agreements that we make. And so Faery, being a current, stands outside of that community. Its energy is that of the natural world around us, which is not human.

HELIX: The natural world doesn't have a concept of good and evil, right and wrong.

TRACI: No. We eat because we're hungry, and that requires killing. But killing, as a human being within human agreements, is a violation of our ethical codes.

HELIX: If your ethics don't come from the Faery tradition, where do your ethics around witchcraft come from?

TRACI: They come from myself. I'm human, and part of the human community. There are agreements we've made as a larger human community that I was not part of making. But nonetheless I was born into those agreements, into society.

Ultimately, the ethics that make sense for the practice of Faery are situational ethics, ethics that are about being in balance. And that's a whole big kettle of fish, which is what the Faery tradition is wonderful for: helping you as a human discover yourself, all of your parts. That's one of the Faery catchphrases that float around in the wider world: "knowing yourself in all your parts," which include all those little hang-ups that make us react in unconscious ways. My ethics arise from within myself, from knowing myself, being spiritually clean, from knowing what my obligations in the wider community are.

HELIX: From knowing yourself and being in relationship, and valuing relationship, I assume. You've talked a lot about community already.

TRACI: Yes. I identify as an animist, which for me is about being in relationship with all persons, human and other-than-human, and that's what I think being a witch is about. You build relationship with those persons—and when I use that term "persons," I mean it in an animistic sense, that a person is a consciousness to which I can relate or that can relate to me. I think that's how we work, humans especially; we work by being in relationship.

HELIX: We talked earlier about what it means to respect others' wildness. Can you talk about that in the context of relationship with human and other-than-human persons?

TRACI: Within Faery, we have the concept of sovereignty. We're all sovereign, all emanations of the Star Goddess. That sovereign state is about being your divine self, realizing your own divinity. "God is a person like myself," that's something Victor said. Respecting that wildness within other persons is the way we respect their divinity. As an animist, I view the Star Goddess mythology as meaning that we are all creations out of that Big Bang, which is Her orgasm, Her ecstatic orgasm, self-produced. Then all persons, every thing that my eye sees, they are divine, and also wild. The cosmos is a wild being. Wildness is divinity, and divinity wildness.

I respect that by first recognizing my own wildness. And if I am divine, that means you are divine, that means everyone is divine. I want respect shown to me, therefore I show respect to others—to Other. I want Other to respect me.

And yet this isn't a delicate respect. It's a ferocious respect where I'm going to respect you to *know* yourself, and I'm going to respect you to speak up and speak for yourself; I'm not going to interpret for you. It goes deeper than the niceties of "May I take your coat?" and "Would you like a drink?"

HELIX: So wild creatures can be expected to be independent, to advocate for themselves, to be assertive about their needs and desires. Let's say everyone in a room is going to behave like that. What does a community of people who are all living in their wildness look like?

TRACI: Where is that community? Let's go live there. [*laughing*] There's a saying among Faery witches that there should only be one of us per community! Maybe we can't all live like that, I don't know. To be wild, it's not necessary to be rude and mean. We've all made some agreements. We've made these agreements that, for example, if I kill you, I'm going to get into trouble! If I steal from you, I'm going to get into trouble, right? We've also made those commitments with one another in lesser ways, like, in my white Southern subculture, we generally agree that yelling at one another is not very nice.

As human-persons living in community, we can speak to one another without screaming and yelling and throwing things [*laughing*]—so we can be *wild,* in that we can speak our truth, and be authentic and set our boundaries. We can say what we need and want from one another without the ugly behaviors or violations that are unjustly called "wild."

HELIX: So what I'm hearing is that people who are fully embodying their wildness still can and do make agreements with each other in order to live peacefully in community.

TRACI: Definitely.

HELIX: So what happens in such a community when someone starts disrespecting someone else's autonomy?

TRACI: On a small scale, if you have a personal relationship with the person who's being disrespectful, you'd talk to them about it. On a wider community scale, the group would have to come together to make a decision about the issue. If the offense was really grave, you'd have to shun that person from community. It's the same as in any human relationship—marriages, friendships—if after a time you cease to respect and honor the agreements you've made together, then you can't be in relationship anymore. Just like in the wider society—if someone commits a grave offense, like taking someone else's life, they've violated a very strong agreement and have to be removed from community.

HELIX: I think a lot of people hear the term "wild" as meaning "uncontrolled." But that's not what I'm hearing here... I'm hearing about independence and self-knowledge, ferocity, strength, not about hurting others.

TRACI: No, no. It's not about being unkind or acting maliciously. It's not behaving in a way that's out of control. Being out of control certainly wouldn't benefit an other-than-human person living in their natural habitat. If they're not in control of their behavior, they're not going to eat! They're going to scare away their prey or be spotted themselves by the hunter.

         What I mean here by wildness is really inherent essence. We as humans tend to layer a lot of stuff—social conditioning—on ourselves so that we stifle our essence, our divinity, our authentic selves. "Wildness" would be our true nature, stripped of stifling cultural baggage.

HELIX: There are ways of enculturating people that restrict and strangle. But there are other ways to socialize people that provide a structure for growth, for developing their humanness and their capacity for relationship. When I think about parenting... You socialize your children because it's required for their happiness.

TRACI: Definitely. If you don't socialize them, you'll make them unhappy adults. They won't find their place in their tribe—in this large tribe that we've built for ourselves, our society. That's what a Faery witch does: struggles with the paradox of how to be this authentic, wild individual living within a society that has certain agreements. Our legal, social, moral, and ethical agreements may require things of us that run counter to what our authentic selves want to do. Holding that paradox is very Faery, and really that's also what it is to be human, and that's what it is to be every other-than-human person who lives in a group. There's always a certain sacrifice of individuality for the group, compromises that need to be made.

HELIX: So if you were to take on a Faery student—and I hear you saying that for you, Faery is more a way of being in the world than a set of practices—what would you be looking for in that student?

TRACI: I would be looking for someone who wants to know their authentic self. And that might be it—all they need is a genuine interest in doing that work. And I'd want to make sure they're stable in some way. Nobody has to be perfect, but I'd want their emotional state to be relatively consistent.

HELIX: So we're not talking about someone who's still in adolescence.

TRACI: No, no. Now, I know that within my lineage, there are people who have begun training students when they were older teenagers. But for myself personally, I would not. I do think that there is a place for younger people to do this kind of work. I have children, all young adults now, and certainly I was incorporating witchcraft practices into our daily life when they were younger. But I wouldn't formally teach an adolescent. It's very problematic to do so in our culture. They're not legal adults.

HELIX: Young people's identities are often in such freefall in adolescence, and even into early college age.

TRACI: Yes. There's no way for an adolescent to be stable. The nature of adolescents is their hormonal imbalance. They are *supposed* to be all over the shop. [*chuckles*] I wouldn't take someone on for Faery training if I couldn't see a track record of some stability, the ability to maintain employment, the ability to maintain relationships. And some of what I'd be looking for is just a good reputation in their community.

HELIX: Is it important to you that a student be respected in their community, be considered an ethical person?

TRACI: It would be for me, yes. Because Faery is about family. It's not about learning Witchcraft 101. It's an initiatory mystery tradition. There's only one initiation, and if I'm training you, you're headed there. It's a very intimate place, initiation. I would not initiate anyone unless I were prepared to call them my sister, my lover, my brother in the Craft. So, yes. It would be important to me that they have a good reputation. [*laughs*] 'Cause they're going to be representing my *family!* Would you want to marry someone that your whole family is going to be ashamed of?

HELIX: So when you say "stable," I'm guessing you don't mean that you're looking for someone who has never been traumatized or has never struggled with depression—

TRACI: Oh, no, no. I'm not a psychologist, though, so I would want to make sure that any potential student already had work like that in hand. I wouldn't want to push anyone over an edge. Because Faery digs, Faery's a very raw kind of current, and it may not be right for everyone. But if there is anything going on, an illness or similar—I would hope to find out about it, because Faery training is really about bringing someone into your family. Eventually you have to share that kind of thing—you *know* one another.

HELIX: So that's what's needed from the student. What do you think is needed from the teacher? What kind of container would you be creating if you were teaching someone Faery?

TRACI: Transparency, as much as possible. It is a mystery tradition, so there are secrets until you're initiated. Bur transparency as far as what I expect, who I am, where I'm coming from. There is a power differential between teacher and student because it is an initiatory tradition. I will always be in a place of power over that student because I'm an initiate, until they—if they—become an initiate themselves. It falls to me to make sure I'm in balance, and that I'm aware and thinking about the fact that there's a power difference. As much as I might say, "Speak your mind, share what's going on," they may hold something back because I'm the initiate and they're wanting something from me, training or initiation or whatever that thing is. It falls onto me to think about that.

Now, some things I *can't* reveal. I have to hold that power. I have to hold the fact that I have power over them, and that's one way that Faery differentiates itself from Reclaiming, which is an offshoot tradition. Reclaiming is all about shared power. Faery does not share power until you're an initiate. So I have to own, as an initiate, that I have power over that student. Just like as a parent, I had power over my children, who were in my care.

When you're a parent, sometimes a child wants to do something that you know they can't, and you just have to hold your power. You're in it, you have the power over them. It's about being ethical. So, how are you a good teacher? Well, how are you a good parent? It's really the same question.

HELIX: Is the power differential between teacher and student static, or does it lessen as the student approaches initiation?

TRACI: I would love to say that it lessens. But it really doesn't, and the reason it doesn't is that it's an initiatory tradition. And no matter how fantastic of a witch the student is, they're not an initiate. Whatever that thing is that you hunger for when you're a student—your teacher may tell you, "We're all powerful witches!" but in your heart, you're saying, "Yeah, but I'm not an initiate yet!" [*laughs*] So no, it's static. We may be equal in ability, we may be equal in lots of things, the student may even be more successful in the world than I am. But in the tradition, in the Faery lineage, I'm still the initiate, so I have power over them because only I can give them the prize they're seeking.

HELIX: It's easy to think of initiation as a prize when you're a student. But on the other side, as an initiate, it's hard to think of it that way.

TRACI: Yes. I don't personally think of it as a prize, but I know I did when I was a student! [*laughs*] And I don't think there's anything you can say to dissuade a student from thinking of it that way. As a student, I felt like initiation would be an acknowledgement of my work. As an initiate, I can say, yeah, no. It's not like that at all. But I feel it would be a disservice to the student not to acknowledge that that's how they're feeling.

Again, it's like being a parent. You don't tell your child, when they tell you that they're cold, "You're not cold!" It's respecting the student's feelings and honoring what they're saying to you, respecting their personhood, respecting their wildness. As an initiate, you want to model for your students: this is what authenticity is. It doesn't include telling another person, "You're not having that experience." They *are* having that experience! That's how students often feel, that initiation is a prize that they're achieving. As an initiate, it's incredibly disrespectful to look back down from my place of power and tell them, "That's a wrong thought!" [*laughs*] Should they feel that way? Well, I wish they wouldn't. But I did. Just like with teenagers.

HELIX: They think adulthood is a prize. But adulthood is a lot of work and responsibility.

TRACI: And none of us felt that way when we were teenagers.

HELIX: No, adulthood looked like freedom. I'm wondering if there's a parallel here with Faery initiation. Is initiation a responsibility that looks like freedom?

TRACI: [*laughs*] I think it *is!* As initiates, we do have a tremendous responsibility. It's the question we asked ourselves as students: "What is the work of this God?" What is the responsibility I have as an initiate? That's the work of this God. It's probably different for each and every one of us. But it's a responsibility, like adulthood is a responsibility. It's not fun and games, man. [*laughs*]

HELIX: And it's a mystery, so it's impossible to communicate across that barrier. To the student, it's a prize, and to the initiate... words fail. Just like it's impossible to really describe what it is to be an adult to someone who's young. They don't believe you when you tell them how hard it is.

TRACI: It's a mystery. It's a rite of passage.

HELIX: I wanted to bring up the Iron and Pearl pentacles, which are some of the most widely known conceptual tools from the Faery tradition.

TRACI: Well, you referred to them in one of your first questions when we were talking about wildness and being in relationship. Being in relationship to the self as an individual, and being in relationship to community, with our obligations to society and our smaller groups—those are the two pentacles, the Iron and the Pearl.[3] The Iron is the red blood in our bodies, and the tool is about being in relationship with your Self, knowing how to relate to that wild self. Knowing it, knowing who you are. And the Pearl is about agreements with community. There are some Faery teachers who use those two tools, and they're great for helping to understand those concepts. But they've gone out of the tradition and are being used lots of other places. Whether or not they're good tools in those places, I don't know. I'm not experiencing them

---

[3] For more information about these tools, see *Evolutionary Witchcraft* (2005) by T. Thorn Coyle.

there. But not all Faery teachers use them. They are passed by particular teachers who find them effective.

When you're learning a skill, like riding a bicycle, eventually it becomes automatic. For me, the pentacles have become automatic. That's not to say that there aren't initiates out there for whom these tools remain fresh and alive. But I think there is a danger—in this digital culture we're in, where information is shared so widely and quickly, these tools have gone very far and in some circles are used in an automatic way. They've become rote.

HELIX: And if they are used in a rote way, are they no longer helping the user to embody the energy they were constructed for?

TRACI: Yes. It can become like the rosary. And I don't want to offend any Catholics, because there are Catholics who can say the rosary in a very intentional way, and it's powerful for them. But just as in any spiritual tradition, you can have a tool in that tradition that becomes just something you're repeating so you can get out of there. I could fight with a student to get them not to use these tools in a rote manner, or I could create something else. The purpose of such tools is to get them in touch with their own individual wildness, look at the constructs that culture has laid on them, and choose to remove those constructs—or choose to remove them and then put them back on again.

HELIX: I do like the word "tools" for the pentacles, because it emphasizes that they are not, themselves, the tradition. I think that's confusing to people outside of Faery; they think that the tools make the tradition.

TRACI: There isn't anything that *is* this tradition other than initiation. There aren't even any gods that are necessary to this tradition. The initiation is Faery. That's it.

HELIX: But even the initiation can be very mutable... and so, all things slip away, all structures slip away! [*both laughing*]

TRACI: Back to that wild essence.

HELIX: Do you think that being initiated into the Faery current requires a sexual initiation? We may have to loop back and talk about what Faery means by Sex.

TRACI: Yes. Yes, it does require sexual initiation. Sex is life force. Sex is the ecstatic energy of life that banged out in that condensed moment, the moment that created the expulsion of those first two elements. And in the Faery mythology, that's the Star Goddess and her masturbation. So Sex is ecstatic union with the energy that is all of life as we know it. To enter that mystery, you have to enter through Sex. Which is probably why Sex is the first point on the Iron pentacle. It all comes through Sex, and it's Love that leads you there.

HELIX: I think that's another widely misunderstood aspect of Faery. You just described Sex as it's meant in the Faery context very well. I personally like the word "Eros" for it, because too many people, when you say "Sex," just think "genitals." And that's not all that we're talking about here.

TRACI: Yes, yes. Maybe the concept is more like the Tantric understanding. We're struggling here with our limited English vocabulary, and so we're left with "Sex."

HELIX: So in Faery, the initiation can't work unless it's sexual, because we're understanding sexual energy as the very energy of life. If you can't open yourself to the energy of life, the initiation can't even happen. People in American culture are very bound up about their bodies and about touch and sexuality, and it seems like part of the process of training in Faery is to release those bonds, to free that life force. Can the process of preparing for a sexual initiation potentially restore power that's lost through unhealthy kinds of enculturation about the body?

TRACI: Yes, yes, I think it can. We do have a lot of body shaming and sexual inhibition in our culture, a lot of shame around sexual behavior and sexuality in general. And conversely, we use sexuality as a tool for marketing. Sexuality is commodified. We have these two poles that both represent imbalance.

Thinking in terms of the Iron Pentacle, using the concepts of Rust and Gilt as ways of talking about unbalanced principles... we have sexuality in a very rusty state, restricted by shame and guilt; and also sexuality in a gilded state, made flashy and co-opted for the purpose of manipulation. These ways of expressing sexuality are not Iron, they're not pure and don't touch our core.

The core of who we are, that innocence of sexuality... it connects back to the way we are when we were children. Little kids explore their own bodies and don't view it as good or bad or anything. They have no morality or ethics around that. They touch themselves for a pure pleasure, and it's all Iron, all in balance. That energy is just how life is. But then we as humans lay meaning on that, meaning derived from culture or from our own understanding, and not all of that meaning is positive. Some of it is quite harmful.

Because Faery is about reconnecting with our wild essence, it is really helpful for healing. There are tools for looking at how we're out of balance in certain areas of our lives, and if we have hang-ups in any area, then we can't flow freely because we're feeling shame or guilt or fear. I know for myself, as a survivor of childhood sexual abuse and a survivor of spousal abuse, it's been really powerful for me: uncovering where, even to this day, I'm still impacted by those experiences, how they laid shame on me or influenced what sexuality means to me. It's been powerful to take the space in my life to think intentionally—to ask the question, "What is my sexuality?" Is it just about being "sexy" the way American culture says I should be "sexy"? Or, if I really think about it for myself, what do *I* think about my sexuality, outside of what my culture says? How do I feel in my body about that, what do I think in my mind? Are the two in sync with one another? And if I just sit and listen deeply, do I hear something else altogether that's beyond body or mind? So yes, very powerful for examining and exploring sexuality in a safe and robust way.

HELIX: One of the questions I know the reading audience is going to want to understand is this... So, say you're teaching Faery. There is a teacher and a student. There is a static power dynamic between that teacher and that student, and you both are stable adults. Part of the training is to look at the agreements that are being made with society and to look at the enculturation laid on the self and to loosen those layers, strip them away, and seek the primal beneath. It sounds like a very vulnerable process. How is it that the potential initiate can come to the initiation container and find it both vulnerable and safe?

TRACI: The initiation container may not feel safe. It may feel scary as hell! [*laughs*] But it's the safest place imaginable. It's a safe place to explore your Self. But that doesn't always equate with feeling safe. Being safe is not the same as feeling safe. We can feel a lot of things and have a lot of thoughts based on those feelings, but it doesn't make them true. I can feel ugly, but that doesn't make it true. I can feel stupid, or that nobody loves me, but it doesn't make it true.

There's this extreme risk aversion happening among Americans right now. Kids aren't allowed to play outside for fear of predators; their parents are being arrested for letting them play outside without constant supervision.[4] We've gotten confused about the difference between feeling safe and actually being safe. The United States has the lowest crime rates in forty years right now. Kids are not in danger from predators while playing outside, but their parents feel incredibly unsafe about it.

When you're studying witchcraft, you may sometimes not feel safe. But if you've done your due diligence as an adult, and you have evidence that your teacher is working from a place of competence and integrity within this tradition... It may still feel scary at times. But that doesn't mean that you're going to be hurt. If you can't let go of that fear, then you're not ever going to go through that initiatory gate. And at some point you do have to let go, because there is a power difference. They know things that you don't.

HELIX: And that's why you're studying. So when a student is approaching that initiatory place, what do you do to be as sure as you can be that this student is consenting to what is going to happen—that their agreement to come to that place and experience that initiation is valid? How do you ensure that they don't feel pressured?

TRACI: The same way you perceive your kids as they're growing up. If a student is understanding their own unique, wild

---

[4] For more information, see http://www.freerangekids.com/.

essence and living from that, then they are going to exhibit it in their behavior. Not just in your training, not just when you're together in circle, but they're going to be showing it at their job, they're going to be making changes in relationships, they'll be shaping their lives in a way that reflects their true self, as opposed to living in the shackles of what they've been taught. Of course, they may want to keep the things they've been taught, but they need to make a choice about whether those things match their authentic self. You know that by watching, just like you do with your kids. You know they're ready to move out and live their own lives when they're responsible with money, when they're doing their own laundry, when they can look at their friends and realize who's a good friend to them and who isn't. It's the same kind of thing. You know by their behavior.

HELIX: So the teacher knows the student is able to consent to the initiation because their behavior is that of an adult. How can a student judge if a teacher has their best interests at heart?

TRACI: Probably the same way that a teacher judges whether they want to take a student. Is the teacher responsible? Are they respected in their community? Are they stable? Are they ethical, living within the ethics of their communities? Do you see them acting in moral ways, according to their own internal moral compass, if that differs from the ethics of the wider society?

A student *should* be judging, because this is a family. You're going to be brought into a family. You, as a student, better look and see who it is you're training with. And if you aren't prepared to marry that person, be that person's sister or brother for life—maybe multiple lives—find a different teacher.

HELIX: There has to be *love*.

TRACI: Yes, love! As we say, before Sex, there's Love; before Love, there's Sex.

HELIX: So initiation comes in the context of a substantial relationship, between people who already know each other on an intimate level.

TRACI: For me. I know within this lineage, there have been teaching circles where people have been initiated before training. It would be disingenuous not to say that that had occurred, and maybe still does occur. But for me it would be, because of the nature of the initiation. It could be that in certain circumstances, or in certain times, it felt different to initiate early. But that doesn't feel appropriate to me now.

HELIX: There have also been times when people liked to start romantic relationships by having the sex first, in a rush of excitement! With the idea that the one-night stand might blossom into something stable.

TRACI: Oopsie. [*both laughing*]

HELIX: Though sometimes those romances work out. But it's a far riskier way to go about it.

It wouldn't be appropriate to talk about the initiation itself in any great detail. But since Cora Anderson has written a bit about the Faery initiation for publication, I feel okay asking this: Is the Faery initiation as you understand it open to, for example, gay, lesbian, and transgender people; people who are monogamous; people who are disabled and can't function sexually? Can all these people potentially be initiated?

TRACI: Of course. The lineage is open to all those people. In the Faery mythology, Sex is not about heterosexual, genital copulation. It's about Sex as life force. It's a much bigger construct than what our society tends to mean by "sex." And it's not about heterosexual procreation. So yes, to all those things. As far as the initiation itself, it's a mystery, and elements of it should not be shared by any initiate with those who have not been through it. I know that Cora has said publicly that there are procedures available for people in different relationship situations. She's mentioned Rites of the Heart, which includes sex with one's own partner, or committing to a sexual act in the next life if one does not have a partner or is unable or unwilling to have sex. So there are lots of avenues for the candidate, but ultimately, the initiation is about Sex and sexual energy.

HELIX: The definition of Sex here is very broad and encompassing, and it can be expressed in many ways. And we're talking about a very individual experience, something that should be shaped to the individual's needs and desires.

TRACI: Yes, absolutely. That's the job of the initiate to have that conversation with the student.

HELIX: The idea of sex between a "teacher" and a "student" is a very touchy point for Pagans right now. But when you talk about that possibility, I hear you using very specific definitions of those words. You're not talking about paid tuition or classrooms, you're talking about an already intimate one-on-one relationship between adults.

TRACI: Yes. And at some point, you have to leave it to the students to ask their teachers hard questions. And if they don't, what are you going to do or say? They're adults.

HELIX: I've certainly had friends in various Pagan traditions study
          with teachers who I didn't believe were ethical. My friends
          had access to all the information that I had access to, and
          they made their own decisions. Sometimes they got hurt,
          and it was painful for me to watch. But it wasn't up to me
          to tell them what they can and can't do.

TRACI: Yeah. You'd be trying to become their caretaker. And
          that's not respecting their wild essence! They get to make
          those choices.

Traci is an initiate of the Anderson Faery tradition. She makes her
permanent home in Texas, but she also maintains a strong connection
to her Irish ancestors and has lived for several years in Ireland. Traci is
passionately committed to maintaining sexual initiation as an option
for initiates in her tradition. In addition to her work as a Faery witch,
Traci's thoughts about consent in the Craft are informed by the
feminist witchcraft tradition of Reclaiming, her healing process from
childhood sexual abuse, and her twenty-nine years of parenting.

Context. Consent. Contact.
An Animist Approach to Consent
Theo Wildcroft

Let us begin with some personal context, to demonstrate where I stand within the debate, and among the diverse communities we can label with the word 'Pagan'. Depending on the listener, I might describe myself as a Pagan, but more accurately as a druid. Most accurately, and most often, I will call myself an animist. I call myself this because my religion is formed of human and other-than-human interaction, of bodies and their ecology.[1] It is shaped by what I can see, smell, hear, feel, touch, and hold. Life flows through everything within my reach. I know that every action we make is a connection: a contact somewhere, somehow, to some entity that experiences some form of life, human or other. I truly believe that every connection holds the potential for experiencing the miraculous. Thus I believe that every act is, in some way, sacred. This is deeper than belief. This is bone-deep knowledge. Like many bone-deep facts of existence, it resists easy explanation and justification. This is my organising principle, my working hypothesis for life itself.[2][3]

Within that life at present, I spend my days writing about, researching, and teaching body-mind practices. I am (more than just) a yoga teacher. My personal spiritual practice is day-to-day rather than

---

[1] See Graham Harvey's (2006) groundbreaking and accessible work on the defining features of indigenous and new animism.

[2] Maxine Sheets-Johnstone (2011) uses existing neuroscientific findings to explain how consciousness is born in sensing and responding to one's environment. Therefore, we are first and foremost animate, relational beings.

[3] See Tim Ingold's (2011) influential work of anthropology for an exploration of meaning-making as a function of moving and being in the world.

high holidays, embodied rather than esoteric, and earthy in nature.[4] It is enacted alone, in family, with my grove, or with my tribe.

I use the word 'tribe' to describe the loose and shifting group of friends and loved ones that I spend time with whenever I can. We meet at summer camps, regular gatherings and occasional rituals. Almost all of the rituals that I attend begin with holding hands and end with hugs. It is with my tribe that I get naked, I dance, I hug, and I hold.[5] We share sweat and tears, song and laughter. We come together in circles and sweat lodges, tents and long barrows. In all these activities and all these spaces, verbal consent for physical contact is rarely requested. There is a common, erroneous assumption in most Pagan communities that everyone will be comfortable with hugs and no-one minds nudity.[6] But I realised that despite this, I feel more boundaried and nurtured and more respected in Pagan contexts than almost anywhere else. Every human community endures incidents of harassment and even violation. Every culture includes people who consciously or unconsciously transgress consensual boundaries. Pagan communities are no exception, but with Pagans, I have felt physically safer than in any other context outside of my own home.

Consent is an issue we need to discuss and address together. Yet let me state clearly first: Pagan culture, as I have experienced it here in Britain, tends to be inherently respectful of the rights of individuals to self-determination. In navigating consent, that counts for a lot. Indeed, after a long summer of tribal camps and rituals, autumn at home leaves me craving the ocean of safe affection I have been unconsciously swimming through. I feel like a sea creature left behind by the tide. At these times, I miss my tribe with my skin as much as my heart.

---

[4] Graham Harvey's (2013) more recent study is concerned with the idea that religion has less to do with beliefs, and much more to do with the habits of everyday life. This concept is growing in support among scholars of religion.

[5] The academic study of religion is also increasingly interested in the place of physical bodies in lived religion (Furey, 2012; LaFleur, 1998).

[6] Naked hugs are, however, rarely appropriate.

Safeguarding

Contact. Consent. Context. Like a lot of people, many of them women, I have endured all kinds of non-consensual physical contact across my lifetime. I grew up in a home where my control over my physical body was routinely violated. As a young adult, I had to learn where to place my own boundaries on what felt like safe contact within all kinds of relationships. I was lucky, in that I had good friends and respectful lovers to help me. Now, as a person, as a teacher, and as a safe-guarder of others, consent is still a live issue with a complex history for me.

In the wider British culture, there is ever more awareness of the possibility of harassment and abusive behaviour in almost all contexts where human beings meet. This holds true online as well as in person. Survivors and victims of interpersonal violence feel increasingly safe and supported in speaking out, sharing, and naming their aggressors out loud. Our stories detail the everyday contexts in which extraordinary transgression can flourish. Speaking out spills much-needed light on all the ways in which even well-meaning people can become complicit in covering up abuse. It continues to enlighten us as to the ways in which assumptions around physical contact can cover up sinister advances by manipulative individuals.

There is, therefore, ever more sensitivity to the boundaries of consent. In many of our professional and personal contexts, we are taught to check before we reach out and touch, embrace and hold. In my early yoga teacher training, I was taught to check in some way for consent before I ever placed my hands to adjust a student's posture. Asking for verbal consent is a talisman we frequently use to ensure no-one is getting hurt or feels unnecessarily uncomfortable.[7] Policies and practices of explicit verbal and written consent are more than bureaucratic inconveniences. They are what we have to help us

---

[7] See Marich (2014) for a more nuanced exploration of consent protocols in yoga classes that can be usefully applied to any situation where shared learning might include shared touch.

navigate in those distressing times when things go wrong. Legal consideration is officially applied to how and where consent can be given in almost all interpersonal physical contact outside of the home. This is especially vital when we care for children and vulnerable adults. But a policy on its own is never enough without a culture of respect to support it. Many professional environments with clear anti-harassment policies can still be uncomfortable places to work.

Creating Safe Space

Consent. Contact. Context. We can all be vulnerable in a given environment. We can all be swayed by the overwhelming nature of sub-culture and peer pressure into consenting to things we might later regret. Mostly, we hope, this is a minor matter. We hug someone not because we feel close to them, but because everyone else has been hugged. We feel odd being the only one not doing something. We want to belong, so we follow the crowd. Occasionally this can lead to more worrying situations. After at least one workshop in a Pagan context that I know of, a participant revealed in retrospect that she hadn't felt she could refuse to be touched. There had been no attempt to ignore her wishes. But somehow the workshop leader hadn't made the context feel safe or relaxed enough for one participant to be the only one to opt out. Because of this, she, the workshop leader, and her fellow participants were all equally upset by how events had played out. Each one felt betrayed by how the others had navigated consent.

In such situations, later problems may be avoided if facilitators take the time at the start of a session to explicitly discuss issues of consent. Ground rules for physical contact can be established. When starting out, we should be careful to welcome all levels of participation equally. This includes those who say "no thank you" as much as those who say an enthusiastic "yes please" to our planned activities. It is important that we have low-risk, low-contact alternatives that most participants will feel comfortable doing. I try to make it clear in my own sessions that people are expected to find their own relationship to the practices I offer. Those who study with me regularly are accustomed to modifying my instructions, or even sitting out and observing. My task in response is to provide alternatives, and ensure students are safe whatever they choose to do.

Aside from the policies and practices that we need for workshops, camps, and organisational activities, we have an understandable reluctance to subject Pagan spaces to bureaucratic measures. Many of us seek to create sacred space and time that feels like being with intimate friends, and friends don't sign release papers before holding hands. We come together, in the common druid prayer, "heart to heart and hand in hand." In ritual contexts, there is a tension between our roles as safe-space-keepers, boundary-holders for people who we do not yet know, and the desire to welcome back dear friends into our physical presence.

Heathen or Druid, Wiccan or Shaman, Pagans are usually affectionate people. We are physical, life-affirming people. Reaching out and making real, physical contact is important to us. But this general rule has many exceptions, for many reasons. Pagans are also diverse, in practice as well as belief. We find much to celebrate in our individuality and our eccentricity. To do this, our gatherings must also be welcome places for those who express their closeness to others in less physically intimate ways. How do we keep the friendliness, the playfulness, the relaxed and unambiguous presence of bodies within Pagan contexts, and still play safe?

It's important, because it's part of who we are to each other. It's culturally significant—a part of our self-defined difference as Pagans from other people. Once I met a beekeeper in the context of his role within our local beekeepers' association. We talked, we were friendly, and we parted each time with a handshake. One day, I picked up some honey from him for a visiting shamanic teacher of mine. For the first time, we met knowing we were both Pagans. This was the only thing that had changed between us. This time when we parted, we hugged.

Living in Relationship

Context. Contact. Consent. The etymological commonality between all these words comes from a Latin prefix "con-" or "com-," meaning "being-with."[8] It has an even more ancient Proto-Indo-European root. In literal detail, context is that which is woven together. Contact: that which touches together. Consent: that which we feel together. These concepts[9] have original definitions and primal meanings resonant of more and less respectful interpersonal connections.[10] They remind us of all the ways in which we bring ourselves together. Consent is not merely a question of acts—a list of that which is consented to by each individual. It is a process of interpersonal negotiation encountered every time we reach out beyond our boundaries towards another being.

As an animist, I know myself as a porous, negotiated being. I do not experience my hands as less sentient than my brain.[11] I know that most of my cells are non-human, and that different parts of me have different thresholds of comfortable, consensual contact than others. Put simply, there are parts of me you can touch, and parts of me you can't. I know that my gut has very definite ideas about how I should interact with the world, especially any part of it I choose to ingest. Put clearly, my mouth will touch what I will not swallow. If this sounds intimate, know that when I am alive, awake, and present to this reality, then everything in life is indeed intimate to me. Remembering, reconnecting, and being-with is the heart, centre, and purpose of my evolving spiritual practice. Each breath is an ecological exchange, an

---

[8] For a beginner's exploration of the etymology of the English language, www.etymonline.com is a fantastic free resource.

[9] concept: that which is taken in and held

[10] connection: that which is joined together

[11] Eugene Gendlin (2004) developed the ecopsychology practice of 'focusing': exploring lived experiences of the body as a therapeutic tool for self-knowledge and transformation. Adrian Harris (2013) is a pagan researcher and researcher of eco-paganism developing this as a technique for deepening our relationships with the natural world.

act of intimacy. Each breath is a consensual communication[12] by my person-as-human within the larger body of the earth. I am myself, and that self is a shifting, birthing, dying, transforming colony of cells and ideas and sensations that chooses in this life to be one being. I am myself, and that self is a single being in a shifting, birthing, dying, transforming colony of beings and forces and experiences that chooses in this life to be one planet.[13] Within this context, consent is understandably complex.[14]

In reality, all touch, indeed all connection, transmits intent. With prior explicit consent or not, you can touch another being in a way that feels respectful, even reverent, or in a way that feels aggressive, possessive, or objectifying. That is not to say that how you receive touch is always how it is intended. But there are subtleties in how we connect. How receptive are we to another's physical responses as we reach out to them? Is there eye contact at any point? Is there a moment's pause to allow another to pull away? And there are many subtleties to touch itself. Even how you hold hands with another reveals more than you know. The wrist that is in front, by habit or design, usually holds the most control[15] over the direction you both will travel in together.

I was trained to touch bone-to-bone, heart-to-heart. It's difficult to explain, and much easier to demonstrate. It is a way of touching that meets another deliberately. It holds the intention to come together in a direct, explicit way, rather than feeling hesitant, apologetic or surreptitious. Early on, I discovered to my surprise that explicit, firm touch is a kind of contact that feels much less invasive than hesitant or indirect touch. Hesitant touch transmits concern[16] or fear to another. It can provoke the instinctive desire to pull away.

---

[12] communication: that which is shared by all or many

[13] David Abram (2012) is one of the best writers to capture this sense of a participative, relational existence.

[14] complex: that which is encircled and embraced

[15] control: that which checks against or verifies

[16] concern: that which is sifted together

The clear intent to honour and respect another. A pause. Seeking rather than assuming a response. A firm touch. When all these are present, explicit verbal consent can be unnecessary. Some of my work is with vulnerable, non-verbal children, often deep into the autistic spectrum. I touch to direct movement, to explain, to induce and demonstrate new bodily experiences. I touch to coax activity and even to share affection. I never embrace a child who hasn't explicitly consented to it, and a child should never feel they have surrendered control of their body. Nevertheless, our sessions are physical in nature, and consent often cannot be verbally given. It must be continually[17] negotiated. The same processes inform every physical, spiritual encounter I experience: from partnered negotiations in ecstatic dance, to the closeness of a sweat lodge. These processes are animism-in-action. Consent, again, is that which we manage to feel together.[18]

Meeting with Honour

Contact. Context. Consent. How we can learn to negotiate a constant[19] non-verbal process of consent has implications for our processes of other-than-human contact. As Pagans, this has repercussions for the greater part of our religious practice. Can we listen to the response of the wind when we invite it into circle? Can we feel the withdrawing of sap before we cut the bark? Can we understand the look we receive from rook, or rabbit, or beetle as we cross paths? We are part of their world, as they are part of ours. In our interactions, this world deserves more than to be treated as a resource, a home, and a mystical symbol.[20] An eagle, a stone circle may have a meaning for me, but this bird, this rock, this place resound with

---

[17] continual: that which hangs together

[18] Deidre Sklar (1994) considers mimesis as an anthropological research skill. When we move like others, do we understand them better?

[19] constant: that which stands together

[20] Stephan Harding's (2006) classic book argues that treating the earth as if it is animate is both intuitively natural and ecologically more sustainable

meaning for and of themselves. Not every interaction is determined or controlled by humans alone.

Along this path of meaningful consent lies a greater capacity for empathy and fewer misconceived assumptions about all beings, human and other-than human. We begin to treat with persons and all their inherent personhood implies, rather than with objects, and all that objectification involves. At this deeper level consent is conceived as spiritual practice. It is an act of reverence and devotion to the life of all things.[21] At the edges of understanding, consent begins to turn inwards as well as out. Do we listen to the eyes' call for rest, or push them onwards into the night? Do we hear the cells' call for liquid, or forget to drink during the day? Do we hear all the silenced voices of the body, or drown them out with shiny and sugary distractions? Like many spiritual practices, the path is not easy, obvious or comfortable.[22] Our inner and outer worlds are not usually harmonious spaces, for reasons often beyond our control. To truly feel the violence as well as the miraculous that is present around and within us takes courage. In complete honesty, this is not a connection I can endure all of the time. But with each step along the path, spiritual practice naturally evolves into a political, as well as personal act.

As already stated, the inherent tendency for Pagans to respect individual rights to self-determination is a fundamental place to begin. Each individual, however we define personhood, has the absolute right to explore, set, and communicate autonomous boundaries between themselves and the world. And as each individual, and their ecology, is constantly evolving together, they also have the absolute right to change and move those boundaries in ways that are confusing,[23] illogical, and capricious. "No" always means "no"; it is not invalidated by a previous "yes". Consent is not a legal piece of evidence, standing

---

[21] Emma Restall Orr (2008) is one of a number of pagan thinkers to discuss an honouring of all life as the foundation for ethical living

[22] comfort: that which transmits strength

[23] confuse: that which is mingled to the point of being indistinguishable

for all time; it is a process. Does "no" still mean "no" when uttered by a child, or when it is a clear but non-verbal response? Does the right to refuse stand even when its meaning is clear, but the person is other-than-human? Can an animal refuse consent to its treatment? Can a tree? How about a river? Where does consent end?[24]

In contemplating[25] consent, we learn to negotiate not just connection but the dynamic flows of interpersonal and intrapersonal, human and other-than-human power. Where our boundaries are weaker than we would like, we support ourselves and others in learning how to say no. We examine the many ways in which we all suffer and we all commit[26] acts of aggression. We discover the ways in which we can find the courage to heal and evolve together. Consent is not a shield we use to protect those who might be broken from those who break them. With care and self-awareness, with strength and forgiveness, it can be an endlessly rewarding process in which we learn from both sides to evolve our own relationships with power, reverence and abuse. This evolution takes place within our more-than-human body, and within the body of society, and also in the bodies of tribe and planet and ecosystem.[27] We turn away from the temptation to separate light from dark. We refuse to banish every abusive impulse and act as something done by others in the name of evil. We do not claim absolute purity for ourselves. We face our shadows and we evolve. We end cycles of abuse wherever we can. We heal however we can. When we do so, we embody the warriors of our tribes.

---

[24] Scholars are only just beginning to ask whether other-than-human beings also have religious experiences. Some animals, for example, have been shown to mourn death and hold specific taboos (Schaefer, 2012).

[25] contemplate: that which is near to the temple

[26] commit: that which sends or puts together

[27] For an examination of the relationships between the personal, cultural and societal (structural) in forces of oppression and liberation, see Thompson (2005).

Moments of Contact

Consent. Context. Contact. In our natural world, edges and boundaries are the most fertile and productive of places. Between field and woodland, sea and shore, and even pavement and wall, diversity thrives and life proliferates.[28] In the pause between desire and fulfilment, we can find oceans of self-reflection in which we learn more about what we are truly reaching for. We can remake consent itself, ritualising the very moment of connection. We can make eye contact that honours both the sacred autonomy of the self that asks and the self that responds. We can make reverent our relationship to the space we leave for either side to engage or withdraw. There is a depth of anticipation in consent as a spiritual practice that recalls us to the miracle of all life, of all connection. And all it takes is a single moment of mutual awareness. All it asks is empathy: the intention to feel together before we come together.

It will, as likely as not, be an imperfect, flawed experience. We will continue, in our enthusiasm, confusion, and even fatigue to make assumptions about who we can hug, and how to hold hands, and who wants to see us naked. In our mundane life, in our gatherings and our solitary moments alike, we will get it wrong. Worst of all, there may be people waiting to take advantage of our assumptions to abusive ends. When this happens, may our policies and practices, our culture and our community,[29] be there to catch and hold, to help us heal and learn from these mistakes. And may none of us be too badly scarred in the process, for too many of us have been hurt already.

The gift of shared sacred practice, be it in circles or sweat lodges, is a repeating, regular chance to reclaim a different, more conscious[30]

---

[28] One of the twelve key principles of a permaculture design system, based on the observation of natural systems is: use edges and value the marginal as having increased diversity and productivity (Holmgren, 2002) (Mollison, 1990).

[29] community: the many or all that shares together

[30] conscious: that which knows together

way of being with human and other-than-human-persons, with the world-within as well as the world-without. The most transformative, most numinous moments of ritual and practice are those in which the whole world is alive to us, and we within it. It is that singular experience when we are reverently aware of the robin's concern above, and the chicks hissing in their nest, and the ivy that conceals it—and in the same moment that all of this is one-life as well as it is many. It is that shining moment when the sun rises, and the drumming rises and the voices in the circle rise with it—and everything in us sings out at once. At these times, if we are not striving to be truly conscious of how we touch each other, how can we call our actions sacred?

May we reach out reverently and make contact, one to one and one to many. May we find connection and understanding across the boundaries of species and language. May we come together allowing for the autonomy of each of us, finding unity at the heart of life's diversity. And with each contact, each touch, and in every context we weave together, may there be a pause in which the whole self, the whole universe could be remade, to find consent: that space in which we feel together.

Bibliography

Abram, D. (2012). The Spell of the Sensuous: Perception and Language in a More-Than-Human World: Knopf Doubleday Publishing Group.

Furey, C. M. (2012). Body, Society, and Subjectivity in Religious Studies. 80, 7-33.

Gendlin, E. (2004). The new phenomenology of carrying forward. Continental Philosophy Review, 37(1), 127-151.

Harding, S. (2006). Animate Earth: Science, Intuition and Gaia. Totnes: Green Books.

Harris, A. (2013). Gendlin and ecopsychology: focusing in nature. Person-Centered & Experiential Psychotherapies, 12(4), 330-343. doi: 10.1080/14779757.2013.855135

Harvey, G. (2006). Animism: respecting the living world. New York: Columbia University Press.

Harvey, G. (2013). Food, Sex and Strangers: Understanding Religion as Everyday Life: Taylor & Francis.

Holmgren, D. (2002). Permaculture: Principles & Pathways Beyond Sustainability. Hepburn, Victoria: Holmgren Design Services.

Ingold, T. (2011). Being Alive: Essays on Movement, Knowledge and Description. Abingdon and New York: Routledge.

LaFleur, W. R. (1998). Body. In M. C. Tayler (Ed.), Critical Terms for Religious Studies. Chicago: University of Chicago Press.

Marich, J. (2014). 12 Simple Ways to Make Your Yoga Classes More Trauma Informed.   Retrieved 18/02/2015, from http://www.decolonizingyoga.com/12-simple-ways-make-yoga-classes-trauma-informed

Mollison, B. C. (1990). Permaculture: A Practical Guide for a Sustainable Future. Washington: Island Press.

Orr, E. R. (2008). Living with Honour: A Pagan Ethics. Winchester: O Books.

Schaefer, D. (2012). Do Animals Have Religion? Interdisciplinary Perspectives on Religion and Embodiment. Anthrozoos, 25, p173-p189.

Sheets-Johnstone, M. (2011). The primacy of movement (Vol. 82). Amsterdam Me: John Benjamins.

Sklar, D. (1994). Can Bodylore be Brought to its Senses. Journal of American Folklore, 107(423), 9-22.

Thompson, N. (2005). Promoting Equality. Basingstoke: Palgrave Macmillan.

Theo Wildcroft teaches and writes about the places where physical, spiritual, and ecological practice meet. As a queer, anarchist animist, she is happiest in the edges of things. She is a specialist in yoga for special needs and a doctoral researcher in religious studies for the Open University. She believes that social and environmental justice are the bedrock of any truly worthwhile religious practice, and that yoga in Britain is not like anywhere else. She helps to run Rainbow Futures' Druid Camp and has served the British druid community in various ways for more than a decade. Find out more at www.wildyoga.co.uk.

Seeking a Morality of Difference
A Polytheological Approach to Consent
Julian Betkowski

The great strength of polytheism is its foundational embrace of difference.

It is misleading, I think, to understand polytheism as simply pluralist, that is to say merely tolerating the presence of multiple viewpoints, since pluralism can still be brought under the power of a singular universal. Pluralism may be understood to accept only a trivial variation that reflects an underlying unity. Difference could then be rendered only as a surface effect, unworthy of serious consideration. Such a shortfall of pluralism can be seen in regards to political identity. American pluralism, which praises the diversity of cultures and religions that make up the nation, also requires the subjugation of that diversity to the political unity of the state. This may then lead to the creation of outsiders and pariahs, as seen with the internment of Japanese Americans during the Second World War, and the real dangers faced today by many Muslim Americans. Pluralism operates in such situations as merely a more covert force of homogenization, requiring the suppression of real difference in favor of a synthetic unity. Pluralism, I suggest, lends itself to these sorts of cynical uses, wherein apparent diversity is used as a cover for a coercive homogeneity.

Thus, my construction of polytheism is a radical departure from such a pluralist view. *It turns toward difference not as a surface effect, but as a key defining feature of reality.* From such a polytheistic view, then, every identity is unique and irreproducible. Differences, even approaching the infinitely small, reign. Equivalence and exchange then become artificial concepts that obscure our vision of the world. Thus, I am less concerned with understanding how things are alike, than with coming to terms with the ramifications of difference.

Morality derived from a belief in our universal similarity is not particularly powerful. If we only do unto others as we would have them do unto us, then we establish only a retributive sense of morality. The injunction to take an eye for an eye, for example, operates only by reenacting the crime upon the criminal, restricting bad behavior only by instilling a narrow desire to avoid personal suffering. This is a morality of exchange, where one act is repaid with another, creating a vicious economy. The action and the beings upon whom it is performed are assumed to share a basic equivalence, so that one can be substituted for another to reestablish order and enforce justice.

Or if we recognize fellow beings as worthy of our respect based only on similitude, how then do we interact with a being that presents us with some substantial difference? What happens when similarity grows weak? Depending on how narrowly we define the similar, all sorts of ethical difficulties may emerge. Racism and misogyny can be understood as a failure of similarity-based moralities, since difference from an idealized type then permits violence, oppression, and subjugation. How far from the ideal likeness may we stray before a morality of sameness breaks down?

Similarly, consent, defined by similarity, requires some form of equality across the parties involved. If we are bound by a morality of sameness, then we are forced to disregard the very real differences that exist between beings, and instead seek to model ideal behavior only on what is shared between them. Differences in gender, physical ability, or age are not considered, and we are left to puzzle over why breaches of consent occur between undifferentiated human beings. If we focus only on similarities, then we overlook the differences and inequalities that shape our relationships and influence the ways that consent emerges and shifts.

In order to understand consent, we must first understand difference and inequality as the basis of our moral framework. I see great profit in grounding our moral understanding not in any similarity that we share with our fellow beings, but in the differences that define and distinguish us. Such a morality revolves around encountering the others and entering into relation with them. *The world as we experience it is filled with variations and intensities, and a true embrace of difference recognizes this as a defining feature of our world.* The trick, then, is the task of navigating these differences and inequalities, in parsing the asymmetrical relationships that we constantly find ourselves involved in.

Love

To begin, I turn to love. I am not at all interested in the spiritual clichés that masquerade as love. I seek instead something more robust. In her essay from 1959, *The Sublime and the Good*, philosopher Iris Murdoch defines love as:

> ...the perception of individuals. Love is the extremely difficult realisation that something other than oneself is real. Love, and so art and morals, is the discovery of reality. [1]

This construction of love is bound up in the world and oriented outward. It is essentially curious and inquisitive; it drives us to expand ourselves and open ourselves up to the world around us. Properly realized, this is a love that perpetually affirms difference and otherness, that motivates us to inspect and inquire into the world around us, and that drives us into relationships with the manifold beings that compose our world. Held by such a love, we recognize the uniqueness and irreducibility of the beings we encounter and come to terms with the brute fact that regardless of our similarities, even the smallest differences have a profound impact. Murdoch further explains:

> What stuns us into a realisation of our supersensible destiny is not, as Kant imagined, the formlessness of nature, but rather its unutterable particularity. [2]

This love is not mere feeling, as theologian Martin Buber explains:

> Feelings accompany the metaphysical and metapsychical fact of love, but they do not constitute it; and the feelings that accompany it can be very different. [3]

When understood as the discovery of reality, as the realization of the realness of the beings that we encounter, love is freed from its romantic constraints. It operates now in a realm that while linked to

---

[1] Murdoch, p. 51.

[2] Murdoch, p. 51-52.

[3] Buber, p. 66.

emotion, is not governed by it. *This is love not sought for the pleasure it produces, but for the richness that it produces in our lives, in the lives we encounter, and in the world itself.*

Further, love is not simply passive, but drives us to engage with the world around us: theologian Paul Tillich says, "The immediate expression of love is action."[4] A love that escapes the constraints of mere emotion is an embodied attitude, an orientation toward the world that we are constantly enacting. The discovery of the world is an ongoing process, one that we deliberately choose to perform. The performance of love further embeds us in the world, and invests us personally in the beings we encounter.

While the love that I describe is not the romantic feeling that we commonly describe as love, this is not to say that it is entirely abstracted and detached. We embody and enact it; it takes hold of us and drives us. Love is passionate, if it is genuine. Tillich insists:

> Passion is not real without a bodily basis, even if it is the most spiritual passion. In every act of genuine faith the body participates, because genuine faith is a passionate act.[5]

Again, in the words of Martin Buber:

> Love is the responsibility of an I for a You: in this consists what cannot consist in any feeling—the equality of all lovers, from the smallest to the greatest and from the blissfully secure whose life is circumscribed by the life of one beloved human being to him that is nailed his life long to the cross of the world, capable of what is immense and bold enough to risk it: to love man.[6,7]

---

[4] Tillich, p. 133.

[5] Tillich, p. 124.

[6] Buber, p. 66-67.

[7] Buber uses the terms "ich" and "du," which are often translated as "I" and "Thou". Du is the intimate form of you in German, but no longer has a direct equivalent in English. However, Walter Kaufman, whose translation

We become responsible for those around us; their lives are knotted up with ours, and we cannot extract ourselves from their experience, nor can they remove themselves from ours. Indeed, our most basic understanding of the world becomes predicated on our collective, mutual investment in the world and the beings that compose it. "Inscrutably involved, we live in the currents of universal reciprocity."[8] *Driven by love, we recognize the insurmountable presence of the beings that surround us.*

Embodiment and Inequality

Love does not flatten all of being into some generic mass. Indeed, understood as the discovery of reality, as our investment in the world, love directly acknowledges through our experience the diverse intensities and inequalities that are spread across being. In truth, we run up against difference every day of our lives. The nature of our embodiments presents us with variations and inequalities at the very foundation of our being in the world. The relationships that we find ourselves in, those that we deliberately cultivate and those which are created by society, further enhance or mitigate those inequalities. We cannot denounce or deny them; love forces us to acknowledge them completely. *In recognizing that other beings are real, we must simultaneously recognize their uniqueness and individuality, their essential difference, their inequality with the beings with whom they cohabit the world.*

Our manner of being in the world is conditioned by our bodily endowments. While we can bring our wills to bear and through exertion expand the range of our potential experiences, we ultimately run up against physical limitations. We humans will never fly as the

---

I utilized here, feels that this translation introduces a distance into Buber's philosophy that runs counter to his overall agenda. Therefore, Kaufman has elected to render "du" as "you" throughout the text in order to maintain the intimacy that Buber requires.

[8] Buber, p. 67.

bat flies, nor will echolocation illuminate our darkened gaze (at least not without some major alteration of what it means to be human).

Most of the inequalities that we confront on a daily basis are not so dramatic, however, as the gulf between man and bat. Our height, weight, sex, physical prowess, the clarity of our vision, our age, and myriad other factors impact our participation in society and the world. Pre-existing social conditions, many of which rely on arbitrary physical traits, further enhance or restrict our freedom of motion. Our bodies, as the conduits through which we navigate the world, both expand and limit the total range of our possible experiences. This range is further modified by the relationships that we both cultivate and find ourselves embedded in.

As embodied beings, we must acknowledge the impact that our bodies have on our motion through the world. *We must recognize the way that other bodies shape the lives of those inhabiting them.* Love enables this dual recognition, of our embodiments and theirs. In turn, the inequalities of embodiment present opportunities to expand our understanding of the world around us. The discovery of reality, the expression of love, is actualized through our encountering difference, through our running up against inequality.

Difference and inequality are insurmountable features of our experience because of our embodied being. There is no simple relation of one to one when encountering experiencing beings. Every being remains unique: different and unequal. No substitution could possibly be made of one for another. Our capacity for experience is then expanded through the apprehension of other beings. We enlarge ourselves, become more fully a part of the world, through our engagement with the unique beings that surround us, and thus we contribute to the expansion of the lives of other beings as well. Love, then, manifests as a particular participation in the world; it seeks to maximize the total potential of experience, the ever-increasing apprehension of the real. Our reality is expanded through the reality of other beings.

Conflict

Love, however, cannot eliminate conflict. Conflict is real. No mere principle can erase it. In a world full of diverse beings, various needs, desires, interests and agendas are bound to clash. We cannot fall back on simple relativistic apologetics by insisting that everyone is right in their own way, or arguing that each person simply shares in some portion of universal truth. It is not enough to assert that conflict is actually an illusion to be dissolved, if only a large enough perspective could be achieved. *Our experience of the world demonstrates that there are points of view, desires, needs, and agendas that cannot be reconciled.* There are conflicts that emerge from conflicting truths that cannot be resolved, conflicts embodied and lived by actual beings.

Embracing difference, we recognize conflict as an essential feature of our world. If we accept difference and inequality as defining characteristics of our being in the world amongst others, then recognizing the inevitability of conflict follows naturally. Again, the relationships that affect our lives further mitigate or enhance conflict, just as they restrict or promote our individual freedoms. The relation of self and other, the realization and expression of difference, lay the foundations of conflict. It is in conflict that inequality becomes most fully realized, as here, the power of one may be brought to bear to foreclose upon the freedoms of another.

Tension then emerges in the mediating of these essential, irreconcilable conflicts. Conflict presses us immediately up against difference and forces us to acknowledge the presence of beings other than ourselves. It is the shock of love, to encounter a being that brings us up short, that catches us off guard in its difference from ourselves. Love, it is true, cannot eliminate conflict; however, it can infuse and permeate conflict. Through love, conflict becomes a means of understanding the world. We recognize the other that we run up against as real, as legitimate, if we have adopted love as an orientation toward the world.

Conflict presents us with the opportunity to see the world through the gaze of another. In conflicts where no reconciliation is possible, we are challenged with seeing the world in a completely new way: the world transformed into an alien place for us to explore anew. It is possible, in these circumstances, not to reconcile or apologize for the conflicts, but for all parties to undergo a process of transformation. The original conflict may be redefined as each opponent opens themselves up to the possibilities with which the other side presents them. *Infused with love, conflict becomes an opportunity to further expand our knowledge of the world, to discover more and more.*

Power

Saying "yes," and genuinely meaning it, is predicated on the possibility of saying "no" with absolute authority. What does it then mean to say "yes" in a world defined by difference, inequality, and conflict? While love may govern our movement through the world, it offers us no insulation against the predations of others who are not so guided. *Power is the hidden term in all discussions of consent.*

Love may serve as our orientation toward the world, but we must recognize that the very difference that we seek out and revere guarantees that we will encounter others who think, feel, and behave differently than we do. We will encounter others who revere other ideals and are guided by other principles. The transformative power that love holds over conflict may change us, but we have no assurance that those who oppose us will be similarly altered.

The inequality that defines our experience of the world insures that power will be likewise dispersed unequally. That power may be used to foreclose the freedom of weaker beings. Consent is severely compromised, since even the perception of coercion is enough to render it void. We seek others' consent to act upon them, but we must be aware that consent is always provisional as long as inequalities exist within the relationship in question. The consent we seek from others, as well as that we give, is conditioned by the power structures that surround us, by our inequalities and differences.

Into the conception of the world as founded on difference and inequality, power appears to reintroduce an economics of being that I rejected with similarity-based morality. The powerful are capable of foreclosing upon the weak and slicing them away from the fullness of their being. Inequalities in power determine the mobility of beings in the world and the degree to which they can impinge upon the beings around them. Recognizing power, then, appears to recognize an economy of being, since the powerful can create and enforce systems of exchange that operate against those subservient to them.

Love cannot eradicate conflict; nor, properly understood, should it move us to try, since it recognizes conflict as a necessary element of being in the world with others. However, love can permeate conflict, transforming us in the process. In the same way, while love cannot erase power, it can transmute our relationship to it. Love, the discovery of reality, moves us to protect others' being and basic freedom.

Love is the rejection of power over other beings. It serves instead to maximize the total power spread across the web of being. This maximization is achieved through resistance to the concretion of power into singular nodes or structures. Power is understood as proportional, and linked to context. The expansion of the power of one being does not necessarily decrease the power of another being, but alters the relationship in which both beings find themselves. Rejecting power over others, love then seeks to regularize, as much as possible, the dispersion of power across various beings, in relation to their inherent differences and inequalities. *Love strives to keep power perpetually mobile and decentered.*

Thus, love makes inequality irreducible: difference becomes a marker of identity and value in and of itself. Variations in power are understood to be transitory characteristics of being, and so the equivalence and exchange that power seems to reintroduce are once again recognized as artificial. Power is not an irreducible quality of being. It is contextual and established through relationships with other beings. The basic power that we possess through our bodily endowments changes over time as we ourselves change. Our environments, the other beings that surround us, as well as the tools that we can bring to bear all influence the amount of power that we wield at any given moment. While in one context, we may be quite powerful, in another we may be weak, and those transitions can occur instantaneously.

We cannot ignore, either, the social constructions that influence power, from the political agreements that underpin the authority of states to the economic agreements that allow for the functioning of trade. Racism and misogyny both demonstrate the disconnection of power from one's irreducible being, since in both cases, the limitations to one's power arise not internally, but are applied from the outside by oppressive social forces. Power is not a quality possessed, but a transitory resource: bestowed and withdrawn. *A power that is mutable and elusive cannot be used as a constant marker of valuation.*

Consent reemerges through the fluidity of power, as power's provisional nature reveals itself as transitory. Consent, understood in this framework, is itself fugitive, always in motion. In love-infused relationships whose power structure is inherently unstable and shifting, seeking consent becomes a reflex action. Consent is then introduced and reintroduced, withdrawn and withheld in accordance with the shifts in power and ability. Love, rendering power a mutable and changing resource, transfigures consent into a perpetual dance.

Synthesis

As Paul Tillich would have it, this is the ultimate concern of my polytheism: love is the discovery of reality. Adopting this engaged, inquisitive love, love becomes the center of our world, and it binds us together in ourselves and our motion through life. Paul Tillich explains:

> The center unites all elements of man's personal life, the bodily, the unconscious, the conscious, the spiritual ones. In the act of faith every nerve of man's body, every striving of man's soul, every function of man's spirit participates. But body, soul, spirit, are not three parts of man. They are

dimensions of man's being, always within each other; for man is a unity and not composed of parts.[9]

Polytheistic love unites us with the world and makes us aware of the differences and inequalities that surround us. It brings us up short when confronted with difference and urges us to see the world again, constantly rediscovering what it means to be in the world with others. I see polytheism, motivated by love, as a constant process: a perpetual unfolding of reality, a bringing into being of new and exciting worlds, of new and challenging ways of being.

In my understanding, polytheism requires us to expand the world more and more, to open ourselves up to the possibilities and transformations with which others present us, and to seek to minimize foreclosures of other beings' freedom. In our relationship with others in the world, polytheism always reminds us that we are bound up in a network, a complicated ever-expanding series of interlocking parts, and that our actions always ripple out further and further.

We are united in love; we are inextricably involved.

References

Buber, Martin. *I and Thou*. Trans. Walter Kaufman. New York: Touchstone, 1996.

Murdoch, Iris. "The Sublime and the Good." *Chicago Review* 13.1: 42-55.

Tillich, Paul. *Dynamics of Faith*. New York: HarperOne, 2009.

Julian Betkowski is an artist and aspiring theologian exploring the ramifications of a contemporary polytheistic life. He believes that for polytheism to be viable in the modern world, it must respond to the

---

[9] Tillich, p. 123.

demands of contemporary society and offer a path forward into the new century. He has recently obtained his Master of Arts in Transpersonal Psychology from Sofia University and is intent on furthering his education and continuing to explore the interface between theology, psychology, and philosophy.

The Charge of the Goddess
Teachings about Desire and Its End, and Their Limitations
Grove Harris

The Charge of the Goddess offers profound teaching on sex, reverence, and desire, but there is much missing in its approach. Pagan culture is positive about honoring the body and enjoying sex, but this can devolve into license rather than freedom if sex is not fully consensual. Both "no" and "yes" have to be respected for freedom to be enjoyed, whether choosing to engage in sex or to refrain, or explorations in between that involve both "yes" and "no." A whole range of pressures may push towards being sexual, and research shows that many young people are having sex they don't want. Advertising, media of all types, pornography, peer and other social pressures all exert influence. And the skills needed to navigate healthy consensual sex go beyond the ability to say "yes" or "no." In addition to connecting with the divine, a healthy consensual sex life requires clarity, presence, trust, self-care, boundaries, negotiating past wounds, and more.

"Yes" and "no" are complicated. In this consumerist, media-saturated age, our brains have been colonized by ads, mainstream media, and commercial music, much of which attempts to create, warp, and judge our desires. It's a mess. We all need to interrogate desire. We've all got expectations, illusions, wounds, fears, and sometimes addictions that distract us from being present and that can undermine pleasure. Fortunately, Paganism is positive about sex and does not layer on guilt or religious repercussions for desires. The Charge honors sexual diversity in the powerful blanket statement that "All acts of love and pleasure are My rituals."

In Paganism, there is no intrinsic separation between sex and religion. The divine can be found everywhere there is love and pleasure, in all forms of flesh, with all sorts of heat, in all sorts of acts. The Goddess is everywhere and sex is divine. Even a compost pile can be a site of spiritual practice; I contemplate the divine in my compost pile regularly. Here is the second half of the Charge as used in the Reclaiming Tradition:

I who am the beauty of the green earth and the white moon among the stars and the mysteries of the waters, I call upon your soul to arise and come unto Me. For I am the soul of nature that gives life to the universe. From Me all things proceed and unto Me they must return. Let My worship be in the heart that rejoices, for behold – All acts of love and pleasure are My rituals. Let there be mirth and reverence within you. And you who seek to know Me, know that your seeking and yearning will avail you not, unless you know the Mystery: for if that which you seek, you find not within your self, you will never find it without. For behold, I have been with you from the beginning, and I am that which is attained at the end of desire.[1]

The first sentence invokes earth, moon, stars, and water, which form an expansive embrace of nature, similar to earth, air, fire, water, and center, of which She is the soul. She is the source and the ending. She calls us to rejoice, with mirth and reverence.

To rejoice is a verb form and so implies action; it is not passive. We are called to take pleasure seriously. In applying the Charge practically, this can mean taking care of our bodies as part of enjoying life and sex. Enjoying the ability to move in general and being able to relax into sensation are both important, and muscle tone is part of pleasure. The strength of pelvic floor muscles directly contributes to sexual pleasure. The ability to enjoy sensations thoroughly does not begin or end in bed; instead sensual awareness can permeate all of life. Attention to enjoying food is important. Rejoicing at each meal is a practice to cultivate, in opposition to American fast food agrochemical meals. Paying attention to the energies that are carried in food, whether in the food itself or the comfort with which I receive it,

---

[1] Starhawk, *The Spiral Dance*, 20th Anniversary Edition (San Francisco: Harper and Row, [1979] 1999), 102-103. This version of the Charge was adapted by Starhawk from the original composition by British Wiccan priestess Doreen Valiente.

increases my ability to enjoy it. Self-pleasuring (a friendlier term than masturbation) is another form of enjoyment, useful for self-knowledge, for independence, for being self-responsible and self-loving. These traits enhance partnered sex. Physiologically, orgasm contributes a nutrient-rich blood flow to the brain that has important health benefits. All of this fits into the broad category of self-care, which is an essential life skill that undergirds rejoicing.

Mirth and reverence are great approaches for life and for sex. To be able to laugh at oneself can make life much more enjoyable, and laughter in bed with a partner tends to be tremendously pleasurable. Its benefits even have a scientific basis: laughter releases significant amounts of endorphins.

Reverence towards one's self means self-esteem, which for many of us is an ongoing work in progress. Generally speaking, patriarchal cultures damage self-esteem, particularly that of women. Self-esteem is a basis for pleasure, at least in how we communicate to others how we want to be treated. My own challenges with self-esteem and sexual development are a significant aspect of my life, with and without partners, and my path is part of what I bring to relationship. Sex can be a crucible for growth of self-confidence and self-esteem, if I maintain my own path and require the same of partners. Pleasure is an evolving adventure; treated with reverence, the adventure is very positive and can evolve throughout a lifetime. This attitude is one gift of Pagan culture.

After naming these pairs of virtues, the Charge addresses spiritual seekers. Not everyone experiences the need for spirit at a core level, but for those who do, the mystery is that *what I seek outside of me I must find within me.* The directive is worth repeating: what I seek I need to find within myself. This instruction is both esoteric and very practical. Instead of giving away my power and looking for something external, I can honor myself and start by growing satisfaction from within me. This is a crucial part of self-care. I don't have to be a "victim" in my life no matter what. I can always step into the solution. If I'm looking for healing, I can respect my own wholeness. If I'm looking for love, I can open my heart and share my appreciation and love with others. If I'm looking for sex, I start by enjoying my own sexiness. If I'm looking for wealth, I give thanks for the abundance in my life. If I'm looking for power, I can exercise to enjoy my own physical strength, and own the power of my "yes" and my "no." And then I attract more of what I want. It's a magical recipe for how to enjoy the gift of life.

The Charge tells me I come from the soul of nature, and I will return to Her. She is the beauty of the green earth and the white moon; She is the mysteries of the waters. I profoundly belong in nature; I am part of the beauty of the earth and the mysteries of the waters. My body is about 60% water; there's no fight between science and religion here. What does it mean to be the beauty of the green earth? I walk the path of the question.

The most challenging part of the Charge is the final statement that one finds the Goddess at the end of desire. A friend declares he's never giving up desire because partnered sex is vitally important to him. The Charge isn't teaching us to abandon desire to attain spirituality, however. This text is positive about pleasure and nature; it doesn't point to a monastic path towards higher spirituality. Sex as a form of sacred communion is more in line with the Charge, even at the end of desire. There's mystery here, about separating out limiting, manufactured desires, fulfilling our more robust desires so that we are replete, and finding the Goddess there too. Here is Starhawk's take on desire and its end:

> In Witchcraft, desire is itself seen as a manifestation of the Goddess. We do not seek to conquer or escape from our desires—we seek to fulfill them. Desire is the glue of the universe; it binds the electron to the nucleus, the planet to the sun—and so creates form, creates the world. To follow desire to its end is to unite with that which is desired, to become one with it, with the Goddess. We are already one with the Goddess—She has been with us from the beginning.

So fulfillment becomes not a matter of self-indulgence, but of self-*awareness*.[2]

Our desires, interrogated and explored, lead us home to ourselves and also to the Goddess, manifested in us. We become aware of ourselves as spiritual, as beautiful and belonging in the green earth. The end of desire is satisfaction, being in the moment, being present to the divine in me and in you. It is being home in Her, in myself, and perhaps with another, rather than fleeing on to the next craving or living in fantasy. The end of desire is wanting my partner, rather than needing her; it is seeing her rather than projecting her. *The end of desire is the place where I want her to be free more than I want her to be or do something for me.* It is a place of surrender, humility, and open-heartedness. It feels good. It's the kind of love that heals as much in the giving as in the receiving.

Love and pleasure are first found within us; the little word "and" is very important. The Charge does not give license to pursue just any pleasure. It's about the intersection of love and pleasure. Love without pleasure, or pleasure without love, are not Her rituals. Both love and pleasure are called for. If I'm not seeing the divine in someone, likely it is best not to be sexual with them. If I'm not seeing the divine in me, I am not self-respecting.

To pursue my own desires and win through to the end of desire, I've got to risk being and revealing me to myself, the Goddess, and to others. This feels like a hero's journey. Here's how I'm walking it lately:

- Asking for Divine protection for my desires. I don't ask for satisfaction per se, as I'm not well-equipped to sort through my multiple desires.
- Seeing my heart as muscle. I acknowledge strength and resilience as well as vulnerability and openness.

---

[2] Starhawk, p. 110.

Image © 2016 by Grove Harris

+ Creating art as offering and exploration. I paint, upcycling used sheets and house paint. I also use molasses to "paint" on sandbars.

- Praying by the ocean. I breathe my prayers into glass marbles and throw them into the sea.
- Yelling at the ocean. I yell, fully expanding my lungs and releasing patterns of fear.
- Sharing deeply with friends. Intimacy can be practiced in many relationships.
- Getting massage regularly. Human touch, and especially skilled therapeutic touch, is definitely one of Her rituals.

The Charge honors nature, pleasure, and fulfillment, but the spiritual path towards Her needs some practical advice. While an active spiritual practice is a pre-requisite for healthy intimate relationships, I need still more skills and guidance. It's not easy to be present to others and to see clearly what they're revealing through their words and actions. It's not easy to honor my own needs and boundaries, and even when I get this right for myself, it keeps changing. Sometimes people seem unconscious of the demands they make on my physical space, my body, and my time. There are lots of opportunities for practicing my own powers of "yes" and "no." Good consensual sex with a partner requires more than spiritual alignment. It requires the boundaries that "yes" and "no" set and affirm. It requires skills at being present, negotiation of past wounds, and trust. It requires a partner.

Here are a useful set of questions, from a guide to dating from a Buddhist perspective, to explore on the way to partnered acts of love and pleasure:

1. Have we talked about venereal disease, AIDS, birth control?
2. Have we managed some conversations about what's going on between us, how we are doing and feeling, and what we are afraid of?
3. Have we handled some level of conflict and acknowledged differences?
4. Is there a balance of giving, receiving, and initiating plans?
5. Are we able to make good eye contact while talking about difficult subjects?

6. Have both of us revealed vulnerable aspects of ourselves and felt respected and accepted?

7. Do both of us feel safe to voice our preferences or accept our partner saying yes, no, a little more, a little less, or not now but maybe later?

8. Are we comfortable touching and exchanging spontaneous hugs and other expressions of physical affection throughout the day?

9. Have we talked over our level of commitment to each other?[3]

These questions qualify the pull of lust by suggesting some specific reality checks.

If potential lovers have not examined their expectations, then someone is likely to get hurt. The Pagan ethic of "an it harm none, do as you will" means attending to the potential for harm to others or to ourselves. Sex is complicated; there are lots of energies and emotions involved, so this basic guidance about what is going on in a new relationship is helpful. Most of the songs I grew up on did not teach me about this; commercial music at that time was mostly about "love is here and now you're gone," which is a far cry from the skills and empowerment needed to fully enjoy partnered sex.

A wise friend of mine, who is exploring new sexual freedom as an adult, says that sex is a conversation. According to him, if all you have to say to someone is "you're so hot," that's pretty limited. With some discussion in advance, sexual partners can be more present to each other and their shared reality, and more free to explore the unscripted conversation of their sexual encounter. Consent to sex, an initial yes, is only the beginning. That conversation will need ongoing permissions (yes) and boundaries (no). If a partner has no boundaries, then it is likely they are abdicating their power, wishing to be taken care of, rather than being fully present. Yes and no are not strictly opposites, but descriptions that may shift and change, and they are continually

---

[3] Charlotte Kasl, *If the Buddha Dated: A Handbook for Finding Love on a Spiritual Path* (New York: Penguin, 1999), p. 126.

needed to navigate middle grounds once a sexual exchange has begun. "A little more, a little less, or not now but maybe later" are all part of that middle ground in consent. Ongoing desire needs some qualification; it is not black or white in practice.

Other Pagan practices can help with being present and with healing from wounds incurred in patriarchal culture. A tree of life grounding meditation, such as can be found in The Spiral Dance, is great for daily practice. Chanting, meditative tools, and spell casting can all help with healing towards wholeness and greater sexual encounters if desired. Very brief descriptions follow:

The Iron Pentacle is a meditative tool that consists of a five pointed star, where the points are all connected by the circle they inscribe and the cross lines among them. Overlaying this image on the body assists with meditation on each point and connecting with the corresponding physical point, the hand, foot, or head. With Sex at the head, Self on the left hand, Passion on the left foot, Pride on the right foot, and Power on the right hand, one can play with the energies of the points. Lately I'm enjoying a walking meditation of stepping out my left foot as passion and "yes," alternating with stepping on my right foot as pride and "no."

Chants can help retrain thought patterns away from negativity and towards more helpful refrains. They are effective sung alone, and are even more powerful sung with a group in ritual. For example, the chant

> My body is a living temple of love
> My body is the body of the Goddess
> Oh oh oh I am what I am[4]

can help heal negative body image and assist with self-acceptance and relationship with the Goddess, which can lead to richer sexual exchanges.

---

[4] Taken from a chant by Michael Stillwater.

Image © 2016 by Grove Harris

The cup of love spell is a powerful way to attract a lover through a simple yet profound process: first cleaning the cup, then filling it up, then placing it on the altar. In *Be a Goddess!*, Francesca De Grandis has written a thick description of this spell with thorough questions for each of the three parts. The spell helps with clearing wounds and expectations from the past, taking responsibility for filling up a vibrant life, and surrendering to help from the Goddess.

The Charge of the Goddess is particularly useful as part of a set of applied religious practices that focus directly on tough issues. A legacy of abuse, sexual violations, problems in bodily esteem, lack of healthy boundaries, and other common challenges need more than the Charge alone.

A major challenge is lack of trust, which can undermine relationships and peace of mind. "Trust" has multiple meanings, including confidence, hope, and reliance, with deep roots that lead back to Pagan perspectives. It is rooted in the strength of wood, in the ability to wait for a lover (tryst), and to druidic vision. Its root "deru," according to the American Heritage Dictionary, means "to be firm, solid, steadfast; hence specialized senses "wood," "tree," and derivatives referring to objects made of wood." These derivatives, besides describing wooden vessels, include tree, trust, betroth, endure, and druid, truce, firm, true, troth, truth, betroth, faith, loyalty, confidence, firmness, tryst (waiting place where one waits trustingly) and druid as "strong seer." Wood has incredible ability to carry water, whether as a tree carries water up to its leaves, or as sawdust absorbs moisture, or wooden bowls carry water. Trust is needed to carry the emotions involved in relationship, like wood carries water. Trust is not just a risk, it is a strength. In its origin, it is a wooden vessel or trough, ready to receive water.

Trust is the ground of sex. It is easier to open in trust. Trust comes from experience, from intuition, and from attention to reality. Answering all those questions prior to sex is a way to build mutual understanding and trust. Trust is a ground for creativity. Laying myself bare through art, whether painting or writing, is similar to laying myself bare in sex. Approaching a blank page, a blank canvas, an empty dance floor, or a potential lover all require guts and trust. Learning to trust makes life easier. Whether trusting the Goddess, my own voice, my choice of color, or my choice of sexual partner, the trust itself makes the creative process, and life itself, easier. When I am not trusting, my struggles increase.

The Charge of the Goddess invites us to trust. She is the beginning and the end, always present, the seen and unseen context of life's journey. She invites us to take the risks of love and pleasure, which are Her rituals. And while additional practices are needed to navigate sexual encounters, the Charge powerfully calls towards a life filled with love and pleasure.

Selected Bibliography

American Heritage Dictionary. Fourth Edition. Boston: Houghton Mifflin Company, 2000.

De Grandis, Francesca. *Be a Goddess! A Guide to Celtic Spells and Wisdom for Self-Healing, Prosperity, and Great Sex*. San Francisco: HarperSanFrancisco, 1998.

Freitas, Donna. *Sex & the Soul: Juggling Sexuality, Spirituality, Romance, and Religion on America's College Campuses*. New York: Oxford University Press, 2008.

Harris, Grove. "Healing in Feminist Wicca." In *Religion and Healing in America*. Linda Barnes and Susan Sered, eds. New York: Oxford Press, 2005.

Harris, Grove. "Composting Our Way Into Renewal." *Huffington Post* March 28, 2013. http://www.huffingtonpost.com/grove-harris/composting-our-way-into-renewal_b_2974275.html

Kasl, Charlotte. *If the Buddha Dated: A Handbook for Finding Love on a Spiritual Path*. New York: Penguin, 1999.

Kraemer, Christine Hoff. *Eros and Touch from a Pagan Perspective: Divided for Love's Sake*. New York: Routledge, 2014.

Lorde, Audre. "Uses of the Erotic: The Erotic as Power." In *Sister Outsider*. The Crossing Press Feminist Series, 1984.

McGowan, Kat. "Young, Attractive, and Totally Not into Having Sex." *Wired* February 18, 2015. http://www.wired.com/?p=1687283

Postman, Steve, and Eric Ganther. *The Cosmic Tribe Tarot*. Rochester, VT: Destiny Books, 1998.

Starhawk. *The Spiral Dance*. 20th Anniversary Edition. San Francisco: Harper and Row, [1979] 1999.

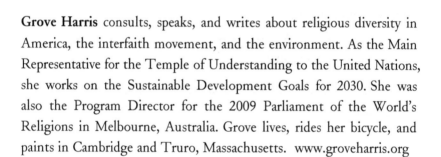

Grove Harris consults, speaks, and writes about religious diversity in America, the interfaith movement, and the environment. As the Main Representative for the Temple of Understanding to the United Nations, she works on the Sustainable Development Goals for 2030. She was also the Program Director for the 2009 Parliament of the World's Religions in Melbourne, Australia. Grove lives, rides her bicycle, and paints in Cambridge and Truro, Massachusetts. www.groveharris.org

Walking the Underworld Paths
BDSM, Power Exchange, and Consent in a Sacred Context
Raven Kaldera

> *You don't like us.*
> *We are the black blotch on the colorful rainbow.*
> *We are the sudden shudder as*
> *Bodies are innocently exposed—the rings*
> *Through the flesh, the pictures in the skin,*
> *Perhaps the marks of knives, of razors, of brands.*
> *Perhaps short-lived marks of crimson and purple,*
> *The colors of royalty. But these are worse,*
> *You think, for they are the slap in the face*
> *That this was no souvenir from a decadent youth*
> *Unless that youth ended just last night.[1]*

I'm a Pagan priest, a Pagan shaman, a Pagan pervert, and the owner of a Pagan slave.

I am firmly ensconced in a religion that claims sex is sacred and abuse is wrong, and I beat two out of three of my partners on a semi-regular basis.

I am firmly spiritually ensconced in a religion that has tried hard, perhaps harder than any other faith, to teach about human equality and walk that talk. I am also a person whose partner says that he is my slave, and I am his Owner.

How does this work, without complete denial of everything that I claim to believe in?

When I was asked to write an article on consent in BDSM and power exchange relationships from a Pagan perspective, I knew that I would have to explain a lot of complex situations, and yet I started out with the lines above, misleading as they seem. I wouldn't be surprised

---

[1] Poetry excerpts all from "This LeatherPagan Tribe," published in *Dark Moon Rising: Pagan BDSM and the Ordeal Path* (Asphodel Press, 2006).

to see them taken out of context and used against me on the Internet less than a week after the publication of this book. Still, I wanted that moment of indrawn breath and furrowed brow. I don't want anyone to assume I'm trying to downplay the strong reactions that many people have to these practices, including Pagans who find out that other Pagans do these things.

Before I unpack the layers of complexity, let's make one thing clear: My sex life is extremely kinky. I won't go into the details—this isn't *that* kind of article—but suffice it to say that if you're not kinky, I've probably performed and thoroughly enjoyed any number of sexual activities that would make you blink and swallow, if not stop listening altogether. I performed them with people who loved the same things I did, and were just as enthusiastic as I was about having them inflicted on themselves—perhaps more so. To date, not a single one of my (willing, enthusiastic, clearly consenting) partners has ever complained about the sex. Me forgetting to put the dinner leftovers away, maybe, but not the kinky, rough, sometimes violent sex.

Being out about my sexual practices, not to mention writing about how they are tied to my spirituality, has made me controversial among Pagans. I've received hate mail and death threats from the more conservative side of this big umbrella, and rumors abound of people I supposedly killed during BDSM rituals. (For the record, everyone has walked away from my hands satisfied and on their own two feet.) Some people have suggested to me that if I hadn't been out about BDSM, I'd be a "respected" Pagan leader instead of a "controversial" one. However, I spent too many years in a closet to want to be there again. Closets are hard on the soul, and they have a tendency to get found out and destroyed, rendering futile all the years of hiding. Since I have the privilege of being out—I have wonderfully accepting partners and child, a home I can't be thrown out of, a job I can't be fired from, and skill at not giving a damn what others think of me, all of which I am very clear are privileges that not everyone else might have—it falls to me to be the out person, the educator, the one who paves the way for others with fewer privileges. So I'm here to talk about consent in these demographics, which in some cases quietly overlap with Paganism, and how this one Pagan integrates these practices with my religious faith.

> *When you said that this was a community where*
> *Anyone could choose to be what they wanted,*
> *Anyone could choose how they would love,*
> *How they would fit their bodies together, you didn't*
> *Really mean it. You didn't mean this,*
> *You didn't mean these choices.*
> *But this is the price of freedom,*
> *Of offering those sacred choices. Sooner or later,*
> *Someone will choose something*
> *That makes your breath stop in your throat,*
> *Your belly turn in fear. You don't like us,*
> *Or our choices, and if anyone can make you believe*
> *That perhaps choice is not such a good thing,*
> *It might be us.*

Early Influences: Kink, Politics and Paganism

Let's start with a little history. The genesis of the Neo-Pagan movement began in the 1960s and 1970s, the era of the sexual revolution, the Equal Rights Amendment, and the blossoming of the civil rights movement. Traditional religious mores were also questioned, especially around the issues of gender equality and hierarchy. In fact, two of the biggest initial selling points of the pack of minority faiths that would eventually be lumped under the umbrella of modern Neo-Paganism were the spiritual equality of women with men (and their full spiritual ordination) and a lack of a centralized bureaucracy to make enforced decisions on dogma.

As a group of theoretically earth-centered religions, most contemporary Pagan traditions developed some concept of the sacredness of the body and sexuality, just as the earth itself was sacred. The sexual values that developed during this culturally fluctuating period were based around equality rather than hierarchy, gentleness rather than force, and freedom rather than shame. While many Pagans found it more difficult than expected to hold to these ideals in the face of their personal baggage, most ardently embraced them.

At the same time, a variety of nascent sexual exploration movements were beginning to bubble up from the cauldron of the sexual revolution. The most obvious of these, on the forefront of sex rights, was the gay liberation movement (eventually to become the lesbian-gay-bisexual-transgender rights movement). For a brief time before the onslaught of the AIDS epidemic, urban gay men developed a culture of sexual freedom (if not downright promiscuity— that revolved around bars, bathhouses, and cruises. Some of these bathhouses and orgy parlors were spoken of by the men who attended them as "temples of sex." The culture of the sacred body was, in its very own way, invading even this outpost of sexual debauchery. This was especially true for gay men who came into Wicca and other Pagan traditions in the 1970s and early 1980s.[2] The new culture of sexual freedom gave gay men license to explore the space of the "sacred body" with no holds barred. As part of this exploration, some gay men turned to more intense practices, often in spaces referred to as "Leather bars" and "dungeons."

Simultaneously, the sexual revolution was opening up new vistas for heterosexuals, including straight Pagans. Free-love, swinging, and other alternative lifestyles, once hidden in the shadows, now claimed their places in the light. The word "polyamory" was coined by the late Pagan priestess Morning Glory Zell of the Church of All Worlds. The forbidden territory of kinky sex, once strictly relegated to exclusive clubs with tightly controlled membership, began to surface and become more public, if not more publicly acceptable. While the underground clubs that practiced kinky sex and sadomasochism did

---

[2] For more information on the influx of gay men in North American Wicca, I recommend that you read Michael Lloyd, *Bull of Heaven: The Mythic Life of Eddie Buczynski and the Rise of the New York Pagan* (Asphodel Press, 2012).

function on a general rubric of consent (despite all fantasies to the contrary), their clandestine nature and their culture of exclusivity tended to detach this lifestyle from everyday reality for many of its practitioners, and thus discourage thoughtful discussion around socially complicated issues.

However, as they came out into the light and attracted newer people, many members of the burgeoning kinky sex support groups began to talk seriously—and publicly—about issues of consent. In the beginning, this was sheer self-defense: the last thing any kinky sex club needed was accusations of rape or assault, even ones that didn't involve the police. The concept of "safewords" —an out-of-context word or phrase used to stop any "scene," or orchestrated episode of kinky sex—had been in use for some time, but it was made regulation in many clubs and strongly encouraged as an across-the-board practice.[3] In the gay male community, writer David Stein created the phrase "Safe, Sane, and Consensual," which became a battle cry for BDSM practitioners across lines of gender and sexual preference.[4] To

---

[3] The practice of having a safeword may seem nonintuitive to many "vanilla" Pagans—why not just say no? The reasons are twofold: First, some BDSM practitioners do sexual roleplay where an individual wants the freedom to cry out, "No! Stop!" or make vague noises of distress and have their pretend "attacker" keep going, whereas saying "red" or "hold" or "dishwasher" is clearly out of role context and obviously means "No, for real, I mean it, stop now." Second, many BDSM practitioners have also discovered that an agreed-upon safeword actually carries more emotional weight and is more likely to be noted and heard when both parties are in an unruly, excited state; it stands out and more clearly invokes an immediate visceral stopping response, especially when both parties are used to the concept and use of safewords.

[4] Personal conversation with David Stein. He has since been criticized by practitioners who feel that it is impossible to judge the safety or sanity of any willing act from the outside, and prefer "RACK," or Risk-Aware Consensual Kink. However, his defence is that he created it in a time before discussions of consent and safety were de rigeur, and casual, spontaneous pickups in bars without negotiation were leading to injuries

be more specific than "kinky sex," the acronym BDSM was created; the different letter pairs stand for "Bondage and Discipline," "Dominance and Submission," and "Sadism and Masochism." Education in safe techniques blossomed, first as a way to prevent accidental injury, but eventually as a smorgasbord of fun ideas to play with. Educational BDSM conferences and gatherings began to spring up across the world.

The first big political clashes of BDSM practitioners with feminist ideology happened in the radical end of the feminist demographic,[5] which was then on the cutting edge of discussing the intersections between abuse, domestic violence, and the negative social patterns into which men and women are socialized. It was a necessary discussion, and one whose time had come. As with many reactions to a long-standing damaging situation, however, there was a period of overcompensation. Even women who engaged in ordinary "vanilla" (non-BDSM) heterosexual sex were under scrutiny: their desire to consort with men was seen as a sign that they had not thrown off enough of their social programming, making them incapable of consent. Consensual BDSM practitioners were seen as brainwashed by society into mindlessly repeating their abuse, or (if they had no personal abuse histories) repeating the violence condoned by their culture.

The battle came to a head during a couple of academic conferences, and it was searingly documented by Margaret Hunt. Responding to her opponents' view that most people are unable to meaningfully consent, she writes:

> Being a historian my thoughts naturally fled back to the past, in this case the sixteenth century: John Calvin in the

---

and STD transmission. His words: "You should have seen what it was like *before* SSC!"

[5] Mind you, I'm not getting down on feminism as a concept; I consider myself a feminist and have for over thirty years. I believe in people's right to choose... whatever sort of sex and relationships they want.

small Swiss city of Geneva. There is no free will, no free choice ... since people had no free choice in the great and hopeless struggle with sin (read "patriarchy"), they needed to be saved from themselves, if necessary by death ... One woman asked, with an air of uncertainty, what had happened to the issue of personal freedom. Hadn't the right to choose, especially around things like sex, once been kind of basic to the feminist movement? ... (The) response was that once you grasp the fact that heterosexuality is pivotal to women's oppression you must also realize how irrelevant issues of free choice really are. She concluded flatly, "Personal freedom is not the sort of concept that would fit into my view of what we can do around sexuality."

At least we know where we stand, I thought. And then I thought: This is not my revolution.[6]

The debates of the 1980s were important and did open up previously unexamined issues about the nature of consent and social brainwashing. However, they also left a legacy of reflexive overcompensation that can still be found in parts of the Pagan demographic, often among people who don't even know the genesis of those ideas. The legacy of reasoning goes like this: *I would never consent to X. If someone forced X onto me, or I took part in X because I felt pressured to do so, it would be unhealthy for me. Therefore, doing X must be unhealthy, period (because I cannot imagine someone sufficiently unlike me for whom doing it willingly would be healthy). Therefore, the only people who would consent to do X must be sick/fucked up/brainwashed by society. If they are any of those things, they must be incapable of meaningful consent around X, no matter their claims to the contrary. Therefore, I cannot accept that anyone who supposedly consents to this is actually consenting. They should be taught the error of their ways, and*

---

[6] Margaret Hunt, "Report of a Conference on Feminism, Sexuality and Power: The Elect Clash with the Perverse," in *Coming to Power*, 3rd edition, edited by SAMOIS (Alyson Publications, 1982).

when they are only willing to consent to the activities that I do not find distasteful, I will believe them capable of consent.

This leads into a spiral of circular reasoning that is both inaccurate and insulting, one that disempowers mature, thoughtful adults who have wrestled with socially unacceptable sexual urges and found safe and healthy outlets for them. It also shuts off communication, because this view is based on fear rather than a reasoned approach to differences.

> *You don't like us.*
> *We confuse you. It was taught that those*
> *Who undergo this pain are broken,*
> *Are weakened, damaged...yet we walk tall,*
> *Holding high our heads. We laugh, we joke, we pursue*
> *Each other, we cook food and tend gardens*
> *And raise children, just like everyone else.*
> *We stubbornly refuse to hear you when*
> *You tell us how wrong we are; your words*
> *Fall empty before the truth spoken by our flesh.*
> *You would hide your children from our eyes,*
> *Our marks, our tongues, the shadows we move in*
> *And out of. Even if you grudgingly agree*
> *That we are strong,*
> *There is no way that we can pretend to be*
> *Innocent.*
> *Yes, that at least, is so.*

Modern BDSM Practices

For denizens of the BDSM demographic today, consent is a holy thing. To run over a stated boundary is sacrilege; beginning practitioners get a faceful of how evil it is to ignore a partner's safeword. Less baldly spoken, but definitely discussed, is the idea that you owe a potential playmate an accurate description of your ability to give and withdraw consent. (More on that problem later.) BDSM practitioners know that consent goes both ways.

That isn't to say that there is never pressure from unethical players. Blatant safeword violations aside, an unethical top may attempt to pressure a bottom into going past their set limits, as in, "Come on, just try it the one time, I think you'll like it! I'll keep you safe!" On the other side, an unethical bottom may attempt to pressure a top into playing with them even if the top is uncomfortable with the bottom's psychological issues, as in, "If you were really as good/skilled/dominant as you say you are, you'd be able to handle me." Both these and other difficult situations do appear from time to time in a dungeon or during a date. The BDSM demographic is so strongly based around the sacredness of consent, however, that the community has a horror of its being violated.

In addition, the culture of BDSM is slowly training its practitioners to be more skillful at talking about sex. For the "vanilla" individual, it's often assumed that there's no need to discuss what sexual activities will be desired or pursued. The assumption is that there are only a handful of basic sex acts, to be taken in a "traditional" order (usually dictated by porn or romantic novels). In some cases, the idea of talking about what's going to happen is considered unromantic and thus undesirable. The ideal is a partner who will magically intuit what you want sexually, and do it in the way you want it without your having to ask or give them direction. (A secondary ideal is probably a partner who just automatically wants to do whatever you want to do, without preferences of their own.) This culture-wide assumption is responsible for many misunderstandings and unclear "maybe-rapes." It's certainly responsible for a lot of bad sex, which then gets blamed on the other person and not the cultural inhibitions.

BDSM practitioners, on the other hand, can't afford such trusting blinders. When "sex" can mean hundreds of activities from cunnilingus to whipping to licking whipped cream off of someone's feet, negotiation becomes crucial if one is even to discern whether two people have interests in common. (Some practitioners make printed lists of their preferred and despised activities, so that they can compare lists and quickly weed out sexual incompatibility.) In addition, when some sexual activities could be physically dangerous if an in-sex communication system of safewords or safe signals is not in place, that awkward period of negotiations becomes a matter of sheer safety. In the process of giving in to this necessity, however, we've learned that not only can it be part of the sexual process (talking about sex can be hot, not a mood-killer), but it doesn't prevent potential romance one bit. Everyone I've ever spoken to who made it into a BDSM community and still dated "vanilla" people has then brought their expanded ethic of sexual negotiation—and the limits of consent—into their "vanilla" dates. They've done this even when it disconcerted potential partners, because it's just that useful a tool.

Even more telling, some children of BDSM practitioners are taught to use safe words at a young age (because the practice is useful for keeping children from wounding each other during rough play), and they are usually encouraged to instigate thorough negotiations with potential dates when their teen years arrive. In my experience, these children of perverts tend to complain about how their "vanilla" dates don't like to talk about sex, and how that non-communication harms their sexual relationship. They also don't tend to have issues about making their consent to any activity, or lack of it, clear and strident. The unconscious splashover of their parents' subculture—with its assumptions about communication and consent safeguards—gives them standards for ethical treatment that some "vanilla" partners might consider unreasonably high.[7]

I believe that the BDSM demographic has a great deal to teach sexual activists around consent, if only those activists could get over the trappings which (superficially and from a distance) seem to resemble abuse. While no local community is perfect, on a meta-community level we discuss consent (and *assent*) more, and with more complexity, than any other demographic. We are not afraid to tease

---

[7] This information gathered via personal conversations with the panelists of "Adult Children of Perverts: How Has Growing Up with BDSM Parents Changed Your Vanilla Sex Life?" Class taught at the Pagan BDSM gathering Dark Moon Rising, 2004.

apart its convolutions, or for that matter, admit that it is a much less straightforward subject than any of us might prefer.

The practice of BDSM also has a subversive side, in that "archetypal" power differentials—binder/bound, inflictor of pain/recipient of pain, kneeling/knelt to, etc.—are sometimes played with as an erotic game. This doesn't always happen; it's not uncommon for people to engage in wholly egalitarian-context sensation play ("Give me a flogging with this soft whip and then I'll tie you up and put clamps on you!"). When "play" power exchange does happen, however, it is thoroughly negotiated. Playing with power roles (which includes fantasy role-play) isn't just a useful way to slowly and safely work through one's fears around a particular unhealthy real-world power dynamic. Over time, it also sensitizes people to unhealthy dynamics in other contexts and helps them to stop, breathe, and act in a conscious, mindful way.

I'm a non-hugger, for a lot of reasons including chronic pain, PTSD, and spiritual taboos. Imagine if the Neo-Pagan subculture borrowed the idea of the "safeword" and made it as ordinary and expected in our circles as it is in BDSM circles. While most BDSM partners create their own safewords between them, it's not uncommon for dungeons to have "house safewords" so that people who don't know each other well and are engaging in casual play can communicate better even if it's someone's first time. Imagine if Pagans instituted "ritual safewords" or "event safewords" for moments when someone wants to refuse some kind of physical contact, but doesn't want to disrupt a ritual or drum circle or even a loud Pagan party with long disclaimers and explanations.

In BDSM circles, the safeword ideally places no blame on either party. *You've decided that you don't want the thing you're doing for whatever reason, you communicate that in a blame-free, neutral way as information, I stop because I honestly want you to give me accurate information, because I want us both to have a good time and I'm not interested in doing something that makes you feel bad. I'll stop and check on you, or change the activity if that's what the safeword indicated. You won't blame me for not magically knowing you needed me to stop, and I won't blame you for telling me. You will take responsibility for communicating your needs, and I'll respond in a way that shows respect for your boundaries. You won't freak out at me and feel violated unless I'm obviously ignoring your safeword and proceeding anyway, and I won't freak out and feel rejected because you didn't want that one thing in that moment.*

This is the way safewords are treated when everyone involved is honest, mature, and committed to making the process go smoothly. Of course, problems do sometimes arise. As with the Pagan demographic, the BDSM demographic has to deal with a constant influx of newcomers who may not attend enough "Etiquette 101" classes (or any) before diving in with both feet, and will not have internalized the above italicized concept. We also have people with social skill impairments who may take longer to pick up on subcultural norms and will need proper behavior spelled out explicitly and clearly. Finally, we also have our percentage of dishonorable people who just don't care who they hurt.

In addition, there can be problems with people whose psychological damage prevents them from clearly communicating their limits during a scene. Generally, most experienced BDSM players will first advise such individuals to find alternate ways to express a safeword. For example, a colored ball squeezed in the hand and then dropped can work for anyone who is temporarily nonverbal, whether due to a trauma experience, a sensory overload, or having a gag in their mouth to bite down on; if the ball drops accidentally, the scene can resume after a momentary check-in. If the individual discovers that they go into a fugue state where even such rudimentary communication is impossible, they are usually advised to avoid BDSM until they have worked through more of their troubles and can take responsibility for communicating limits in a high-emotion environment. BDSM practitioners acknowledge that someone who cannot take that responsibility is a danger not only to themselves, but to their well-meaning play partner. It can be traumatizing for an honorable person to realize that they unwittingly ran over the limits of someone who didn't communicate them, and now they have hurt that person and have no idea how to prevent it from happening in the future.

Moving further, imagine that all open rituals had a period beforehand where people discussed what would happen (initiations aside), and that there was a safeword available for people who wanted to bow out of any activity and a way they could gracefully do that without disrupting the flow or making a fuss. Imagine the HP or HPs saying, "If you think that something might trigger you to the point where you can't communicate, please see me afterwards. We'll try to work something out, but if that's a serious possibility, you might think about only coming to rituals that have no triggering components for you. We're happy to discuss the particulars of each one with you beforehand, but you need to take responsibility for your own safety first."

> *You hold within yourself the image of evil*
> *Created by the ills of society,*
> *How it looks, how it smells, and we*
> *On the surface, seem to be a good match.*
> *We are just close enough to frighten you,*
> *Just far enough away to confuse you,*
> *And you would blot us out rather than struggle*
> *With those contradictions, those ambiguities*
> *That shift the solid ground beneath your feet.*

Sacred Catharsis: The Spiritual Connection

When I began to explore BDSM, I found that a number of my "scenes" began to have a strong spiritual component. As a long-time Neo-Pagan, I did of course believe that sexuality was a sacred thing, but on some level I didn't expect that to apply to BDSM. Sex that can be poetically described with images of fruit and flowers and gentle ocean waves, sure. But sex that is more reminiscent of a lion ripping apart a gazelle—does that count as sacred? Of course it does, but when I brought the idea up in Pagan circles, I found out where I'd picked up that opposing idea, which most Pagans believed implicitly. Leaving aside the Pagans who reacted as if I'd announced that I'd become a rapist, most felt that "spiritual sex" was gentle non-kinky sex—

"natural sex," as they put it. I was engaging in "unnatural sex," and thus any spiritual experiences I might have were simply delusional.

Initially, the BDSM community was no more receptive to combining kinky sex with spirituality. When I brought up spiritual experiences during scenes with other BDSM practitioners, most reacted with either disdain ("I keep my religion out of my sex life!") or cluelessness ("You mean like rubber nun outfits?"). Over time, however, people began to approach me one by one and confide that they, too, had found themselves in similar circumstances. "I was being whipped, and then... *something*... happened. Yeah, it was *something*." Many had experienced the cocktail of chemicals—including the infamous endorphins—that come with carefully sustained non-injurious pain, and they had discovered that those chemicals opened the door to the Spirits as surely as the mushroom cocktail of a South American shaman. Some discovered that allowing themselves to fully inhabit a taboo dramatic role enabled them to fall deeply into a sacred archetype, if only for an hour. Some had made profound discoveries about themselves in the middle of BDSM scenes. Some had visions while undergoing these rituals—and *rituals* they most certainly had become.

I decided to look at research on the matter, and indeed indigenous societies have a number of practices that I refer to as "the ordeal path." These include the Lakota Sun Dance, the Hindu Kavandi ceremony, the Indonesian ball dances, African scarification rites, Maori tattooing, Indian Tantric rituals of taboo-crossing, Filipino Catholic crucifixions, and even flagellation in Catholic monastic orders. Some of these rituals are rites of passage, some are ordeals to prove one's strength and endurance, and some are designed to bring the subject close to their own internal monsters. Some are offerings for underworld deities, and yet others are rituals to enhance the body's endorphin levels and connect with Spirit. Pain, endurance, and psychodrama have been used for millennia as spiritual tools; we in Western culture have simply lost—or thrown away—that thread of knowledge.

To be fair, there's one big difference between the above list of rites (with the partial exception of Tantric taboo-crossing) and what we modern primitives have been rediscovering in our home dungeons: those rituals aren't sexual, and ours usually are. I say "usually" because the last decade has seen an upswing in nonsexual BDSM practices. (This is usually explained to dungeon onlookers by pointing out that, in many cases, emotional and spiritual catharsis are as much or more satisfying than sexual release.) Why did our rediscovery of the Ordeal Path of spirituality grow out of a sexual subculture rather than, say, a culture of potentially injurious sporting activities? I believe that it has to do with the repression of, and confusion around, sexuality in Western culture. Sexuality is one area where all participants must surrender, at least to some extent, if only to the power of passion itself. When you surrender, the locked doors in your psychic basement open up and taboo subjects escape. Most people raised in Western culture carry a morass of fears of death, humiliation, and pain, and fear of sex is usually stuffed in there with them. Sometimes, over time, those fears begin to stick together. In a society where sex is not so taboo, the door to the underworld might open somewhere else. However, for many of us sexuality is the first and most powerful taboo, and sex is the starting point of purification through endurance and pain, the beginning step down into the darkness.

Note that when I say "darkness," I do not mean that these practices are inherently harmful or unhealthy. Rejecting the binary of good and evil, most Pagan traditions generally accept the concept that darkness is associated with the "night side" of consciousness. Our deities are both light and dark, as well as varying shades in between, and we speak of our "dark gods" as sources of transformation, intensity, wisdom, and deep (if perhaps painful) knowledge. They are the Holy Powers that show us difficult truths, guard the Underworlds (both literal and personal), care for the Dead and the Ancestors, and implacably strip away our illusions. We may not seek them frivolously, but we understand their worth and the value of working into the darkness.

I remember the controversy in the early 1980s about whether "dark" deities and goddesses were "too dangerous for modern Pagans to call upon. While some corners of the Pagan demographic still hold to the doctrine of "only Love and Light God/desses," most Pagans have since relaxed and embraced the more holistic concept that all parts of natural existence have their own holiness, including the parts concerned with death, decay, loss, sorrow, blood, devouring, ghosts, and the painful transition from death to rebirth. Gods and goddesses of death and the Underworld are no longer seen as evil, but simply as keepers of a part of the cycle that human beings often find distressing and inconvenient. Most Pagans that I know now believe that Their mysteries, while sometimes difficult, can free one from fear. Rituals and practices that lead one through one's own darknesses and promote healing and self-awareness are no longer considered "too dangerous" for our religion, as I heard them described in those earlier eras.

Ritual BDSM takes this road through one's sexuality, and sometimes emerges into other dark areas that need purification through catharsis. While Pagans who use the Ordeal Path may honor and work with many different deities, it is common for them to center their practice around death-centered Underworld deities such as Hades, Hel, or Ereshkigal; or implacable Hunter deities such as Artemis or Herne; or forbidding war deities; or even psychopomp deities who lead others in and out of the dark places. Other Pagans honor self-sacrificing deities such as Frey or Dumuzi, or deities who were forced into (or chose) ordeals that eventually led to wisdom and power—Odin, Persephone, Sedna, and many others.

The late Morning Glory Zell, who converted from a disapproving anti-BDSM force in her Pagan community to a delighted practitioner, wrote about a vision of the Goddess that she had during a BDSM scene:

> She told me that what I was seeing here was nothing less than Her own generational experiment with the domestication of sexual violence in the human species ... By focusing on sexually imprinting an influential sector of the young of this species, the Dream Gaea is trying to turn our inevitable violent biological impulses from deadly abuse to a stylized, playful form of courtship behavior, the way birds and some mammalian species have modified aggressive fighting

postures into dance movements. More animals survive this "mock violence," and can pass on their genetic proclivities to such modified behavior. This courtship tactic is part of a very large strategy that encompasses martial arts, fencing, and organized non-lethal gladiatorial sports like football, and many other ways in which we can turn our raw animal violence into forms of Art or Play. Repressed, primordial reflexes rarely remain there; denying that they exist doesn't make them go away. Back in the 1960s, the eminent animal behaviorist Konrad Lorenz wrote a book called *On Aggression*, which postulated that our species was in fact attempting to evolve beyond warfare by evolving stylized social behaviors such as bowing, shaking hands, and organized sports. I believe he was correct, but just did not go far enough.[8]

If we are to continue to value sexual openness, Pagans need to adopt, teach, and make acceptable a level of clear negotiation, responsibility, and respect for consent that rivals (and perhaps even exceeds—I can dream, right?) that of the BDSM demographic. We need to have a way to both maturely solicit and maturely refuse sexual aggression, without the confusing veil of shame or fear that shuts down our communication and sets people on both sides up for failure.

At the same time, we need to respect that many of our deities are more interested in bloody truths than social niceties. They will continue to push some of us toward catharsis by any road that moves us. In ancient times, such practices were usually confined to "mystery cults," although some cultures showcased them as public rituals. We who follow the Ordeal Path understand that this road isn't for everyone, but what road is? We know that throughout recorded history, some people have always been drawn toward such rituals. Even if the path we take winds through strange territory our ancestors never

---

[8] Morning Glory Zell, "Dark Ecstasy: Dancing With the Shadows of Our Future,".in *Dark Moon Rising* (Asphodel Press, 2006).

could have imagined, how we get there, and thus touch the deities and spirits, is less important than that we actually, sincerely do so.

> *We point to your revered past and laugh,*
> *Showing you books in ancient flesh, symbols*
> *Cut with blades of stone, needles of bone,*
> *The sacred plants burnt to ash and rubbed into the blood,*
> *Blood, blood, the altars ran with it and we*
> *Add our own to that ancient scarlet flow. We point to*
> *Woden on the Tree, Inanna stripped and beaten,*
> *Persephone raped, Gullveig three-times burned,*
> *Fenris, Loki, Prometheus chained, the Corn-King*
> *Cut down and threshed and devoured, Shiva's corpse*
> *Disemboweled by his skull-hung mistress as She*
> *Makes use of His dying member, and all*
> *The other dark hands that did the deeds.*
> *These are our Gods,*
> *We say, and They are your Gods too*
> *Whether you will or no.*

A Step Further Down the Road: Power Dynamic Relationships

The term "power dynamic relationship" describes personal relationships where one person has a negotiated amount of power over the other. This can extend only to a specific scene, to the entirety of someone's sexual life, or to other negotiated areas of life; or in some cases, it can extend to having authority over everything about that person. The words used to describe these relationships are both controversial outside of the BDSM demographic and hotly debated inside it. They include, in order of the extremity of authority transfer: Dominant/submissive (D/s), Master/slave (M/s, which can also be written Mistress/slave although a certain percentage of female M-types prefer "master"), and Owner-property (O/p).

The intracommunity debates regarding these terms are largely around definitions. Where, for example, does one draw the line between submissive and slave, or slave and "human property"? Can one person define themselves as a "slave" for an hour? What if that definition offends someone who has willingly given themselves up to live under another's rule and feels that the first person's temporary self-definition trivializes their choices? Are such choices personal or relational—for example, can one self-identify as a master or slave even if they are unpartnered, or is that like claiming to be a husband while single and unmarried? The debates are made more difficult by the fact that these terms are strongly eroticized by the people who claim them, which gives them little incentive to abandon the term when shut out by someone else's definition. On top of this, not all people who practice negotiated power dynamic relationships under these definitions practice kinky sex. The M/s/power exchange demographic and the BDSM demographic are actually somewhat separate groups (with, in some cases, separate conferences and events) that have a lot of overlap, with the non-overlapping parts of each pointing hairy eyeballs at the other.

Pagan debates around these labels tend to focus on the terms' historical uses. The feminist-leaning Pagan demographic often associates non-egalitarian relationships with historical oppression, especially of the "traditional patriarchal marriage" variety. The word "slave" doesn't go over well there, even when proudly proclaimed by an assertive, collar-wearing individual who is willing to argue for their label as a valid identity. The attitude of many people outside of BDSM or power exchange demographics is that those words (or at least Master, slave, Owner, and property) should only be used to refer to nonconsenting chattel slavery, either historically or currently occurring in oppressed areas of the world; according to this view, the consensual nature of these post-sexual-revolutionary relationships makes the labels inappropriate. Others fear that these individuals are simply unhealthy, with a controlling partner having duped a weak, codependent individual into accepting their authority... because why would anyone healthy actually consent to live in such a relationship?

Again, this attitude assumes that people who seek out power dynamic relationships are all damaged and never thoughtfully consider their desires. In actuality, the demographic of people who are deliberately cultivating such relationships is growing all the time, and for the most part, they don't look like "traditional marriages" at all. That movement is gaining its own conferences,[9] education,[10] outreach, international support groups,[11] and schools of theoretical thought— and, surprisingly enough, there is a strong undercurrent of spirituality among some of its communities. Power dynamic relationship conferences are loaded with educational classes about communication, trust, discipline, self-awareness, chosen family, and the place of many different kinds of love. Since the first conferences originally came out of the gay leather community, they tend to be queer-friendly and accepting of many styles of custom-made relationships. While some share space with BDSM classes and practitioners, more are now acknowledging that not everyone in an "authority transfer" relationship practices kinky sex.

When mindfully designed, power dynamic relationships are generally more deliberate and less assumptive than egalitarian ones. This happens for the same reason that sustainable polyamorous relationships build in a higher level of communication than most monogamous ones: complex, effective communication is necessary for the relationship's very survival. If a power dynamic relationship doesn't have a structure for communication, problem-solving, and the building (and rebuilding) of trust, it simply won't last. Modern power exchange educators stress finding what will make these relationships healthy, sustainable, and fulfilling for everyone involved. When Pagans

---

[9] The Master/slave Conference in Washington, D.C.; the M/s Gathering in Wilmington, Delaware; and the Power Exchange Summit in Columbus, Ohio.

[10] As well as the conferences themselves, there are two educational "titles" that have yearly competitions at various local events, and the winning couples compete for international titles: the Master/slave title, and the Power Exchange title. Both are strictly for education: the winners teach about power dynamic relationships in their area for a full year for any group that asks them, and they are funded by the local conferences.

[11] Masters And slaves Together (MAsT): http://www.mast.net.

and others criticize the "traditional marriages" of the 1950s and before, they are criticizing relationships that avoid self-examination and depend on a specific social pattern to fall back onto in times of difficulty. In contrast, we modern "masters and slaves" build our relationship structure based on the needs of the people involved rather than that of a cookie-cutter social standard, and we do so either between ourselves or at most with a small community of peers around us.

That isn't to say that no one is wandering around damaged and unthinking, full of baggage that they hope such a relationship will mend. There are plenty of those people, and many wander in, see what we're talking about, and then leave, chasing their two-dimensional porn fantasies. Sometimes they stay and realize that power dynamic relationships require a lot of self-work. A community with a high level of thoughtful conversation around alternative relationships (not to mention a strong GLBT presence in some areas) tends to self-select for a certain type of person. However, the power exchange demographic is still far behind the BDSM demographic in its outreach, and that includes outreach to Pagans. The Pagans I know who live full-time in power exchange generally find it easier to put together a Pagan rite at a BDSM or M/s conference than to speak up about the structure of their relationships at a Pagan gathering.

At the last power dynamic relationship conference I attended, there was a spiritual sanctuary, a candle-lighting ceremony for the ancestors and beloved Dead who had passed that year, two classes discussing ways of creating a spiritual discipline of relationship, and a liberal interfaith service (run by myself and attended by a Buddhist monk in full robes who was also a gay leatherman and Master). While many power dynamic practitioners shun anything religious, the spirituality movement within this demographic is now strong enough that we require an ongoing conversation about how to be respectful of those both with and without a spiritual focus.

A fair percentage of the "woo-woo crowd" in this demographic are Pagans, and we spend time discussing how the sacred archetypes of our ancestral past inspire us and show us ways to structure the spiritual discipline of deliberately unequal relationship. There are deities who rule and deities who serve, spirits of honor and leadership and spirits of service and sacrifice. There is Ganymede who carries the cup for Zeus, and Ninshubur who carries a sword for Inanna; there is Neti who guards the gate for Ereshkigal, and Mordgud who guards the gate for Hel, her Norse counterpart; and many others. It's especially important that we have examples of strong and competent deities who have chosen to serve another, as they demonstrate that choosing to be in a subordinate position does not mean that one is weak or stupid— or not valuable to the leader whose path they make easier.

Due to its coming-of-age period in the rebellious, free-floating 1960s and 1970s, Neo-Paganism does not have traditions of monasticism or clearly defined discipleship. We tend to think of the former as a vehicle for repressed individuals to avoid the world and their bodily urges, and the latter as a vehicle for exploiting the gullible. While there have been some reprehensible (and highly public) situations of this type in America in the past fifty years, many of us who found ourselves having unexpected spiritual experiences in our power dynamic relationships would say that those are perfectly good babies who should not be tossed out with all the dirty bathwater. As one Pagan who sought the disciple's path put it:

> Eventually I accepted that I could not meaningfully surrender my ego to a discipline that my ego had constructed. This was a 'sheepfold of my own devising' ... For a long while, I had assumed that the struggle to understand the divine will and form one's own conclusions about spiritual matters was an essential part of spiritual development. I believed that simply following someone else's rules was an immature expression of spirituality, and that a meaningful spiritual connection transcends the need for such rules. From an intellectual and political perspective, I would still prefer to believe this. However, for me, years of this kind of philosophical inquiry did not bring me one bit closer to God. It did not make me a better person. It did not aid me in making good choices with my life. It did not provide comfort in difficult times. For some

people, it does all these things, but not for me. When faced with decisions of spiritual import, I continually became mired in doubt and confusion. This approach just doesn't go anywhere for me. It is not my path.[12]

For the right person, spiritual discipline—and specifically, the choice to live willingly under the rule of another—can be a way to trade breadth of experience for depth of experience. For the right person, taking power in a sacred way—understanding that the other person is like a piece of land that you are stewarding, and that you will be held accountable by the Holy Powers for how they proceed—does not encourage laziness or corruption, but instead inspires them to strive to be more worthy every day. Just as I see my eighteen acres of woods and fields as a sacred trust with a living spirit, and I have a strong responsibility to find the best possible compromise between my needs and making that land the best that it can be, so I also see the relationship between myself and my slaveboy in the same light ... and I know that my Gods watch, and judge.

For such a relationship, informed consent requires more than a mutual stated desire. It is the responsibility of the submissive/slave/person who will take orders to submit themselves only to someone they trust deeply and find worthy of serving, to do their due diligence, and to abandon the situation if it shows itself to be harmful to them. It is the responsibility of the dominant/master/person who gives orders to remember that this is a chain of command, and they are not at the top of it. That position belongs to the Gods, or if you're a non-theistic Pagan, the Universe and its cycle of return on your deeds. It is the responsibility of both parties to allow trust to develop slowly, at its own pace, because both sides need to consent to each new shift of authority. (It isn't always

---

[12] Joshua Tenpenny, "Finding the Slow Path." Published first in *Spirit of Desire: Personal Explorations of Sacred Kink*, edited by Lee Harrington (Mystic Productions LLC, 2011), and then in *Sacred Power, Holy Surrender: Living A Spiritual Power Dynamic* (Asphodel Press, 2012).

the person taking orders who has to say, "Hey, wait, hold on, I'm not ready for this part yet!")

What Paganism Can Learn From Us

When we teach about power in our communities, we need to teach skill at being in authority and skill at being subordinate. When we fail to discuss how to honorably use power and to what code the powerful should be held, it's rather like teaching abstinence and hoping the kids will just refrain from having sex. Certainly the spiritual practice of striving for radical egalitarianism is honorable in its own right, and it is its own kind of renunciation; one could think of it as a sort of power-celibacy. But to hold radical egalitarianism up as the "best" option is the equivalent of advocating that everyone take vows and give up sex entirely. Nonhierarchy is the appropriate path for some people (and Pagan groups), but not everyone. It's true that history is littered with bad examples of hierarchical relationships and societies, but that doesn't mean that power exchange can't be done cleanly. It just means that it requires a lot of work.

Earlier in this article, I mentioned that BDSM play often sensitizes people to unhealthy uses of power in ordinary life that they would otherwise have let slide. This is doubly true for people in power dynamic relationships—and we, too, have something to offer to consent culture. We dissect questions that are often left untouched. *How does one cleanly consent to be under the authority of another in a healthy way?* (This is a situation that many egalitarian people find themselves in every day, in the workplace or classroom.) *How does one cleanly take responsibility for matters of importance in someone else's life?* (This, too, can come up in an egalitarian relationship during difficult moments or because of illness and injury, and people in those relationships often fail to explicitly negotiate where they will take responsibility for each other, which can result in all kinds of confusion and hurt feelings.) *How does one sort out one's baggage, figure out how much selfishness is a good thing and where one crosses the line, figure out how to keep from offering up to another what one doesn't yet own fully for one's self?* (This, too, can be an issue for everyone in intimate relationships.) *How does one surrender the ego without losing the soul, and how does one accept the perilous and precious gift of that surrender without having to pretend to be perfect?* These questions are the frontier boundary of our work of reclaiming power-over, clearing away millennia of tarnish and crud, and searching for the bright gem beneath. *There is nothing that cannot be reclaimed and healed. Say it again and again. Believe it.*

Imagine, if you will, if every one-on-one relationship in Pagan religion which might contain a power differential—especially the often-cited "high-risk" teacher-student relationship—was negotiated with regard to areas of authority and expectations in the straightforward, everything-on-the-table way that a modern mindful power dynamic relationship is hashed out. Imagine if, rather than trying desperately to eliminate all power differential, it was simply acknowledged and discussed, with structures of recourse put in place in case those who take orders are dissatisfied, and the person in charge taught how one should conduct one's self honorably when given the gift and terrible privilege of power over another person. While there's nothing wrong with having a horizontal power structure and a commitment to radical equality in one's group, that's not what everyone wants or needs. Instead of assuming that the best way to lead is to take as little power as possible, a Pagan consent culture of many paths should be teaching people how to use it wisely, and what they ought to expect from someone in charge.

This summer will see the very first Pagan Power Exchange gathering, where people who practice both deliberately unequal religions and Pagan religion will meet and discuss how our relationships intersect with our spirituality. There will probably be naked consensual slaves—and clothed ones, for that matter. There will probably be people they address as "Master" or "Mistress" or "Sir" or "Ma'am"... or "Lord" or "Lady." There will definitely be ritual that celebrates honor, service, devotion, leadership, and surrender. We'll see what kind of strange fruit grows from this new seed, and we'll spread those quietly throughout Paganism—not because we want everyone to do what we do, but because we want people to be able to look at all power dynamics with clearer eyes. This act can only benefit us, because when we are seen without personal and social distortions, we are harder to demonize. It can also only benefit the world.

> *That word, "primitive," we see it differently. No room*
> *For idealized, pretty tales. Our ancestors*
> *Scrambled and crawled across thorns*
> *To survive, to do more than survive, to find these*
> *Crumbs of wisdom that are our inheritance.*
> *And if we think that under our*
> *Smooth exteriors and shining toys we are*
> *Any better, any less flesh that gives way to thorns*
> *Then we are merely blinded fools,*
> *And we deserve the pain unlooked-for*
> *Rather than the ordeal we choose*
> *With open arms, with open heart,*
> *Legs spread wide to take in holy lightning,*
> *Going as to the bridal bed in joy.*
>
> *For we have bared our throats to the Darkness*
> *And lived to draw the map.*

Raven Kaldera is a Pagan priest and minister of the First Kingdom Church of Asphodel, a Northern Tradition shaman, an astrologer, an ordeal master, a devout polytheist with many Gods and spirits, a polyamorous transgendered intersex BDSM and M/s activist, and the author of too many books to list here. He is dedicated to Hela and Shiva and guides people down the shadow roads... and safely back out again.

Saving Iphigenia
Escaping Ancient Rape Culture Through Creating Modern Myths

Thenea Pantera

"You work with the *Greek Deities?*" A friend asked me, with a grimace on her face.

It's not the first time I've gotten that reaction from someone. Usually, I reply, "I'm with Hermes." Somehow, after that, people seem to be a bit relieved, and move on to another subject.

Sometimes they press me further, "I get why Hermes, but why the Greek pantheon? Like, Zeus? And Hades? As a woman, how can you *touch them with a ten foot pole?*"

Greek Paganism has a problem, and that problem is ancient rape culture. There's a lot of sexual assault in ancient Greek mythology, and it's not generally treated like a crime by the myth-makers. Cassandra is punished for withdrawing consent. Hera punishes rape victims. Every single male deity in the pantheon is responsible for at least one sexual assault, with the exception of Ares, who is a perennial villain in Greek mythology.

Please don't misunderstand: there is much to recommend ancient Greek culture and its mythology. Many of the stories are beautiful and still relevant today. These are Deities to whom hospitality is important. I feel strongly that they want to be trusted and to be welcome in our homes. While the mythology portrays rape culture, it also portrays great acts of mercy, divine accountability and justice. Yet, how can I ignore the violent attitudes that the ancient culture had toward my gender?

By looking into mythologies of the past, anthropologists learn about what a culture valued. Mythology is a symbolic language through which cultural values and cultural experiences are expressed. People associate their Deities with what they think is important, and the ancient Greeks were unapologetically misogynistic. They had their filter, and it sharply colored how they experienced and portrayed their Deities. *In short, I don't think the Deities ever supported misogyny or rape.*

Our values have changed. Our symbols have changed. What Greek sexual mythology meant to the ancient Greeks, it no longer means to us. Over this chapter, I plan to show what our modern theological problems are. I will explore how we are misunderstanding the gods because of the shifts in values and symbols that have occurred over the millennia. Lastly, I will suggest some possible strategies for tackling problematic myths.

Killing Rape Culture in Our Theology: "Maybe the Deities Don't Have to Be Good?"

In modern Western culture, there is a certain underlying notion that the people with the power get to make the rules. The Koch brothers can buy off a political party and write their own tax policies. Corporations get to decide what a fair wage is. It is a world where might makes right.

This is exactly why we have a problem with rape culture. The dominant culture believes that if you had the power to take something, you must have somehow deserved to get it. If we get caught and punished, then we must have deserved that, too. It's why people laugh when they see pictures of tuxedos Sharpied onto drunk people who have passed out, rather than feeling immediately horrified. It's why there are so many apologists for police brutality.

Unsurprisingly, then, a fair number of people buy into the notion that our Deities do not need to be upright, just, or good. After all, deities answer to no higher authority. Who could stop them? These worshippers *excuse* the actions of deities that are not in line with modern values. The theological idea that "might makes right" is compelling to many, and not only because it resonates with our experience of more mundane powers like Walmart or British Petroleum. It lets us take the myths at face value rather than grappling with the shift in values that has occurred over two and a half millennia.

Some Greek Pagan clergy have said that Deities may do what they like with their followers because they are Deities. This may include forcing psychic intimacy and doing violence to humans, sexual and otherwise. One must pacify the Deities with offerings, they argue, to prevent this from happening. They point out that rainstorms do not need to be fair, nor do volcanoes, and that the Deities are similar in this regard. They are not role models. We cannot rely on them to set a good example.

This thinking uses power and authority to excuse violence. The Deities are entitled to be violent because of their power and authority. *If you are powerful enough,* you don't need to think about how anyone feels. *If you have enough authority,* you don't need to consider the dignity of the vulnerable. This, to me, sounds a whole lot like, "You can't convict those boys of sexual assault, they come from good families and they are important members of the football team," which, according to the defendants in the Steubenville rape case, was a perfectly legitimate reason to excuse sexual brutality.

This thinking is poisonous because Deities are not the only beings ever to find themselves with power or authority. They are not the only beings ever to be in a position where they can hurt someone and get away with it. We need to take questions like, "Am I powerful enough?" or "Will I get away with this?" out of the reasoning process if we want to escape the gravitational pull of rape culture.

How can we articulate the responsibility of one being to show respect for the autonomy of another, if power is no longer a part of the question? I would frame it like this:

> If you harm, violate or abrogate the will of another being, the action you take is something which inherently degrades and diminishes you. Authority and power cannot protect you. Instead, it worsens the crime, and the degradation.

Ancient Greek Religion Expected the Deities to Defend Our Values

In ancient Greek Paganism, not only did mortals look to the Deities to know right from wrong, they also looked to their Deities to be the enforcers of justice. Their belief in the Deities animated their sense of virtue and hospitality.

These [people] exceeded all men in pride and impiety; and Zeus, desirous of putting their impiety to the proof, came to them in the likeness of a day-laborer. They offered him hospitality and *having slaughtered a male child of the natives,* they mixed his bowels with the sacrifices, and set them before him, at the instigation of the elder brother Mainalos. But Zeus in disgust upset the table at the place which is still called Trapezos, and blasted Lykaon and his sons by thunderbolts.[1]

These men were punished for "pride," but please note what the act of pride was: it was infanticide and cannibalism. In the ancient Greek mind, impiety, eating people, and violations of hospitality tended to be equated. The reasoning went, if you don't even honor the Gods, you certainly can't be trusted to follow the laws of decency toward your fellow man.

This myth is far from the only one in which Zeus, or Zeus and Hermes together, show up disguised as vulnerable individuals seeking hospitality. The notion that any stranger who happens into your home might be a deity animated people's sense of obligation to be decent to others while offering them succor. Correspondingly, those who did not honor the Deities were suspected of other wrong doing as well.

We must ask ourselves, "How can building a culture of consent be seen as synonymous with honoring our Deities?" One straightforward answer is that any person we touch without permission, assume the gender of without permission, or discriminate against ~~could be a deity in disguise, too.~~ is Divine.

Would it even enter your mind to touch a Deity without permission? The common ancient belief that Deities disguise themselves as humans to test us can also animate our modern Greek Pagan morality.

---

[1] Pseudo-Apollodorus, *Bibliotheca* (trans J.G. Frazer), 3.8.1-2. *Theoi Greek Mythology.* 2nd century CE. Available at http://www.theoi.com/Text/Apollodorus3.html.

Our Symbols and Our Values Have Changed: Hades and Persephone

To illustrate the shift in symbols and values I've been talking about, I want to look at the Hymn to Demeter and the story of Persephone's abduction by Hades.

Here's the synopsis: Zeus arranges a marriage between Hades and Persephone. Persephone and Demeter are not consulted. Hades collects Persephone, and Demeter becomes angry with Zeus. Demeter uses her nature powers to smoke Zeus out. Zeus relents and sends Hermes to fetch Persephone. Hades somehow makes Persephone eat Death-Fruit, and so Persephone has to spend the dry season in the underworld.

To a modern reader, this really looks like Hades is a bad guy, maybe even a rapist. To an ancient reader, however, the relationship between Hades and Persephone looks quite different. To begin to explain how this myth might have read to an ancient Hellenic Pagan, we need to start by understanding the ancient Hellenic view of what marriage was and how it worked. Please note the following:

> Hermes [...] found the Lord (Hades) inside his palace, seated on a funeral couch, along with his *duly acquired bedmate.*[2]

The words 'duly acquired bedmate' set this apart from the many, many incidents where a male deity physically forced himself on an unmarried woman. Hades, in good faith, did everything that it was considered proper for a Greek man to do in order to acquire a lawful bride. If we were to translate this myth, substituting our customs, Hades would have dated Persephone for a year or two, taken Persephone out for a fancy meal, gotten on one knee, and offered her a diamond ring. Then, after exactly a one-year planning period, they would have gotten an officiant (maybe Hera) to conduct a wedding at the Olympian version of the Ritz Carlton.

---

[2] Homer, "Hymn to Demeter" (trans. Gregory Nagy), lines 342-343. 7th century BCE. Available at http://www.uh.edu/-cldue/texts/demeter.html.

Those are our customs. They did not exist in ancient Greek culture. According to ancient Greek culture, Hades did everything right. Had the Greeks practiced different customs, Hades would have followed those instead.

An ancient Greek marriage happened in three phases. The first was the *Engue*, or betrothal, which was arranged between the *Kurioi*, or fathers of the groom and bride, respectively. If the groom was considered an adult in his own right, the arrangement could take place between the groom and the father of the bride.

The bride was not considered to have any legal agency. She did not need to be present for the betrothal. The ancient Greeks did not have a notion of a woman as a being whose consent, or lack thereof, was in any way meaningful. In the marriage of Hades and Persephone, the betrothal was arranged between Persephone's father (Zeus) and Hades.

> I begin to sing of Demeter, the holy Goddess with the beautiful hair.
>
> And her daughter too. The one with the delicate ankles, whom Hades seized. *She was given away by Zeus*, the loud-thunderer, the one who sees far and wide. Demeter did not take part in this, she of the golden double-axe, she who glories in the harvest.[3]

labyrs? ✗

The central event of the Athenian wedding is the process of loading the bride into a chariot and transferring her from her father's house to the Oikos of her husband. The final step in this process is the man carrying the woman over the threshold of the home.

oh!

> He was riding on a chariot drawn by immortal horses. The son of Kronos. The one known by many names. He seized her against her will, put her on his golden chariot, and drove away as she wept.[4]

well it's still a bit dodgy

---

[3] Ibid., lines 1-4.

[4] Ibid., lines 18-20.

The very last part of the marriage ceremony was a showering with fruit or nuts.

> But he gave her, *stealthily,* the honey-sweet berry of the pomegranate to eat.[5]

Did you ever wonder how a person manages to cunningly commit some action that ends in, "Oops, I got fruit in your mouth?" The idea makes a lot more sense if you imagine Hades throwing pomegranate seeds at his new bride to celebrate her arrival. That clearly doesn't make sense in the context of lines 360-380, but it's an idea that I think bears exploring.

To the ancient Greeks, there was nothing unusual in the marriage of Hades and Persephone. This was simply how marriage was done in Greece during the seventh century BCE, and of course the silly women were going to be upset. Women just don't know what's good for them.

Spend a moment imagining a woman hearing the Hymn to Demeter and wistfully recalling how she, too, wept bitterly at her marriage, missing her mother terribly. Then, she smiles, thinking of how she built her own household and gave birth to the children she loves. This was a reality for almost every Greek woman, a reality as inevitable as death. In fact, being forced into a marriage she did not choose was the good outcome, comparatively speaking. Is it any surprise that forced marriage shows up in Greek mythology?

Why Kore? Because she is every unmarried woman.

Why Demeter? Because she is The Mother.

Why Hades? Because, in the end, death carries us all away by force, whereupon we go to live in the Household of Hades. Death mirrors an ancient Greek woman's experience of marriage almost exactly. *wow*

Hades stands in for The Husband in this tale. That does not mean that he invented the Greek marriage ceremony, or even that he approves of it. The language and symbolism are put into his mouth, stealthily, by people who are now long dead, but the myth lives on,

---

[5] Ibid., lines 371-372.

Persephone myth—not just going to the Underworld, but dying

carrying with it an echo of the terrible oppression that many Greek women faced.

Despite all that, Hades did not commit rape. The action was *marriage*. The fact that Persephone was able to return to her mother at all implies that the marriage had not yet been fully enacted. We can assume that Hades figured he had all the time in the world for his bride to warm up to him. Ancient Greek culture was one in which only men got to decide their destinies, and in which rape was seen as a demonstration of a can-do attitude, ambition, and virility.[6]

In a parallel fashion, it was considered inappropriate for women to *be raped*. The men were just victims of Eros. The women shouldn't have been outside in the first place. If you doubt that last point, go look at some ancient Greek pottery. Notice that all the women are pale and all the men are dark? That is because men were free to roam outside, while a modest woman stayed in the house. This explains why, in the *Odyssey*, the suitors of Penelope never assaulted her: only a woman outside was fair game. Note that in Greek myths, some very large number of victims are nymphs or other female spirits of the outdoors. The rape myths existed, in part, as cautionary tales to remind women not to go out unchaperoned.

So what do we do with the myth of Persephone? What do we do with other myths like it? We have two basic choices: we can accept that our Deities are stuck in a cultural mindset nearly 3,000 years out of date, one that is anti-woman and pro-rape; or we can decide that our deities do not and did not support these facets of Greek culture, despite the lack of primary source text material to prove that.

If we choose to believe that the Deities do not hold identical values to humans living more than two thousand years ago, we must

[handwritten margin note: She was outside gathering flowers]

---

[6] For more on this topic, see Carla Schodde, "Rape Culture in Classical Mythology," *Found in Antiquity* Oct. 6, 2013. Available at http://foundinantiquity.com/2013/10/06/rape-culture-in-classical-mythology/.

begin to be more judicious about the images that we rely on to connect to our Deities, whether they be in pictures or in words.

Approaches to Evolving Mythology

If a religion is blessed to survive long enough, it will eventually find its values and its mythology to be in contradiction. Religions that have survived a long period of time respond to this problem in a variety of ways. I am not going to tell you which of these will work for you, and there are more options than those included in this chapter. My hope is that this discussion will at least provide a starting point.

Abstract Interpretation

One approach to dealing with the discrepancy between ancient Greek values and symbols and our own is to simply account for the differences when interpreting mythology. This means not only understanding that the same symbol may take on different meanings, depending upon the time period and region of the world we are discussing, but also respecting the ancient Greek symbols in their own context.

In other words, when you are trying to understand a myth, it really doesn't matter what a chariot may mean to you, or in the Tarot, or in Norse mythology. For the purposes of understanding a Greek myth, you must understand what chariots meant to the ancient Greeks. This requires an in-depth understanding of Greek culture, Greek art, Greek philosophy, Greek customs, and Greek values.

From there, we can look at what the myths are trying to say on a deeper level and, moving past the instinct to interpret myths as things that deities actually did, explore what virtues the deity stood for and how those same virtues may be applied to modern life.

Rather than directly changing how we understand the story, we view the story as a sort of cipher, not literal in the slightest, but rather an encoded message from the ancient past. This approach also frees us up from any temporal narrative. If a deity stood for a particular thing at one time, they can stand for it again.

An example: The myths of Zeus raping women, of which there are many, may have symbolically connected to his role as the deity who brought the rain. The words often spoken at the *engue*, "I give this woman to you for ploughing," show that human procreation and the growth of crops were symbolically related. Rainy season, in a Mediterranean climate, was the season where seeds placed in the Earth would begin to grow. We need not understand these as literal rapes. Rape, as a symbol, was in vogue at the time, and it represented the fructification of nature. Even if we do understand these events as literal rapes, ancient Greek culture must be taken into consideration. Rape was considered praiseworthy, a proof of virility and ambition. As symbols, these events allude to Zeus as a powerful, victorious and virile God.

The advantage of this is that we no longer have to place value judgments on the actions that deities do in mythology. The Deities are real, but their actions are symbols that the ancients used to describe them. *The disadvantage* is that this approach is sort of a temporary fix. If you look for books of ancient Greek theology, you won't find much. In ancient traditions, theology isn't really separate from mythology. When culture changed, the myths changed. In a sense, this kind of solution to a theological problem, often employed by Christians, fixes the problem by holding the sacred stories at arm's length like a pair of stinky socks. Inevitably, it wears thin, and people looking to imaginatively engage with the Deities will want to "get back to basics." When that happens, we're back to square one.

The Story between the Lines

Here I look into other cultures for cues as to how to deal with a problematic mythology. Unlike Greek Paganism, Jewish religion sees the words of its mythos as unchanging and infallible. Consequently, Jews' response to narrative elements that don't make sense or that don't resonate with them is to use the text as a jumping-off point and to draw out strangeness in the wording or the circumstances. They call these interpretive stories *Midrash*, putting them in a separate category from the original stories in the Masoretic Text. Still, if you ask a Jewish person about a story, they may tell a Midrashic tale as though it was written directly in the Torah. By using this method, they've achieved a synthesis of old and (relatively) new. In some cases, the meanings of the myths are turned on their heads.

Lucian did something similar in the second century CE with his *Dialogues of the Gods*.[7] While satire, much of the *Dialogues* does seem to be in response to obvious questions in Greek mythology. The questions that plagued the ancients were often "How can these two versions of the myth both be true?" and "How can other cultures believe in different deities?" Writings like these, however, can be used to fill in the gaps between myths, and perhaps explain why certain things are not as they seem.

An example, in the style of Lucian:

> *Hermes:* Persephone, I was thinking. It's unfortunate that you only have a husband for a third of the year. If you were looking for a two-thirds of the year husband, I am available.
>
> *Persephone:* Hermes, you are dear to me, but I would never be unfaithful to my husband.
>
> *Hermes:* Firstly, I can't reckon how it's unfaithfulness. You can't spend that time with him no matter what you do. Secondly, you didn't even choose him.
>
> *Persephone:* Tell me, Hermes, have you never lied to your father? Zeus fears Demeter. Should I not? Of course I told her that Hades grabbed me away by force. My mother, a Goddess of Life, never would have approved of my marriage to the God of the Dead.

The *advantage* to this approach is that it keeps us grounded in the old canon while updating our understanding.

---

[7] Lucian, "Dialogues of the Gods." *Theoi Greek Mythology*. 2nd century CE. Available at http://www.theoi.com/Text/LucianDialoguesGods1.html. (Really, you should just go read the whole thing.)

The *disadvantage* is that while this approach might rectify problematic myths, it does not create new ones to support our values.

Re-Writing

The ancient Greeks wrote and re-wrote their myths. Certain myths crop up in Hesiod and Homer with different versions. The Orphic poems have a third version. Myths also changed over time. To understand how the ancients changed their myths, let's look at the myths of Iphigenia.

> To him then spake in answer the king of men, Agamemnon: [115] "[...] I am minded to make amends and to give requital past counting. [...] And if we return to Achaean Argos, the richest of lands, [Achilles] shall be my son [...] Three daughters have I in my well-built hall, [145] Chrysothemis, and Laodice, and Iphianassa; of these let him lead to the house of Peleus which one he will, without gifts of wooing, and I will furthermore give a dower full rich, such as no man ever yet gave with his daughter."[8]

Many consider Iphianassa to be the same person as Iphigenia. In roughly 450 BCE, we have Aeschylus revising this myth in his *Oresteia*: Iphigenia is sacrificed by Agamemnon, rather than being married to Achilles. In roughly 400 BCE, Euripides writes the play *Iphigenia in Aulis*, wherein Iphigenia is betrothed to Achilles but then sacrificed to Artemis. Between 500 BCE and 400 BCE, the version wherein Iphigenia is killed by her father to honor a deity was the popular version. By the second century of the Common Era, however, this view falls out of favor:

> Now I have heard another account of Iphigenia that is given by Arkadians and I know that Hesiod, in his poem

---

[8] Homer, *Iliad*, Book 9 (trans. A.T. Murray), 114-149. *Theoi Greek Mythology*. 8th century BCE. Available at http://www.theoi.com/Text/HomerIliad9.html.

Artemis made
Iphigenia into
Hekate?.
moon
Luna

Catalogue of Women, says that Iphigenia did not die, but by the will of Artemis, is Hekate. With this agrees the account of Herodotos, that the Tauroi near Skythia sacrifice castaways to a maiden who they say is Iphigenia, the daughter of Agamemnon.[9]

Here we can clearly see how a myth evolves when it is told in different ways by people with different values. Note that the human sacrifice element is being directly addressed, even though the earliest source does not include it. Notice how the story-tellers who came after did not simply ignore the sacrifice element, but corrected it. In other words, different people throughout Greece believed different things. Stories were shared, spread, changed to suit the needs of the people, and then later scooped up by historiographers who included versions they liked and ignored ones that didn't fit in.

If we cling to the essential virtues that the Deities are Deities of, and think about what a myth is trying to say based on a firm understanding of Greek culture, we should be able to hold on to the same Deities while telling different stories about them. In so doing, we wind up with myths that are congruent with our values and that make sense to us, based on how we use and interpret symbols.

An example, in the Style of Pausanias:

Now I have heard another account of the marriage of Hades and Persephone, that is given by the Bostonians. It is said in Boston that Demeter had been warned by an oracle that her daughter should never speak to the God of the underworld, or else she would lose her place among the Olympians. Demeter feared for her daughter and warned her never to knock upon the Earth. One day, Kore was curious and disobeyed her mother. They say that a handsome God sprang from the Earth with beauty like a youth, but with yet a

---

[9] Pausanias, "Description of Greece," (trans. W.H.S. Jones), 1.43.1. *Theoi Greek Mythology.* 2nd century CE. Available at http://www.theoi.com/Text/Pausanias1C.html.

full beard, and Persephone was instantly smitten. The two conspired to elope with the help of Zeus. Yet another version is told in Silicon Valley, where they say that she was kidnapped only because Hades could not spend long in the world above, but once Persephone was in his domain, he offered the fruit and gave her a choice.

The *advantage* to this approach is that it allows mythology to become diverse and dynamic again. It potentially restores Polytheism to its former glory, where multiple interpretations, even completely new retellings, become sacred.

The *disadvantage* is that getting people to view mythology in this way is an uphill battle. We also risk losing perspective and forgetting our roots. It also focuses our attention on fixing the flaws in the old myths rather than creating new ones.

Continued Mythology

This continued mythology approach is most easily seen in the Bible. In the first five books, the Hebrew deity is portrayed as extreme and severe. Over the course of the books that follow, the nature of that deity shifts and becomes less severe until he ultimately punishes a prophet for wanting him to destroy a town. Later, the Gospels added further interpretations and dimensions in the form of story.

While this kind of linear narrative is almost impossible to impose on ancient Greek mythology, the spirit of it—of keeping the old myths while adding new ones that show the nature of the Deities *today*—is another possible approach.

An example, in the style of Pseudo-Apollodorus:

At one time, the Johns of New Orleans exceeded all other men in pride, entitlement and violence. Seeking to put their impiety to the test, Aphrodite put on the guise of a sex-worker, taking Hermes with her, who disguised himself as her guardian. Three men attacked Hermes, who took an apparent fall, then circled Aphrodite meaning to take what they had come for without paying, or even asking first. The Goddess,

in disgust, caused them to drown in their own salty spittle.
Hermes summoned snakes from the sewers, covered in slime,
to slither over them as they perished.

The advantage of this approach is that it creates myths that
directly address our modern concerns.

The disadvantage is that it does nothing to redeem the old myths
unless linking narratives are written to explain how the Deities
acquired these values which we now hold to be evidently just.

Some Closing Thoughts

While some might find the ideas I've presented in this article a bit
radical, I hope I have shown that there is good historical precedent for
a new mythology approach. It has been used to good effect by P.
Sufenas Virius Lupus, who created a mythology that specifically
affirms the experiences of transgender and gender-diverse individuals
as sacred in eir book, *All-Soul, All-Body, All-Love, All-Power: A
TransMythology*.

I genuinely believe that what does not grow and change is
dead. If we bring our tradition into the present with a living, evolving
mythology that resonates with progressive values, I believe that we will
have happier Deities and a brighter future.

Thenea Pantera is an educator, writer, potter, and priestess of Hermes.
She is a founding member of Pandemos, a diverse collective of pagans
and polytheists from various traditions that come together to honor
Hellenic Deities just south of San Francisco Bay. Her views are not
meant to represent the entirety of Pandemos. She is firm in her belief
that a successful Greek Pagan community will be one in which
multiple theologies are supported. Thenea also writes about spirit
work, theurgy, magic, and more on her blog at
magickfromscratch.com.

Is "Tam Lin" a Rape Story? Yes, Maybe, and No.
A. Acland

(*Editor's Note: Contemporary Pagans draw on a variety of myths and folktales for their religious practices. For some, these stories offer insight into the nature of deities, spirits, the land, and humans' relationship with them; for others, they are read archetypally or psychologically and so primarily reveal the spiritual nature of human beings.*

The sixteenth-century Scottish ballad of "Tam Lin" is an important source for Pagans who feel drawn to folkloric tales of Faerie. A. Acland's essay reconciles love of this ballad with a rejection of rape culture. In doing so, it models ways that Pagans and others might constructively interpret beloved myths that have become ethically problematic.)

Introduction

There are many versions of "Tam Lin." Even the longer versions of the ballad contain only so many verses, with much of the activity presented in either snapshot or symbolic fashion. Determining what is and isn't going on in the narrative, therefore, can often be a matter of interpretation. One of the important interpretive issues is whether the initial sexual encounter between Janet and Tam Lin is consensual or not.

This topic is a difficult one. "Tam Lin" is a story that can be read as a romance, as well as one that centers on the actions of a headstrong and brave female character. It is deeply beloved by many people and has been retold in many formats. Readers may come to the ballad from any number of paths, with a variety of expectations. They are therefore often dismayed or disgusted to read versions of the original ballad that depict the sexual encounter between Janet and Tam Lin as non-consensual, as this detracts from the ability of the reader to enjoy and embrace the story. Janet is an unusually bold and fearless female character for traditional literature, and having her cast in the role of rape victim is a serious hurdle to overcome. Having the titular Tam Lin depicted as a rapist can make it difficult for readers to invest in his rescue. In order for the story to remain relevant to a modern audience, we need to understand its troubling aspects in their historical and narrative context. Even more important, however, is the possibility that these aspects may not be truly integral to the story.

Does Tam Lin rape Janet? If so, what purpose is served by presenting the sex as non-consensual? Are there other potential interpretations of the encounter? How does the way the ballad frames the interaction between Janet and Tam Lin change the presentation of Janet and Tam Lin's characters? What changes in the interpretation of the story when we change our understanding of this interaction? How can the modern reader love the ballad of Tam Lin without perpetuating the rape culture aspects that seem to permeate some versions?

Disclaimers

First disclaimer: This essay will discuss interpretations of sex and consent in a sixteenth-century ballad, including attempts to understand the beliefs about sex, consent, and rape that underlie the story in their historical and narrative contexts. Many of these beliefs will be offensive from a modern perspective. Examining these beliefs does not constitute an endorsement of them, nor does it condone the behaviors they lead to. Neither does the examination or criticism of these beliefs constitute an attack on the ballad or disparagement of those who love it. We have to examine our stories critically and honestly in order to understand them. Striving for understanding is, itself, a form of love.

I am writing under the assumption that the reader will be able to distinguish the identification of reasons for which rape may occur in the ballad from real-world victim-blaming or excuse-making. I also assume that the reader appreciates that ballads recorded in the sixteenth century about faeries who sacrifice people to Hell are unlikely to constitute a reasonable guide to sexuality or socially responsible frameworks of behavior.

Second disclaimer: I am an obsessive fan of the ballad, not a historian, folklorist, student of comparative literature, or academic in any other field or background directly relevant to the examination of folk ballads. The following is not intended to be an exhaustive examination of the topic, nor is it an academic article with references for every assertion. Correction, clarification, and addition from others, however, is welcome and encouraged, because more information is better. (The URL for my website is included at the bottom of the piece.)

Third disclaimer: This essay discusses only the presentation of the sex in older versions of the ballad in an attempt to understand the origins and meanings of aspects of the story. Modern reworkings of the ballad and all prose retellings are out of scope, as the later versions build on the foundation of the earlier ones and not the other way around. The purpose of Janet's pregnancy in the story or the purpose of establishing a specifically sexual relationship between Janet and Tam Lin is also beyond the scope of this essay. This actually is a large enough topic that I'm only going to scratch at the surface even with those limitations.

Yes

He's taen her by the milk-white hand,
  And by the grass-green sleeve,
  And laid her low on gude green wood,
  At her he spierd nae leave.
When he had got his wills of her,
  His wills as he had taen,
  He's taen her by the middle sma,
  Set her to feet again.
She turnd her right and round about,
  To spier her true-love's name,
  But naething heard she, nor naething saw,
  As a' the woods grew dim.
  - "Tam Lin" version Child 39G[2]

---

[2] "Tam Lin," *The English and Scottish Popular Ballads,* ed. Francis James

The first answer here is yes: "Tam Lin" is a rape story. Sex without an enthusiastic "yes" is an assault, and quite a few versions of "Tam Lin" are fairly straight forward about Tam Lin not seeking consent. It would be dishonest to say that what is going on in some versions of the ballad is not rape. Tam Lin has sex with Janet without her consent, therefore this event is rape, therefore "Tam Lin" is a rape story.

Having established that, the next question is why? What purpose is served by having the sex be non-consensual? What narrative purpose is served by this act? There are a number of narrative tropes surrounding rape in stories, and several of them apply or can be applied to "Tam Lin" as a rape story.

Punitive or corrective rape is rape as punishment for a transgression. In the ballad, maidens are warned not to go to Carterhaugh. Janet disobeys this command, disobeys the cultural edict to not take material from a faerie wood without asking permission, and does not apologize when confronted. Because she has transgressed these laws and standards, she is raped as a punishment. Historically, in stories which involve punitive rape, the woman's later pairing with the rapist is often presented as a humbling of the woman. She is subjugated to the man's stronger will and brought back into line with the dictates of the culture by obedience to him thereafter. Shakespeare's *The Taming of the Shrew*, for example, falls into this category.

Symbolic rape is rape as part of an act of sympathetic magic. Janet has plucked flowers from the woods, "deflowering" the tree. She is therefore herself deflowered in return. While the initial verses of the ballad indicate that Tam Lin may take other forms of payment for entry to his woods (rings, green mantles), these alternatives are never presented as options for Janet. She may be seen to have invoked this particular response by her wording of "ask no leave of thee", causing Tam Lin to ask no leave of her in return. While it is difficult to have sympathy for someone who applies this logic to rape in the real world,

Child (Boston and New York: Houghton, Mifflin and Company, 1882–1898).

in the ballad world it may be that Tam Lin has no choice in his actions; bound by the magic of faerie, he may be required to respond to her actions with an assault. There are many stories from the same period that do not hold their protagonists responsible for violent actions committed while under enchantment (those transformed into dragons, for example). Because they are bound by magic, their actions tend to be seen as involuntary. Regardless of Tam Lin's choice in the matter, it is possible to view symbolic parallels between her actions and his.

In cultures that prize a woman's pre-marital virginity, a woman who has engaged in sex before marriage may be considered unsuitable for marriage afterwards. One of the ways of addressing this transgression was to force the woman to marry the man with whom she had sex, whether consensually or not, thus making it possible for a man to "steal" a wife through raping a virgin. This notion of forcible marriage to protect against a perception of pre-marital sex has extended, in some cultures, to include situations where a woman may be forced or coerced into marriage with a man who has abducted her, regardless of whether or not sex occurred. In this context the term "rape" may signify situations of forcible sexual intercourse, as well as abductions of women to obtain them as wives (*The Rape of the Sabine Women*,[3] for example). In this framework, Tam Lin's 'theft' of Janet's virginity (rape as sex act) could be seen as a symbolic prelude to her later 'theft' of him from the Faerie Queen so that Janet may marry him (rape as abduction).

Seductive rape is rape as a means of romance, in which the rape is intended to cause the woman to fall in love with her rapist. A man who rapes a woman has asserted his sexuality over hers, effectively claiming her for his own; stories may depict his overwhelming passion inspiring a similar passion in her, a forceful sexual awakening. In cultures that do not value a woman's sexual agency, seductive rape can

[3] Dhwty, "The Rape of the Sabine Women," *Ancient Origins* 30 Mar. 2015. Available at http://www.ancient-origins.net/news-history/rape-sabine-women-002636.

be used as a means of "permitting" a woman to have sex without violating the culturally imposed stigma of seeking out sex. However distasteful, it is nonetheless true that some cultures prefer stories where a woman falls in love with her rapist to stories where she seeks a sexual relationship of her own free will.

The distinctions presented above—between punitive, symbolic, and seductive rape—may be partially false when applied to the ballad of Tam Lin, as elements of several or all of them may be present. Tam Lin's rape of Janet may be a symbolic act triggered by plucking flowers, but also a humbling for being defiant, and a seduction that leads her to love Tam Lin.

Some versions involve more suffering on Janet's part than others. Janet may be left alone afterwards to wander in a darkened forest, sometimes for days. She may be left shamed by Tam Lin's actions, or frowning, though the emotional response is not generally depicted as any more negative than that. She may appear unfazed and start planning how to bring him home immediately. Or she may return home disheveled, and while the ballad's lines about her looking pale and wan are usually taken as indications of pregnancy, they may also be signs of emotional distress following a trauma.

Regardless of the reason or combination of reasons for the rape in "Tam Lin," Janet is generally portrayed as defending Tam Lin to her family, referring to him as her true love, and hesitating little in committing to his rescue. He suffers no ill consequence for the non-consensual act. In the versions of the ballad where the sex is depicted as non-consensual, the assault is not seen as a barrier to later romance and devotion between Janet and Tam Lin.

While not a viewpoint likely to appeal to modern sensibilities, historical stories may very well promote a view of sexuality, and women's sexuality in particular, in which it is more acceptable for a woman to be raped and a man to commit a rape than it is for a woman to violate cultural taboos, particularly with regards to sex and chastity, and still be portrayed as an admirable character. This viewpoint also frames Janet as primarily reactive rather than active; rather than having

her actions reflect her own choices, she must save Tam Lin in order
to provide herself with a suitable marriage partner after a rape.

Maybe

Consider the following verses that frequently start out versions of
"Tam Lin":

> *O all you ladies young and gay,*
> *Who are so sweet and fair,*
> *Do not go into Chaster's wood,*
> *For Tomlin will be there.*
>
> *Fair Margret sat in her bonny bower,*
> *Sewing her silken seam,*
> *And wished to be in Chaster's wood,*
> *Among the leaves so green.*
>
> *She let her seam fall to her foot,*
> *The needle to her toe,*
> *And she has gone to Chaster's wood,*
> *As fast as she could go.*
>
> *When she began to pull the flowers,*
> *She puud both red and green;*
> *Then by did come, and by did go,*
> *Said, Fair maid, let aleene.*
> *- "Tam Lin" version Child 39D*

Now, the opening to another ballad:

> *Queen Jane sat at her window one day*
> *A sewing a silken seam*
> *She looked out at the merry green woods*
> *And saw the green nut tree*
> *And saw the green nut tree*

She dropped her thimble at her heal
And her needle at her toe
And away she ran to the merry green woods
To gather nuts and so
To gather nuts and so

She scarce had reached the merry green woods
Scarce had pulled nuts two or three
When a proud forester came striding by
Saying, "Fair maid, let those be"
Saying, "Fair maid, let those be"

"Why do you pull the nuts," he said
"And why do you break the tree?
And why do you come to this merry green wood
Without the leave of me?
Without the leave of me?"

"Oh, I will pull the nuts," she said
"And I will break the tree
And I will come to this merry green wood
I'll ask no leave of thee
I'll ask no leave of thee"

He took her by the middle so small
And he gently laid her down
And when he took what he longed for
He raised her from the ground

He raised her from the ground
   - "The King's Daughter Jane"[4]

---

[4] "The King's Daughter Jane," *The English and Scottish Popular Ballads*, ed. Francis James Child (Boston and New York: Houghton, Mifflin and Company, 1882–1898).

Likewise:

O may she comes, and may she goes,
Down by yon gardens green,
And there she spied a gallant squire
As squire had ever been.

And may she comes, and may she goes,
Down by yon hollin tree,
And there she spied a brisk young squire,
And a brisk young squire was he.

"Give me your green manteel, fair maid,
Give me your maidenhead;
Gif ye winna gie me your green manteel,
Gie me your maidenhead.'

He has taen her by the milk-white hand,
And softly laid her down,
And when he's lifted her up again
Given her a silver kaim.
        - "The Bonny Hind"[5]

These latter two ballads, for all of their initial similarity to "Tam Lin," are much more closely related to each other than either is to the faerie ballad. Neither contains any supernatural elements, and both are stories where a young woman, gathering objects in the King's woods, is raped by a man who then turns out to be her long-lost brother.

In "The King's Daughter Jane," the woman responds to the rape by wishing she were dead; in "The Bonny Hind," she does kill herself, causing her brother to bury her body secretly and claim, upon coming home covered in blood, that he'd been out hunting deer (hence the 'hind'). Both stories are unambiguously rape stories, with little to the tale other than the set up for the rape, the rape itself, and the

---

[5] "The Bonny Hind," ibid.

consequences after. While "Tam Lin" can certainly be viewed as a rape ballad, there is generally at least some substance to the story beyond the rape, for what little redemption that offers.[6] These stories do not even have that level of complexity.

(As an aside, it's horrific that these ballads assign the consequences of the rape entirely to the women, while the men are presented as having no regrets beyond having raped the 'wrong' woman. "Don't rape unknown women because you might be related to them" is a pretty lousy message.)

In her excellent 1970 paper "The Opening of 'Tam Lin'," E. B. Lyle describes these verses—presenting the woods, the longing woman, and the desire to run off to pluck flower or nuts—as originating in the other ballads. She argues that the verses were grafted onto "Tam Lin" as part of the combinative process that is common to folklore.[7] Lyle uses the wonderful phrase "vigorous parasitic growth" to describe the intrusion of these verses into the ballad, where they are then perpetuated at the expense of the overall story.

Based on Lyle's argument, one could suggest that the similar verses in "Tam Lin" constitute an imposition of rape onto a story in which there was not originally a rape present. If these "parasitic" verses have distorted the story, and the stories from which they originate are unambiguously rape stories, then their major effect is to push the initial sexual encounter between Janet and Tam Lin towards an interpretation of rape.

This is not a conclusive argument; it's entirely possible that whatever verses originally opened "Tam Lin" before these verses were added were no better, and claiming otherwise is necessarily speculation. It's also not quite honest to claim that verses that can be shown to have originated elsewhere aren't really part of the story. Cross-contamination is as common in ballads as with bacteria, and any

---

[6] The version that folklore collector Francis James Child labels 39L is a notable exception to this pattern.

[7] E.B. Lyle, "The Opening of 'Tam Lin'," *The Journal of American Folklore* (Jan-Mar 1970: 83[327]): 33-43.

particular version of a story that is told often enough becomes a legitimate version of that story, distasteful or not. We cannot disavow versions merely because we dislike them.

However, if we assume that the existence of these verses independent of "Tam Lin" are evidence that the ballad did not initially include such explicit indications of rape, the ballad can be re-examined to see what other interpretations are available.

(Lyle takes the position that the parasitic versions are entirely an addition, rather than a replacement, and would start "Tam Lin" with the observation of Janet's pregnancy. I'm opposed to this interpretation, as I think it both unlikely for a story to start with the protagonist inexplicably pregnant, and because the circumstances surrounding the pregnancy do matter in understanding the interactions between Tam Lin and Janet.)

No

> *Janet has kilted her green kirtle*
> *A little aboon her knee,*
> *And she has broded her yellow hair*
> *A little aboon her bree,*
> *And she's awa to Carterhaugh*
> *As fast as she can hie.*
>
> *When she came to Carterhaugh*
> *Tam Lin was at the well,*
> *And there she fand his steed standing,*
> *But away was himsel.*
> *- "Tam Lin" version Child 39A*

If the scenario where the woman who goes to Carterhaugh seeking only flowers is raped is a result of the intrusion of rape ballads into the story, what other interpretations of Janet and Tam Lin's encounter are supported by the ballad, putting aside those verses?

One of the more obvious possible interpretations is that Janet goes to Carterhaugh specifically to seek out Tam Lin, and even more specifically, to seek a sexual encounter with him. Perhaps there was some similarity between this hypothetical lost opening and the structure of the rape ballads that allowed the latter to supplant the former: a woman travels to a wood and meets with a young man there, although the nature of their meeting can now be called into question and potentially reframed.

The ballad's setting is an important clue to this interpretation. While the rape ballads are set in a generic King's Woods or unnamed forest, "Tam Lin" places the story specifically in Carterhaugh, a location invoked in several other faerie stories. It is the site for faerie sightings in "The Wee Wee Man,"[8] and it is only a few miles away from the Eildon Hills, where the Queen of Elfland meets and carries away Thomas the Rhymer.[9] In other words, Carterhaugh woods is a location already established as liminal and inhabited by faeries, and anyone traveling there deliberately can be presumed to be aware of its nature.

It is also worth noting that Janet wears a green kirtle to Carterhaugh. Green is symbolic of fertility and growth, and it is a color considered unlucky to wear in the presence of faeries, likely to get their attention ("The fairies' fatal green" in "Alice Brand"[10]). Green is also a color associated with sexual liberty, as seen in some ballads where a woman, upon leaving or being left by her lover, puts on a coat of green. (See also the tradition of "grass widows," a term applied to women who were never formally married to their partners, or never

---

[8] "The Wee Wee Man," *The English and Scottish Popular Ballads,* ed. Francis James Child (Boston and New York: Houghton, Mifflin and Company, 1882–1898).

[9] "Thomas the Rhymer," ibid.

[10] Sir Walter Scott, "Alice Brand," *The Lady of the Lake* (Edinburgh: John Ballantyne and Co., 1810).

formally divorced from an absent partner. The "grass" may derive from the idea of illicit trysts in the fields.)

Janet is often depicted as performing acts of grooming, such as braiding her hair, which are more in line with a person anticipating an interaction than someone engaging in solitary flower or nut harvesting. More importantly, in some versions of the ballad Janet is not going to Carterhaugh in general, but going specifically to a place where Tam Lin is likely to be present—near the location of a holy well (an area further associated with faeries or enchantment[11]), or even near where his horse is standing. These verses, unlike the parasitic rape ballad verses, are unique to "Tam Lin," and they may be vestiges of an older introduction.

Under the terms of this scenario, Janet is not encountering Tam Lin by accident or as a faerie reprisal, but attempting to locate him. Her plucking of the roses could now be seen as a deliberate provocation, and her challenge to him when he appears to her is not insolence but invitation: I am your equal, and I am making a choice. She has donned clothing meant to evoke fertility and summoned what she believes to be a faerie knight in an enchanted wood.

The scene that follows in the more complete versions of the ballad involves Janet's family observing her pregnancy (some versions omit this). We can guess at what happened, then, without needing the explanatory and unpleasant verses that remove consent from their encounter. In this context, however, Janet's praise and defense of him to her family appear as further evidence that she thinks well of him and has voluntarily chosen him.

If my love were an earthly knight,
As he's an elfin grey,
I wad na gie my ain true-love

---

[11] For examples, see *Holy and Healing Wells,* 30 Mar. 2015. Available at https://insearchofholywellsandhealingsprings.wordpress. com/category/scotland/.

For nae lord that ye hae.
  - "Tam Lin" version Child 39A

Later, when Tam Lin and Janet meet again and she is seeking herbs to induce a miscarriage, he may greet her with phrasing such as:

O why pou ye the pile, Margaret,
The pile o the gravil green,
For to destroy the bonny bairn
That we got us between?
  - "Tam Lin" version Child 39G

"How daur ye wauk alane," he said.
"amang your father's tries
For spoiling o the bonnie babe
That we gat merrilie?"
  - "Tam Lin" version Crawfurd[12]

Tam Lin's tone may not be cheerful, but his characterization of the pregnancy as a mutual accomplishment, and their earlier encounter as something merry (another common variant is "play"), suggests that he is recounting a consensual act that both parties found enjoyable, participated in equally, and look back upon with fondness. Janet's response once again identifies Tam Lin as a lover:

If my luve were an earthly
As he's an elfin rae,
I coud gang bound, love, for your sake,
A twalmonth and a day.
  - "Tam Lin" version Child 39G

---

[12] Andrew Crawfurd, "Tam Blain," *Collection of Ballads and Songs*, ed. E.B. Lyle, Volume 1 (Edinburgh: Scottish Text Society, 1975).

...or she makes an enquiry about his eligibility as a partner:

"O tell me, tell me, Tam Lin," she says,
"For's sake that died on tree,
If eer ye was in holy chapel,
Or Christendom did see?"
       - "Tam Lin" version Child 39A

Earlier in this essay I touched on these elements as potentially part of the rape culture aspects of "Tam Lin". Perhaps, I suggested, the ballad portrays a rape without acknowledging the trauma of rape. I am including these elements again here in fuller detail to make the opposite argument, as I feel that they more strongly support the opposite assertion: that "Tam Lin" was not originally a rape ballad at all, but the story of a woman who has voluntarily sought out and fallen in love with a man and has had consensual sex with him. In these verses, Janet does not object to interaction with Tam Lin or renounce his right to interest in the pregnancy. Instead, she objects solely to his inability to join her in the mortal world. If Janet and Tam Lin are acting in the latter parts of the ballad as if the rape had never happened, then the simplest explanation is that it didn't.

Janet's seeking out of Tam Lin in the ballad's later verses, when she goes to rescue him from the Faerie Queen, may very well parallel earlier, now lost, verses where she initially sought him out in Carterhaugh. Tam Lin is Janet's lover, to whom she is devoted, and whom she chose for herself for her own desire and her own purpose. This sort of parallel repeated structure is common in ballads, and Janet seeking out Tam Lin initially reinforces her seeking him out on Halloween, therefore making more sense in the narrative structure than an accidental initial meeting would. Both journeys are acts of defiance, expressions of self-determination, and acts of love. "Tam Lin" as a story of two lovers is more in keeping with the ballad's characterization of Janet, the later language between them, and the narrative's overall themes.

Given how strongly the rest of the ballad presents Janet as a woman who is defined by bravery and defiance, the decision to initially depict her as a pliant victim of a sexual assault does her a disservice. Rape culture—and therefore rape ballads—perpetuate narrow, confining options for the expression of women's sexuality; they function, at least partially, to limit women's sexual freedom and expression. To my mind, it is likely that some earlier, ancestral version of "Tam Lin" had Janet deliberately seeking out her lover in the woods. Later culture, in order to make the story conform to a more narrow, restrictive, and punitive view of women's sexual agency, introduced the rape ballad aspects to "correct" the immorality of a woman deliberately seeking sex outside of marriage, and with a man considered unnatural and unholy.

Janet is undeniably the center of the story, and therefore interpretations of her tend to reflect the morals of the culture that continues the ballad, even if the story is distorted in the process. To a culture that does not allow for a heroic female character to seek out premarital sex, it is preferable to depict the sex as non-consensual rather than to endorse immoral behavior. A Janet who is raped (whether punitively, symbolically, or seductively) and must rescue her rapist as a form of penance is preferable to one who is sexual, willful, and self-determined. We can recognize that this sort of thinking is abhorrent to modern readers, and we can stop perpetuating it.

In short, the transformation of "Tam Lin" into a rape ballad is itself a punitive rape of the story.

The story is stronger and more loving when Janet retains her agency, her active sexuality, and her willfulness. The Janet who faces down knights in the hall who try to shame her, who faces down the Faerie Queen, and who faces down every horror she must embrace at the crossroads at midnight deserves better than to be interpreted as passive and conforming. She should not be cast as merely reactive, responding only to the directives placed on her by others, but as guided by her own wishes and desires. While earlier times may have tried to make the story into one of a woman who is forced into her role, we can remove that distortion.

Conclusion

While I believe the arguments I have outlined here are true, and I hope that they are persuasive to the reader, I am certain that "Tam Lin" is a living ballad, and that living ballads change. Regardless of whether or not you agree with the presented conclusions about the past history of the ballad, we, as storytellers and readers, retain the ability to interpret and shape the story as we carry it forward into the future. We can refrain from perpetuating the harmful tropes that I have argued are an artificial intrusion of rape into the story, regardless of whether or not we agree that they are artificial. There is nothing in the story that relies on their presence, and a good deal that contradicts their message. Both the story and readers of it are better off without the rape aspects of the ballad. As we love the story, we can hold on to what is real and true.

Acknowledgements

Thank you to my incredible beta readers/editors, Sonya Taaffe and Christine Hoff Kraemer, without whom this essay would have been much less focused and much more riddled with errors.

A. Acland has been researching and curating information on the Scottish ballad of "Tam Lin" since 1997 and runs the website Tam-Lin.org.

Godspousery and Consent

Sebastian Lokason

From 2004-2010 I was married to Frey, a Norse god and one of the Vanir, a god of prosperity, fecundity, and peace. In late 2010 that relationship ended, and I had some dalliances with various entities. Then, in 2014 I began an intimate relationship with a demon named by lore whom I refer to in my public writings as "D," as he has asked me to not publicly identify him. D and I were handfasted in March 2015.

If you're reading this wondering how a human can be married to a deity, there is historical precedent for it. Greek mythology is full of stories of Hellenic deities having intimate relations with humans. Within Norse paganism, there is a story in the lore of a priestess-wife of Frey; there was also a man wedded to Thorgerda the giantess (possibly Frey's wife Gerda), who adorned her statue. In the Middle East, djinni are said to seduce humans; some Sufi traditions of the Middle East assert that a harmonious relationship between a human and a djinn brings many spiritual benefits. As late as 17th century Scotland, people having faery lovers was considered common. I could go on and on, but needless to say, this is not a new thing.

Over the last several years, humans marrying deities has become a more frequent practice. Godspouses are still a minority within greater Paganism, but we are not unheard of. Falling in love with a deity is not that different from falling in love with a human. Maintaining an intimate relationship with a non-corporeal entity does present challenges—for example, many godspouses necessarily have to develop the ability to communicate with spirits, and sexual activity often involves some combination of astral journeying and masturbation—but all relationships are work, and most of us (myself included) will tell you that the challenges and workarounds are worth it for the quality of the relationship: the experience of wonder, mystery, ecstasy. To be beloved of one of the Powers is to drink deep of the Well of Wyrd, to eat from the Tree of Life. There is nothing else like it.

Unfortunately, there are some challenges with this path beyond the obvious ones of figuring out how to have a tangible relationship with an invisible person, and I feel some caution is advised.

The first is that this path is not for everyone. That might be obvious to a lot of you, but I have found that many new to Paganism, and new to the path of being a devotee of a particular deity, will encounter godspouses first (since we tend to be the most vocal about our deities, so if you're looking for information on a specific deity, and especially on devotional practice to that deity, you are probably going to run into information written by a godspouse sooner rather than later), and may take away the idea that one has to be married to a deity to be properly devoted to them. In reality, there are many kinds of relationships people can have with the Powers. Romantic/sexual relations are just one type of relationship. People can be in a parent/child relationship, teacher/student relationship, or friendship, or even be "patroned" in the classic sense of a deity or spirit guiding one's livelihood (such as an artist devoted to Wayland or Brighid or Hephaestus, or a merchant devoted to Hermes, etc.). But if you are new and easily impressionable, you may be led to believe that becoming a godspouse is the most proper way to devote oneself to a deity. Not only is this not the case, but may be very much the *wrong* path for you, and it may strain your relationship with that deity. Relationships with the Powers are different in their own ways, but they are sometimes not so different from relationships with humans: to have a sincere and lasting connection with a person, you can't force the relationship; it needs to develop organically. That is even more true of making connections to the Powers.

The next caution I would offer is that if you enter into this sort of relationship, it needs to be with consent, and that needs to be informed consent.

Over the last seven years or so I have heard a disturbing number of accounts of deity-on-human abuse. There are people who feel they were pressured into marrying a deity by the entity in question, or were harassed by that entity until they gave into demands for sex or marriage. This is bad enough, but there are those within the devotional polytheist community that will express problematic attitudes if one reports non-consensual experiences with a deity, including victim-blaming ("suck it up"), minimizing (being told you're "overreacting," "making a big deal out of nothing"), and trivializing ("you're too sensitive," "it's not about you"). Some devotional polytheists believe that non-corporeal entities are bigger and more powerful than humans, and thus always right, and anything they decide to do to humans is always justified. I have known at least a couple of people who have reported being raped by deities and said that "they needed it," that it "taught them a lesson." My response to this: would you say that a 300-pound man hitting a 100-pound woman is okay because he's bigger? Would you say that a parent severely beating their very young child is okay because the parent is older and "knows better"? It's not suddenly okay if a deity does it. In my opinion it's even less okay (and let me be clear—abuse is not okay, period) if a deity does it, because with great power comes great responsibility.

This is not to say that all deities abuse humans. It has been my experience, however, that many people get into Paganism nowadays without an occultist background and thus miss important training such as how to discern spirits, how to ward oneself and one's home, and how to banish spirits. There are malevolent "bottom feeder" entities who know this and are adept at impersonating deities to prey and feed on humans. However, whether a spirit is a deity or an astral predator impersonating a deity, you have the right to say no to any demand an entity makes of you. You are not obligated to go along with whatever a deity wants just because they're "bigger" and "more powerful." You do not owe anyone sex. You do not owe anyone marriage. If an entity is pursuing you and you're uncomfortable with it, you have the right to turn them down. Moreover, the acts of sex with a deity, or marriage to a deity, are acts of devotion, and true devotion is only given with a sincere and willing heart. Devotion cannot be forced. A deity relationship born of sexual harassment and abuse is not a devotional relationship. It is definitely not a true marriage; it makes a mockery of the oaths and energetic bonds of marriage.

If you are approached by a deity for this type of relationship and your heart says yes... informed consent still applies.

If you do marry a deity, you are not obliged to have sex with them. Of the dozens of godspouses I know, most of them choose to be sexually intimate with their Beloved and enjoy it. But a few are not sexually intimate with the deity, for whatever reason, and that's perfectly okay—their relationship is one of companionship. Marriage does not equal sex. Romance and love does not equal sex. Likewise, sex does not equal marriage—it is possible to have a sexual relationship with a god that is just sex! Giving pleasure and ecstasy is its own act of devotion. So if you have sex with a non-corporeal entity, you are not obliged to marry them.

I would also advise reading about the relationships of different godspouses (many of which are publicly documented on the Internet on blogs), and maybe talking privately to some godspouses if they are open to discussing the topic with you (however, do not just assume that all of us are, even those of us who are public about it). People's relationships with their Beloveds will vary, but something that most of us tend to have in common is a tremendous amount of sacrifice, our lives being "set apart." I would love to tell you that it is totally possible to have a non-corporeal spouse and live a "normal" life with a corporeal partner, a 9-to-5 corporate job, not looking outwardly "weird" or "different" to a single soul, but in the many dozens of stories of godspouses I've heard, the overwhelming majority of us are marrying into an entire package of dedication, consecration, initiation, and purpose. Not all of us are priests, many of us are not in community service roles at all, but instead our service is love and support to our Beloved—but this is still a full-time job, and one that leaves its mark.

If you marry a deity, you are in for interesting times. Your life will not be the same. You yourself will not be the same in a year, in five years. Are you prepared for this? Do you love your Beloved so much that you will burn for Them, like the phoenix, and learn to fly? This is what you are marrying when you are human and marry a deity. You are marrying energy, you are marrying presence, you are marrying the wyrd tied to this deity. You are marrying an entire experience of living mythology. Learning how this impacts people in different ways can help prepare you for your own journey.

My final note of caution with regards to godspousery and consent is about the community itself.

As noted earlier in this essay, a percentage of devotional polytheists, which include godspouses, think that deity-on-human abuse is okay, and this tends to go with a host of problematic attitudes. Many new godspouses will look to other godspouses for guidance, which is not wrong in and of itself—a few of my closest friends are themselves godspouses. But a number of folks who fancy themselves spiritual servants, mentors, teachers, or community leaders of some sort are in it for the wrong reasons—they may themselves be healers with unresolved wounds, damaging others and thinking they are helping.

I have run into godspouses who will, in their attempt to help newer godspouses, exercise a sort of authoritarian control— telling you that mundane hobbies and interests are "a waste of time" and should be given up, or that things like art are only valid if connected to your devotion in some way. They may tell you frequently that your "signal clarity" is off if your personal gnosis and *doxa* doesn't match up directly with theirs. They may offer you unsolicited "godphoning," saying something like "your deity told me to tell you that you need to be doing this thing that just so happens to line up with this thing I've told you that you should be doing, and you've told me you can't do it for what I think are stupid reasons." They may truly think they are passing on a message from that deity, as opposed to being manipulative. This is something to watch out for.

Most egregious is the phenomenon wherein someone offers to be trance-possessed by your Beloved so you can have sex with Them. This is not always abusive—I know of a few cases of spirit-workers who are in a relationship with each other (or at least close enough that intimacy between them isn't unwelcome) and also involved with deities. One might act as a vessel for the other's deity-spouse for ritual or recreational purposes, and I have heard this reported as a happy, beautiful experience. However, there are also several cases I know of where one person (often older) pressured the other (often younger and less experienced) to have sex with them while their deity was supposedly being horsed, because "it's what the deity wants." In some of these cases, the person went along with it but felt gross afterwards, or didn't go along with it and still felt gross.

This is a particularly nasty form of spiritual abuse because it may not be immediately obvious that you are being preyed upon. Indeed, the person doing the pressuring may think that they are performing a legitimate service. But if you're being pressured into sexual activities that you don't want, it's not okay. I have also known of people who have experienced someone claiming to be possessed by their deity and being sexually inappropriate with them while under "possession," and this is also unacceptable. Those presenting themselves as being possessed by your deity may also be abusive and manipulative in non-sexual ways, such as engaging in verbal and/or physical abusive, then claiming to have no knowledge of their actions ("the deity did it"). They may pressure you or lay guilt trips on you to do things that make you uncomfortable or may even go against your values (especially if these are things that the deity has never brought up with you before).

The problem of people claiming "possession" as a way to manipulate and abuse others is not unique to godspouses, but godspouses are a more obvious target for this kind of abuse due to the intimate and highly personal nature of their deity relationship. If you find yourself on the godspouse path, please be careful. Make sure that the relationship you are entering into is consensual. Guard yourself against those who would exploit your relationship, even if they might mean well. To marry a deity is a beautiful, sacred thing; D says I am his home. That home is a shelter, a refuge... that home is necessarily a safe space.

Sebastian Lokason has been a Pagan and occultist for over twenty years. He is one of the forefathers of the Vanatru movement, and in addition to his work with the Vanir, he is a demonolater. He blogs at Patheos, PaganSquare, and WordPress, has written several books, and is also an artist, astrologer, and Reiki Master. He lives in New Haven, Connecticut with a demon companion and their cat.

Part II:
Responding to
Abuse and Assault

The Third Degree: Exploitation and Initiation

Jason Thomas Pitzl

When I was 18 years old, a woman my mother's age took my virginity in the name of religion. It was the culmination of months of "grooming," where I was fed a fantasy of power, responsibility, and sense of being the protagonist in a vast unfolding drama. Whatever misgivings I had going into the situation, and they certainly were there, they could not withstand the carrot/stick of power's promise, and the threat of being cut off entirely from a world I wanted desperately to be a part of: to be a Witch and High Priest.

Let me back up a bit. I grew up socially awkward, but fundamentally normal, in Omaha, Nebraska. The Omaha I remember, from the 1970s and 1980s, was overwhelmingly Christian in its orientation. The Jewish family at the end of my grandmother's block were considered quite exotic by our standards, and we certainly had little notion of anything outside of the ambient cultural Judeo-Christianity that largely held sway. Despite, or perhaps because of this, I became intensely interested in pre-Christian mythology, devouring Edith Hamilton, Thomas Bulfinch, Robert Graves, and whatever else I could get my hands on.

Myths, for me, were exciting. They told of a world of romance, passion, extremes, and highly involved divine powers. Perhaps, as a victim of routine schoolyard bullying, this thought appealed to me the most, or maybe it was simply a yearning for a more visceral religious experience than the vacation Bible school classes my grandmother would occasionally enroll me in. Still, I nominally considered myself a Christian because the myths weren't real, and because there wasn't any other option to be had.

All of this changed when I moved to Illinois at seventeen, to live with my father and, I hoped, to start a new life removed from everything that was Omaha. It was there that I was adopted by a circle of close friends, and where the fortuitous loan of a book about Wicca blew my mind. Suddenly, everything I knew was a lie. The old gods weren't just phantasms latched onto by primitive ancient minds, and you didn't just have to settle for the Christian party line. There was, I learned for the first time, a counter-current to what most everyone thought and felt about the numinous.

I suppose "zeal of the convert" is the best way to explain my early months as an aspiring Wiccan. I devoured everything I could get my hands on, built a giant altar in my bedroom, performed a dedication ceremony, went out and bought a large pewter pentacle to wear to show my allegiance, and was no doubt somewhat annoying to the friends who had introduced me to the faith. I even insisted on wearing a pouch of spiritually significant stones while having my appendix removed. This was all pre-Internet, so we were limited by the books we could find, the metaphysical stores within driving distance, and the elders who might be willing to give us instruction. Without the networking tools we have ready access to now, elders were especially hard to find.

When I look back at the young Pagan I was, I suppose "driven" was the word to describe my explorations. I was seeking a purpose; I wanted confirmation of my beliefs; and I wanted it all now. None of this is unusual for a teenager exploring their faith, but it does render one vulnerable to predators.

Working that summer at a local Renaissance Faire, I met several other Pagans outside my small circle of friends for the first time. I was introduced to a woman who I thought would be the mentor I wanted—a woman who, she said, was an initiated High Priestess, and had recently broken off from her old High Priest (whom she described as abusive, which may have been true), and who said she was open to training a replacement.

In retrospect, it all seems so foolish. I find it hard to write this narrative without interjecting my present self. Even now, the deluded haze I was in is raw in my memory. I ignored my friends. I broke up with a girl I was dating, because she dared call my relationship with the High Priestess "co-dependent." I was utterly wrapped around the fingers of the Priestess, and perhaps worst of all, I was becoming imperious and haughty, sure that I was tapping into a well of power and knowledge beyond the understanding of my peers.

Then came the initiation.

A week before the ritual, the High Priestess told me: If I wanted a 3rd degree initiation from her (to the highest rank), I had two choices. Either I could perform the Great Rite "in True"—a sexual ritual—with her; otherwise, she would have to use all of her spiritual strength to initiate me without that aspect, but the effort would subsequently erase any memory she would have of me. Those were my choices: sexual initiation, or religious obliteration.

This choice was supposedly a message from the Goddess channeled directly through the Priestess. I believed her. By this point in our relations, channeled messages from the Goddess had become a more and more frequent means of control. I believed utterly in them. I believed it was the Goddess speaking whenever the Priestess's eyes rolled back and she changed her voice and demeanor.

The initiation itself was anti-climactic. I crossed the threshold of my own sexuality in a tawdry, fumbling, mess of a pseudo-ritual. In my bedroom. In my Dad's suburban condo. I remember clearly that she didn't know the words of the ritual—for some reason that stuck out. Despite my youth and my nervousness at actually going through with this—my performance anxiety nearly derailed everything—I, at that moment, became a Wiccan High Priest (or so I hoped). "The Great Rite in True." I believed the Priestess was quoting the Goddess when she said she felt the "pangs of love" as I spent myself.

After the initiatory ritual, I felt I had too much invested to back out now. What I went through was simply one unpleasant thing, one sacrifice, and it was certainly worth it for the spiritual destiny I had to fulfill, right? But then I got the word, literally (I thought) from On High: I would have to continually service my High Priestess sexually, in the name of our faith. My work was not done.

Fortunately, this happened on only one more occasion. I remember it very clearly, because she channeled the Goddess during "the Rite," and afterwards, I asked Her: how long do I have to keep doing this?

The ending of this story is not that interesting. My best friend held an intervention, saying that I would lose her friendship should I continue down this road. Despite feeling honor-bound, I realized I had to break free, and did so. The High Priestess, rebuffed, haunted the edges of my life for a while longer, then finally ran away from her own family, to live in an different town. I remember having what I suppose would be termed a panic attack when I spotted her the next year at the Renaissance Faire. I begged my boss to move me to a different station. I never saw her again after that.

Years later, she contracted some illness and died. A friend of the current young man she was dating delivered to me a sketch book of mine, which the High Priestess had held on to for all those years.

I really had nothing to say in response. The wide-eyed seeker was no more. I still sought knowledge, but my trust was a jaundiced thing for a long time. I scrapped my "initiations" and my prideful attitude, and started back down the road of my faith a changed young man.

Why did I stay a Pagan? A Witch? Partly because even then I understood that my abuser was not my faith. The core of my faith survived despite the emotional ordeal I went through. My innocence was gone, but not my sense of wonder at an enchanted world. That was enough to continue.

I like to think that, today, I am fully healed from these experiences. But that's not entirely true. I had to quit a coven I thought about joining because the fact that they worked skyclad (naked) was immensely triggering. As a journalist in my religious community, writing about sexual predators in our midst has been, at times, difficult. Still, writing this down is a sign that I may finally have closure on this tale.

Note:

I would like to add that no established modern religious Witchcraft tradition, whether they are of a relatively modern lineage or one of the British traditions that emerged into the public eye in the 1950s, engages in sexual initiatory rites as a norm. Sexual rites in these contexts are undertaken rarely, and only with the full and informed consent of all participating. What happened to me is the result of one person abusing their position and authority for their own ends.

If you feel you might be in a position where your trust and religious oaths are being used in ways that are abusive, or exploitative, please get out as quickly as you can, seek the proper authorities, and talk to counselors and advocates who are experienced in guiding individuals through the emotional and spiritual damage done.

This essay is reprinted from Medium.com by permission of the author.

Jason Thomas Pitzl is an artist and writer living in Oregon. His writing has appeared in a number of places over the years, including the 2013 academic anthology *Pop Pagans*, for which he contributed a chapter. Other writing credits of note include editorials for The Washington Post's "On Faith" project and his founding of *The Wild Hunt*, a journalism outlet focused on modern Paganism.

As an artist, Jason has participated in several shows and briefly ran a gallery project for the Urbana-Champaign IMC. An ongoing visual diary of his works in progress can be found at epimetheusstudio.com. His work is figurative, expressionistic, and is often heavy with personal symbolism. He is currently the Programming Director for Faerieworlds Events, which runs the Faerieworlds Festival in Oregon, MythicWorlds in Seattle, Washington and FaerieCon in Maryland.

From Fear into Power: Transforming Survivorship

Sarah Twichell Rosehill

I am a witch whose first significant magical act was to take the ring my abuser gave me and throw it into the releasing fire at Twilight Covening, my community's fall gathering. For me, being a survivor and being a witch are intimately intertwined, and magic and community were both central to my healing.

My abuser taught one of my extracurricular activities when I was a teenager. He was often charming, and I worshipped the ground he walked on in the way that only a fourteen-year-old girl can. He also had a controlling disposition and a nasty temper, well-masked by a veneer of concern for his business, for the team, for appearances. I said yes to his advances and spent the next ten years doubting myself, coiling myself against dangers I didn't even trust myself to perceive.

There are two things that are simultaneously true about my situation, and looking back, coming to peace with this tension was central to my healing. One is that what happened to me was wrong, as any sexual relationship between a child and a teacher must be. The other is that it was complicated. Age and power dynamics weren't the only factors in my inability to meaningfully consent; my own insecurity and need for attention were also part of it. There are ways in which I was lucky, like never being physically forced. These things don't alter the simple truth that what happened was wrong, but they did make the abuse into something hard to see clearly, and they added confusion and self-doubt to the list of things between me and healing.

It's hard to describe what it feels like to be both desperate and terrified to change, but that was how I came to magic. Anamanta, the magical tradition I've learned in the EarthSpirit Community, teaches that we all have a shape, made up of knots tied in threads of the energy that creates and sustains the universe and everything in it. I am lucky to have a shape that includes excellent parents, a great education, a love of words and music, and deep loyalty. It also has other things: I'm impatient and easily distracted. I love certain kinds of intensity. And I am a survivor.

Anamanta also teaches that loosening the knots that make up our shape opens up our perceptions and enables experiences of mystery. As a young witch, I found this equally thrilling and terrifying. I longed for change—to feel less scared, to find a path towards intimate relationships, to trust my own judgement, to know that I was okay—and I was also afraid that if I loosened up even a little I would break, or dissolve, or somehow just disappear. Control felt like safety.

The tool I discovered at my first Twilight Covening, serendipitously, was releasing, and I had plenty to let go of. But I also encountered trance, which gave me the opportunity to have experiences beyond the bounds of my self; the use of words to reinforce or undo aspects of our self-perceptions; and the power of symbol and metaphor to communicate meaning beyond the level of thought. These generative tools provided an essential counterweight: ways to engage with the spaces left open as I let go of painful patterns.

As I began to work magically with my own shape, perceiving it and making room for the possibility of change, it became clear to me that trying to take my abuser to court was going to be an important part of my journey. Partly, I was motivated by the desire to protect others: the grapevine told me that my abuser was continuing to have inappropriate relationships with young women. But I also felt the need to do this for myself: to face my own terror down and see what lay beyond. The reality that there was no way out but through became inescapable for me.

I was lucky to make strong connections early in my affiliation with EarthSpirit. I found a magical mentor at my first event, Twilight Covening, and his wife was the person who sat with me in the district attorney's office while I gave my testimony, the one who took me home and let me roll out pie crusts and play with her sunny toddler afterwards. A survivor in the community was one of my earliest teachers and was frequently my best source of reassurance that everything happening to me was normal. I also had a brief relationship inside of the community, and while it had many flaws, I felt completely safe in it, which was itself a tremendous gift.

Ritual also provided me opportunities to explore my edges. At my first Twilight Covening, I was asked to make a mask, write words that described me on it, and then wear it into the crowded dining hall. The task seemed impossible, but it was incredibly important to someone longing to be seen. At my second Twilight Covening, I worked in a support role for the Visioning Ritual, a long, physical journey where participants encounter beings, the natural world, and themselves. Part of the preparation for this work involved walking the ritual route in the dark, something that terrified me. There were a dozen of us making the walk, and my teachers wisely sent me in the middle so that there would be people both in front of and behind me. They also never expressed any doubt that I could do it—as, of course, I did.

My community also did a number of things right. Most importantly, I always felt supported in my boundaries. One year, I attended an outside event with some community members, and someone on their event staff suggested that I should dance topless at the fire circle. It was, by any standard, a mildly inappropriate remark: it was objectifying and my choices weren't any of his business, but it also wasn't in any way directly threatening. If someone made that remark to me today, I would have a very direct conversation about it, but I wouldn't expect to feel afraid. Nonetheless, I was in a vulnerable place, waiting for the district attorney to tell me if they would pursue my case, and it was enough to send me into a tailspin. The people I was attending with went to the organizers, and by the time I understood what had happened, it was clear that the person in question was no longer going to be welcome on the staff. In retrospect, this seems to me both clearly correct and also hugely important: I got the message that my reaction was not only okay but understandable, and that I was supported by community leaders.

I don't want to gloss over the challenges that I know, as a leader now myself, are inherent in this kind of situation. I was lucky in that my abuser was someone from outside my community. I was also lucky that EarthSpirit had already grappled with a case of intra-community abuse years before I came along and thus had already had many of its own reckonings. I was lucky to connect quickly and deeply with people heavily involved in EarthSpirit, to join their event staff within eighteen months of my first gathering, and therefore to have people who advocated for me not just in a general way, but in a specific, personal one. And I was lucky to have many teachers and mentors who were willing and able to be generous with their time, teaching, and energy through the most difficult years and beyond.

In the end, although I'm tremendously grateful to my community for holding me through this wildly difficult work, I'm also grateful for something else: I was allowed, in the eyes of the community, to move on. After spending most of a year doing a great deal of public crying, it eventually became clear that my case would not be prosecuted, and I made my peace with that. Even the attempt gave me strength and confidence in a way that nothing else could have, and my healing continued, supported by the fact that no one expected me to continue to be hurting and vulnerable forever. I was allowed and even encouraged to keep shifting my shape, finding my way into teaching and facilitating ritual. And ultimately, finding my way through my own history and then forward inside my community led me into my own power.

Sarah Twichell Rosehill is a witch, writer, foodie, semi-competent knitter, and aspiring photographer. Formally trained in Anamanta and Feri, she is influenced by everything from fairy tales to popular gurus. She has been teaching, planning events, and facilitating ritual with the EarthSpirit Community (www.earthspirit.org) for over a decade.

In the Midst of Avalon
Casualties of the Sexual Revolution
Katessa S. Harkey

Summary of Events

Marion Zimmer Bradley (1930-1999) was a celebrated author of science fiction and fantasy. Her works have frequently been hailed for their inclusion of Pagan, feminist, and LGBTQ philosophy. Her epic novel *The Mists of Avalon* has been particularly beloved in the contemporary Pagan movement. The book reinterprets the Arthurian cycle in the light of feminist Pagan ideals.[1] Scholar Carol Fry reports Bradley consumed all ten volumes of *The Golden Bough* at the age of fourteen, piquing her life-long interest in the occult.[2] This is also the age at which she began writing.[3]

The reversal of gender roles in the alternate history fantasy presented in *The Mists of Avalon* compliments the works of feminist historians and folklorists in the tradition of Margaret Murray. While Bradley considered herself to be a Christian,[4] she was involved in developing alternative religious perspectives. Rachel E. Holmen (who became editor of Bradley's *Fantasy Magazine* following her death) wrote in a memorial piece, "One of her hopes, while writing '*Mists*', was to encourage Christians to value the contributions of women to religion."[5]

---

[1] Carol L. Fry, "The Goddess Ascending: Feminist Neo-Pagan Witchcraft in Marion Zimmer Bradley's Novels" (*The Journal of Popular Culture* 27.1 [1993]: 67-80) 72-74.

[2] Fry 77.

[3] Fry 71.

[4] Fry 77.

[5] Rachel Holmen, "Marion Zimmer Bradley: June 3, 1930 - Sept. 25, 1999," *Marion Zimmer Bradley: A Biography* (Marion Zimmer Bradley Literary Works Trust, c. 1999) 1. Available at http://www.katinkahesselink.net/his/bradley-mzb-bio4funr.htm. Note: this

During her life, Bradley supported and promoted the newly-emerging Pagan faiths as viable, healthy alternatives to overly-patriarchal religion. Elements of Pagan practice may be seen in other of Bradley's works. As noted by Fry regarding the use of psionic power in Bradley's Darkover setting:

> The manner in which power is generated is quite suggestive of Neo-Pagan coven practice. Individuals sit together at a table, pouring their psychic energy into a jewel... The arrangement has obvious similarities to coven practice in creating what Pagans call "high magic" and to the "cone of power" raised by the coven, right down to the fact that both the coven (in most cases) and the matrix group are led by a woman...[6]

While Bradley's relationship with the convicted pedophile Walter Breen caused some scandal at the time of his final arrest, the facts of the case have rarely been publicly discussed until recently. On June 3, 2014, Tor published an article by Leah Schnelbach on its website (later removed) in tribute to the dead author on her birthday. This post neglected to mention Bradley's documented complicity in her husband's criminal sexual behavior.

Comments on the article drew attention to Stephen Goldin's website, which hosts the first two of Bradley's sworn depositions. These are from a 1998 civil suit brought by one of Breen's victims, Goldin's step-son.[7] In them, Bradley testified that she knew of Breen's activities[8] and publicly defended him.[9]

---

source no longer available in its original location on the Marion Zimmer Bradley Literary Works Trust page.

[6] Fry 71.

[7] "Deposition of Marion Zimmer Bradley," *MZB Deposition 1 & 2* (The Superior Court of the State of California, 1 Jan. 1998). Available at http://www.stephengoldin.com/MZB Website/MZB Depositions 1&2.html.

[8] Deposition of Marion Zimmer Bradley 1:13:11-19.

The convention organizer Deirdre Saoirse Moen posted a critical response on her blog[10] and commented negatively on the Tor article. When she later contacted Moira Greyland (Bradley's daughter, with whom she had worked in prior contexts) for comment, Greyland's email response revealed that Bradley had not merely been complicit in her husband's activities, but had herself engaged in abusive behaviors.

With permission, Moen published Greyland's email along with two of her poems in a new blog entry. Entitled "Mother's Hands" and "They Did Their Best," both are poignant works.[11] The first graphically describes abuse of a physical, psychological, and sexual nature.

> *The bathtub scene makes me see red*
> *With water closing over my head*
> *No little girl should fear to die*
> *Her mother's fury in her eye!*

The second describes the community's lack of response to Greyland's suffering.

> *For the party line now*
> *Is to claim that somehow*
> *Everybody somehow did their best*
> *So the ones who did wrong*
> *Goes the new New Age song*
> *Aren't to blame, we should lay this to rest.*

---

[9] Deposition of Marion Zimmer Bradley 1:28:10-17.

[10] Deirdre Saoirse Moen, "Marion Zimmer Bradley Gave Us New Perspectives, All Right," *Deirdre Saoirse Moen: "Sounds Like Weird,"* 3 June 2014. Available at http://deirdre.net/marion-zimmer-bradley-gave-us-new-perspectives-all-right/.

[11] Deirdre Saoirse Moen, "Marion Zimmer Bradley: It's Worse Than I Knew," *Deirdre Saoirse Moen: "Sounds Like Weird,"* 10 June 2014. Available at http://dsmoen.livejournal.com/544470.html.

A later interview given by Greyland's brother Mark confirms her version of events.[12]

Other blogs and sites began to report Greyland's revelations. Fans and (now) former fans of Bradley's work were particularly disgusted and outraged. On June 16, blogger Natalie Luhrs summarized community sentiment (all emphasis in the original):

> And, as is clear from the Breendoggle documents, everyone in their vicinity knew what was going on. What is even more clear, because of the years involved, was that many people knew for a long time. And, for a long, long time–the time it takes to ruin a generation of lives–the community still did nothing to stop him.
>
> Let me repeat that. EVERYONE KNEW IT.[13]

Still, some commenters urged caution, pointing out that blogs are not reliable sources of information. Others worried it was a hoax of some kind and questioned whether the author of the email truly was Moira Greyland. Given the years since Bradley's passing, a few found the timing of the accusations suspicious. These concerns were answered when the story was picked up by a major news outlet. As reported on June 27, 2014:

> Greyland, writing to *The Guardian* via email, said that she had not spoken out before "because I thought that my mother's fans would be angry with me for saying anything against someone who had championed women's rights and made so many of them feel differently about themselves and

---

[12] Chris Starfire, "Secret Keeper No More: An Interview with Mark Greyland," *Starfire Studio*, 13 July 2014. Available at http://starfire-studio.com/markgreyland.html.

[13] Natalie Luhrs, "Silence Is Complicity," *Pretty Terrible* 16 June 2014. Available at http://www.pretty-terrible.com/2014/06/16/silence-is-complicity.

their lives. I didn't want to hurt anyone she had helped, so I just kept my mouth shut."[14] [15]

As word spread, the accusations proved difficult for the science fiction and fantasy (SF/F) community to digest. This community includes Pagans influenced by Bradley's work, who frequently reported a sense of betrayal.[16] Responses thus far have primarily been in the form of online commenting and blogging. While many have expressed horror and outrage, others have explored the relationship between the author and the body of work. Skeptical responders have questioned Greyland's motives and whether posthumous accusations are verifiable or appropriate.

History

In order to understand these revelations and the community responses, we must examine events in relationship to one another and in historical context.

Bradley was born in 1930 in Albany, NY. She grew up in poverty during the Great Depression but exhibited early academic keenness

---

[14] Alison Flood, "SFF Community Reeling after Marion Zimmer Bradley's Daughter Accuses Her of Abuse," *The Guardian* 27 June 2014. Available at http://www.theguardian.com/books/2014/jun/27/sff-community-marion-zimmer-bradley-daughter-accuses-abuse.

[15] *Editor's Note:* Since this article went to press, Moira Greyland has published an essay providing additional details about her sexual abuse by both parents. Greyland attributes her abuse to her parents' utopian belief in human beings' inherent pansexuality, a conclusion that leads her to condemn same-sex marriage. See "The Story of Moira Greyland (Guest Post)," *Ask the Bigot*, ed. Katy Faust, 23 July 2015. Available at http://askthebigot.com/2015/07/23/the-story-of-moira-greyland-guest-post/.

[16] Jason, Pitzl-Waters, "Marion Zimmer Bradley, Abuse, and Cautionary Tales," *The Wild Hunt: A Modern Pagan Perspective* 26 June 2014. Available at http://wildhunt.org/2014/06/marion-zimmer-bradley-abuse-and-cautionary-tales.html.

and a love of the written word. She was married to Robert Alden Bradley from October 26, 1949 to May 19, 1964; they had one son, David Robert Bradley (1950–2008). Beginning sometime in the 1950's, Bradley became involved with the lesbian organization Daughters of Bilitis. Regarding her marriage, Holmen reports:

> Her son David asked later why she and his father had stayed married for so long, when they were so obviously incompatible; she replied, "He knew he could trust me with his money and we never ran out of things to talk about." And their conversations led to better novels that sold easily to publishers.[17]

In May 1960, Bradley published a story in *The Ladder,* the magazine of the Daughters of Bilitis. Its protagonist is a lesbian wife and mother in a similar life situation to Bradley. She struggles to come to terms with her feelings of being an outcast to both queer and straight culture.[18]

During these early years of the SF/F community, fans carried on lively correspondence through individual letters, local newsletters, and more widely published "fanzines." Mailed correspondences served as the primary means of communication among the emerging organized communities that collectively called themselves "fandom." Management of the mailing lists was one way to gain power and clout within the community. Groups organized locally and to put on larger convention events.

Prolific authors such as Bradley learned early on that connecting to this community was the key to success. It was through networking by correspondence that she entered a relationship with Walter Breen. She would only later move to his geographic vicinity.

---

[17] Holmen 1.

[18] Lauren Jae Gutterman, "'The House on the Borderland': Lesbian Desire, Marriage, and the Household, 1950-1979" (*Journal of Social History* 46.1 [2012]: 1-22) 2.

A member of Berkeley fandom, Breen was already known to the community as a pedophile. Parents and members of the community were so disturbed by his behavior that they organized to have him banned from attending the 1964 WorldCon in Oakland, CA, Pacificon II. WorldCon is a traveling event at which the Hugo awards are presented, something like the "World's Fair" of the SF/F community.

A member of the WorldCon committee named Bill Donaho published a newsletter sent to a hand-picked group of twenty-eight involved community members and organizers. Entitled "The Great Breen Boondoggle, or All Berkeley is Plunged into War," it contained a recounting of Breen's actions, a consideration of options, and a plea for input and aid in the process. Though it was marked "DNQ" (Do Not Quote), the contents of the document became known to the general fan community in Berkeley. In the following passage, Donaho graphically renders his eyewitness account of Breen's interactions with a 3-year old girl.

> I recall one occasion—a fairly large gathering at the Nelsons—in which he also used a pencil, rubbing the eraser back and forth in the general area of the vagina, not quite masturbating her. (Walter is incredible.) Many people were somewhat displeased by this—most particularly her parents. No one thought he was actually psychologically damaging P----- (she being so young)—obviously ----- and ----- would have interfered if they thought he had been—but the spectacle was not thought to be aesthetically pleasing. Years later Walter found out about the reaction and said, "But why didn't somebody say something! I wouldn't have dreamed of doing it if I'd thought someone *objected*."[19]

As a result of the distribution of the letter and the attendant controversy, Breen was banned from the convention in question.

---

[19] Bill Donaho, "The Great Breen Boondoggle or All Berkeley Is Plunged into War," *Breendoggle Wiki*. Available at http://breendoggle.wikia.com/wiki/Breendoggle_Wiki.

However, the community was so divided over the issue that groups and friendships were broken and some boycotted the convention.

Donaho faced personal and political consequences for his choices. Bjo and John Trimble, also WorldCon organizers, solicited articles and published a fanzine entitled *The Loyal Opposition*. A "symposium" fanzine distributed to two lists, the document disputed the factual accuracy of Donaho's statements.[20] The totality of these events and circumstances came to be known as a byword in fandom parlance as the "Breendoggle."

Donaho's letter went on to state that when Breen was notified of the situation, he threatened to sue. Breen additionally claimed that if he were banned from Pacificon II, Bradley would also not be attending the event. Donaho reports varying positions in the community regarding Bradley. As she was well-liked, some wanted to hush the issue up so that she wouldn't find out; some thought she knew and was being excessively tolerant, while others wondered if she should have been warned. Donaho did not mention anyone thinking that Bradley might know of and share in Breen's proclivities.

During the course of these events, less than one month after her legal divorce on June 3, 1964, Bradley married Walter Breen. In *Before Stonewall*, scholar of LGBTQ activism Donald Mader reports that they were married in February 1964,[21] making the time-frame of Breen and Bradley's actual (as opposed to legal) relationship a matter of dispute.

Mader, who knew Breen personally, further recalls:

> He literally left a larger-than-life impression... This impression was the result of a remarkable force of personality

[20] Bjo Trimble, "Summing Up," *The Loyal Opposition*, 18-21. Accessed via NelC, *Random Acts of Senseless Stuff* at http://nelc.dreamwidth.org/313708.html.

[21] Donald Mader, "Walter H. Breen (J.Z. Eglinton)," *Before Stonewall: Activists for Gay and Lesbian Rights in Historical Context*, Vern L. Bullough, ed. (New York: Harrington Park, 2002: 312-322) 315.

that made Breen the center of attention in any gathering—be it a coin fair, a science fiction convention, or a movement meeting—of his prodigious intellectual energy, and, it must be admitted, of a carefully cultivated flair for the outrageous.[22]

While it is difficult to pick fact from fiction in Breen's accounts of his early life, there can be little doubt of his intellectual capacities and broad range of talents. He gained the most success in the field of rare coins (numismatics). He is also remembered for his contributions to the field of the history of homosexuality in an era in which such sociological approaches to gayness were unprecedented.

Breen was a proponent of "Greek love," the concept that intergenerational male-male relationships are not in themselves hurtful to the younger partner and may be helpful in the context of a loving relationship. It was this ideology that informed his historical scholarship in the work *Greek Love*, published in 1964 under the pseudonym J.Z. Eglinton. The book was edited by Bradley and dedicated to her as "my beloved wife."[23] In two parts, the work first dealt with the apologetics of the subject, then delved into the history of the matter.

Breen and Bradley continued this collaboration on his *International Journal of Greek Love*. This publication was similar in activist intent to the Lesbian publication *The Ladder*, to which Bradley contributed (often under the name "Miriam Gardner").[24] In the first issue of Breen's journal, Bradley published an article entitled "Feminine Equivalents of Greek Love in Modern Fiction." While in its language, the work is careful to keep references to fantasy and the page, it is difficult not to infer Bradley's opinion on the matter from her participation in the project.

---

[22] Mader 313.

[23] Mader 315.

[24] Ruth M. Pettis, "Bradley, Marion Zimmer," *GLBTQ: An Encyclopedia of Gay, Lesbian, Bisexual, Transgender, and Queer Culture*, 2005. Available at http://glbtqarchive.com/literature/bradley_mz_L.pdf.

It is important to note that at the time, majority opinion still placed homosexuality into the same general category of "sex deviancy" as pederasty or pedophilia. At the fomenting of the gay rights movement, some prominent members were simultaneously involved with efforts to normalize this type of sexual interaction and considered it part and parcel of gay liberation. One example was Harry Hay, founder of the Mattachine Society and co-founder of the Radical Faeries. He later joined and was a vocal supporter of NAMBLA (the North American Man/Boy Love Association) throughout his life.[25]

The present proponents of the "Greek Love" world view see their opponents within the GLBTQ community as "assimilationists." Activists in organizations such as NAMBLA claim that harm occurs only when intergenerational relationships are interrupted or shamed. Consider Bradley's own words from the aforementioned essay:

> Tragedy, however, seems not to be inherent in such a relationship... but occurs only when (1) the relationship is misunderstood and interrupted by outsiders, or (2) the older woman fears or rejects such an attachment.[26]

It may be ascertained from the depositions that in the following years, Bradley and Breen lived a highly bohemian lifestyle. Their household regularly hosted visitors, house guests, and a rotating cast of "stray" children and young people.[27] An unknown number of these experienced abuse at Breen's hands.[28] Bradley was frequently away, traveling to events and conventions. Her romantic partner[29] and

---

[25] David Thorstad, "Harry Hay on Man/Boy Love," *North American Man/Boy Love Association* (2003), 1. Available at http://nambla.org/hayonmanboylove.html.

[26] Marion Zimmer Bradley, "Feminine Equivalents of Greek Love in Modern Fiction" (*International Journal of Greek Love* 1.1: 48–58) 56.

[27] Deposition of Marion Zimmer Bradley 1:27-34.

[28] Deposition of Marion Zimmer Bradley 1:50:22–1:51:12.

[29] "Deposition of Elisabeth Waters," *Elizabeth Waters' Deposition, 10/16/97* (Superior Court of the State of California, 16 Oct. 1997) 1:18:21-25.

secretary, Elizabeth Waters, helped manage her intertwined business and household affairs, which spanned several properties. Goldin notes that Breen met Kenneth Smith and also his next unnamed victim at conventions during this period.[30]

In July of 1989, Moira Greyland informed her psychiatrist that Breen had been molesting a young boy named Kenneth Smith. When Greyland was questioned by the police, it came to light that the abuse had been taking place since 1984, when Smith was between the ages of 8 and 11. Breen eventually pled guilty and was sentenced to three years' probation. Kenneth Smith's mother brought a civil suit. Smith needed extensive psychological care as a result of his trauma.

In 1989, Breen began molesting another unnamed boy. Breen was arrested in 1990 and sent to prison, where he died in 1993.[31] In 1997, Smith turned 21 and hired a new attorney. Bradley and Waters were added to the civil suit, citing negligence. (It is in regards to this suit that their depositions were taken.) As noted in the transcript, Bradley had by this point suffered strokes[32] and was on antidepressant medication.[33] In August of 1999, a settlement was reached in favor of Smith. On September 25, 1999, Bradley died of a heart attack.

The Controversy

It is problematic when a prominent individual is accused of wrongdoing posthumously. Commenters have expressed that Bradley is no longer here to defend herself from the accusations. While this is technically correct, Moira Greyland's story is not new. In her

---

Available at http://www.stephengoldin.com/MZB Website/Elizabeth Waters' Deposition, 10_16_97.html.

[30] Stephen Goldin, "Timeline of Events," *Marion Zimmer Bradley: In Her Own Words*, 1999. Available at http://www.stephengoldin.com/MZB Website/Marion Zimmer Bradle---Timeline.html.

[31] Goldin (1999) 1.

[32] Deposition of Marion Zimmer Bradley 2:67:25.

[33] Deposition of Marion Zimmer Bradley 1:8:3.

deposition, Bradley testified that Greyland had told her Breen had molested her.[34] Notably, one of the stipulations of Bradley's deposition was that no questions would be asked regarding her relationship with her daughter.[35] In her deposition, Bradley's partner Elizabeth Waters testified to an incident Bradley had admitted to her:

Q. What did Marion tell you about that episode?

A. That Moira kept biting Patrick, and she couldn't think of any way to stop her, so she tied her to a chair and threatened to pull out all of her teeth with pliers, and Moira became hysterical, and Marion untied her and let her go, and Moira never bit her brother again.[36]

While in most cases there is insufficient evidence to determine whether posthumous claims are justified, this particular case is exceptional in the depth and breadth of documented evidence, including sworn testimony.

One reason that the community may be finding these revelations difficult to digest is that Bradley represents a rare type of culture hero. A noted lesbian and author of activist literature, Bradley distinguished herself in a troubled era and in a field dominated by men. Moreover, her books appealed to a general audience, not only a female readership. Her SF/F works seemed to express an unprecedented ethic of free love and tolerance by sexually pairing partners of varied gender, number, and species.

Bradley's public persona was carefully crafted. She seemed to live the lifestyle every fan dreamed of in one of the burgeoning centers of alternative culture. In short, Bradley presented a picture of the progressive SF/F "new woman."

Furthermore, Bradley was well-known and liked in fandom for personally supporting a market for young and aspiring authors; she helped many launch their careers. Just as the shine of celebrity rubs off

---

[34] Deposition of Marion Zimmer Bradley 2:105:19-22.

[35] Deposition of Marion Zimmer Bradley 2:64:8-16; 1:19:1-6.

[36] Deposition of Elisabeth Waters 1:169:4-5.

on those associated, so too may any infamy. This reality might help explain the dismissal of earlier accusations as exaggeration or politically motivated slander. As stated by Jim Hines, one such author who has become successful:

> I'm proud of those stories. I believe the *Sword & Sorceress* series was important, and I'm grateful to Bradley for creating it. I believe her magazine helped a lot of new writers, and her books helped countless readers. All of which makes the revelations about Marion Zimmer Bradley protecting a known child rapist and molesting her own daughter and others even more tragic.[37]

The more recent accusations cut Bradley's professional image to the core and reveal a truth no one would wish to see in a figure he or she had previously idolized. Goldin posted the depositions in 2000. Since that time, the information contained there has generated little interest or commentary. If it were not for Moira Greyland coming forward in June of 2014 regarding the abuse she suffered, it is possible that the court of public opinion might never have been called for Bradley's legacy.

Separating the Artist from the Works

The context of the recent controversy was originally the Tor memorial birthday piece that failed to note any of Bradley's misdeeds. The belief that due diligence on the part of a reporter ought to have uncovered the matter sparked Moen and others to respond. Even if the author of the piece or Tor were aware of the controversy, were they under an obligation to mention the accusations of abuse in a piece intended to honor Bradley's work? Now that further ills have

---

[37] Jim C. Hines, "Rape, Abuse, and Marion Zimmer Bradley," *Jim C Hines* 23 June 2014. Available at http://www.jimchines.com/2014/06/rape-abuse-and-mzb/.

come to light, must these be noted as well? In other words, what shall be the legacy of Marion Zimmer Bradley?

The remaining disputes around the subject point to a broader ethical and philosophical conundrum. That is, to what degree is the work of art tied to its creator? Some commenters were so horrified by what they had learned about Bradley that they threw away her books—some even going so far as to burn them. Others said they didn't know what now to do with the books or expressed disgust at the thought of re-reading them.

This aversion response indicates a sense of psycho-spiritual tainting by association. Certainly there is the social factor to consider: what others might think if they see Bradley's books on one's shelf. However, giving or throwing away a problematic book is a different act from making special arrangement to light it on fire. The latter behavior indicates at least a purgative impulse, if not intentional ritual separation. The book is treated as a symbol of the artist or his or her influence.

As has already been noted, however, the works themselves live a life quite apart from the circumstances of the author who produced them. Many Pagans, members of the SF/F community, and queer people found characters with whom they could identify in Bradley's books. This in and of itself sent a comforting message to those who often felt like outcasts in their day-to-day lives. Have not the works done material good? And how could this be so if a work were somehow impressed with the evil influence of an evil author?

In online discussions, various other historical authors and artists with unsavory personal characteristics have been brought forward for comparison. Horror author H.P. Lovecraft (1890-1937) is one repeatedly mentioned figure, possibly because he shared with Bradley a number of similarities in biographical and career detail. His is a useful example for looking at the logic used in such comparisons, though the specific details vary.

Like Bradley, Lovecraft both incorporated elements of occultism and influenced occult culture through the fiction he wrote. He created a setting open for development by others and carried out correspondence with young genre authors,[38] thereby encouraging the development of the early SF/F community. As products of the time, however, Lovecraft's works frequently reflect his racist views,[39] often evoking fear of "miscegenation" (the mixing of the races) and genetic degeneracy.

Despite these social justice problems in his work, Lovecraft is honored as one of the formative voices in American horror. His open-source world remains one of the few collective settings available and attracts many young authors to "the Mythos." He is regularly celebrated with annual conventions and cultural events. Ethical arguments of this type conclude: if we are to castigate the works of Bradley for her unpopular and now-outdated views, should we then also dispense with Lovecraft (or whomever)?

Challenges to this type of argument generally detail the differences between the cases. In the Lovecraft example, there is no evidence that the author acted upon his views in a criminal way. Nor has it been alleged that he or his views caused negligent or abusive harm to individuals within the community that read his works. Furthermore, Lovecraft is not now, nor has he ever been held up as a culture hero in the field of social justice. His racist views are well-known and regularly noted by critics and commentators of his works. Finally, while Lovecraft's views come through only in his fiction, Bradley also presented her views in persuasive essays, as in her article for *The International Journal of Greek Love.*

In Bradley's fictional works, her views on sexuality are hidden from scrutiny behind elements of the fantasy. Questionable sexual acts or relationships are normalized by placing them in the context of ancient or alien cultures. These choices lessen the need for the reader

---

[38] "H.P. Lovecraft," *Biography.com,* A&E Television Networks, 2015. Available at http://www.biography.com/people/hp-lovecraft-40102.

[39] Arun Rath, "Horror Of Horrors: Is H.P. Lovecraft's Legacy Tainted?" *NPR* 4 Oct. 2014. Available at http://www.npr.org/templates/transcript/transcript.php?storyId=353737040.

to critically examine incidents of rape, incest, or pederasty. (As a good feminist analyst of the time, one would have been precluded from passing judgment on other cultures by the standards of one's own.) As noted by Rosenberg,

> Zimmer Bradley writes that "The little blue-painted girl who had borne the fertilizing blood was drawn down into the arms of a sinewy old hunter, and Morgaine saw her briefly struggle and cry out, go down under his body, her legs opening to the irresistible force of nature in them"... Without the context of Zimmer Bradley's personal history, it is possible to read this sentence as a description of an ancient religious practice that is unsettling both in its depiction of an altered state and behavior that contemporary readers would not find acceptable. In the context of her testimony, and an article she wrote about sensual relationships between older and much younger women in literature, we lose the reassurance that the author shares our moral and ethical presumptions.[40]

Bradley was no stranger to written erotica meant to titillate the reader. Her novel *The Catch Trap* features an illicit affair between two gay trapeze artists, twenty-three and fifteen years of age. While technically classifiable as gay historical fiction,[41] the novel was selected by Salmon and Symons as the sample work in a research study of slash fiction.[42] In the novel, the illicitness of the sex is itself a subject of the

---

[40] Alyssa Rosenberg, "Re-reading Feminist Author Marion Zimmer Bradley in the Wake of Sexual Assault Allegations," *Washington Post* 27 June 2014. Available at http://www.washingtonpost.com/news/act-four/wp/2014/06/27/re-reading-feminist-author-marion-zimmer-bradley-in-the-wake-of-sexual-assault-allegations/.

[41] Erastes, "Review: The Catch Trap by Marion Zimmer Bradley," *Speak Its Name* 7 Jan. 2010. Available at http://speakitsname.com/2010/01/07/review-the-catch-trap-by-marion-bradley/.

[42] Catherine Salmon, and Don Symons, "Slash Fiction and Human Mating Psychology," *Journal of Sex Research* 41.1 [2004]: 94-100.

work. The very first sexual encounter between the two characters raises questions about consent. As noted by reviewer Erastes:

> Tommy is fifteen when he's first approached sexually by Mario, so people who find anyone having sex under 18 as distasteful are going to want to avoid this. I admit I found it mildly disturbing—not because of Tommy's youth even in the times that this was set—but because Mario's first approach came over as little more than "interfering" with Tommy when he was in no position to object (they were sitting in the back of a moving car)... It didn't matter to me that Tommy was accepting of this back seat advance, Mario knew that Tommy could hardly scream "get off me!" and so in this case I did, as I said, find it a little creepy, even though Tommy didn't mind.[43]

Nevertheless, Erastes recommends the book as "an Essential Read for anyone serious about writing gay historical fiction." He was either unaware of or chose not to mention any scandal surrounding Bradley, and he notes confusion as to why the novel is out of print and rare, given its quality.

Bradley was adroit at generating sexual tension through the breach of taboos around consent, and this skill is at work in *The Mists of Avalon,* which many readers have found to be sexually exciting. However, the question remains as to whether reading the book (or similar materials) may influence readers' attitudes, and also whether such an influence was Bradley's intention.

What would Bradley have said of the matter? As reported from Fry's interview:

> I asked Bradley if she felt an obligation to raise readers' consciousness levels with her work. She answered, "Yes I do. I think every writer does. Every writer puts their [sic] very strongly held feelings in what they write, and it's much easier to do in a novel than in a pamphlet." But she also said[,] "I

---

[43] Erastes 1.

think if people have too many convictions, they should hire a hall or a soapbox. I don't think too much political consciousness is good in a novel."[44]

Conclusions

Due to the occult themes inserted early into the developing genres of science fiction and fantasy, the origins of the Pagan and SF/F communities are inextricably bound up with each other. Practitioners in the one are often fans of the other. Formative occult authors such as Aleister Crowley and Dion Fortune also turned their hands to fantasy fiction and imbedded occult wisdom in their narratives. The two groups have evolved concurrently alongside one another into the overlapping community that we know today.

Both Pagans and SF/F fans have also typically been more tolerant of other "outsiders" in society, such as sexual minorities. While neither community segment is monolithic in its views, political leanings within these communities in America have been consistently progressive (or at least alternative to the mainstream).

While "progressive" philosophy now embraces an ethic of consent as defined by today's ethical understandings, these ideas did not appear whole-cloth. The notion of consent developed over time as research revealed what types of sexual experiences are harmful and why. As we examine the "Breendoggle" communication, we see an organizer candidly expressing the confusion that accompanied the sexual revolution. Direct witnesses of Breen's abuses did not know whether they felt badly about what they were seeing because the activity was bad, or because they had been told to believe it was bad. Homosexuality and pedophilia had been lumped together by mainstream mores for so long that, to the fan community, it seemed possible that Breen's proclivities seemed repugnant solely because of learned prejudice. If their reactions were based on learned prejudice,

---

[44] Fry 78.

repudiating Breen would have been at best intolerance and at worst bigotry.

Over time, the tide of opinion about whether pedophiles should be considered part of the GLBTQ community turned clearly against inclusion. At that point, however, Breen's presence was an open secret in fandom and in the community at large. His connection to Bradley may also have lent him some protection. In essence, he was "grandfathered in." As a direct result of the community-wide social uncertainty, an unknown number of children were harmed. It was not until many years had passed—and community members had experienced the harmful impact of predation—that any legal action was taken to remove Breen from the community. These proceedings began not because an adult in the situation moved proactively, but because Moira Greyland spoke to a mandatory reporter.

The current controversy around Bradley is not only a reaction to the most recent revelation that Bradley abused her children. Its vehemence stems from communities encountering an uncomfortable chapter in their history and in the development of consent culture: a period when, especially among those struggling for GLBTQ rights, there was genuine uncertainty about whether adult sexual attention toward children was harmful. Whatever the ultimate fate of Bradley's legacy, we need to tell our history truthfully so that the mistakes of the past need not be repeated.

Katessa S. Harkey is the Storyteller and co-founder of Spiral Cult Circus, a Hermetic ritual theatre collective in Portland, OR. As a second-generation organizer in the SF/F events community, she has been assisting at conventions since childhood. She also serves as a kitchen coordinator to various festivals held at Windward Education and Research Center. Her ministry includes sex-positive activism, performance, spiritual education, and shamanic guidance. She is polyamorous, ecosexual, and a member of the LGBTQ and BDSM communities. Trained in musical theatre and educated in Women's

Studies, Katessa works to create vibrant and inviting alternatives to American mainstream culture.

Responding to Abuse in the Pagan Community
Cat Chapin-Bishop

The first perpetrator of child sexual abuse I ever reported committed suicide.

I'm aware that there are those who, on hearing that, will say, "Well, good! One less pervert in the world." Unfortunately, the world is not as simple as that. This was back in the mid-eighties, and I was still an intern in psychotherapy. My client was a single parent, the mother of two young boys, barely scraping by, in part with the help of a boarder—who, it turned out, had sexually abused both the boys.

"But it was only once!" the mother said. "And I watch them all the time now. It has never happened again!" But, of course, it had happened again, and more than once. We found that out after I did what the law required and made the phone call to child protective services. Later that day, CPS called at the family's home to interview the room-mate. And later that night, he went into the garage and hung himself.

It was one of the boys who found his body.

To him, this man was not "a perpetrator." To him, this was the man who had taken him fishing and helped him with his homework. Because while the abuse had been awful, it had not been all there was to this man's presence in the boy's life. His feelings, like life itself, were complicated.

So the mandated counseling to help the boys recover from sexual abuse became counseling to help them cope with sexual abuse and the suicide of a member of their household. And for a time, everyone in that small family had to struggle with the added burdens of guilt and financial hardship caused by this death.

I do not in any way regret making that report. I do not believe that taking a young boy fishing wipes out the harm of abusing him, nor that paying part of a family's living expenses erases the guilt of sexually abusing a child. But the story points out the trouble with making sweeping generalizations about perpetrators. Those who prey on children are also friends, family members, wage-earners; and sometimes they are artists, musicians, teachers, or members of a spiritual community whose work is missed when they are removed from those communities. It is dangerous to caricature offenders as all alike, easily spotted, or wholly monstrous.

The trouble is, if we begin to believe that all perpetrators of child sexual abuse are like comic-book villains, we risk becoming blind to the cases that don't fit that simple picture. Our communities may begin to make excuses, to minimize, rationalize, and deny the abuse. We say to ourselves, "But she was a teenager—she could have stopped it," or "He's not like those other perpetrators—it was only because he was drunk (had just lost his job/ had been divorced/ was depressed)." And then we may not pick up the phone and make the report—or we may not enforce a community statement that says we have a "zero tolerance policy" around sexual abuse. Or we may try to "fix" an abuser through compassion and good intentions, without understanding that those are not the tools needed for this particular job. To prevent that, we need to go beyond rhetoric and slogans, and understand the real world of perpetrators and their victims.

So what we do know about perpetrators?

They are, overwhelmingly, male. Women can and do sexually abuse children, but it is far less common.

They are no more likely to be gay than straight, despite years of right-wing propaganda to the contrary. However, being gay does not mean that someone is not a perpetrator; there is no relationship between those two things.

They may well be minors themselves; the problem of sexual abuse of children by older children and teens is probably under-reported, and can be difficult to tell from "sexually reactive behavior" in which children act out abuse they may themselves have experienced. (Effects on the victim may be very similar, though the prognosis for the perpetrator may be very different. This is one case where seeking help, and not turning away from a perpetrator because he is not what we have been led to expect, can make an enormous difference for everyone.)

Some perpetrators will largely confine their abuse to members of their own family; others will offend primarily against unrelated children. Some will have only a handful of victims, but many will abuse hundreds of children over the course of their lives.

Perpetrators are almost always survivors of childhood sexual abuse themselves. Often, they are sexual offenders in multiple ways. They may well have ongoing sexual relationships with adult women (or men) at the same time that they are abusing children. They often (though not always) abuse drugs or alcohol, sometimes as a way of lowering their own inhibitions against committing a crime.

Often they will have a habit of objectifying the targets of their sexual interest; this is associated with an increased likelihood of reoffending. Generally they lack empathy for others, and particularly for children, but this is not always obvious.

It can be hard to get good information on recidivism among perpetrators of sexual abuse, because most studies rely on criminal convictions, which self-reports of convicted perpetrators reveal to be far fewer than the number of victims offended against. What is clear is that sexual abusers of children have a high rate of repeating their crimes.

Treatment does lower that risk, but only if it is specialized offender treatment. Counseling from sources other than specialists in this field seems to have no effect in lowering the risk of reoffending, and this is one area where no ethical pastoral counselor should even think of offering their "help" as a substitute for reporting abuse officially and having an offender complete a specialized offender treatment program. Unless you have been trained in this specific area of practice, this one really is over your pay grade.

So who are the victims of child sexual abuse, and what are some of the effects of that abuse?

They're a lot of different people, it turns out.

About 20% of adult women and 5—10% of adult men recall having been sexually abused as children. Boys are more at risk of abuse by non-family members, possibly because boy children tend to be more mobile and independent of their parents' supervision in our society. Some research shows risk is evenly distributed across age groups, but other studies find that teenagers are especially at risk—an important thing to keep in mind, as there can be a tendency to blame the victim where teens are concerned. It's important to remember that, though teenagers can engage in consensual sex with other teens, they still lack the knowledge and resources of adults, and there is always a power imbalance between an adult and a child. Perpetrators take advantage of that power imbalance to manipulate victims of any age. And there are other vulnerabilities perpetrators look for, to exploit among their victims. We know that children who have been victimized in other ways, or whose families are affected by poverty, substance abuse, or violence are at higher risk for sexual abuse.

Whatever makes a child more vulnerable, in other words, makes them more vulnerable to sexual abuse. The lingering effects of having been abused as children can include depression, PTSD, and a higher risk of substance abuse, suicide or self-injuring behaviors into adulthood. Children who have been sexually abused may show prematurely sexualized behavior, and there is an elevated risk of being re-abused or sexually assaulted among children who have experienced sexual abuse.

It is worth mentioning that even when there is clear evidence that penetration has been part of sexual abuse, in only a small fraction of cases will there be genital injuries of that penetration. This is important to understand, so that we do not refuse to accept the testimony of victims that is not corroborated by physical injury.

Sexual abuse is definitely harmful—but it may not be harmful in the ways we've been taught to expect. And while children are in no way responsible for their own abuse, some responses to having been sexually exploited, such as early sexualization, may be misunderstood by adults in a way that allows us to dismiss their testimony. We need to be careful to remember that victims of sexual abuse are complicated human beings, and no more likely to fit one mold than any of us.

What do we know about helping survivors of childhood sexual abuse to heal?

There are a number of things we as a community can do to support survivors in their recovery after sexual abuse. Research shows that some very simple things can make an enormous difference to how well survivors heal from the most horrific abuse: things like, when a victim reports their abuse to an adult in authority, that adult takes them seriously and acts on the report.

Counseling can be important, of course, but there is definitely a place for just standing by survivors and showing empathy. Research suggests that other important factors in healing include having at least one non-abusive adult a child can confide in, and having a community that responds with what might be called moral clarity, making it clear immediately that, no matter what, children and teens are not to blame for their own abuse, and that sexual abuse is always the responsibility of the adult. It turns out that simply being clear that the sexual abuse of children is wrong is of enormous benefit to survivors. We do not need to burn perpetrators in effigy to support survivors.

That's a good thing for a lot of reasons: threats of violence against perpetrators, for example, may not be reassuring to a victim, but instead, can stir up feelings of guilt or fear—fear for themselves, as survivors of another form of violence, or for other adults in the child's life, who may have been threatened by the abuser as a way to secure the victim's silence. Instead, reporting suspected abuse to the authorities, if that is still possible, and firm, consistent limit setting with those we reasonably believe to have sexually exploited children— regardless of the age of the victim, regardless of whether force was used, or whether the victim confided the abuse in an adult at the time or much later—is likely to be more helpful then vengeful rhetoric or acts of violence.

What else can we, the Pagan community, do to make our gatherings and groups safer for the children and teens who attend them?

In this area, there is a lot that we can do.

1. We should structure programs for children and teens to minimize the risk of abuse at gatherings.

This one is pretty straightforward. Many gatherings are now large enough to have children's programming, and that's great. However, we need to think about these programs as potential risks. Perpetrators are often drawn to positions where they can interact with kids, because access allows opportunities to abuse.

To limit that, we need to do what other religious organizations and reputable child care programs do: make sure that children are never left in the company of just one adult. All children's programs need to have more than one adult staff member with kids at all times. In addition, we need to make sure that kids' programs happen in locations with lots of visibility and easy access for the parents. For instance, one of my favorite gatherings features a large rec hall just off the main dining hall. Both rooms are a hub of constant activity during the event, and the children's programming happens mainly in that rec room, with parents and other community members constantly passing through. It adds a note of cheerfulness to everyone's experience... and it means that the whole community is aware of what is happening with the kids all the time. Not conducive to abuse!

2. We should institute mandated reporter training for all gathering staff, along with education on perpetrator behavior and warning signs.

Many Pagan religions feature initiatory oaths of secrecy, and Pagan leaders often need to observe confidentiality around the identities of participants in community events in light of the religious discrimination which many of us still face. However, there is a difference between protecting initiatory secrets and maintaining the confidence of Pagans in sensitive positions and preserving secrecy around suspected child abuse. Mandated reporter laws in every state require clergy, counselors, and child care workers to report all suspected incidents of child abuse—physical or sexual—and neglect.

Notice, the standard here is suspected abuse—not proven, not confirmed, but suspected abuse.

Staff at a Pagan gathering, Pagan clergy in the performance of their duties, and staff who provide programming for children and teens at community events are required as a matter of law to report when they suspect abuse has occurred to any underage person. Everyone whose work will put them in contact with the community's children needs to be aware of their duty to report suspected abuse and neglect to that state's child protection services, and the organization's procedure for doing so.

Not only is this the law, but I believe there's a moral case for following this law without exception. I can't tell you how painful it has been for me, as a counselor, to hear over and over again from adult survivors of child abuse that they had told a trusted adult what was happening to them, only to have that adult ignore their confidence. The sense of betrayal caused by abuse is only deepened when an entire community seems willing to look the other way.

I understand that we may be tempted to short-circuit the legal channels for abuse. We may not want to trust them. However, we are not trained investigators in this field; we are not in a position to truly protect kids from abuse without help. We are in no position to evaluate even the most sincere-sounding promises by an abuser that they will seek help. No matter how counter-cultural our values may be, in this one area, I firmly believe we need to follow the legal process for signaling the state that a child may be in danger.

3. We should create trained community ombudsmen to reach out to children and families affected by sexual abuse or sexual violence.

It's great to have mandated reporter training for staff at events, but Pagan events are large, sometimes overwhelming, sometimes bewildering things. There can be hundreds of strangers all around, and very few of us, surrounded by strangers, feel comfortable asking for help in a time of crisis. Newcomers to a community may not even know where to turn for help.

GC –outside
person or group to
help with cases?
PAGAN CONSENT CULTURE   221

The time has come for all large Pagan events to have clearly identified contact people who make it their job to be welcoming and accessible, and to serve as the first contacts for incidents or individuals that cause concern, whether or not they rise to the level of sexual assault or sexual abuse. Needless to say, these people should have additional training, probably including in some form of counseling. They will need to be calm, grounded, and very familiar with the resources of the area where any events are being held, and they will need to have the ear of the gathering's coordinators and the community's leaders. Finally, and most importantly, their job will not be to act as finders of fact—no individual is in any position to do that. Instead, their job is to make sure that problems get noticed, victims get supported, reports get made, and records are kept—confidentially between the gathering's leaders and any official investigators.

4. We should not attempt to create a secondary court system to determine the ultimate guilt or innocence of accused perpetrators.

This is a difficult thing. We need at one and the same time to take seriously allegations by children and teens who report their abuse, and we need not to attempt to act as finders of fact. While false reports of abuse are exceedingly rare—at least as rare as false reports of other serious crimes, according to the FBI—they do occur. Moreover, it is one thing to believe the testimony of victims themselves, and another to allow rumors and friend-of-a-friend accounts to rush us to judgement.

This is not only for the sake of the accused. Not only are we, as a community, unable to provide the system of checks and balances that allow defendants their rights to fair trial, we are also unable to provide the level of expertise that properly trained investigators bring to their work with abused children. Ironically, if we rush to create a parallel system to mete out justice, we may endanger the rights of both victims and the accused at the same time: we can both deprive the accused of a fair process within our communities, and also contaminate the evidence so that even solid grounds for a conviction will be inadmissible in a court of law.

Fact finding just isn't our role. When there is reason to suspect child sexual abuse, we need to hand the ultimate finding of fact over to those who have the resources to do the job properly.

5. We should empower local organizations to respond to suspicion and to concerns, through mandated reporting, banning, and/or watchful waiting for persons of concern.

While it's not the role of our communities to be substitutes for the legal system in determining guilt or innocence, we do have a role to play in judging what actions we need to make on a local level to protect our kids, and also to be sure that our leaders and teachers are held to a high standard of ethical conduct. We need to establish clear guidelines in our local communities for removing persons of concern from positions of trust within the community, with or without a criminal conviction, when there have been credible, specific allegations of misconduct made. I'm not talking about banning individuals based on vague rumors or the notion of guilt by association. But I am talking about times when there have been repeated reports of troubling behavior made against a person, as reported by the people who were directly involved.

This may seem like a contradiction to my recommendation not to attempt to adjudicate questions of guilt or innocence on our own, but in fact, it is not. Because, while we really need the standard of innocent until proven guilty where someone has been accused of a crime, whether we grant or refuse the privileges within our own communities is a different matter. There, our standards will be different from those of a criminal court. Not only will a different level of proof apply to our own hearings, but a different standard of behavior may be needed, too. I would suggest that the higher the position of trust granted someone, the higher the standard of behavior we will hold them to.

Among our leaders and teachers, despite the fact that we have no means of our own of establishing guilt or innocence, credible reports of child sexual abuse at a minimum create an appearance that is at odds with our community's ethics. And in the case of a leader or a

N

TAPA Policy

Preach

teacher, allowing them the privilege of holding themselves out as representatives of our religious traditions while they are under investigation for sexual abuse is simply inappropriate.

Likewise, given the high rates of recidivism among perpetrators, we may want to think twice about allowing anyone access to gatherings where children will be present, who has either a past conviction of any form of sexual exploitation of children, or who has been the subject of repeated, specific allegations from within the community, with or without any criminal convictions.

6. On a national and international level, we should encourage full, open disclosure of objective indicators of risk, like arrests for charges related to pedophilia.

We should report allegations as allegations where legal processes have been initiated, but not in the absence of legal action. On some levels, this is very unsatisfying: how can past victims hope to warn future victims when a perpetrator who has never been arrested or convicted moves from one place to another? On another, it is a way of recognizing the reality that we will never know every potential source of harm within our communities, while allowing our budding news services to function as they function best—as news services, reporting only what is subject to confirmation, only what is objective. Trading in rumor may serve justice one day, but it will thwart it the next. Without the greater knowledge of one another we can only have within local communities, we will have no way to prevent the kinds of abuses that many of the critics of the current wave of coverage fear: vague accusations that may polarize us, without actually making our communities any safer.

We live in a world of complexity, and as much as we might like to think otherwise, we are not separate from even the most dysfunctional aspects of our society as a whole. Child sexual abuse is a part of our modern world, and sadly, it will remain part of the Pagan community as long as that continues to be true.

The good news is that we are not helpless. We can do more to protect victims, and to keep perpetrators from using our communities to find and access victims. It's not enough; surely, we all wish we could do more. But it is a good deal more than nothing.

As we work together to heal the world as a whole, may our efforts within our own communities take root and flourish.

This article is reprinted from The Wild Hunt: A Modern Pagan Perspective *by permission of the author.*

Cat Chapin-Bishop became a psychotherapist in 1986, and she has had over 20 years of experience as a counselor specializing in work with survivors of childhood sexual abuse. She served as the first Chair of Cherry Hill Seminary's Pastoral Counseling Department and designed the earliest version of CHS's Boundaries and Ethics course, which is still central to the program there. Cat has been a Pagan since 1987, and a Quaker as well as a Pagan since 2001. Her writings can be found online at *Quaker Pagan Reflections.*

Sexual Assault and Abuse Prevention
Safeguarding Policies for Pagan Communities
Kim and Tracey Dent-Brown, with the Triple Horse Coven

You wake up one day, switch on your phone and computer, and are instantly bombarded with messages, texts, and emails. An acquaintance from your local Pagan community has been arrested, but it's not clear why. *How can we support this person? What's going on? What is the charge?* It's not someone you were particularly close to, didn't even like much, to be honest. *But we have to stick together.* More news emerges; they have been arrested on suspicion of a serious sexual assault. *Shock. Disbelief. Who, where, and when?* Okay, this is not someone you were best friends with, but this is unbelievable.

Days go by, and the circumstances become clearer: a complaint from one of the accused person's students, who had been at their home for teaching. Out of the blue, a second complaint emerges from a completely different person, then a third. *What is this? Are these copycat claims? It's unthinkable someone from our community could do this right under our noses.* Months drag by before a trial. Witnesses and forensic evidence, plus videos and diaries kept by the accused, provide confirmation: this was a repeat sex abuser who identified vulnerable potential victims, befriended them, groomed them, then assaulted them in private—often in ritual space.

The accused is found guilty. After the verdict, people in the community voice things like: "I never felt safe around them" ... "There was always something creepy" ... "There was that odd incident at the weekend camp" ... "The signs were always there."

This case is fictional, but cases like it have happened in Pagan communities around the world (as well as in communities of other faiths, of course). After the event, there are always questions about how it happened, what could have been done differently, how the community can prevent it happening again. If it hasn't happened in your Pagan community yet, this chapter is your opportunity to ask these questions *before* such an event occurs rather than afterwards.

The authors of this chapter include professional therapists and researchers. We have several goals for this chapter. We know from our work that some features of potential and actual abuse in the wider community apply equally well to the Pagan community, and we outline these here. Next, we examine some of the specific Pagan attitudes, practices, and mind-sets that make it easier or more difficult to keep each other safe. And finally, we provide practical safety measures that we would suggest for the Pagan community at large.

We are part of a small, tight-knit Wiccan coven, but we are also part of a much wider Pagan community in and around a city in the north of England. This kind of loose, open community is how most people come to Paganism, and it is the setting where many remain— in the UK, the USA, and elsewhere. Frequently, newcomers first join open, publicized meetings in public places where they can test the water (in the UK, these are often named after their location and called 'pub moots'). Invitations to open rituals or to more private meetings in people's homes may follow ('house moots'). Semi-public events like conferences, workshops and camps—sometimes free and open to all, sometimes charging a fee and more or less private—add to the range of experiences available in the wider Pagan community. We have friends and craft kin in Europe, Australasia, and the Americas who describe a similar range of settings, from an intimate *Hexencafe* in Amsterdam to the huge and bustling PantheaCon held annually in the USA.

To get us started, we invite you to consider the following scenarios, fictionalized but based on experiences we have had:

+ *A newcomer to a public moot held monthly in a café is introduced by the moot organizer. Later that evening, another member of the moot comes to sit by the newcomer, who has said they are looking for a coven to join. The established moot member tells the newcomer that their sex magick group is looking for new members, but that the initiation is a sexual one. The newcomer does not return to the next moot.*

+ *A long-established Pagan camp is "clothes optional." In the dinner queue, one attendee accidentally bumps up against the person in front of them. Apologies are exchanged. The next meal, the same thing happens. At the third meal, the person who is being bumped realizes the same person is queuing behind them yet again. They leave the queue without eating.*

◆ *At a Pagan conference, a well-known Pagan personality is in the bar the evening after their speaker session. Plucking up courage, a member of the audience from their talk approaches them. They chat, the personality buys some drinks, and then invites the audience member to carry on the party up in their hotel room. The audience member wants to say no but fears being seen as prudish (if the offer is a come-on) or paranoid (if it is not).*

◆ *A house moot on the ethics of open sexual relationships is being run in the home of a couple. After the discussion, people stay to eat and drink, then leave as the evening wears on, except for one person who remains. This last person relates how much of a turn-on they found the discussion and tells the hosts that they have been looking for people who are into swinging, dropping vague hints about how they might be attracted to one or both members of the couple. When they get no encouraging response, they eventually leave, baffled.*

These are scenarios which may have resonances for you; perhaps you have experienced something similar. They are at the milder end of seriousness, well below the threshold for any kind of criminal activity, and yet they leave a sense of unease along with a feeling that it is difficult to know how to respond (if at all) to such events. This chapter will suggest how we might make minor boundary violations (and more serious ones) less common, as well as providing a framework for what to do if they should nevertheless occur.

What We Know about Abuse in the Wider Community: Dynamics and Consequences

As Pagans, we hold the worldview that everything is connected to everything else. Accordingly, we cannot treat our community as being separate from the larger communities around us: "As above, so below". To a greater or lesser extent, we are all products of the cultural cauldron we are born into. Our primary attitudes, values, and norms are well established by an early age, and we inevitably bring these cultural templates into the communities we create and inhabit as Pagans. We don't exist in a hermetically sealed bubble, unaffected by the world outside (not even when in a magic circle), so what do we know of issues of consent and abuse from the wider world? We will begin by looking at more serious and obviously criminal cases than the examples given above.

Some of us writing this chapter have worked therapeutically with survivors of abuse. We know the experience of sexual abuse is very common in our clients, but study after study shows that it is not uncommon in the general population either. A recent large analysis[1] with a sample of nearly ten million informants worldwide shows that about 18% of adult women and 8% of adult men report having been sexually abused as children. These figures have been repeated too often, in too many independent studies, for there to be any doubt about their accuracy. The prevalence of sexual assault after childhood is somewhat less but still significant; one study reported 10% of women and 1.4% of men describing non-volitional sex.[2] The consequences of these experiences are variable. It is *not* the case that everyone who is sexually abused or raped is permanently, irreparably damaged; many people are resilient, and they can and do recover from such trauma. But experiencing such abuse does increase the risk of developing later life problems; survivors can be more likely to develop mental health

[1] Stoltenborgh et al (2011), "A Global Perspective on Child Sexual Abuse: Meta-Analysis of Prevalence around the World," *Child Maltreatment*, vol. 16 no. 2, p. 79-101.

[2] Macdowall et al (2013), "Lifetime prevalence, associated factors, and circumstances of non-volitional sex in women and men in Britain," *The Lancet*, vol. 382, issue 9907, pages 1845-1855.

difficulties, relationship problems, addictions, and eating disorders, and they are more likely to commit suicide.[3]

Research on the general population can also tell us something about the dynamics of abuse and how these situations are likely to occur. These are the conditions we need to look out for: the precursors and early warning signs of problems. Abuse is hardly ever carried out by strangers; the predator leaping out of the bushes is largely a bogeyman myth. When an adult is sexually assaulted, 73% of perpetrators are known to the victim; 38% report a friend, 28% an intimate, and 7% a relative.[4]

So far we have been discussing the prevalence and effects of abuse in wider society. What about the dynamics of abuse? One myth is that everybody who was sexually abused as a child is at risk of becoming an abuser. This statement is true only to the degree that *anyone* (survivor or not) could become an abuser. While it is the case that many adult perpetrators of abuse were abused as children, it's also the case that most survivors of abuse do *not* themselves become perpetrators.

anyone could be an abuser

One model of how perpetrators operate was developed by David Finkelhor in the 1980s and is still influential.[5] Finkelhor proposes that an abuser has to overcome four hurdles:

+ They must be motivated to abuse
+ They must overcome their own internal inhibitions (shame, knowing right from wrong, empathy for others)
+ They must overcome situational barriers (procedures or systems that protect potential victims)

---

[3] Briere and Elliott (2003), "Prevalence and psychological sequelae of self-reported childhood physical and sexual abuse in a general population sample of men and women," *Child Abuse and Neglect*, vol 27, issue 10, pages 1205-1222.

[4] U.S. Department of Justice, *National Crime Victimization Study* (2005). Available at http://www.icpsr.umich.edu/icpsrweb/ICPSR/series/00095.

[5] Finkelhor (1984), *Child Sexual Abuse: New Theory and Research* (New York: Free Press).

◆ They must overcome the individual victim's own defences
(by coercion, physical means, etc.)

In subsequent sections we will discuss how attempts to abuse
might play out in a Pagan context, and how we can use this
information to better protect our communities and everybody within
them.

But the four hypothetical situations at the head of this chapter are
much milder than the criminal abuse we have just been discussing.
Are these situations in anything like the same league? Is a serial
pesterer just one step away from being a rapist? We propose that it is
precisely because the hypothetical situations are less serious that we
need to intervene at this level. Many people reading this will have
come across these or similar situations, even if they have never come
across frank sexual abuse or rape. And it is situations like this that
occur at level 3 of Finkelhor's model, the time when society and
community might become aware of a problem and have the chance to
intervene. Almost all abuse happens in secret, private settings, when
the perpetrator can rely on not being disturbed to overcome the
victim's defences (level 4). How much better never to get to that point!

Even if the slightly uneasy, creepy, hard-to-pin-down situations
never develop into blatant abuse, we feel that the Pagan community is
ill-served by tolerating them. Love and trust are sometimes cited as
Pagan ideals, and the development of a loving and trusting relationship
with a group is compromised by boundary-testing behaviour of the
sort outlined in our examples. Does this mean a joyless, sexless,
prudish pall needs to descend over Pagan communities? Far from it!
To paraphrase Doreen Valiente, "All acts of love and pleasure are our
rituals." Abstinence, celibacy, shame, and accusation may be employed
to address abuse concerns in other communities, but we can do things
differently as Pagans.

Special Considerations for the Pagan Community

The findings of studies such as those mentioned above strongly
suggest that the sexual abuse of children and adults is fairly consistent

across all nationalities, cultures, ethnicities, religions, and subgroups within these. There are some variations, but no group is immune to sexual abuse, and there is certainly no reason to think Paganism might be that exception. There are no specific data on Pagans because Paganism remains a very small subculture, and no studies have looked at abuse in Pagan communities. But absence of evidence for sexual abuse in Paganism is not evidence of absence. On the contrary, believing that we are somehow different, special, or immune (as the Catholic Church did for many years) only breeds a situation where abuse is more likely.

Many Pagans feel isolated or disconnected from the wider non-Pagan community by their spiritual beliefs. When finding like-minded people who share at least some of these beliefs and experiences, Pagans may experience relief, joy, and a sense of belonging, often for the first time. It can then be extremely difficult, especially for newcomers, to attend to the difficulties that inevitably arise in this sought-after community. The pull to conform can be strong.

Historically, we Pagans have had to defend ourselves from the stereotypes and prejudices others hold about us: we are not devil-worshipping sorcerers stealing around in the dead of night, turning milk sour, and practicing foul rites. It has been difficult to acknowledge our own community shadow when our energy has been invested in defending ourselves from the shadow other communities have projected onto us. Thirty years ago in the UK, Pagan families and communities faced a nationwide panic about "Satanic ritual abuse."[6] In places from urban Rochdale to far-flung Orkney, children were taken into care, parents arrested, and questions asked in Parliament. Thankfully, it all came to nothing. There was no abuse, there were no baby-breeding covens, and there were no prosecutions. Instead, history has shown that in terms of groups and organizations, the Catholic Church and Local Authority run schools and Children's Homes have

---

[6] LaFontaine (1998), *Speak of the Devil: Allegations of Satanic Abuse in Britain* (Cambridge, UK: Cambridge University Press).

presented some of the greatest dangers to the physical, sexual, and emotional safety of children and young people.

In the light of such moral panics, it is understandable that Pagans have wanted to dramatically disassociate themselves from such unethical behaviour. The concept of the "'new age" "white witch" is in some ways a product of this process. Unfortunately, although the ritual abuse scare of the 1980s proved groundless, more recent cases such as those of Peter Petrauske and Jack Kemp[7] and Redvers Barnard[8] indicate that the Pagan community is not immune. Petrauske and Kemp were found guilty of a string of offences against young girls, many carried out in the context of a ritualistic magical setting. Barnard—who attended court daily with his pentacle assertively on show—was sentenced to twenty-two years in prison after being found guilty of three rapes and many more sexual assaults carried out in the context of his "white witchcraft". Some will argue that these are exceptional cases, and that by definition, people who commit such acts are not true Pagans. By casting them out and denying that they have any connection with our community, we think to keep ourselves safe from their taint.

But casting them out does not leave us untainted. These men carried out their activities for years as part of a wider circle of people described in the *Independent* article as Pagans. Untypical and exceptional they may be, but the world at large has no problem identifying them as Pagans and witches, nor in describing the abuse as happening in a coven setting. Of course, these problems are not limited to the UK; in early 2014 the well-known US musician and

---

[7] "Pair jailed over witches' coven 'ritualistic' sex abuse," *The Independent online edition*, 14 December 2012. Available at http://www.independent.co.uk/news/uk/politics/pair-jailed-over-witches-coven-ritualistic-sex-abuse-8417739.html.

[8] "'White witch' who raped and abused young girls over three decades jailed," *Manchester Evening News online edition*, 4 March 2015. Available at http://www.manchestereveningnews.co.uk/news/greater-manchester-news/white-witch-who-raped-abused-8766069.

Pagan elder Kenny Klein was arrested for possession of child pornography.[9] The case sent shock waves through the community, but as we write in summer 2015, it has not yet come to trial. Are we more likely to detect another of these cases if we believe that "no true Pagan" would do such a thing? Or are we more likely to detect it if we accept the truth: that every corner of every community is at equal risk, regardless of class, religion, gender, ethnicity, or location?

If we accept that our world is interconnected, then we must also accept that our communities exhibit many of the same patterns and dynamics that exist in the rest of the world. We have already learned how to navigate that wider world with an implicit body of knowledge and skill that lies predominantly out of our awareness. This type of social learning applies to all humans and at its best, it contributes successfully to social growth and harmony. At its worst, it perpetuates inequality, prejudice, and fear of those that are different. This leads to oppression and violence towards others.

The wider world in which our Pagan community sits is one that habitually undervalues anyone who isn't white, male, straight, or wealthy. This value system is frequently expressed as violence and abuse, with women and those from minority groups being on the receiving end. Ultimately, this has resulted in a culture where rape and abuse are tolerated or denied, and where the victims of such violence are systematically and organizationally blamed, shamed, or frequently punished. It would be unusual, therefore, if this dynamic was not also an inherent part of our Pagan communities. This reality can be extremely difficult for many Pagans to acknowledge, particularly when we hold an image of ourselves of being open-minded, accepting, and outside of mainstream cultural norms. Our love of the earth, our sense of spirituality, and our reverence for the divine embodied in all of us sits at odds with the common stereotype of abuse and abusers.

---

[9] "New Orleans man booked on 25 child pornography charges," *New Orleans Times-Picayune online edition,* 26 March 2014. Available at http://www.nola.com/crime/index.ssf/2014/03/new_orleans_man_booked_on_chil.html.

Power with

However, it's important to remember that we are talking about a scale or continuum of attitudes and norms that can foster more extreme behaviours.

The issue of power is crucial here. In general, society's pervading dynamic is one of "power over" rather than an egalitarian "power with." This orientation to "power over" can indeed be seen within our Pagan community. Think about the structured hierarchies still prevalent in many covens and working groups and the obvious pecking orders (informal, but nonetheless powerful) seen in open rituals and festivals. If we add the issues of secrecy and tight confidentiality around many of these activities, we have a potentially fertile ground in which abuse could flourish. Not every hierarchical group will necessarily experience abusive relationships, of course, but care needs to be taken to safeguard against it happening.

Paganism by its nature breeds secrecy

The absolute reality, though, is that abuse *will* happen somewhere. As we said earlier, abuse of adults and children happens in all parts of society, and the Pagan community is no exception. To this extent, then, we are no different from the wider society. Indeed, the occasional need for secrecy and pseudonyms; the informal, dispersed, and autonomous nature of Pagan practice; and the occasional vulnerability and uncritical approach of some seekers might even make our community a place where there is more need for caution. Having said this, however, there is much within Pagan culture that may also act as a protective factor. These elements can be vital sources of support for a consent-oriented culture.

Pagan groups tend to be tolerant, inclusive, permissive, and non-proselytising. Many Pagan paths emphasise a strong relationship with the natural world, and they often celebrate cycles of growth and fertility. Human sexuality is celebrated in all its forms, not hidden away shamefully or ignored as irrelevant. Our experience of Pagan communities is that they tend to be celebratory, sex-positive places where shame and guilt have less power than in the outside world, and where strong-minded assertive individuals flourish even if (and often because) they in some way swim against the mainstream. While we have no published data to back up these assertions, they are some of the reasons we sought out a Pagan path in the first place, and having found what we were looking for, they are reasons that we stay. Some paths emphasise a strong (even primary) role for women and the divine feminine, and some groups have minimum age requirements for potential members. These are not the features of a cult-like system where secrecy, charismatic leaders, and arbitrary rules go unchallenged. Most people who have tried to organize a Pagan event will confirm that trying to force groups of Pagans to behave in a particular way is doomed to failure!

Many Pagan groups value personal growth and development, the idea of personal responsibility, and the concept of rising to challenges from within and without. Wicca has its system of eight paired virtues (honour and humility, power and compassion, strength and beauty, mirth and reverence). Druidry has its nine virtues (wisdom, piety, vision, courage, integrity, perseverance, hospitality, moderation, and fertility). Asatruar have their own nine virtues, including honour and discipline alongside hospitality and self-reliance. These may give us some clues as to how we might continue to be free, playful, and passionate while also being respectful, moderate, and disciplined. These virtues are not polar opposites; rather, each is necessary for the other. Joy without boundaries is uncontained, neglectful, and selfish. Boundaries without joy are sterile, lifeless, and imprisoning. Boundaries *with* joy comprise the twin pillars of severity and mercy within the Kabbalistic tree of life, joining humanity with the divine.

What Can Be Done? Guidelines and Suggestions for Action

We do not intend to duplicate Cat Chapin-Bishop's chapter in this book, but we invite you to review its recommendations, as they form an excellent foundation for action. Using these as a start, and our Pagan virtues as a reference point, how could Pagan communities, festivals, moots, and conferences help to raise the barriers at all four levels of Finkelhor's model?

1. Reducing motivation to abuse

This is the hardest level on which to intervene. Intervention at the level of society is the only approach here, including doing research into the causes and precursors of a tendency to abuse. But where there is an actual abuser, there must be treatment provided so that they have the opportunity to address the causes and change their levels of motivation. Our job as Pagans and as citizens in wider society is to vote for governments who are willing to fund this kind of work, rather than simply locking people away for a time, then releasing them unchanged.

2. Reinforcing internal inhibitions (shame, knowing right from wrong, empathy for others)

Let's make this easier by asking not "How we can we help a potential rapist to shore up their inhibitions?", but rather "How can we all develop a state of mind that makes us more likely to take others' consent very seriously?" This approach takes the responsibility away from any potential victim (and isn't that the right way to go, rather than expecting potential targets of unpleasantness to do all the work?).

Uncomfortable though it is to say, reinforcing inhibitions requires Pagan men in particular to step up. We must acknowledge that centuries of privilege, alongside our on-average greater physical strength, size, and weight, have put us in a position of power. We may not want that, we may try to reject it, but we can't change it any more than we can change the colour of our skin. We need to develop the virtues of humility, compassion, moderation, and discipline, and we need to ask our brothers and sisters to challenge us when we fall short. When we are challenged, we need to drop our defences, painful though this is, and look within to see what we could have done differently. Becoming aware of our own power and privilege is something all of us can do differently. If you are male, or white, or middle-class, or a longstanding member of your community, you have power and privilege which you could (even unwittingly) wield

[handwritten margin note: we have the obligation to be careful]

carelessly. If you are many or all of those things, count your blessings and be even more careful.

A second thing we can all do (in positions of power and privilege or not) is to take consent much more seriously. As well as strengthening our inhibitions against negative actions, let's also increase our willingness to take positive ones. Principally, let us be braver about consent. If as Pagans we are assertive, unconventional, willing to take personal responsibility for our actions, passionate, and at home in our bodies, why not be brave, explicit and open in asking others about whether they want what we want, too? There are many easily available sources of information about affirmative consent—any Google search will uncover them. Most suggest that valid consent should be ongoing, explicit, informed, enthusiastic, active (not passive), and mutual. Much has been made by some who profess to be confused about what this means, but it should be simple, as demonstrated in a wonderful and popular post by blogger rockstar·dinosaur·pirate· princess.[10] She uses the metaphor of asking if someone wants tea:

[handwritten margin notes: Ongoing, explicit, informed, enthusiastic, active, mutual]

> You say "hey, would you like a cup of tea?" and they go "omg fuck yes, I would fucking LOVE a cup of tea! Thank you!" then you know they want a cup of tea.
>
> If they say "No thank you" then don't make them tea. At all. Don't make them tea, don't make them drink tea, don't get annoyed at them for not wanting tea. They just don't want tea, ok?
>
> If they are unconscious, don't make them tea. Unconscious people don't want tea and can't answer the question "do you want tea" because they are unconscious.

Our third and fourth tricky hypothetical situations at the start of the chapter become much easier. The onus is on the person wanting intimacy (of any sort) to ask for it, clearly and unambiguously. If we

---

[10] "Consent: Not Actually that Complicated," *Rockstar Dinosaur Pirate Princess* 2 March 2015. Available at http://rockstardinosaurpirateprincess. com/2015/03/02/consent-not-actually-that-complicated/.

[handwritten margin note: read]

can get to a situation where it's okay to ask, and it's okay to say no (or yes, as appropriate!) without shame or fear on either part, then how much easier will things be? If there is no request for intimacy, then intimacy is not on the agenda, and we can party on right at the level we are. If there is a request, and the person being asked feels equally okay about responding with a "yes" or a "no," then everyone is empowered and safe and knows where they stand.

More than that, as another blogger points out, the process of seeking consent is not some sterile negotiation like haggling over a financial deal. As long ago as 2010, the online community Feministing posted a blog called "On the Critical Hotness of Enthusiastic Consent,"[11] making the point that the process can itself be sexy, arousing, and the complete opposite of the tedious way it is often portrayed.

"I'd really like to make love to you."
"Gods, I've been thinking the same thing—my tent, now!"
What's not to like?

3. Strengthening situational barriers (procedures or systems that protect potential victims)

This is the area most ripe for action, because it is where communities, groups, covens, organizing committees, and so on can have influence. We make the following suggestions—by no means exhaustive, and we hope that these may spark ideas for readers in positions of community influence.

Newcomers to Paganism often make use of public moots as an entry point. If you run such a moot, consider explicitly stating in your public information that newcomers will be ~~welcomed but not~~ imposed

---

[11] Erin, "On the Critical Hotness of Enthusiastic Consent," 2011. Available at http://feministing.com/2010/10/27/on-the-critical-hotness-of-enthusiastic-consent/.

upon. Give the name of an organiser who can introduce newcomers and to whom they can turn for advice and support.

Moots are often advertised on public websites, Facebook, Witchvox, in magazines, etc. If you edit such a site or publication, state that newcomers should be given the name and contact details of an organizer. Consider making it a condition of advertising that moots undertake to keep newcomers safe and introduce them carefully to the Pagan community.

When advertising rituals open to the public or semi-open to the wider Pagan community, be explicit about the scope. Because people will have heard of skyclad working, make it clear that everyone will be clothed! When running a camp or conference, make explicit rules about topics such as nudity, consent, drugs and alcohol, violent or threatening behaviour, and so on. Issue these in written form to everyone, and make it a condition of attendance that they agree to abide by them. Identify named ombudsmen to whom people can go if they are concerned. There should be an attitude of zero tolerance towards physical and sexual violence, with organisers reserving the right to exclude anyone from the camp if expectations are not met. This possibility should also be stated on the event information.

All event staff (paid or voluntary) who are responsible for children and young people under the age of consent should be criminal records-checked.

If an event, or a sub-event within a larger setting, is going to have different rules and expectations than is the general practice, this should be made explicit. There is nothing wrong with a space dedicated to intimate touch, or free love, or multiple partners, or BDSM, where those who enter can be assumed to be okay with witnessing or being approached to participate in those activities. The rules of negotiation and consent still apply to everyone in the space, however; entering the space does not constitute consent to touch.

At a clothes-optional event, being naked does not imply consent to being hit upon. Attending the naked disco does not mean agreeing to sex (or even dancing) with anyone else who attends. Make this clear, organisers.

[handwritten: take time out]

If someone is pushing boundaries, organisers should intervene. This does not mean acting as judge and jury, but it might involve asking someone to take a time out. Having a clear mechanism for this process will mean organisers need not worry about others taking the law into their own hands.

4. Reinforcing the individual victim's own defences (to coercion, physical means, etc.)

If the rest of the Pagan community does nothing at levels 1-3, the potential victim ends up being entirely responsible for defending themselves. The more active the community has been at earlier levels, the less likely it is that action at this level will be needed.

Organisers of moots, conferences, gathers and groups: make it easier for people to say "no" by insisting in advance, in your literature for your event, that a "no" must always be respected.

[handwritten in left margin: Amanda, make an emergency list of numbers]

In advance, identify trained volunteers with a mental health, rape crisis, or similar background who can intervene to support a victim. Call on these people for help immediately if someone has been hurt or abused.

At formally organized events, understand the system of mandatory reporting so that as organizers, you know when events have gone beyond your capacity to intervene and you must inform the police or Child Protection Services.

Some might dismiss these cautions and restraints as "health and safety gone mad". However, those of us who have experienced abuse or assault know only too well the pain, distress, and potentially life-long difficulties these experiences can create. It is time to demonstrate that openness, consent, and dialogue can simultaneously increase both our freedom and our safety. The stronger the boundaries, the safer the space within them; we know this from when we create sacred space. If we really can support our community in challenging and changing the cultural norms we have inevitably brought with us from the world outside, then not only does this give us a place of safety and growth, but it also supports us in becoming agents of change in the wider world. As below, so above! *So mote it be*

Kim Dent-Brown is a Senior Lecturer in Psychology at a university in the north of England and is a practitioner of Cognitive Analytic Therapy. He worked for twenty-five years in mental health in the UK's National Health Service, often with adult survivors of child sexual abuse.

Tracey Dent-Brown is a Gestalt Psychotherapist specializing in the area of trauma and abuse who practices in both private and National Health Service settings. She also teaches and supervises other counsellors and psychotherapists.

Kim and Tracey are both members of a Gardnerian Wiccan coven with whom they have co-written this chapter. **The Triple Horse Coven** was founded in 1996 in East Yorkshire as a training group. The coven now consists mainly of experienced 2nd and 3rd degree Priests and Priestesses dedicated to creating a safe space within which to explore the boundaries of magical working and experience. This chapter is based on that exploration.

The Rite and Right of Refusal
Sexual Assault Prevention and Response in Communities and at Festivals
Diana Rajchel

The Art of No

Consent culture begins with no. This is not the "no means yes" that created daily nightmares for women in the past. It also extends far beyond the chant "No Means No."

This "no" is the art of no, the skill, the execution, the essence. It happens during that act of clear communication preceding either foreplay or amicable departure. "No" is the double-edged core skill of all good sex. In saying no, people learn to communicate their honest needs. By learning to accept no, people learn how to define boundaries between themselves.

"No" applies to far more than just sex. Culture permeates our environments like oxygen, and the atmosphere around body sovereignty has become toxic. Somehow, the body, that sacred space that defines our boundary between the self and the outer world, has become a subject for public comment. Given the entitled attitudes people show when commenting on bodies—too thin, too fat, why that outfit?—it's unsurprising that physical and sexual assaults happen so often: 1 in 5 women and 1 in 71 men experience rape in their lifetimes.[1]

Consent culture consciously infuses the cultural environment with the skill of sending and receiving "no," and from there it changes the environment to one of safety and acceptance.

While the world of the sex-positive focuses on saying "yes" to honest desires, "yes" to self-knowledge, and "yes" to celebration of the

---

[1] Centers of Disease Control and Prevention, "National Intimate Partner and Sexual Violence Survey: Summary Report" (Atlanta, GA: National Center for Injury Prevention and Control, 2010): 124.

kinky, weird, and transgressive, it does not always celebrate the right of refusal. Perhaps it's the naïve assumption that all decent people understand that they should check before they do something with another person's body. Perhaps it's because consent is, most of the time, a well-packaged art form among the kinky. It's not just an in-bed conversation as you go; it involves questionnaires, check-lists, and even referral letters and background checks from current and prior partners.

Paganism, as a group of religions that honor, elevate, and celebrate sex as nature acting within us, usually welcomes kinky folk. However, the vanilla still outnumber the kinky even among Pagans. For most people, it's a crapshoot of religious history, personal history, and location of birth as to what (if any) realistic education about sex and relationships happened.

Sacred sexuality looks so very much at the freedom to say "yes" that the enthusiasm of discussion at times obscures "no" However, like yin and yang, God and Goddess, light and dark, the ability to consent and deny, the sovereignty of the body is necessary for us to have and maintain full spiritual balance.

One thing recent history has taught us: even Pagans sometimes forget to teach their daughters and sons the importance of "no," and some still fail to listen when those children try to use this important tool. Until the right of no—the *rite* of no—is fully integrated into our cultural practices, our quest for spiritual, sexual, and emotional freedom remains incomplete.

Boundaries and Their Violation

In consent-culture relationships, boundaries are explicitly-stated limits concerning touch, talk, and time. Some Pagans might associate these social rules with what they call the laws of hospitality.[2] According to those laws, when one person remains as a guest in

---

[2] Fenian Niafter, "The Tradition of Hospitality," *Ancient Worlds* August 26, 2005. Available at http://www.ancientworlds.net/aw/Article/617978.

244 CHRISTINE HOFF KRAEMER AND YVONNE ABURROW

another's home, he/she does so with the implicit expectation that neither host nor guest will come to harm during that time. This means that both parties can dwell under the same roof without fear of rape, murder, theft, or cruelty.[3] The same concept applies to the human body. The body houses a soul, and when that soul engages with other souls, that being should receive hospitable treatment. When one person interacts with another, especially in an intimate way, they must treat that person's body as an honored guest.

Scene negotiation, a practice of BDSM culture, might also benefit those of more mainstream tastes.[4] Scene negotiation is a conversation where the involved parties talk about what they enjoy and don't enjoy. No sexual activity occurs until after this discussion; nothing is left to guessing. Rather than "destroying the mystery," as some outside the culture may argue, this conversation elevates the experience of sex. Having pre-defined boundaries lets both parties relax into their chosen roles, freeing them both for a fuller, more intense experience. Unfortunately, as recent headlines point out, there are still members of the BDSM community who sometimes violate this trust by taking on acts not previously agreed.[5] When something happens without specific prior consent (and consent may be obtained in the moment with enough trust), in consent culture, it is a form of assault.

Many still see honest sexual talk as shocking, if not necessarily taboo. The conversations are all the more difficult because we may unwittingly uphold mainstream culture's most destructive values by misconstruing them as virtues. For example, the overculture often promotes violation of boundaries as a virtue. This thinking weaves

---

[3] John Beckett, "The Limits of Hospitality," *Under the Ancient Oaks* July 20, 2014. Available from Patheos.com at http://www.patheos.com/blogs/johnbeckett/2014/07/the-limits-of-hospitality.html.

[4] lunaKM, "The Basics of Negotiating a Scene," *Submissive Guide* August 26, 2009. Available at http://www.submissiveguide.com/2009/08/basics-negotiating-scene/.

[5] Tracy Clark-Flory, "When Safewords Are Ignored," *Salon* January 28, 2012. Available at http://www.salon.com/2012/01/29/real_abuse_in_ bdsm/.

into figures of speech, in the way we reward workplace competition, and in what we perceive as romantic ideals. Many culturally posed examples of "go getters" are actually examples of rape culture.

Some common phrases illustrate how we as a culture reward boundary violation:

- *"Don't take no for an answer."* This comes up in many situations as a motivating phrase about personal or professional success. In capitalist culture, sales people get all sorts of training on overcoming objections. The reward is immediate: they get money and status by manipulating people away from "no." In fictional accounts, the character often succeeds even in situations where "no" has the stronger case. Repeatedly, the male "loser" (presented as poor, unattractive, or in some other arbitrary way undesirable) gets the girl through persistence that crosses the line into stalking.

- *"It's better to seek forgiveness than permission."* This rationalization denies the right of refusal. The adage twists the autonomy it intends to promote by encouraging the theft of others' autonomy. Perhaps this thinking is how people excuse exploitation of the unconscious.

- *"I have a right to because I'm your husband/mother/doctor..."* Here, a person claims vested authority that trumps the desires of another fully functioning adult. In consent culture, people operate from agreements and boundaries. No one has this kind of authority over another human being.

- *"Do what you can get away with!"* Several years ago, a student paper published a cartoon showing a sexual "move" where a woman on all fours is having sex with one man, and he sneaks out so another man can slip in.[6] Being subjected to sex with a person other than

---

[6] Anna North, "Purdue Student Paper Runs Instructive Rape Cartoon," *Jezebel* September 20, 2010. Available at http://jezebel.com/5642689/purdue-paper-runs-instructive-rape-cartoon.

the one you gave consent to is *absolutely* rape—even if it's not overtly violent. Yet mainstream news outlets labeled this cartoon as controversial rather than as offensive. Since those who joke about violent and violating behaviors are, statistically, far more likely to engage in them, the easy dismissal of the cartoon in the media distressed many people.[7] Often, when someone highlights the violating nature of the above thought-patterns, predictable pushback happens.

+ *"It's just words. What about free speech?"* Violence, especially cyclical violence, begins with words.[8] An abusive person requires his or her target to be off-balance. Think of words as the shortest route to producing the high that an aggressor gets from bullying. An example of this happens in the pick-up artist scene, a subculture of (usually) men that deliberately target women with low self-esteem as sexual targets.[9] Along with using Neuro-Linguistic Programming (one style of conversational hypnosis) as a means of manipulating consent, these "artists" also "neg" the person objectified—usually in the form of a back-handed compliment intended to make that person strive for the objectifier's approval.[10] While the articulation of political differences may offend in a superficial way, most do not make other people feel immediately

[7] G. Tendayi Viki, Manuela Thomae, Amy Cullen, and Hannah Fernandez, "The effect of sexist humor and type of rape on men's self-reported rape proclivity and victim blame," *Current Research in Social Psychology* 13, no. 10 (2007): 122-132.

[8] Teresa Chandler Sabourin, "The role of negative reciprocity in spouse abuse: A relational control analysis," *Journal of Applied Communication Research* 23:4 (1995): 271-283.

[9] Tom Chivers, "Pick-up Artists, Online Seduction and Dating Tips," *The Telegraph* January 14, 2010. Available at http://www.telegraph.co.uk/women/sex/6987982/Pick-up-artists-online-seduction-and-dating-tips.html.

[10] Ibid.

threatened or unsafe. When someone approaches a person with uninvited comments about that person's body, personal choices, or personal potential, those words constitute violence. Abusive people choose violent words to manipulate a person into tolerating the escalation to physical violence. Those who are skilled in verbal abuse can change the structure of a person's brain in the process.[11]

+ *"But it's not violent touching..."* Violence begins with violation, not with bruises. While situational context can change the standards for uninvited touch—people in long-term relationships tend to develop their own language for touching, consent, no, and stop—in most situations, anything beyond a tap on the shoulder to get someone's attention (or tackling them to get them out of the way of oncoming traffic) is an overstep. This includes handshakes, hugs, kisses, massages, and any other physical contact. You need not do away with these gestures, but creating a habit of asking verbally first enhances everyone's sense of safety.

Despite much subcultural mythology to the contrary, Pagans are not universally forward-thinking about gender equality. While some of this is generational—equal to one generation is unequal in the next—most inequality comes back to the day-to-day poison of mainstream thinking about sex and gender. The priestess may have authority in the circle, but outside of it, she's as likely to experience undermining criticism as any other member of the overculture perceived as female. These challenges to her authority often appear in quibbling, social violence, and petty politics. All of this sociopolitical chicanery comes back to boundary issues—and the failure to respect every man, woman, or other's right of refusal.

---

[11] "Living with a Psychopath: When the Mask Slips." *Masks of Sanity.* Available at http://masksofsanity.blogspot.com/.

Practices for Establishing and Checking Boundaries

Every person must establish boundaries in every relationship. This process requires communication and may require learning new ways to communicate. Boundary-setting is necessary in many aspects of forming a relationship, not just during sexual negotiation.

The First Impression

Boundary-setting in a sex-positive environment begins at the first moment two or more people interact. It does not matter what the setting is—in a dungeon, online, at a flower show, at a ritual—the rules of first meeting remain the same: keep your hands to yourself. Do not touch another person without direct consent. If you wish to touch, ask first. "May I shake your hand?" "Are you a hugger?" This is difficult for some, especially those to whom handshakes are automatic, almost informal. Yet even this casual gesture causes people with illnesses or trauma issues trouble on a regular basis. It is much easier to give the person space to refuse, and to honor that refusal.

The Platonic/Casually Social

Even in established platonic relationships, boundary-setting and resetting happens as emotional intimacy waxes and wanes. For example, someone leading a ritual may wish to touch people—for anointing, for blessing, or on impulse. The same rules that apply to instructors teaching group classes at a gym should apply to public rituals: *always ask first, and explain the purpose of the requested touch.* If a ritual relies on any physical contact, no matter how casual, participants should be informed before the ceremony begins that touching of any kind can happen. People may not want to join hands or sip from the same cup if they are ill, may prefer to avoid anointing or sharing food because of allergies or, especially in situations where they are new to the group, they may need to establish some trust before they can accept casual touching.

The Erotic

Now that you have to keep your hands to yourself, how do you get to the sex without traditional flirting skills? The easy way is to ask, *after establishing an appreciation for the human being inside the body that attracts you.* A sex-positive proposition also means accepting "no" as an act of freedom that deserves celebration. The truly sex-positive enjoy sexuality and attraction without feeling entitled to the sexuality of others.

How to Ask

There are specific ways to ask for sex, a date, or romantic contact. The simplest—and still the most terrifying—is just to say so. "I enjoy your company and would like to be sexual with you. Do you have any interest?" Such an invitation should not include excessive detail. If the person refuses, friendly interaction can continue free from any sense of violation.

If the person is interested in such interaction, then an open, honest, sober discussion about details and activities can occur. Making sure you both agree on the specific interactions will not only ensure that you both want to share the same experience, the establishment of consent makes terrific foreplay. First, it frees people to talk to each other about what they enjoy. Second, it gives each person a chance to tell a prospective lover about sensitivities and preferences, information that can enhance the encounter.

Building Trust/Rebuilding Trust

Most people do not set out to bully or prey upon other people. They operate on assumptions and fail to rethink those assumptions on a regular basis. Most boundary violations stem from simple cluelessness, often rooted in generational cultural shifts. In previous decades, the new availability of birth control forced people to rethink the roles and capacity of cisgender women. These changes in sexual freedom have also brought about changes in what kinds of touch are acceptable. In the early twentieth century, touching still involved significant taboos and often came with a proscribed choreography. People from the '60s and '70s, however, came from a generation where touching and hugging were upheld as world-changing virtues— sometimes even to the extent of forcing hugs or other affection. Today, many people do not have clear guidelines about touching or not-touching, leading to uncertainty and confusion. Additionally, Pagan and other groups may include people who have trouble with empathy for non-predatory reasons, such as Asperger's syndrome or past traumas. This makes touch and connection complicated, and that difficulty grows as any group grows larger.

These challenges all come together at Pagan festivals. Some place expectations upon newcomers without prior discussion. In an attempt to be welcoming, people may hug, touch, or behave in an overly intimate manner, sharing stories about sex or personal lives that strangers may feel uncomfortable hearing. Those new to a Pagan environment—or any environment—need a reason to trust the people they meet. Clear expectations, explaining what will happen in a ritual or activity beforehand, checking with people about touch first, and fulfilling pre-established expectations build that trust.

In the absence of centralized authority, Pagans of past generations relied on a vouch system and welcomed new friends wholeheartedly based on a friend's word alone. However, this system allows too-easy manipulation by predators, especially as the community has grown from small groups into festivals and conventions. Pagans need to change our up-front behaviors when welcoming in new people by practicing clear communication, and we need to train ourselves in contingency plans when someone enters our midst and violates the atmosphere of trust.

Reissuing consent and rebuilding trust requires that all parties acknowledge a breach of trust. Only after acknowledgment can real progress happen. In the case of romantic relationships, all the people involved might need to visit a therapist. In the case of social neglect— say, ignoring a victim that reported a problem—the individuals within the organizational bodies must acknowledge and discuss what happened, then choose methods for changing that group environment to make it welcoming and safe for those invited. For instance, if an assault occurs during a festival, and it comes out that organizers dismissed the concerns of the victim or witnesses, the festival needs to take steps to re-establish trustworthiness. Assaults in these environments happen because the unconsciously created social context gives them room. Creating a safe, consent-culture gathering requires an awakening process. If this process has not already begun when an assault happens, the result is a harsh wake-up call.

Predators

A small percentage of the population seeks domination at any cost, making the establishment of trust and consent all the more difficult. Often these predators find ways to exploit our social norms and deeply-held convictions for their own benefit. Americans especially tend towards low-context behavior: that is, behavior that does not require initiation into complex codified meanings to understand. There are fewer rules, etiquette, and rituals to use in daily behavior than there might be in high context cultures. Low context cultures tend to preserve privacy less while high context cultures preserve it more. In the case of Americans, many take pride in obvious displays of who they are and what they expect of others. Yet most carry within them a cognitive dissonance when it comes to sexuality: hundreds of years of religious and social taboos surrounding reproduction, pleasure, and gender make us especially vulnerable to exploitative behaviors.

In this dissonance, predators hunt.

Predators in the Pagan community operate like predators in any other community: they appear to be one of the people they target. If not in a leadership role, a predator may still appear as vocal, active, and committed. Since Pagans often provide hunting grounds in the form of unregulated festivals and conventions, it is easy for those looking for people to exploit to manipulate Pagan social norms. Letting children run free at such events may seem like a celebration of trust and freedom, yet it also leaves them vulnerable. Engaging in fertility rites with physical acts of love is wonderful—but semi-public rushes of ritual energy can create situations where it appears acceptable to pressure others for sex.

Predatory individuals tend to think in terms of "hunts" and "games." A typical predator begins with two methods: either that of belittling, like the aforementioned pick-up artist methods; or with seduction and flattery, first of the group, then of a specific target within the group.[13] Often charming, this person actually may seem anything but socially awkward. Many have a degree of charisma or at least a patter, a self-story that is grandiose and heroic. It is only as time progresses and people challenge their story that their character may emerge bit by bit. One of the weaknesses of the Pagan community that such a predator may exploit is a collective tolerance for social awkwardness. Because so many people within Paganism have disabilities or life experiences that make social situations challenging, when a predator does something unacceptable, the behavior may be excused as awkwardness or blamed on a generational concern, such as the feelings that the changing roles of men and women produce.

After a scandal, people hunt high and low for predators while wondering where they went wrong. Ultimately, only time and careful observation can reveal predators. Most function in cyclic stages:

- Seduction
- Manipulation
- Verbal assault/Emotional assault
- Manipulation/seduction
- Escalation to physical assault, including sexual assault[14]

After the initial seduction, a predator becomes a drama-seeker. The need for constant stimulation means that any peaceful moment gets disrupted. Tantrums occur, petty differences constantly raised, and the predator spreads chaos, often in a way that people might not immediately think to trace that behavior back to him/her. The

---

[13] *Masks of Sanity.*
[14] Ibid.

following are some common techniques used by such predators. Please take note: many people who have psychological wounds may also participate in a few of these behaviors, especially during periods of stress. Spotting a predatory person means looking at consistent use of all or close to all of those listed below.

+ *Gaslighting*: Convincing the target of the truth of something patently untrue. "It's your fault this happened..." "I never said that..." "Why am I always the one that gets picked on?" This leaves the target mistrusting his/her own judgment and perceptions.

+ *Projection*: Accusing the target of the actions and intentions of the perpetrator. "I can never express my opinion without you attacking me!"

+ *Passive Aggression*: The use of sarcasm and sullen behavior to communicate hostile feelings without actually expressing these thoughts. This encourages the target to cater to the predator's mood.

+ *Self-Victimization*: Predators often make themselves out to be victims. This may take the form of bringing up past trauma, verifiable or not. They may also borrow from the projection technique where they make themselves out as the wounded party when called out on bullying behavior.

+ *Blaming others*: From the predator's worldview, nothing is ever his/her fault. Mistakes are attributed to other people or on circumstances. Favorite scapegoats emerge over time, usually someone who recognizes the predatory behavior and attempts to call it out.

+ *Self-pity*: To the untrained ear, self-pity may sound like remorse. Ultimately, however, a predator talks about all the difficulties of his/her life without acknowledging their agency in making choices.

+ *Withholding*: A predator may try to control groups or individuals by withholding information. The information could be personal, financial, or civic. This tactic works especially well on Pagans because of misunderstandings about traditions and traditional secrecy.

+ *Secrecy/Triangulation*: "Don't tell so-and-so I said this..." often starts a chain reaction of strategic negativity. This method stirs mistrust and infighting within a group, leaving the predator free to hunt.

The techniques of predators are recognizable once you understand the behavior. Unfortunately, confronting the predator does next to nothing, especially if the person doing the confronting is already a victim. Predatory personalities, even in the process of admitting wrongdoing, cycle blame back onto every person around them using denial and projection. They typically do whatever they can to protect their behavior, and will not own up to anything that requires a change of behavior. Even if that person ends up in prison, gets caught on camera incontrovertibly engaging in the questionable activity, or gets called out in public, s/he will neither change nor own his/her behavior. A person with psychic wounds, however, when confronted will respond with genuine consideration of his or her actions. While knee jerk denial may happen, introspection does follow very soon after. Because of this difference, and because the truth takes a small amount of time to come out, it is important to allow time after confrontation to observe the person's reactions and processing.

Predators can be quite effective at resisting accountability. Some of this we can attribute to the predator's successful manipulation, but a significant influence also comes from conventional thought. We routinely accept predatory concepts embedded in overculture, such as "Don't take no for an answer" and others mentioned above. To try to prevent predatory behavior, the only effective option available is to educate ourselves. We desperately need to call out and rethink those aspects of our culture.

Prevention is always easier than cure. Changing the culture of festival and group environments, and establishing rules that ensure all people (including children) are heard and fairly considered, does far more to create a safe environment than does simply getting rid of the person engaging in questionable behavior and resuming business as usual. The organizers/safety keepers of a group may present a document describing required conduct to someone who is engaging in predatory behaviors—and the reaction to that required conduct will likely reveal where that person lies on the spectrum between wounded and abnormal. Given that a true predator refuses to change behavior—and has a high likelihood of recidivism, simply going on to the next place to engage in harmful actions—all too often removal/banning from the festival grounds and community is the only safe option. If it seems unclear whether the person is truly devoid of genuine empathy, however, a group may present the option of readmission after a course of therapy, working with a 12-step program, or something similar. Often an actual predator will begin the steps of therapy, but then at some point refuse to complete that work. A person with legitimate wounds will find the self-confrontation helpful and is likely to complete the work.

When an Assault Occurs

Most festivals do not have a plan for when someone reports a sexual assault. Worse, some organizers quickly resort to self-protection, shoving assault reports aside with statements that "the proper authorities were contacted." Since rape kits often go untested and allegations of rape can be hard to prove even with witnesses, it's important for a group to take additional steps. A good organization should have a set procedure for investigating what happened and a procedure for curative action based upon those determinations.

When alleged victims come forward, it is important to ask intelligent questions, act in a manner that honors the victim, and neither validate nor dismiss anyone's assertions. Making sure the victim feels safe and does not suffer more than he/she must in order to testify, and protecting the victim from excess public comment and criticism, all uphold that person's dignity. Any procedure adopted by an organization needs a review annually to ensure it remains relevant based on social concerns of the time. All these practices help ensure that victims are heard and that the organization is prepared to uphold justice within a community.

When investigating assaults, organizations should have a set procedure and set questions to ask. Pagan organizers are not law enforcement agencies, but they do have responsibility within the communities they establish.

One such procedure might be:

+ Ask the questions stated below and provide the victim with a contact for a rape crisis center.

+ Be sure you update your understanding of rape and consent. Submitting to an unwelcome interaction because of fear or social pressure is not consent. A claim that the victim is promiscuous is not consent. Being drunk is not consent. Unconsciousness is not consent.

+ If the person is in a relationship with the person accused, treat it with the same concern given to someone assaulted by a stranger. Most rapes happen between people that know each other, and this can occur even in long-term relationships.

+ Establish a policy to deal with accused predators. This involves asking that person to avoid the alleged victim, observing the potential predator's general behaviors, and possibly asking the person to leave. Often predators will flatter decision-makers but also viciously attack anyone seemingly immune to his/her overtures.

Here are sample questions to establish what happened and to determine what to do. These apply regardless of a person's gender, sexual orientation, or other expressed identity, including socio-economic status.

- When?
- Do you want to go to the police?
- Are you going to go to the police?
- Are you safe?
- Are you able to get somewhere safe?
- Can you say who?
- If you were unconscious, might you have been drugged? Will you consider being tested for opiates?
- What do you need to see done?

Take the victim at his/her word—and if they are in a place to do so, take this person to the police and ask for a rape kit if appropriate. While the kit may well go untested, getting that evidence as soon as possible may help depending on the circumstances of the crime.

Sexual assault is not limited to penetration, although often that is the only legal concern to the police. Any act of non-consensual touching with sexual intent is a form of sexual assault, just as non-consensual touching without sexual intent may qualify as assault. If this situation arises, seek potential witnesses, but do not rely solely on their testimony. Predators are clever manipulators and may have found ways to induce cooperation in victims and witnesses.

Let's be clear about why this issue is so very, very important: *rape hurts people*. Even rape that happens to the unconscious hurts victims—almost all realize something violent happened afterwards. The trauma of rape goes much deeper than hurt and uncomfortable feelings. Trauma steals a person's sense of autonomy and safety. The damage to a person's body from rape can be life-long.[15] The damaged ability to trust can also affect that person's ability to have healthy

---

[15] Susan M. Frayne, Katherine M. Skinner, Lisa M. Sullivan, Tara J. Tripp, Cheryl S. Hankin, Nancy R. Kressin, and Donald R. Miller, "Medical profile of women Veterans Administration outpatients who report a history of sexual assault occurring while in the military," *Journal of Women's Health and Gender-based Medicine* 8:6 (1999): 835-845.

relationships forever.[16] Such trauma undermines and can even destroy communities.

When an assault occurs at a festival or event, it's important to put assessing harm to individuals ahead of the organization's reputation. No organization is ever more important than personal sanctity. Without that physical sanctity and safety, the event does not merit the trust required to continue. In fact, unless the organizers act rightly to restore trust by addressing the assault, the harm done to the community by the trauma of an assault may make it impossible to continue the event.

No procedure can screen out every potential predator. However, making Pagan events (or other public gatherings) difficult places for predators to manipulate others will help. Establishing policies based on consent-culture principles can help all attendees know that they have a right to safety within that space, and that they can reasonably expect the support of the community should something violate that safety.

Establishing a true, sex-positive environment begins with "no." We must teach people how to say "no" —and how to accept it. This practice will allow community and interpersonal trust to grow. Those who attend festivals can introduce their consent-culture practices, teach workshops, or initiate conversations about the best methods of expressing consent culture. Those involved in organizing festivals and conventions can begin the arduous work of establishing safety measures.

Changing culture isn't easy. The creation of a genuine, sex-positive consent culture has many stumbling blocks set before it. Still, a safe environment that produces better social and sexual interactions for everyone is a vision well worth the work.

---

[16] Patricia A. Resick, "The psychological impact of rape," *Journal of Interpersonal Violence* 8:2 (1993): 223-255.

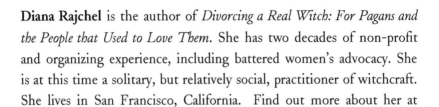

Diana Rajchel is the author of *Divorcing a Real Witch: For Pagans and the People that Used to Love Them*. She has two decades of non-profit and organizing experience, including battered women's advocacy. She is at this time a solitary, but relatively social, practitioner of witchcraft. She lives in San Francisco, California. Find out more about her at dianarajchel.com.

Sex-Positive, Not Sex-Pressuring
Consent, Boundaries, and Ethics in Pagan Communities

Shauna Aura Knight When I first discovered that I was Pagan and started attending public events, I heard Pagans say, "Pagans believe in harm none," "Pagans are very accepting of GLBTQ people," "Pagans welcome poly and kinky people," and "Paganism is very empowering for women." However, when I began traveling and teaching leadership skills to Pagans, I heard a much darker story. Almost every time I teach a leadership workshop, I hear about a local coven leader who sexually harasses people, pressures adult students for sex, or sexually abuses minors.

Unfortunately, the most common response in Pagan groups—as it is in many mainstream organizations—is to engage in victim blaming: whistleblowers are dismissed as troublemakers trying to "stir the cauldron." This reaction doesn't address the problem, or even acknowledge it. For me, the goal is to build—and live in—a healthier Pagan community. For clarity, when I say "Pagan community" I'm referring to the overlapping communities that fall under the umbrella of the Pagan subculture.

I've heard wisdom from friends engaged in the Twelve Step process: It's impossible to address a problem until you admit the problem is there. And another piece of wisdom from the field of strategic design: You can't solve the problem until you know what problem to solve, and the solution to the problem is often held within the accurate definition of the problem itself.

What's the Problem?

Many Pagans identify as sex-positive, yet we are still raised with the same sexual hang-ups as the dominant culture. Thus, we have many cultural shadows to contend with. In an attempt to rebel against the dominant culture, many mistake acting in an over-sexualized way for being sex-positive, unaware that their behavior may make others feel pressured sexually.

This problematic behavior is exacerbated by the general lack of respect for boundaries present in both the dominant culture and at Pagan gatherings. At Pagan events, you can see a baseline of poor boundaries in action when people hug or touch others without their permission. Further, when someone does assert their boundaries, they are often told they are being a prude or a spoilsport. Such an environment makes Pagan communities particularly vulnerable to predators who take advantage when groups disrespect individuals' boundaries.

Unfortunately, most Pagan groups lack methods to deal with predators, particularly when they are in leadership roles. Another challenge is the long history within the broader Pagan community of conflicts between Pagan groups. This setting makes it difficult to tell if someone's being a whistleblower on sexual harassment, or if it's just a bad breakup that went public. In either event, when someone speaks up, they are often dismissed.

Sex-Positive vs. Sex-Pressuring

To build a culture of consent, it's important to understand the difference between sex-positive and sex-pressuring. The Center for Sex-Positive Culture offers this definition:

> The sex-positive movement is an ideology which promotes and embraces open sexuality. The sex-positive movement is a social and philosophical movement that regards all consensual sexual activities as fundamentally healthy and pleasurable, and encourages sexual pleasure and experimentation.

Sex-positivity is the idea that there's nothing wrong with sex if it's safe and consensual; this is in contrast to the dominant culture's belief that homosexuality, polyamory, BDSM, or any alternative sexual expression are "bad." and sex is shameful unless it's for procreation.

Sex pressuring, on the other hand, shames people *into* sexual expression. Some examples include: "You're a prude if you don't get naked around the bonfire," or "You're not really sex positive if you don't want to have kinky sex." Being over-sexualized doesn't inherently make someone sex-positive.

Sex-positive does *not* mean:

- You must have sex with everybody in your group
- People can pressure you to get getting naked
- You must be okay with having sex in front of other people
- It's okay to aggressively flirt with or physically touch anyone just because you think they're hot
- You can use your position as a group leader or teacher to get people to have sex with you
- You have to dress sexually or have lots of sex

Consent, and especially enthusiastic consent, is one way of ensuring positive, healthy sexuality. But how do we make consent-seeking normal within our communities? What makes sex such a difficult topic to address?

Cultural Shadows

Shadow work is core to leadership and personal growth. The essence of shadow is the tension between genuine, basic human needs and what our culture has deemed "bad." My understanding of the concept of shadow comes from Jungian psychology as filtered through various articles, books, and teachings from my mentors. Shadow is often composed of things that we learned were "bad," and so we reject the notion that we need (or do) them. I think of shadows as the things we're really afraid people will hate us for if they were discovered. Sometimes, we're so afraid of this happening that we don't even allow ourselves to *know* that we do those things.

Because we can't cope with the idea that we do "bad" things, we often do them unconsciously. Sometimes we first become aware of our shadows by observing distasteful behaviors in other people. If we become self-reflective, we may realize that *we do it too*.

Any time we have basic human needs that we're told are shameful, we both want that thing but also hate ourselves for it. The individual's ego, the identity, tries to negotiate getting the person's needs met with what they believe is "right" or "wrong." Ego doesn't deal well with anything that would make us "bad." Thus, ego tries really hard to shove shameful needs into our psychic/mental dungeon.

For most humans, sex is a basic biological need. And yet, cultural messages often tell us that we should be ashamed of our desire for sex—except, of course, when that desire is being exploited for commercial gain. Wearing sexy clothing and having sex will get you labeled as "promiscuous," as a "slut," and as a "whore," and yet advertisers use imagery of half-naked, sexualized people in order to sell things. Most of us have to encounter this juxtaposition every day: we see sexualized, commercialized images meant to spark our sexual desire, along with moralizing messages about that desire's shamefulness.

When we find ourselves trying to fulfill needs that we have learned are "bad," as we inevitably do, it can send us into a shame spiral. If you want sex, and then you have sex with someone and feel guilty, that's shadow in action. Shadow becomes particularly problematic when it starts to produce addictive or compulsive behavior, such as compulsive cheating or sexual harassment.

When we're taught that our essential needs are shameful, we learn maladaptive strategies to try and meet those needs. Those strategies usually fail, but we engage in them again and again.

Sex-Pressuring Shadows

In the sexually-free Pagan subculture, shadows around sexuality get complicated as many people try to identify sex as "good" and "positive," and then pressure other people to be sexualized. People are often called prudes or uptight for wearing too many clothes or turning others down for sex. This behavior is important to notice: Any time someone is trying to shame someone else, there's shadow work at play. My guess is that the people in the Pagan community doing the most sexual pressuring are feeling a great deal of shame and guilt about wanting sex. They are trying to convince *themselves* that sex is "good"—and failing.

Here's a personal tightrope that I find I walk as a leader and teacher within the Pagan community. Years ago I told some festival organizers that I didn't want to dance naked around the fire, much less have sex by the fire in front of everyone, and that I'd prefer privacy. I was told, "You'll get used to it, once you ease up." I was told I'd have to get over being such a prude. I was frequently teased for wearing long-sleeved shirts to Pagan gatherings even when I explained that my skin is sensitive to sunlight. Now, I believe that people should be respected regardless of what they wear or don't wear. Yet, as a teacher, when I'm choosing what to wear at a class or a festival, I feel the pressure that those shaming comments created. I fear that if I wear "sexy" clothing, I will be seen as promiscuous, and thus not respected as a Pagan leader and teacher. At the same time, I also don't want to be labeled a prude.

I debated for a long time whether or not to use a pen name for my paranormal romance novels. I acknowledged that some might lose respect for my work teaching leadership by using the same name. In other words, I still face the same negative judgments within the Pagan community that I do in the dominant culture, just with the added pressure to not be a prude.

Sexual pressuring, while often explicitly saying that sex is good, still plays out the cultural shadow that sex is bad. Any time we're being pressured to do something, our basic boundaries are being violated.

Boundaries, Consent, and Limits

To begin to address the issues of consent, we need to understand boundaries and limits. The way I approach boundaries and limits comes from one of my mentors, Dr. L. Carol Scott. Boundaries are our edges. Our bodies end at our skin. Our thoughts and desires end at our skin too. Just because you want to touch someone doesn't mean they want that, and just because you want someone to be attracted to you doesn't mean they are.

Here are some examples of treading on others' boundaries:

- Hugging without asking
- Offering unasked-for advice
- Pressuring people for sex
- Groping
- An inability to say no, or accept when someone else tells us no

Setting a limit is when we enforce a boundary. Boundaries and limits can often be most easily understood by the words "no" and "yes." Think about a time when someone has asked you to do something and you felt pressured to say yes. Maybe you said yes because you didn't want to hurt their feelings. We often say yes when we want to say no because of the way refusal is taken in our culture. Regardless of the speaker's intentions, the word "no" is sometimes perceived as a total rejection, not as a simple refusal of a single proposition. The statement that, "No, I can't help you move into your new apartment," for example, might be heard as "No, I don't like you, I've never liked you, and really, nobody likes you." This is a fairly common norm, though I'd offer that it's an unhealthy one and it will take active work to shift this perception of the word "no."

We are taught to say yes to be polite, and we are also taught to manipulate others into saying yes. When "no" means we ourselves are being rejected as people, and "yes" means others like us, consent becomes problematic. The emotional consequences of saying no become very high-stakes.

Most people are not good at hearing no. Earlier in my life, neither was I. As a Pagan event planner, I used to pressure people to take on roles in events I was organizing. Eventually I came to understand that I was being manipulative to get people to say yes and that I wasn't respecting their boundaries. I've worked to make more space for people to say no, though it means I plan far less grandiose events than I used to.

Similarly, I've worked to get better at saying no to others, despite the potential that people will perceive the word no as a wholesale rejection.

Hugging and Boundaries

At almost any Pagan gathering, you'll see people reach out for a hug without asking permission to touch the other person. If someone were to approach me for a hug, and I were to set a limit and gently say, "No, thank you," that person would more than likely feel stung by rejection. I've heard people say, "Pagans hug, you'll get used to it." Yet whether or not we have the right to accept or refuse a hug is an important issue of physical boundaries and consent. Poor boundaries and cultural pressure to say yes create a gray area where we might continue to say yes even when we're uncomfortable. We might find ourselves allowing physical touching or other behavior that borders on sexual harassment, but in a pressured environment, it can be difficult to figure out where the line is. The pressure to hug creates an ambient environment that is tolerant of harassment. And we don't want to be the prude, we don't want to be the spoilsport. So we don't speak up.

People who don't like casual physical touch don't need to be "fixed," In a consent-focused culture with better boundaries and respect for limits, it would be easier to offer a drama-free opportunity to hug or not hug without judging someone for it.

Other kinds of physical touch without consent can become harassment. At a Pagan conference, I was suddenly hugged from behind. I had no idea who was behind me and had to hold back my body's automatic reflex to turn and shove. It turned out to be someone that I know, but that didn't matter. I wasn't asked for my consent for that touch. I talked to a friend who had the same thing happen. She was in the vendor room when someone came from behind to hug her. She said, "That better be my husband." A nearby vendor smirked and said, "Or someone really cute." How—in any way—does a person's appearance make it okay for them to touch you without consent?

You might see these behaviors as just innocent hijinks. However, they create a gray area that makes it hard to determine what's over-enthusiastic affection from a friend and what's sexual harassment.

Boundaries and Respecting "No"

When I review certain situations, I often see where I wanted to say, "I'm not okay with this," but I didn't because I was afraid of offending people and being labeled the party pooper. And that's the communal problem we have—it's the peer pressuring that we don't even realize we're engaging in that encourages people to allow touching and other behavior that they don't want. When I have experienced these things, I haven't always spoken up, because... these people are my friends, right? They don't mean any harm, I'm probably just oversensitive, right? Nonetheless, uninvited touching can be a form of sexual harassment.

At the same conference I mentioned above, several friends were drinking one evening and invited me to hang out with them. They were tipsy, and they decided to spray my cleavage with chocolate whipped cream, then told their friend to lick it off. Before I could even think to say no, I was being touched in a way I hadn't consented to. My whole body went into shock, and I couldn't speak. It took me several days before I really was able to process what had happened and feel angry about it. At the time, I felt that I was the one with the problem because I was too uptight.

As long as we see a person holding boundaries as *someone who is ruining the group's fun,* we're going to keep running into these problems. What would happen if we, instead, honored and respected others' boundaries? If we asked them if it was okay before trying to hug them, if we respected someone's decision to not drink or not have sex without teasing them? What if, instead of complaining about all the nasty jokes we can't tell or worrying about how boundaries are going to spoil our fun, we think of the healthy communities we keep saying we want to be part of?

Touching people without their consent is not sex-positive. Telling people they are ruining the group's fun and that they are ashamed of their sexuality because they don't want to be groped in public is not sex-positive. Further, when we don't enforce our own physical boundaries, or when we're afraid of speaking up for fear of offending someone, that opens the door for worse predatory behavior.

I have a few friends that are very physically affectionate. They like to take your hand or grip your shoulder or lean in for a big long hug. They don't mean to make anyone else uncomfortable. But if we don't talk about consent to our well-meaning friends, if we don't work to respect each other's physical boundaries, we're making more room for the genuine creepers to slip through the cracks.

We have to learn to say "no" with the knowledge that our "no" is going to be respected. Only if "no" is respected does "yes" have any meaning.

Predatory Pagan Leaders and Teachers

Sadly, leaders, teachers, and others in positions of power sometimes sexually harass or abuse others. Many people ask me, "How do I stop an abusive group leader from hurting people in the community?" The truth is, in most situations you can't force someone to stop leading a group. Even if an illegal act has been committed, such as a rape, it can be hard to prove to the courts or the community. In most cases, though, abusive Pagan leaders aren't breaking any laws, they are just taking advantage of their group members.

The diversity and counterculture identity of most Pagan groups confuses the question of ethics and morals. One argument I frequently hear from Pagans is, "Well, who decides what's appropriate and inappropriate? I don't want to be the thought police." Following the laws of the land may offer an ethical guideline. However, as a Pagan activist, I don't always support (and sometimes actively speak against) laws I don't agree with, such as laws that make same-sex marriage illegal or restrict access to abortion. And again, some abusive behaviors aren't necessarily addressed by any law.

To the question of, "Who decides?" the answer is pretty easy: you do. Each Pagan group, each individual tradition, or each solitary practitioner, gets to decide these things for themselves, for their own group. What's acceptable in your group might not be acceptable in mine. I'm writing here from the perspective of my own personal ethics, which may be useful as a guideline for you or your group.

There are a variety of potential abuse scenarios in Pagan groups, ranging from unintentionally creepy behavior or boundary pushing, to emotional and verbal abuse, sexual abuse, rape, and even sexual abuse of minors. I believe that using a position of power as a priest/ess, group leader, teacher, or author to manipulate people for sex is unethical.

Sexual Harassment and Avoidance

Sexual harassment is often brushed off in the dominant culture, and at Pagan gatherings I'd say even more of it gets ignored. I have experienced and witnessed group leaders who were inappropriately touchy-feely. They were always hugging people without asking—usually a long, full-body contact hug—or draping their arms on people or touching their hands, or overtly flirting. There's nothing wrong with hugging, touching, or flirting, but when the person being flirted with is giving body language that says they are uncomfortable, and the person keeps at it, that behavior doesn't support good boundaries or the notion of consent. Continuing to hug, touch, or flirt after the person has said no or has clearly shown that they are uncomfortable is harassment.

I admit, I've often engaged in avoidance behavior when being touched without my consent. I break eye contact, I shrink my body away, I hope it will end. Afterwards, I minimize what happened instead of directly confronting the harasser.

Many in the Pagan community have become complicit in a leader's sexual harassment. There's one Pagan leader in a Midwestern city who is notorious for being a "letch." I've heard this over and over: "Oh, don't mind Person A. He'll hit on any young, pretty woman. Let me know if he gets too fresh." This remark is always said with a fond or slightly exasperated smile. Yet several other members of the community have explicitly asked me if there's a way to stop this leader's harassment without standing up to him and causing a "witch war." The answer to that? Not really. As long as the broader community makes excuses for a leader's poor behavior, it will continue.

In other situations, friends and peers of the harasser will sometimes silence victims by saying, "Oh no, Person A couldn't possibly do that. You must have been mistaken." Essentially, they cannot believe—cannot even consider—that their friend would violate others that way. This tendency is an unfortunate aspect of human psychology. Basically, our brains don't like to process information that contradicts what we already know (or think we know). Even presented with evidence of harassment, our knowledge that Person A is a "good guy" will prevent us from being willing to acknowledge the new evidence. This inability to process new information results from the cognitive dissonance created by the conflicting information.

The tendency to uncritically defend loved ones is a type of poor boundaries that I refer to as the *ego annex*. When you write a book, create a work of art, or plan an event, you feel like part of you is in that thing/event you helped create. Your boundaries don't end at your skin, they annex that thing that you did. Similarly, we tend to annex our friends, our family, our covens, any groups we are a part of, as part of us. Unfortunately, just as our own egos don't deal well with being identified as a "bad," we don't deal well with someone we've "annexed" being identified as bad. Most of the time we'll get defensive and dig in our heels instead of looking at the evidence.

Abuse and Predation

When we look beyond harassment, there are deeper issues of abuse. While predators sometimes come across as "creepy," more often they are the charismatic, shiny leader/teacher. Such leaders may target newbies and more vulnerable coven members or event attendees. These leaders are the people who intentionally use their position of power to manipulate people into having sex.

Predators of any type typically target the most vulnerable person in the room. They will often target the youngest person or the person who has poor self-esteem or is shy or nervous. When the person initiating touch is consistently in a position of power or influence over the people they are touching, that's a red flag.

Such manipulative leaders come in a variety of guises. In some cases, they are coven leaders that overtly tell group members that they'll need to have sex with them to stay in the coven or to advance to the next level. (I'll address actual sexual initiation later in the essay;

in this context I'm talking about leaders and teachers that are manipulating people for sex.) In my teaching, I have heard from many people who have been pressured by a coven leader for sex. I've even heard of several different groups where the leaders invited minors (age 12-15) into a teaching coven and then pressured them to have sex with the HP/HPS.

My own former romantic and teaching partner used his position as a group leader and teacher to have (or try to have) sex with members of our community in Chicago, as well as when we traveled and taught. He implied that he and I were polyamorous (we weren't). After our final breakup, women came to me and told me that he made them so uncomfortable they stopped attending events. Others apologized to me and admitted they'd had sex with my partner but hadn't realized at the time that he was cheating on me. Abusers like this can be difficult to spot because they frequently are very charismatic and often have done a lot of great work for the community.

Power Dynamics and Leadership Ethics

You might be thinking, "If someone flirts with me and I have sex with them, how is that abuse? I consented, right?" The manipulative grooming strategies many abusers use can make consent complicated. And if we're discussing minors under the age of consent, even if they say yes to sex, their consent isn't legally valid. Here's my personal ethical code. If I'm in a position of power, it's unethical for me to have sex with people I'm leading and teaching. I have a policy that I won't date people who are students or ritual participants.

Imagine I've just facilitated a deep, transformative, ecstatic ritual. We've gone to the Underworld and faced our shadows. Participants have big cathartic moments. After the ritual, a participant comes up to me. I find him attractive. He asks me out. Though he is the one initiating things, is it ethical for me to date him?

Absolutely not.

Ritual participants are in a vulnerable headspace, and with students there's a power dynamic. Much like if I were in the position of being someone's boss, or being someone's therapist, there's an unequal power balance. There's too much potential for abuse.

Now, it is possible to grow a healthy peer relationship with people I have met when they were students, attendees, or members of a group I led. If I have worked with someone and established a peer dynamic, then it might be feasible to date that person eventually. I advocate leaning on the side of caution.

The issue here is power and charisma. As a leader and teacher, it's difficult for me to know if someone is attracted to the real me or to the teacher/ritualist, or if the person has poor self-esteem and has latched on to me as the "shiny" group leader. It would be easy to take advantage of someone in that dynamic, even if I were trying not to. Imagine, then, how very easy it is for a predator who is deliberately manipulating others with their position of power to take advantage.

Grooming and Abuse

Grooming is a word for the manipulative process predators sometimes use to break down their victim's personal boundaries to influence them into consenting to sex or other situations that they are uncomfortable with. There are scenarios where I may have consented to sex—but I was also manipulated or lied to. Sex in this context is consensual, but unethical; issues of consent and manipulation are related (but different) areas of sexual misconduct. The primary scenario I will explore is a group leader pressuring an adult into having sex with them, but the abusive grooming process can happen with minors, and it can happen in less overt power dynamic situations as well.

Grooming is taking an inch, and another inch... and another. This particular process creates an environment where people might do things they otherwise wouldn't have done.

Here's a scenario of leader exploits student: You join a coven. You're brand new, wet behind the ears. You start attending classes; you're inspired by your new spirituality but overwhelmed by how much you don't know. The coven leader sets up an intense power dynamic with praise and shame. They are powerful and magnetic and lauded as an authority by other students. Group members vie for the leader's approval. You are awed by how much they know. You want them to like you because you are a people-pleaser.

Often there is a hot/cold dynamic of shaming ("No, that's wrong! That's not how you balance your chakras!") and praising ("Good, that's an excellent spell-working!") Eventually the praising becomes more personal and leads to a sexual proposition. In some cases, the leader's attention becomes a prize to be fought over, and the whole group may begin trying to outdo one another to get sexual attention from the group leader. This dynamic breaks down victims' boundaries and sense of self to get them to consider doing things they ordinarily wouldn't.

The relevant point is that abuse like this comes in inches. Nobody just agrees to have sex with the group leader. Instead, you are manipulated into thinking that it was your idea. It's when the victim's whole sense of self-identity hinges on the approval of the leader that this dynamic unfolds. When someone manipulates another into sex, it's not sex-positive. It's abusive.

Sexual Initiation

I am on the fence with this. I know of some groups that have done sacred sexuality work where the leaders/teachers are very clear about the setup of the group and the expectations, and they focus on personal development and boundaries before any physical contact. In those cases, it's possible for things to be done ethically. However, I'm also aware of sex temples that recruit people into abusive cults.

Some Pagan traditions require sexual initiation for the mysteries to pass to the new initiate. Is there ever a way to ensure there isn't a power dynamic with potential for abuse? If there's any overt or even tacit pressuring, I don't know that valid consent can be ensured. In one tradition I've heard people say, "You don't have to do the Great Rite in actual, *but it's a shame if you don't*." That's a tacit pressuring. Those in support of sexual initiation often say, "But sexual initiation is one of our most sacred traditions and mysteries!" I would offer that there are any number of religious and cultural traditions that are ancient and held as sacred, and yet are not ethical in a modern context.

What I do know is that there are, unfortunately, a number of groups and group leaders who use the "sexual initiation" trope not for actual sexual initiation work, but just to manipulate people into having sex.

Handling Sexual Misconduct in the Pagan Community

There isn't a good way to stop a group leader who is abusing their group members. Most Pagan groups have no hierarchy controlling whether or not a particular person can lead a group. Rules won't stop predators from abusing. These circumstances present a number of challenges in seeking ways to deal with these issues.

If you are dealing with the potential abuse of a child, the issue must be taken to the police immediately. Do not protect the alleged perpetrator just because they are Pagan! In cases when an adult has been raped, however, some victims don't want to go through the nightmare of dealing with police, and rape is still difficult to prove legally. The victim's wishes should be taken into account when deciding whether to involve the authorities.

In many instances, bringing up allegations of sexual abuse or harassment within the Pagan community will almost inevitably lead to a polarized situation. Some will believe the victim, others will blame the victim. Here are a few examples of victim blaming I've either personally experienced from speaking out about my ex, or that I've witnessed others be subjected to:

- "You're just stirring up trouble."
- "Stop tearing leaders down! You're destroying our community!"
- "There are two sides to every story."
- "You have responsibility too. Don't blame everything on them."
- "I can see you're not willing to give mediation a chance."
- "It's time to move forward and stop blaming them."
- "You're just engaging in a power play."

Many victims will not come forward at all because of this shaming. Put bluntly, I'm an author and a teacher. I have some credibility and a public voice in the Pagan community. In other words, I have some social power, and I still faced victim blaming and backlash when I spoke up about my abusive ex. What if you're a newbie, an attendee at an event? Coming forward would involve a much bigger social risk.

Those of us who have been victims face this choice: Speak out and risk your own reputation by people yelling at you for starting a witch war. Or, be silent and thus complicit in further abusive behavior.

Whistleblowing

Speaking out usually gets brushed off as an attempt to start a "witch war," and it is easy for the conflict to become a popularity contest. The person who "wins" is typically the person with more social capital. It's not usually guilt or innocence that causes someone to retreat from the community, it's how much pressure they can take before they burn out. These conflicts leave scorched earth in their wake. I'm not suggesting that you shouldn't speak up if you have been abused. However, you should know what you're getting into.

Some have suggested the creation of some kind of Pagan predator database. Unfortunately, there are Pagans who falsely accuse other Pagans (especially leaders and teachers) of sexual misconduct or other abuse as a method of revenge. In other words, listening to whistleblowers would be easier if everyone told the truth. However, not all allegations of abuse, harassment, or rape are truthful. The Pagan community has a long history of Pagans who lie or exaggerate in order to "take down" a leader. In many instances, it's difficult to fact check and find out what really happened.

Rules, Boundaries, and Information Sharing

It's important for groups to establish rules for acceptable behavior as well as to teach individual group members to grow stronger boundaries and develop a healthier sense of self. Group rules won't stop predators, and workshops on boundaries won't fix predators either. Predators are often acting compulsively. Rules and education work by clearing out the "gray area" and helping people discriminate between friendly touch and sexually harassing behavior. If your group or event clarifies its rules for behavior and its definition of consent, then harassment and abuse also become clearer.

While the creation of national or international predator databases is problematic, I do believe it's important for any group or event to record complaints about members. You'll notice patterns over time even if you don't have enough information from any single complaint. It's also useful for local leaders to share information about potentially problematic people. Word of mouth is not the best way to disseminate information, but it is one of the few methods we have within the small world of the overlapping Pagan communities. It's useful as long as we understand that information passed this way should be taken not as a condemning judgment, but as a warning prompting us to observe that person's behavior.

Paradox

Many abusers are not completely bad people. These leaders and teachers are running events, organizing groups, teaching workshops, and building community. This is partly why people often refuse to believe that their leader could have done something unethical. They will often insist, "But that person does so much good in our community!" In fact, many people engaging in abusive behavior feel genuinely guilty about it. They act compulsively and then apologize: "I'm sorry, I'll never do that again. I'll change." Often they promise to get help, and sometimes they do, for a time. Unfortunately, these types of remorseful abusers can be more dangerous because their periods of reasonableness allow their victims to get sucked back in.

What Can We Do?

If a Pagan predator database isn't really feasible, and if establishing group rules won't stop predators, what can we do? The best thing that we can do is build a culture of consent, of respect for boundaries, of healthy self-esteem. Rules and agreements for behavior within a group or at an event won't stop a predator, but they will make that predator's behavior *far more obvious*. People with healthy boundaries—and people who know that their boundaries and limits are going to be respected because they are in a culture of consent—will feel more comfortable speaking up about behavior that isn't acceptable.

If you are aware that your "no" will be respected and you won't be shamed for being a prude or a party pooper, then you're more likely to speak up to someone about behavior that isn't acceptable, or escalate by taking the issue to one of the event staff.

By understanding consent and the notion of enthusiastic consent, as well as understanding the differences between being sex-positive and sex-pressuring, we can begin to grow healthier boundaries and make truly predatory behavior more obvious. Having solid policies within groups or at events for what behavior is acceptable and what isn't—and enforcing those policies—begins to address harmful behavior within the Pagan community. I also believe that part of building a truly sex-positive culture is learning to talk more frankly about sex, sexual health, and pleasure without shame, but also without pressuring others. If we talk openly about these things, we can take away their shadow power.

What do we expect of our leaders, of each other? What behavior is acceptable, and what isn't? What do we do when a Pagan leader acts in a reprehensible way? How do we hold them accountable? This work requires us to confront our assumptions and ask hard questions. It is no easy task.

Note

This article was inspired by and uses writing from several of my previously published articles, which are available online and also collected in my book *The Leader Within*. Articles include:

"Sex, Ethics, and Paganism," and "Sexual Initiation, Discrimination, Consent, and Rape" (published at www.PaganActivist.com)

"Abusive Leaders, Grooming, and Seduction," and "Harassment and Boundaries" (published at ShaunaAura.wordpress.com)

Resources

Dr. L. Carol Scott, www.lcarolscott.com

The Center for Sex Positive Culture, thecspc.org/frequently-asked-questions/

An artist, author, ritualist, presenter, and spiritual seeker, **Shauna Aura Knight** travels nationally offering intensive education in the transformative arts of ritual, community leadership, and personal growth. She is the author of *The Leader Within*, *Ritual Facilitation*, and *Dreamwork for the Initiate's Path*.

Shauna is also the author of urban fantasy and paranormal romance novels including *The Truth Upon Her Lips*, *A Fading Amaranth*, *A Winter Knight's Vigil*, and more. Shauna's mythic artwork and designs are used for book and magazine covers as well as decorating many walls and shrines. She is passionate about creating rituals, experiences, stories, and artwork to awaken mythic imagination. www.shaunaauraknight.com

Living in Community with Trauma Survivors

Lydia M. N. Crabtree

I have a visceral reaction to the smell of chicken poop. Not an "Ewwwww, that smells!" kind of reaction, though. Chicken poop that has baked in the hot Georgia sun means that there is money nearby.

When I was a girl, after my grandparents could no longer compete with big agriculture, the chicken industry started to convert agricultural farms to chicken farms and trained former farmers to raise and mass produce chickens or eggs. Papa Lee chose chickens.

Chicken poop smells like money. Money was needed to keep Papa Lee and Mama Bridges from selling out to big agriculture as so many in Union Point, Georgia had to do.

Chicken poop smells like home—that white clapboard house where rooms were added as needed and the porch ran the length of the ever-expanding house, where the one living room had been converted into a guest room and there was no heat or air, only the gentle blowing of fans and crackle at the hearth in winter.

Chicken poop means no longer driving the truck to care for beef cows, but walking in waders through the chicken coop to gather dead chickens and then throw them down the makeshift garbage ravine for scavengers, like the family of foxes who lived in the wooded glens of the farmstead. All of this industry, not in a quiet field slowly stifled by a summer's heat, but in a closed-up coop, long and wide as a football field, while massive turbines draw in clean air and blow out the smell of chicken poop: that is the smell that you can sometimes catch on the breeze if you travel down the roads in Georgia on a hot summer's day, while the rest of Georgia's Papa Lees continue to turn to chicken farming as the only means to keep their land.

Sexual trauma survivors have visceral reactions involving all the senses (including the etheric, soul, or psychic sense). Unfortunately for Pagan leaders, there is no way to anticipate those reactions or how they will manifest. Traumatic reactions are steeped in the individual trauma someone faced. For me, chicken poop smells like money and home, but to some in Georgia, the smell is so offensive that they take different roads just to avoid it. When a trauma survivor has a visceral reaction based on a traumatic event, not everyone will find their fear comprehensible. For that matter, the survivor may not understand it either.

One of my personal triggers is having hands near my face. Just this past Thanksgiving, we sat with our family playing a heated game of Uno. My husband sat to my left and was catching the brunt of my merciless Uno play. After the fourth four-card-draw he was forced to accept, he reached his hand out to touch the dog laying between us, and in that moment I braced to be hit. My husband has never hit me, yet it is ingrained in me that when a hand is coming toward my face, violence will be the outcome. I had been feeling sort of bad about the cutthroat way I was playing. The abused child in me was feeling like it should get smacked for playing so hard against my own mate. In years past, these types of incidents would have had me ducking for cover. However, I have been in therapy a long, long time, and I was able to quickly redirect my mind.

"That's my husband," I said to myself, "He will not hit me. I am safe here. There is no violence in this place and never has been."

I covered so well that when I told my husband later about what happened, he was shocked and surprised, not even remembering the incident that was now indelible to me.

It has taken years of cognitive therapy to counteract my fight, flight, and freeze instincts. I have learned how to cover over these incidents so that most people do not even know they have occurred. I have been in a loving and violence-free relationship for nearly fifteen years. All of these things make an incident like this much easier for me to deal with. However, that was not always true.

At a party once, my then-boyfriend, who had never been violent to me, moved to put his arm around my shoulders. Unfortunately, we were in a tight and confined space and before I knew what had happened, I was under the refreshment table trying to figure out how I got there and why. Try explaining that to a bunch of drunk partiers!

When thinking about rituals and gatherings, there are some common-sense things that the greater Pagan community can do to accommodate those who have experienced sexual assault, physical abuse, or trauma. These guidelines will ensure that if difficult situations arise, they can be handled professionally and promptly to the greatest good of all involved.

Fair Warning

The most obvious and important thing that leaders can do is to warn participants if a ritual, gathering, or workshop will deal with issues around trauma, sexual assault or abuse, and/or physical abuse. Even romance novels these days have started providing a one-sentence warning regarding the content. If rape is an element of the story, then that fact is disclosed on the back cover. These statements can be simple and straightforward:

This workshop (ritual/gathering) deals with issues regarding sexual abuse (assault, physical abuse, mental and/or emotional trauma).

This simple warning should be enough to encourage those with serious issues to stay away from these events and significantly reduce the likelihood that a participant will experience an unexpected mental, psychic, or physical response.

That said, fair warning is never as good as avoidance.

Avoidance

Most leaders have not had the specialized psychological training that prepares someone to deal with sexual abuse, physical abuse, or trauma victims. If you haven't had such training, then *do not* hold a workshop, ritual, or gathering around these issues. Only those who are prepared to deal with deep issues around trauma should lead such events.

In Small Groups

For leaders who work most often in smaller groups, the best advice is to have a list of resources from the area available for when you come across those who struggle with experiences of trauma. This list should include a suicide hotline, an abuse hotline, and the names of several reputable counselors who are Pagan-friendly and trained in treating sexual, physical, or emotional trauma. Normalizing seeking help from professionals is beneficial to those who have suffered trauma. Many recovering victims may believe they are crazy or doubt that the abuse really happened. Encouraging them to seek help, and encouraging the perception that getting mental help is no worse than going to a doctor for a physical ailment, is very important.

The strategies described below for large groups may also be adapted for small ones.

Lay Priests and Priestesses

All large events, regardless of topic, should have designated lay priests and lay priestesses prepared to work with anyone who has an extreme reaction to a ritual or workshop. A "lay" priest/ess is a leader and peer counselor who does not have professional certification in counseling or psychology. These people are not participants in the event; they are observers. Their job is to watch the participants and look out for people who have an adverse or acute reaction to the event. If necessary, they should help these participants leave the event, and they should be trained in how to properly care for them. Even the most seemingly innocuous events can impact a trauma victim negatively.

What to Look For

Lay priests and priestesses should look for people who respond with extreme emotional distress to the event they are participating in. They should scan the event both energetically and physically, looking for anyone who has any strong negative reaction to what is happening. This could include agitation, anger, or the inability to settle. It could include intense sadness and crying.

In most instances, doing nothing is the best course of action. If the participant is only bothering one or two persons in their immediate vicinity and seems to be holding their energetic and emotional reaction in check, intervention could cause a larger problem than it solves. However, if the reaction and distress seems to be growing over time and/or signs of panic are setting in (difficulty breathing, signs of extreme sweating and uncontrollable crying indicating that the fight/flight/freeze response is coming to the forefront), then intervention is the best course of action.

What to Do

In ritual space, first cut the door

Approach the person by going clockwise outside the circle and then cut the door directly behind them. Then go two or three persons down from the person in distress and step into the circle. Approach this person directly, trying to get their attention before you are in front of them. If you are unable to do this, then kneel in front of them and look up into their face. Both of these approach techniques are designed to tell the person that you are not a threat to them and have come to help.

Ask them, "Would you like to leave or stay?"

If they respond negatively, tell them gently, "There is a safe place nearby that we can go and you can collect yourself. Only if you would like to ... If you feel better, then we can come back."

Typically, this is all that is needed to get a person in emotional distress to step away from circle or the event. If this doesn't work and the person says that they still do not want to leave, then the lay priest/ess should take a position next to the person in distress and stand *without touching them*, ready to help them leave if they have need.

Have a place within sight of the original event to take the person in distress.

The last thing you want to do is take a person in distress far away from what is currently familiar. A place with a pavilion, if you are at a gathering, or even some chairs within sight of the ritual or workshop are good. This visible setting subconsciously demonstrates to the distressed individual that you have no nefarious plans and are simply trying to give them space and time to collect themselves.

Do not touch!

This seems counterintuitive to most Pagans, but it is extremely important not to touch trauma victims and people in distress. Touch is often associated with violence and violation. When someone is in distress, their ability to discern positive touch and negative touch has been compromised. Lead them to the place where they can sit down and offer them a box of tissues, but do not touch.

Do not pry!

This is not the time or place to try and diagnose. The priest/ess's job, in fact, is not to gather information. It is to sit and share someone's energetic, psychic, and emotional pain without judgment and with love and compassion. This is done by being attentive and allowing the person all the time and space they need to collect themselves. The priest/ess should listen to whatever they say without comment or judgment. This time is about them and not you.

Have water and crackers (rice crackers for people with food allergies), and if the person seems to be unable to ground, offer them both of these. You can offer some of these standard responses:

- There is nothing to be sorry for.
- Don't worry about it. It happens to all of us eventually.
- Take a deep breath with me. Deep breath in. Deep breath out.
- Take as long as you need. We have all the time in the world.
- Would you like a tissue (water, cracker, rice cracker)?

These responses are meant to reassure, not to delve into a person's emotional trauma. That is not the priest/ess's job. Lay priest/esses are not trained to deal with emotional trauma. Their job is to help stabilize a person and have them reengage with the workshop, ritual, or gathering. If the person asks the priest/ess to leave, they should agree and move an unobtrusive distance away. Some participants may choose to leave the event at this point, and the priest/ess should allow them to do so and return to the event.

Female to Female; Male & Female to Male

If the lay priests and priestesses see someone in distress, then the most important thing to do is properly partner lay priest/esses with the person who needs intervention. Lay priest/esses can approach other women in distress alone or in pairs (with another priestess is preferable). As a rule, lay priests should not approach women in distress unless accompanied by a lay priestess. Men who are in distress, however, should be approached by a female *and* male working in tandem. The reasons behind this practice have to do with the statistics around violation.

If the participant in distress is third-gendered or trans* and does not present or identify as strictly male or female, sending a team of trans* or third-gendered priest/esses would be the ideal. If this is not possible, a mixed-gender team is recommended.

For trans* priest/esses, self-identification is what is most important. If a person self-identifies as female and physically presents as female, then they should stick to the suggestions for lay priestesses. If a person identifies as male and physically presents as male, then they should stick to suggestions around lay priests.

For the Protection of Lay Leaders

Organizations that deal with minors, religious groups who peer counsel, doctors, and some education groups have developed best practices for leaders to interact with persons of different genders. These best practices protect lay leaders and the persons they serve.

For safety reasons, it is best to have lay priest/esses work in teams. According to a survey,[1] most perpetrators of sexual violence are men. It is common sense, therefore, to reduce the interaction between lay priests and women in distress. However, the same survey indicates that

---

[1] Patricia Tjaden and Nancy Thoennes, "Prevalence and consequences of male-to-female and female-to-male intimate partner violence as measured by the National Violence Against Women Survey," *Violence Against Women* 6 (2): 142-161.

violence perpetrated against men is mostly perpetrated *by* men. For this reason, having a team with both a male and female available to approach men in distress should cut down the likelihood that the male in distress will feel uncomfortable. This practice will safeguard the lay priest/esses who are there to help.

It would be nice to see Pagan leaders come up with standard best practices that protect leaders, elders, priests, and priestesses from accusations of misconduct and sexual assault. Until this is done, we should have clear guidelines to best direct leaders' interaction with community members.

Above Reproach

People who work with minors should avoid situations where they could potentially be accused of sexual misconduct. This means that, just as doctors often have nurses observe their interactions with patients, it is usually helpful to have an observer present during certain kinds of interactions with community members.

Nearly 100% of women who are raped are raped by men, and 70% of rapes and 86% of occurrences of physical violence against men are perpetrated by men. Therefore, if you self-identify as a man and physically present as a man and deal with minors, it potentially protects your reputation to never work alone with minors of any gender. When dealing with adults, depending upon the situation, having intimate meetings with people of any gender may be best served by working with a partner as well.

If a leader is never alone with a community member, then the leader is much less likely to be accused of sexual misconduct with them. Having another person in the room helps to stabilize the situation. Utilizing technology can also reduce the likelihood that you will be accused of inappropriate behavior. Video chats and phone calls are excellent ways to meet with community members while putting a physical barrier between yourself and those you serve.

Since we lack strong guidelines for best practices when dealing with minors and when doing lay counseling in the Pagan community, the best a Pagan leader can do is conduct themselves in a manner that is beyond reproach. This means not permitting situations that might show that leader in a questionable light. It also means not participating in sexual ritual or having sexual relationships with people who have a perception that you have power or authority over them.

This seems to trip up many different types of elders. Many Pagans seem to have a "no big deal" attitude toward sleeping with students or others in the community who may see them as authority figures. I puzzle over this, given the large amount of social experiments that prove that authority can cause all kinds of behavior that is outside the norm or standard.

In the now well-known Milgram experiment, persons were encouraged to shock people to death simply by the presence of a person in a lab coat, even when the dial clearly told the participant that death was the outcome of the shocks being administered (the 'victim' was actually an actor and no shocks were administered). What is less known is the effect that charisma, perceived good looks, *and* authority have upon individuals. Since most Pagan elders and leaders tend to have a fair amount of charisma and a certain degree of good looks and authority that are either perceived or asserted, they are in a unique position to influence the behavior of those around them. If they could not, they would make fairly poor teachers.

It is these same qualities that potentially enable leaders to be able to talk others into sexual behaviors and relationships that they would not normally undertake. We know that authority affects a person's likelihood of saying yes, as the Milgram experiments clearly demonstrate. We know that looks also influence how people respond to someone. In the social experiment show *What Would You Do,?* (2014), a black man had a more difficult time than a white man at attempting to steal things out of a car. However, when the thief was played by a good-looking, white blond woman who all but confessed to stealing, people helped her steal things![2]

---

2 "Car Theft," *Primetime: What Would You Do?* Season 9, Episode 10 (ABC News, 2014).

The power of looks and charisma cannot be discounted by leaders and Pagan elders. Combined with authority, the mixture is devastating to the social senses. People who would not normally agree to sexual acts will, and this can lead to morning-after regret and a sense of betrayal. In one case study of how this occurs, I interviewed a woman who was a neophyte studying under a male teacher. He was good-looking, seemingly knowledgeable and generous with his time and attention. Eventually, he told her she was ready for her first degree and explained that it needed to be a sexual initiation to "work." She readily agreed, believing that he must be the expert and completely taking at face value what he had to say about the ritual and the act. In her own words, she "had never felt so dirty in her life and couldn't wait to get away from him" once the actual ritual began.

In a Goddess-centric religion, no sexual ritual should leave any participant feeling like they have participated in anything other than a highly spiritual experience. If any person leaves the ritual feeling violated, tricked, used, misinformed, or misled, then the ritual and experience should be counted as a failure by those who led it.

This is not to say there aren't healthy ways to have sexual rituals occur with positive outcomes for everyone involved. The easiest way is to have these rituals occur between already sexually active couples. Leaders can teach both partners what needs to be said and energetically done and then allow the partners to do the working by themselves in the privacy of a ritual room.

When it comes to dealing with people who have previously been sexually violated, elders, teachers, and leaders would be wise to simply refrain from having any kind of sexual relationship with them. Sexuality is confused and muddled for sexual abuse survivors, and very few teachers and leaders have the training necessary to walk a survivor to a place where sexual ritual can be a positive thing. Those leaders who do have training as sexuality counselors will still not engage with a survivor sexually themselves (due to the existing relationship), but will instead partner with a third party who meets with the leader for training before and after. Sexuality counselors have extensive training and take months, if not years, to move toward the actual consummation of the sexual act. They often focus on intimacy issues and desensitization versus the actual act of sexual intercourse.

To put it simply, if you are a Pagan leader and not already a professional sexuality counselor, you do not have the training to engage in a healthy sexual encounter with an abuse survivor. Do no more harm and simply do not deal with these issues. Refer people in need to the appropriately trained specialists.

If you aren't clear about whether or not what you are doing with students and community members is a positive thing for them, ask yourself these questions:

+ Has *anyone ever* complained about coercion after a sexual ritual?

+ Has *anyone ever* cried or shown signs of emotional and mental distress before, during, or after a sexual ritual?

+ Has *anyone ever* accused you of date rape?

+ Do you have ritual sex strictly with people of the gender(s) you are attracted to?

+ In your opinion, do you only have the ability to only have ritual sex with relatively young, good-looking people? Why have you never had ritual sex with someone you aren't attracted to if it is the ritual that is important?

+ Is ritual sex a requirement of your tradition or training without alternative?

+ Do you discuss your sexual activities with other elders, teachers, and leaders you admire, or do you hide this part of your practice?

If you have answered yes to more than one of these questions so far, you should re-evaluate the use of ritual sex in your practice.

+ Are you willing to discuss your sexual activities with other elders and leaders?

+ Are you willing to have this practice be something that is generally known in the Pagan community?

- Do students or community members who come to have ritual sex with you remain in relationship with you and your group after the ritual?

- Do students or community members have someone they are encouraged to talk to before and after sexual rituals? Is that person a licensed sexuality therapist?

- Do students or community members have the opportunity to say no up until the very last moment in a sexual ritual?

If your answer to any of the above questions is no, then you should re-evaluate your sexual rituals.

- Has *anyone* you have had ritual sex with been under the age of eighteen?

If you answer yes to this question, you are in danger of being arrested for statutory rape and should cease and desist immediately.

Chicken manure will always smell like home to me and continue to repulse the traveler passing through South Georgia. I will always worry that a hand coming at my face is going to strike me, regardless of who it is attached to. Only trained and licensed counselors can really help me deal with my past. That is their job and my responsibility.

Nevertheless, Pagan leaders can make participation in community easier for people like me. The practical guidelines above will help Pagan groups better accommodate the needs of those with histories of sexual, physical, mental, and emotional abuse. However, as long as we have Pagan leaders who aren't aware of the social power inherent in their leadership role, and as long as we refuse to put forth general guidelines that protect all community members and teachers, then issues around consent and authority rape will continue. Continued education and the creation of general guidelines are our essential next steps in creating Pagan consent culture.

Lydia "Dia" M. N. Crabtree is an adult incest survivor who has written on issues around family spirituality, spirituality and disability, and spirituality and childhood trauma survival. Her current book project, *Family Coven: Birthing Hereditary Witchcraft,* covers how to make the family unit the first magical group that children experience. She has been featured in other anthologies including *Bringing Race to the Table* and *Rooted in the Body, Seeking the Soul* (both from Immanion Press). She writes for the Patheos.com Pagan channel through her column "Birthing Hereditary Witchcraft." Dia is also the co-founder of the Pagan Pro website, which seeks to make safe Pagan circles by discouraging the participation of abusers through complete transparence of leadership. She is available on Facebook, Twitter, and Tumblr.

Consent in Intergenerational Community
Requirements for Community Integrity
Lasara Firefox Allen

Intergenerational community is community in its naturally occurring form. Although the nuclear family model has splintered the more longstanding model of intergenerational family living, we are all involved in intergenerational community to some extent.

Some of us have close ties with our families, blood or otherwise. Some of us have intergenerational community within our religion, one generation passing lore and teachings along to the next, with those of younger years picking up the work as they are able. Others have the fortune to have our religion and our family as a shared lineage. With increasing longevity in the contemporary Pagan movement, we are seeing families with three, four, and even five generations sharing Pagan faith.

Communities that are not intergenerational are generally not sustainable. Tribes, villages, families, even most religious organizations are intergenerational. Communities that are composed of a single generation will by necessity die out with that generation.

However, when a community is formed around a new idea, principle, way of life, set of spiritual principles, or movement, that community is often comprised of a single generation. Many of these communities are formed by young people who were lit up by a vision of new possibilities. If a community—large or small—that arises around one of these phenomena proves viable, the young folks will age. In most foundationally viable communities, that will mean that some members will have offspring. These children are likely to grow up within the community to a greater or lesser extent.

When it comes to contemporary Paganism, I was one of those offspring.

I come from a lineage of family tradition witches with three active generations in the contemporary Pagan community. My mother is an ordained clergy member, as am I. And whether or not either of my children opt for the Priesthood path, they have been raised Pagan.

Coming of Age in the 1980s

In the late 1980s, I turned eighteen deep in the heart of the Neo-Pagan movement. It was a clumsy moment for our community. The idea of intergenerational relationships hadn't really entirely taken form yet in the counterculture and there was a lot of banter—surely intended to be harmless—about my "coming of age," as in coming up to the legal age of consent.

I could tell you stories—more than a handful—that were nothing short of awful to experience. "There's a line of men waiting for Lasara to turn eighteen!" was said out loud in my presence more than once. My response, also said out loud on occasion, was, "You've got to be kidding. If I wanted to sleep with you I would have by now!"

There were times in hot tubs under the night sky where wandering hands made excusing myself the only safe option. There were nights of debauchery that resulted in muddled, blurred boundaries and self-directed remorse.

In the community in which I came of age, there was a lot of pressure and expectation around sexual availability, non-monogamy, and the righteousness of shared lovers. As a powerful, sexually expressive (if also wounded) young woman, I was taken aside by some of the older women in my community and told that if I was going to "tease" their men (by, for example, dancing skyclad around the ritual fire), that I should also have sex with them. I was called a "ball buster" and "frigid" for refusing the advances of men more than twice my age—men who in many cases I had looked up to as teachers, advisors, family members, and symbols of authority.

My growing into my sexual majority was perceived, in and of itself, as consent. My enjoyment of my body was perceived as an invitation. My expression of my sexuality was perceived, in the worst cases, as an affront, because I was not willing to share it with everyone who wanted to experience it.

I took care of the need for boundaries by exploring my sexuality primarily outside of my spiritual community. The rare exceptions were people who were visiting our community and would be leaving.

To be fair, I had some beautiful times, mostly with those few migrant souls who were passing through. Nonetheless, many of my experiences were hurtful, and in some cases, traumatizing. They wrought in me good cause to address issues of consent in my life.

During the peace, love, and sexual revolutions, in the pendulum swing away from the rules that had previously held the world in place, many of my parents' generation had a severe case of inconsistent—or non-existent—boundary awareness. Looking back on it all, I see most of my negative experiences more as signs of the confusion of the times than actually stemming from predatory intent.

The Pagan community that I see around us today has matured. Slowly we are becoming more educated about consent. Generation gaps are also becoming more pronounced as the first generation of contemporary Pagans hits their sixties, seventies, and eighties.

At the same time, the growth of the movement means more anonymity, which means that predatory behavior can be more easily hidden. Additionally—as has been a problem since the advent of contemporary Paganism—many come into the comparatively permissive social environment of our communities and don't understand that even though the rule structures are different from the ones in dominant culture, there are still rules.

Teaching Children about Consent

As parents, semi-parental figures, and extended community we are ultimately responsible for the wellbeing of the children in our community. Teaching children about consent (or the lack of it) is something that begins when they are born.

From the very beginning of our children's lives, we are modeling and reifying unconscious attitudes about consent, bodily sovereignty, autonomy, and enforcement. In order to be able to teach and model consent in a conscious way, however, we need to address our own ideas regarding consent, including addressing sexual programming and areas of wounding. We need to honor our own boundaries, and model holding them gracefully and powerfully without violating the ultimate sovereignty of others.

The dominant culture is not big on consent-based parenting or teaching. Statements like, "Because I said so!" tell children that they are not allowed a personal boundary, and they are also undeserving of a basic explanation.

When we honor a child's "no," we are teaching them about consent. This comes down to basics, like not forcing children to wear clothes they don't want to wear, allowing them to say no to hugs and kisses, and honoring their desire or need to end a conversation.

Of course this training has to be tempered by one's responsibility to take care of the child and offer them the structure they need. This process can be bolstered by encouraging the development of negotiation skills. Offering children choices helps encourage a sense of autonomy while also learning to collaborate on positive outcomes.

Parents and other caregivers can also encourage development of personal responsibility and collaboration by inviting children to participate in problem solving. When children are brought into the process, they get to help craft an outcome that feels good, while also learning to take the needs of others into account.

We can also teach children about consent by modeling what is known as enthusiastic consent. Try saying things like, "I would *love* to go for a walk with you! Thank you for asking." Or, "I love it when we spend time together."

On the other end of the spectrum, we also need to teach children about predators in age-appropriate ways, particularly how they can help avoid predation. This process is made much easier when starting from a place of a developed sense of personal sovereignty.

And finally, we need to take the stigma out of reporting violations. We need to believe children when they tell us that something doesn't feel right with someone, or that something happened that injured their sense of safety and sovereignty.

Organizational Integrity

We need to create models of consent in our organizations. This process requires educating ourselves on the legal elements of consent by studying local, state, and federal laws. We need to agree on policies regarding consent, including agreements about what happens when a violation occurs.

For some organizations, this will be a complicated process. Collective core values will have to be examined. Groups will need to create formats for addressing grievances or come to agreement on zero-tolerance policies.

We need to examine collective values regarding power structures and consent. In particular, we need to address (on both the personal and organizational levels) the question of sexual consent in intergenerational community. To create intergenerational integrity, we need to take age considerations and the existence of semi-familial/clan/extended family relationships into account, as well as take the implications of long-term relationships to heart. For example, if someone has had any involvement in raising or mentoring a young person over the course of their childhood or young adulthood, that relationship must be viewed in almost all cases though a familial lens.

We also need to address other power differentials. We will need to come to agreement, or at least have discussions, about teacher/student authority structures and relationships, and deconstruct our cultural assumptions about power, authority, and sexuality.

With these conversations in process and structures in place, we need to offer education to our members about consent, and in cases where appropriate, about our specific organizational agreements regarding consent. We will need to create templates for orientation sessions for festivals and conventions, create written policies and share them as part of membership packets, and post them at events.

Community Integrity: Protection and Supporting Next Generations

In the larger community, we need to continue having open conversations on power, consent, personal integrity, and sovereignty. Some of these conversations will naturally be about sexual conduct, but a culture of consent goes far beyond questions of sexual consent. We need to continue examining the areas where the dominant culture has affected our collective process, and also where confusion about the different cultural values about sexual expression within Paganism may have created murkiness.

We must keep in mind that as adults, it is our responsibility to set and stick to boundaries, even when they get less clear for the young people we have seen grow up. It is our responsibility (and if we create it so, it will be our deep and respectful pleasure) to hold safe space for our young ones to grow into their sexual identities in an unguarded and natural way. This can only happen once we make a safe space for this process. This safe space that we create together will allow the healing of our own sexual wounds as well. With dedication to our collective process, we may get to see our young people experience a consent-fueled sexual liberation—a liberation that recognizes "yes," "no," and "maybe" all as valid responses to any invitation.

As my children (nearly adults now) move through the crowds at festivals and conventions, I recognize that my vision is somewhat colored by my own formative experiences. I keep a watchful eye. But I also challenge myself to trust our collective growth, and my own consent-based parenting, and the strength and wisdom of my children.

I know that my children's aunties and uncles—by blood and otherwise—are also watching out, just as I am watching out for my nieces and nephews, and for all the young people in our community, whether I know them or not. We are all watching, because this isn't just a "community"—this is a family.

Lasara Firefox Allen is an author, coach, educator, and activist. A second generation Pagan clergy member and a family-traditions Witch, she is raising her children in the Pagan community. Her first book, *Sexy Witch* (Llewellyn, 2005) is available in four languages and distributed internationally. Her second book with Llewellyn is *The Fivefold Goddess*. Lasara offers courses, workshops, and retreats covering a range of topics; relationships, parenting/family dynamics, sexuality, feminism, body-image, magick, and spirituality. Married to the love of her life and mother to two amazing kids, Lasara and her family live in the wilds of northern California. Find out more at www.LasaraFirefoxAllen.com.

Part III:
Building
Communities of
Autonomy and
Empathy

Mindful Touch as a Religious Practice

Christine Hoff Kraemer

For me, mindful, loving, pleasurable touch is a religious practice, a physical expression of my most deeply-felt convictions about the world. I came to this practice after years of unwittingly abusing my body through restricting my access to pleasurable touch.

Once upon a time, I was a graduate student researching sexual and gender minorities in new religious movements. Ironically, I was spending enormous amounts of time writing about embodiment in an environment that implicitly devalued the body at every turn. I read, I wrote, I talked; I ate and slept mostly so that I could read, write, and talk some more. Although I loved writing and thinking, overall I was miserable. All the parts of me that are *flesh* were miserable.

After I graduated, I decided to take a break from academia and go to massage school. It was an incredibly healing time for me, because I was finally able to live my talk about the sacred body. Doing bodywork enabled me to accept at a bone level my belief that body and mind are really one substance, one energy, one being. I was trained by therapists who brought a deep reverence to their work, who approached each client with great respect and compassion. It was in this context that I started to combine what I'd learned about consent and power in the BDSM community with the kind of therapeutic boundary-setting a bodyworker needs. I learned to bring greater presence to my touch and honed the communication skills needed to work with survivors of assault or abuse.

I came to realize that although contemporary Paganism had wonderful theology about how touch could be sacred—and so did progressive queer Christian theology, which I was also studying—it was the bodywork and BDSM communities that really understood the logistics of making touch ethical and consensual. I decided to bring all those resources together in my book, *Eros and Touch from a Pagan Perspective,* from which parts of this essay are drawn.[1]

---

[1] Christine Hoff Kraemer, *Eros and Touch from a Pagan Perspective: Divided*

What Is the Erotic?

"Eros" or "the erotic" is a state of connected, intimate, fully embodied intimacy, a state that can include the sexual but is not limited to it. As a theological term, "eros" has a long history, but here I'll focus on its use in the twentieth and twenty-first centuries.

Psychologist C. G. Jung defined eros as a relational principle, "the great binder and loosener" within the psyche, among people, and between the individual and the world.[2] He saw the erotic as the desire for wholeness within the self, as well as the desire to connect and interact with others. In Jungian thought, the human self reflects the *imago dei,* the image of God. Eros, then, is a principle of both the human and the divine: the human desire for wholeness is a mirror of divine desire.

Speaking of the erotic in a psychological and theological context, however, may distract us from the fact that it is fundamentally embodied. Poet and feminist Audre Lorde defined the term famously in her essay "Uses of the Erotic: The Erotic as Power."[3] For Lorde, the erotic is the impulse to flourish physically, emotionally, and spiritually. It is a desire for pleasure that drives a person to resist oppression and strive for a satisfying and meaningful life. The erotic can be expressed sexually in the bedroom, but it is also present in every moment of intense engagement with the world, particularly moments that are celebratory or creative.

---

for *Love's Sake* (New York: Routledge, 2013). To increase the readability of this essay, I have omitted many of the footnotes and simplified the content. In *Eros and Touch,* sacramental touch is just one part of an erotic ethics approach to social justice. Interested readers who would like to read *Eros and Touch* but are unable to purchase it or borrow a copy from a library are encouraged to contact me for options.

[2]   C. G. Jung, *Collected Works* v. 10, *Civilization in Transition,* 2nd ed. (New York: Bollingen, 1970), 254.

[3]   Audre Lorde, "Uses of the Erotic: The Erotic as Power," *Sister Outsider: Essays and Speeches by Audre Lorde* (Freedom: Crossing Press, 1984).

Some writers emphasize the erotic as a quality of connection with the natural environment or the cosmos. Theologian Carter Heyward, for example, writes that "My eroticism is my participation in the universe."[4] Writer and literary critic Miriam DeCosta-Willis calls eroticism "[t]he life force that flows like an inscrutable tide through all things, linking man to woman, man to man, woman to woman, bird to flower, and flesh to spirit."[5]

Because of upbringing, conditioning, or temperament, not everyone easily perceives the erotic in their relationships with other people or the land. To feel the pleasurable interpenetration that DeCosta-Willis describes may require a shift in awareness. The shift may be as subtle as tuning a radio to the right station, but it can sometimes require a temporary separation from old patterns of disconnected living.

In *The Spiral Dance,* Starhawk describes a summer she spent as a young person, bicycling up and down the West Coast and camping on beaches. She writes, "For the first time, I lived in direct contact with nature, day and night. I began to feel connected to the world in a new way, to see everything as alive, erotic, engaged in a constant dance of mutual pleasuring, and myself as a special part of it all."[6] For Starhawk, prolonged outdoor living allowed her senses to open to this loving, sensual, interconnected quality of being. Such openness can give everyday life the emotional flavor of a parent cradling a baby, an embrace between long-separated friends, or lovemaking with a trusted partner. It can make the intake of air into one's lungs feel like a caress from the universe.

---

[4] Carter Heyward, Touching Our Strength: The Erotic as Power and the Love of God (San Francisco: Harper & Row, 1989), 25.

[5] Miriam deCosta-Willis, Introduction, *Erotique Noire: Black Erotics,* ed. Miriam deCosta-Willis, Reginald Martin, and Roseann P. Bell (New York: Anchor Books, 1992), xxix.

[6] Starhawk, *The Spiral Dance: A Rebirth of the Ancient Religion of the Great Goddess,* 20th anniversary ed. (1979; San Francisco: HarperSanFrancisco, 1999), 14.

The erotic, then, is a force that operates within the self and between selves. This love for others and the self, expressed concretely through the flesh, opens opportunities for an ecstasy that is our divine birthright.

The Erotic in Society

Our failure to acknowledge the erotic flow of life force in our larger social structures and daily lives contributes to economic and social inequalities, as well as to poor individual and social health. If we consider the right to pleasure to be a basic human right, acts that do not nurture the body become clear ethical violations in a way American society does not currently acknowledge. To quote theologian Marvin Ellison, "Every oppression involves violence toward the devalued body."[7] These oppressions include domestic abuse or sexual assault, mandatory unpaid overtime or sweatshop working conditions, laws criminalizing consensual sex acts between adults or hate crimes committed against minorities. There is a wide range of unethical activities that are brought sharply into focus as crimes when we prioritize bodily autonomy.

Valuing pleasure is also important for our children and for our society's future. Though studies have shown that depriving children of affectionate touch stunts them both cognitively and physically, rules against touch between public school teachers and children have become increasingly draconian, and some schools have even prohibited hugging and handholding between children. In our efforts to protect children from abusive touch, we have subjected them to the abuse of neglect and encouraged a culture where children and adults alike are agonizingly touch-starved—a state that encourages illness, intolerance, and violence. Our failure to value pleasurable touch doesn't just affect those in disadvantaged positions—it hurts us all.

---

[7] Marvin M. Ellison, *Erotic Justice: A Liberating Ethic of Sexuality* (Louisville: Westminster John Knox P, 1996), 15.

Pagans are in a unique position to respond to this situation because, unlike the dominant Christian religious traditions of the Western world, our theologies largely already affirm the sacredness of the body, of sexuality, and of touch. What we lack, however, is the culture and training to put these beliefs into practice in a systematic way. I hope to provide some of the building blocks for such a culture in this essay.

Mindful Touch as a Sacrament

Although increased levels of pleasurable consensual touch will increase our health and happiness, what I propose here is more radical than that. *Loving, consensual touch can be a deliberate religious practice.* When we experience being as fundamentally erotic, we may feel a desire—perhaps even a holy obligation—to facilitate erotic connection between and among groups, between individuals, and within ourselves. A practice of consensual, pleasurable touch—offered formally, as in a ritual of healing, or informally, as in the warm squeeze of a friend's hand—encourages empathy and connection and opens the way to divine love. We are each the eyes and hands and lips of the gods, and in touching each other, we experience our infinite variety and particularity, as well as the life force that animates all of Being.

The practice of making contact mindfully, as both an ordinary and a profoundly holy act, is what I call *sacramental touch.* As we use the term in Western theology, a sacrament is an act that demonstrates the presence of unconditional divine love in the world. While "love" and "the erotic" are not things we can see or lay our hands on, touch is their visible and tangible sign. "Sacrament" captures the joyful reverence and intentionality that a deeper understanding of the erotic can bring to the touch we offer.

A Brief History of Sacramental Healing Touch

The idea of sacramental touch draws on a long cross-cultural history of healing. In the West, the recorded practice of healing through touch goes back to at least 1553 BCE, in the form of the

Ebers Papyrus. Other recorded accounts can be found in the Bible, in the medical writings of Greek physician Hippocrates and the Roman physician Galen, and throughout the history of Christianity. Eastern cultures also feature a variety of touch therapies; in both Chinese medicine and Indian Ayurvedic medicine, various points on the body are stimulated in order to balance its vital forces. These systems have similarities with the ancient Greek theory of bodily humors, which the technique of *anatripsis* ("rubbings") was meant to regulate. In some cultures, techniques similar to what we now think of as massage were used to dispel possession by disease-causing harmful spirits. The traditional systems of medicine described above (and those of Australia, Africa, and other regions) arose as part of integrated cultural worldviews that included the spiritual. In other words, these traditional systems of healing touch are based on specific theologies of the body and its relation to the cosmos.[8]

The contemporary Pagan approach to touch has a great deal to do with healing and with the attempt to harmonize oneself and one's relationships with the natural world. Many contemporary Pagans hold the idea that all living things share a vital life energy, which I have been characterizing here as eros or the erotic, but this philosophy is more generally referred as "vitalism." Vitalism has been a part of many religious movements that focused on spiritual and physical healing, especially in nineteenth and twentieth century America. [9] Contemporary American Paganism was most directly influenced by the vitalistic theories of psychoanalyst Wilhelm Reich, whose name for the energy pervading the natural world was "orgone." Reich believed that orgone could be transmitted from being to being through touch, especially during sexual activity. If the proper flow of orgone was blocked because of emotional or other dysfunction, Reich taught,

---

[8]   Robert Noah Calvert, *The History of Massage: An Illustrated Survey* (Rochester, VT: Healing Arts/Inner Traditions, 2002).

[9]   Catherine L. Albanese, *Nature Religion in America* (Chicago: University of Chicago Press, 1991).

mental and physical disease would result. Reich believed that pleasure is essential for health, and he was hostile toward authoritarianism and patriarchy, all of which made him popular among Pagans.[10]

Along with their interest in vitalistic theories, many contemporary Pagans have drawn on sexual practices from nineteenth- and twentieth-century Western esotericism. The practice of sexual ritual in this era sought to resolve pathologies created by repressing human sexual instincts (as described by Sigmund Freud and others). Occultists who embraced the practice of sex magic did so in search of personal spiritual freedom, but also because they believed that sexual liberation would contribute to a new social order free of racial and gender-based oppression.[11] These social goals were widely shared by mid- to late-twentieth century Pagans.

Such egalitarian goals also motivated the practice of "naturism" or nudism. Naturists believed that nudity erased signs of social rank, encouraged physical health, and increased personal and social freedom. Accordingly, Wiccan publicizer Gerald Gardner emphasized ritual nudity in the form of Wicca that he spread in the 1950s. In Wicca and in a variety of Pagan groups emerging in the 1960s and 1970s, Pagans came to see acts of consensual sensuality and sexuality as moments where human beings actively channel divinity: the "acts of love and pleasure" named in the Wiccan text *The Charge of the Goddess*. Although sex magic and naturism were not understood as directly therapeutic in the same way as, say, chiropractic (which is a good example of a vitalistic therapy), they were nevertheless conceptualized as healing practices—behaviors that restore the harmony of the body with nature and the cosmos and so encourage personal and social health.[12]

---

[10] For more information about Reich's influence on contemporary Paganism, see Chas S. Clifton, *Her Hidden Children* (Lanham, MD: AltaMira Press, 2006).

[11] Hugh B. Urban, *Magia Sexualis: Sex, Magic, and Liberation in Modern Western Esotericism* (Berkeley: University of California Press, 2006).

[12] Clifton, *Her Hidden Children*.

Contemporary Paganism today includes a number of practices that could be considered as sacramental touch. Sexual ritual for the purpose of communing with divine energies (often performed privately) continues in Wiccan and other traditions. Additionally, Pagan and other spiritually-oriented sex workers offer sexual healing services to those traumatized by sexual assault or other abuse, or who are simply struggling with body shame or social anxiety. Some of these sex workers think of themselves as "sacred prostitutes" and understand their work as continuous with ancient temple prostitution. Such sexual healing work can take a variety of forms, from counseling, to hands-on sexual instruction, to performance art. Its goals include helping individuals cultivate pride in their bodies; gain a sense of ownership over their sexual power; liberate repressed sexual energy; learn how to communicate about sex and maintain healthy boundaries; and practice techniques to achieve ecstatic or mystical states, as well as to simply have more enjoyable sex.[13]

Pagans engage in a variety of sensual and therapeutic forms of sacramental touch as part of religious practice. They may use water or scented oil to anoint themselves or each other as a method to bless and heal. For example, the Five Fold Kiss is a Wiccan practice in which words of blessing and kisses are bestowed on various parts of the recipient's body. Some groups also engage in group massage, in which a recipient receives gentle, nonsexual massage from the members of the group while all participants verbally affirm his beauty and holiness. Some groups that use this kind of ritual touch may give the blessing "Thou art Goddess" or "Thou art God" to affirm the divine presence within the recipient's physical form. These rituals may be performed simply as blessings, or as practice meant to dispel shame or encourage healing from trauma.

---

[13] Ellen Evert Hopman and Lawrence Bond (eds.), "Sacred Prostitutes," *People of the Earth: The New Pagans Speak Out* (Rochester, VT: Destiny Books, 1996), 139-51. This chapter features interviews with D'vora and Annie Sprinkle.

Many Pagans also practice modern forms of laying on of hands meant to heal injury or disease. In some Pagan communities, it is common to be trained in Reiki, a spiritual touch practice from Japan that facilitates physical and emotional healing through improved flow of life force. Such practices affirm widespread Pagan beliefs that mental, physical, and sexual health result from the proper movement of natural and/or divine forces, and that appropriate, intentional touch helps to correct and strengthen that flow.

Seeking and Expressing the Divine through Touch

Sacramental touch attempts to raise intentional touch to an art form, one that fosters healing and divine connection. The mindfulness needed for this kind of practice is modeled well by professional bodyworkers, particularly those who already see a spiritual dimension to their practice.[14] Bodywork educator David Lauterstein, for example, is fond of saying that when a practitioner lays her hands on a client, she is laying her hands on an entire history: all the experiences of an entire life, and all the inheritances of that person's ancestors. Because body and spirit are one, to touch another's body is also to make contact with another *soul*—an act that deserves nothing less than awe.

Because of this awareness, bodyworkers are trained to create well-boundaried, safe containers for people to receive pleasurable touch and help them re-educate their bodies in healthy movement patterns. Some of this is accomplished in practical ways: the space is prepared with music and a comfortable table so that it feels relaxing and safe; the bodyworker gets informed consent from the client by having them fill out a form and explaining what will happen in the session; the client is draped with a sheet to set boundaries around parts of the body that are not being treated or will not be touched. But just as important as these physical practices is the mindfulness in which

---

[14] For initial reading on the spiritual dimensions of bodywork, I recommend Deane Juhan, *Touched by the Goddess: The Physical, Psychological, and Spiritual Powers of Bodywork* (Barrytown, NY: Station Hill Press, 2002).

bodyworkers are trained. In his essay series "The Seven Dimensions of Touch," Lauterstein stresses the importance of the bodyworker's intention when first making physical contact with a client. He writes,

> The first element or dimension of touch occurs when we lay our hands upon someone. Just laying down a hand establishes a point or area of contact. [...] This single dimension of basic contact sums up everything so eloquently depicted in Michelangelo's famous Sistine Chapel painting, where God and Adam reach toward each other. The power of this picture is that it depicts with stunning visual beauty the creation of life.
>
> Creation occurs in the moment and in the space of touching another. This is the relationship.[15]

For Lauterstein, when contact occurs—between the divine and the human, or between two human beings—a relationship is initiated that will affect and change both parties. Contact provides the opportunity to establish an "I-Thou" relationship. This term comes from the work of philosopher Martin Buber, who defined an I-Thou relationship as one where neither party is objectified, but where each is fully and lovingly acknowledged in all of their complexity.[16] For Buber, "I-Thou" describes the ideal relationship between a human being and the divine. The qualities of such a relationship—compassion, openness, caring, respect, commitment—form a potential basis for all other relationships. When we make first contact—particularly when touching another physically, but also when first making eye contact— we have an opportunity to begin an "I-Thou" relationship and to make a holy connection.

The embodied nature of relationship is important in Pagan theologies. Many Pagans believe that our deities are immanent in the world and are in a constant state of growth, change, and development.

---

[15] David Lauterstein, *The Deep Massage Book* (Taos, NM: Complimentary Medicine Press, 2011), 44-45.

[16] Martin Buber, *I and Thou* (New York: Scribner, 1958).

Rather than being transcendent—outside of us or the universe—our deities change with us, struggle with us, perhaps even share our flesh. Relationship is an essential feature of the way divinity expresses itself—in the universe in general, and for human beings in particular. When we approach touch sacramentally, we attempt to bring this relational quality of the divine not just into ritual, but into our everyday lives.

When we practice sacramental touch, however, it is important not to neglect our own safety and well-being. While seeking to treat others with love and reverence, it is equally important that I maintain an I-Thou relationship with *myself*. We have an obligation to set good boundaries with those who will not treat us with respect, caring, or even basic politeness. Those who are unwilling or unable to engage in relationships of mutual respect deserve compassion, but not indulgence. Sacramental touch happens most naturally when both parties feel safe.

Distinguishing Qualities of Touch

In the United States and in some other Western countries, touch often feels unsafe because the boundaries between sexual and merely affectionate touch have become blurred. This cultural reality has contributed to widespread touch deprivation, but also to a more subtle problem. Today, many individuals have not learned to make clear distinctions about different qualities of touch; they may assume that all touch is sexual, or fail to recognize sexual touch when it occurs.

This confusion is due to a lack of experience with different qualities of touch. Nearly all cultures condone sexual touch in some form, but sexual touch may only be allowed in specific contexts or between specific classes of people. When highly restricted sexual touch is one of the few permitted forms of touch available, individuals may develop a tendency to perceive *all* touch as potentially sexual. Further, when sexual needs are not being met due to cultural restrictions and inhibitions, sexual frustrations may color other kinds of physical encounters and give even unintentional touch a sexual charge.

Somatic psychologist Phyllis K. Davis sees Americans' confusion of loving touch with sexual touch as a system of pathological thinking that hinders people from getting the kinds of touch they need. For example, people may withhold affectionate touch out of a fear of being condemned as promiscuous or homosexual. Among and between families, adults may restrict their touch behaviors so as not to accidentally encourage adultery or incest, or to avoid accusations of child molestation. Additionally, the cultural tendency to sexualize large areas of the body—often everything but the hands, arms, shoulders, and head—may cause nonsexual touch to be inaccurately read as sexual.[17]

Davis states that "in order to learn to differentiate between hands that touch to turn on, and hands that touch to convey comfort and affection, [individuals] must experience both."[18] In her practice, she has found that most individuals find it easy to make distinctions between kinds of touch when they are taught directly. In group workshops, she asks participants to choose partners for a touch exercise in which one partner touches the other while focusing one by one on the emotions of tenderness, anger, detachment, and sexual arousal. The receiver attempts to identify each touch without being told which emotion is being expressed. Having removed the expectation that every touch is potentially sexual, most individuals are able to begin making clear distinctions either immediately, or with a few repetitions.[19]

Deliberately developing the ability to distinguish types of touch—and being clear with our own intentions when we touch another person—helps to ensure that both persons in the exchange will have a positive experience. It is common in our culture for people to initiate sexual touch out of a desire for affection. When both individuals in a

---

[17] Phyllis K. Davis, *The Power of Touch,* revised edition (Carlsbad, CA: Hay House, 1999 [1991]), 85-88.
[18] Davis, 86.
[19] Davis, 22-23.

relationship have a larger menu of kinds of touch to choose from, they are more able to identify their desires and negotiate a physical encounter that satisfies them both.

Touch Deprivation

Touch deprivation has well-documented effects on our health, psychological and physical. Most Americans are impacted by it, as we are socialized to touch very little compared to many other countries. One cross-cultural study looked at how frequently friends sharing a meal touch each other in an hour, on average. Puerto Ricans touch around 180 times an hour, French friends 110 times, and Americans a mere two times.[20]

So what exactly does touch deprivation do to us developmentally? The most dramatic evidence is in the rates of infant deaths in orphanages in the late nineteenth and early twentieth centuries, which in some American cities could be as high as 90%. The condition was called *marasmus,* meaning "wasting away." Those babies who did survive past the first year of life were severely physically retarded, a condition now referred to as "deprivation dwarfism." At length, the cause was determined to be a combination of understaffing and neglect. The prevailing psychological opinion of the time advised not "overhandling" babies, lest they become spoiled. Additionally, due to understaffing, staff generally only had time to clean and feed the babies, not to handle them or play with them. When extra staff were added at such orphanages to cuddle the infants, mortality rates dropped dramatically.[21]

---

[20] Davis, 80.

[21] R.A. Spitz, "Hospitalism: A follow-up report," in D. Fenichel, P. Greenacre & A. Freud (Eds.), *The Psychoanalytic Study of the Child,* Vol. 2 (New York: International Universities Press, 1947), 113-117. See also Ashley Montagu, *Touching: The Human Significance of the Skin,* Third Edition (New York: Harper & Row, 1986 [1971]), 99.

Animal studies have demonstrated that tactile stimulation is a biological requirement for infant mammals of all kinds, not just for human infants. For many species, a baby animal must be stimulated in the abdominal area by the mother's tongue, or it does not begin to urinate or defecate and so dies. Other animal studies have shown that pleasurable touch is the key element that causes mammals to form an attachment with their caregiver. Monkeys who were isolated when young developed a variety of hyperactive, apathetic, and violent behaviors that appeared much less frequently in monkeys raised by their mothers. Further, isolated monkeys who later had offspring showed abusive behaviors toward their young with much greater frequency than their socialized counterparts.

In other studies, rats that had been handled extensively in infancy showed increased immunological responses—and therefore, greater resistance to disease—that persisted into adulthood. Rats who were handled frequently and affectionately not only showed calmer, less anxious, and friendlier behavior, but also survived surgical procedures at a much greater rate than their less-handled siblings. Another rat study showed that affectionately handled rats grew faster, showed greater problem-solving ability, and responded to stress with less anxiety. Frequent nurturing touch during the developmental period, it appears, increases the ability of mammals to endure physical trauma, as well as tending to produce an even temperament.[22]

Some researchers have suggested that depriving human beings of touch can have a wide-ranging social impact. For example, cross-cultural studies by neuropsychologist James Prescott correlate low levels of affection shown toward infants with violent behavior in adults.[23] Other findings, however, suggest that the effects of early

---

[22] More information on animal studies can be found in Ashley Montagu, *Touching: The Human Significance of the Skin,* Third Edition (New York: Harper & Row, 1986 [1971]).

[23] Davis, 109, referring to James W. Prescott, "Body Pleasure and the Origins of Violence," *The Futurist* April 1975 and Prescott, "Alienation of Affection," *Psychology Today* December 1979.

neglect can be mitigated by touch in adolescence and later in life. Studies conducted by researcher Tiffany Field showed that increasing the amount of safe, boundaried touch that disturbed adolescents receive may help to relieve symptoms of mental illness. In one study, adolescents institutionalized for psychiatric disorders received massage for half an hour every day for a week. Their levels of stress hormones dropped, their sleep patterns became more regular, and incidents of inappropriate sexual and other behavior decreased, leading to earlier discharges from the psychiatric program.[24]

Given the evidence that touch is necessary for human development, policies prohibiting touch in public schools do not bode well for children's health. Touch deprivation may be one of the culprits behind increased rates of hyperactivity in children, as well as a contributing factor in anorexia and other eating disorders in adolescents and adults. Other studies suggest that by forbidding affectionate touch between students, school authorities may be creating social situations that encourage bullying, gang violence, and abuse in dating relationships.

Cultivating a Spiritual Practice of Touch

To declare that pleasure is both necessary for our health and our divine birthright is a first step towards the practice of sacramental touch. To be able to *feel* this truth emotionally is a second. But once the mind and the emotions have committed to the practice, the body must get involved, and here a bit of study and practice will not go amiss. For those of us who are dealing with a lifetime of feeling awkward about touching, books and classes on massage and other kinds of healing touch may provide tools to achieve particular qualities of touch. Davis, for example, relates an anecdote about an overly enthusiastic hugger in one of her workshops, a large and cheerful man whose hug knocked out her breath and popped one of her ribs. No doubt the man wanted to convey warmth and a lack of sexual intent, but leaving Davis winded was probably not the effect he had

---

[24] Tiffany Field, *Touch* (Cambridge, MA: MIT Press), 61.

intended![25] If we approach touch as a religious practice, it must be taken seriously as a *practice*—something that we commit to, study, repeat, and refine. A commitment not just to touch, but to touch others *well,* is part of sacralizing touch in our lives.

When I urge readers to cultivate an educated touch, however, I do not mean that if touch cannot be done well, it should be avoided. Rather, I hope that greater intentionality, knowledge, and consciousness around touch will help readers overcome shyness or awkwardness and reach out as their hearts move them. It will also help to ensure that the touch that they initiate will be received warmly and with pleasure.

Honoring Boundaries

With touch, spontaneity must be mixed with empathy, connectedness, and respect. If we seek to touch others as a sacrament—to touch them in a way that initiates an I-Thou relationship between divine selves—it is important to honor others' boundaries and make sure we have their consent to touch them. As someone who has often been anxious about imposing on others, I have benefited greatly from the explicit consent involved in giving or receiving bodywork. A professional bodyworker will interview the client before the first session and explain how the session will proceed. Clients have the opportunity at that time to set certain body parts or certain kinds of touch as "off-limits" for whatever reason. Whether giving or receiving, I find myself much more comfortable and confident after this direct exchange of expectations.

In the BDSM community, explicit negotiations around touch are also the norm. Books on kink often provide lists of activities that potential partners can fill out and exchange, indicating their likes, dislikes, limits, and potential interests. This kind of negotiation is also common in the polyamorous community, where feminist sexual ethics have been a powerful influence. Many polyamorous people are aware

---

[25] Davis, 201.

that, due to gender-related socialization patterns in our culture, both men and women frequently struggle to say no to sexual advances they do not want. It is clear that this problem must be addressed from both sides: the person who is approached must develop the assertiveness needed to say yes or no with confidence, while the person who is approaching should seek clear consent and be emotionally prepared to be rejected. At polyamorous gatherings, newcomers are often encouraged to ask verbally before touching, especially when approaching someone they do not know. The ability to ask, "Would you like a back rub?" and receive the answer gracefully is considered a sign of simple good manners, while a flirty "May I kiss you?" can often come off as romantic.

Such verbal conventions also help to ensure (though by no means guarantee) that neither party engages in sex they do not want. Even sensitive and caring people can misread a partner's body language when in the throes of passion, especially if the partner has mixed emotions rather than being entirely unwilling. It is a painful thing to learn that a partner feels guilty, embarrassed, or uncomfortable after what the other person thought was a pleasurable night; it is even worse to find oneself in a pattern of silence, repeatedly having sex that one does not want in an attempt to avoid hurting the other person's feelings. When frequent verbal communication is part of a relationship from the beginning, conversations about sex become normal and expected, and the highly-charged silence that can arise around unsatisfying sexual encounters is less likely to form.

The art of gaining verbal consent, once mastered, is rarely inappropriate. With a little practice, the question "Would you like a hug?" can come to seem natural. In certain situations, however, it may also be necessary to assess consent nonverbally. Based on the context in which I am meeting someone for the first time, I may open my arms to offer a hug. Usually the offer is accepted when the other person opens their arms in return. Occasionally, however, I am offered a handshake instead—a clear signal about that person's boundaries. Such boundary-setting is not a personal rejection. When another person has stricter boundaries around touch than I do, most likely those boundaries have nothing to do with me as a person, and much to do with how they understand appropriate behavior (with new acquaintances, with people of a certain gender, with non-family members, etc.). By shaking a new acquaintance's hand instead of insisting on a hug, I honor who they are and how they are coming to the relationship that is about to form.

When assessing consent nonverbally with someone new, it is important to watch the other person's body language and facial expression and aim for the lowest common denominator—the type of touch that both parties signal they are comfortable with, *which may be no touch at all.* When first meeting, it is most important that contact be genuine and comfortable. I refer the reader to Staśa Morgan-Appel's essay (included in this volume), which recommends practices for communities seeking to be as accessible as possible for people with disabilities or severe allergies, survivors of trauma, and others for whom any kind of physical contact may be problematic.

If we seek to touch as a religious practice, we may wish to increase the amount of touch in ours and others' lives, as well as its intimacy. It is important, however, that we do so in a way that increases our connection with others rather than alienating them. Physical contact is not something to be pushed on others, no matter how "good for them" our science or our theology says it will be. A sacramental touch is always extended as an invitation, not as a demand.

Seeking Consent in the Midst of Unequal Power Relationships

We all live in a web of unequal power relationships. Our society has rules, often unspoken, about who can exploit or commit violent acts on others' bodies, and these rules are based on hierarchies of gender, race, class, gender identity, and other characteristics. The reality of social injustice can make it very difficult to secure enthusiastic consent to many kinds of interactions, especially ones involving touch.

To say that an adult person with access to education, jobs, and basic political freedoms *cannot* give consent to sex, however, invalidates their expressions of desire and threatens to strip them of the power they do have. As discussed in the introduction to this collection, we need the ability to distinguish between *exploitation* (where vulnerability is taken advantage of) and *coercion* (where the use of force removes the possibility of consent). The classic exploitative relationship in feminist literature would be women's participation in the pornography industry. Such participation is rarely coerced, and some women find enjoyment, empowerment, and financial benefit through making pornography. However, many women take up making pornography because of financial need and social pressure. These pressures do not necessarily invalidate their consent, but they do make the situation ethically questionable because of the women's vulnerability and the difficulties they may experience if they attempt to leave the situation. In the pornography industry, not all participants have a robust exit strategy, which is a necessary part of ethically negotiating a hierarchical power relationship.

Importantly, the existence of a power dynamic in a relationship—even an erotic relationship—does not make it inherently exploitative. Feminist ethicist Cristina Traina has explored unequal erotic relationships beginning with the perspective of motherhood. For Traina, the relationship between a nursing mother and an infant is one of the most deeply erotic relationships a human being can experience—and it is also one of the most unequal, with the infant utterly at the mercy of its mother, unable to set any boundaries around sensual touch. Yet we tend to view the mother-infant relationship as one of the most desirable and important kinds of bonds that human beings can experience. In fact, without a loving relationship with a caregiver in early childhood, children may develop attachment disorders that prevent them from engaging in loving, mutual relationships for the rest of their lives. Traina argues that if the loving touch exchanged in the mother-infant relationship is desirable—as seems obvious—then erotic relationships in a power dynamic must not be inherently unethical.[26] The challenge, then, is to discover what makes an unequal relationship exploitative and what makes it healthy.

When negotiating consent across a power dynamic, we can:

- ◆ ensure that power differentials are explicitly acknowledged and that the possibility of exploitation is discussed on an ongoing basis. BDSM vocabulary can be helpful for identifying, describing, and negotiating hierarchical power dynamics in all kinds of social relationships.[27]

- ◆ seek relationships that allow for power to move fluidly between the participants. Rigid power inequalities where there is no room for negotiation and no exit strategy may compromise both partners' ability to give enthusiastic consent to the relationship in general and to touch in particular.

- ◆ honor urges to engage in relationships of dominance and submission as part of our primal human wildness and look for ethical, healthy ways to channel them. The explicit negotiations and use of safewords involved in BDSM are helpful in creating a safe container for these desires to be expressed.

- ◆ deepen our capacity for empathy and the capacity of our children and students. Empathy as defined in research psychology is the ability to share the perceived emotion of another person. Empathy training has been found to increase group cohesion, improve individuals' social skills, and encourage tolerance and teamwork within diverse groups.

---

[26] See Cristina L.H. Traina, *Erotic Attunement: Parenthood and the Ethics of Sensuality between Unequals* (Chicago: University of Chicago Press, 2011).

[27] I recommend *The New Bottoming Book* and *The New Topping Book* by Dossie Easton and Janet W. Hardy, as well as works on BDSM by Raven Kaldera.

◆ support social justice movements that seek greater political, social, and economic equality, thus addressing the rigid social hierarchies that put so many of our relationships on unequal ground.

Transforming Our Own Relationships with Touch

To honor others' boundaries and needs, we must first honor our own. In seeking to care for others, I have sometimes ignored my own needs and treated myself as less important than the person I was caring for. But I too deserve to be a Thou, not an It. If I do not care deeply about my own thriving, I am throwing away the gift of my embodiment. How can I genuinely turn to another and affirm "Thou art God/dess" if I cannot see God/dess in myself?

Although receiving professional bodywork is an excellent method of seeking out safe, pleasurable touch, amateur classes or working through a massage book with a friend can be equally effective. Delightfully, taking classes in massage usually provides opportunities to receive touch, as one's classmates need bodies on which to practice. When the amount of touch that one receives is substantially increased, the reduction in anxiety, elevation of mood, and increase in general well-being that results can be substantial.

For those whose busy lives do not allow time and space for taking classes, Davis' *The Power of Touch* includes a number of exercises designed to increase one's comfort level with touch, and which can be done at any time with a friend or loved one. Some exercises include reflecting on one's personal history of experiences with touch, beginning with childhood; observing and describing one's current touch habits and behaviors; initiating small, casual touches with strangers to observe their reactions (and one's own); exchanging backrubs or foot massages with friends; experimenting with different kinds of sensation with a loved one (scratching, rubbing, stroking, tickling) and asking for feedback; asking for a hug when in a familiar group; cuddling with a partner with the lights on and off and observing the differences; and much more. Above all, Davis encourages her readers to seek out others who are willing to experiment with and talk openly about physical contact. These allies can provide essential support in transforming one's own relationship with touch.

Certain volunteer opportunities can also challenge and expand one's own touch boundaries. Hospitals sometimes need volunteers to cuddle or massage newborns, and homes for the elderly often welcome volunteers to spend time with their residents. In my work as a massage therapist, I have visited assisted living centers to give neck and shoulder massages to the elderly. In many cases, the fact of my touch was just as important to my lonely clients as the reduction in muscle tension. The elderly are a particularly touch-deprived population, especially those who are unpartnered. When we offer touch to those who are deeply in need, we open to the profound healing capacities of ordinary touch and of our own capacity to channel divine love.

Touch others, then, as a sacrament, a holy rite in which divine love is tangibly felt; for your hands are the hands of the gods; your eyes full of compassion or yearning are theirs, and from your loved ones' eyes they look back; your kisses of affection or lust will be pressed on the Goddess's own lips. *"For I have been with you from the beginning, and I am that which is attained at the end of desire."*

Christine Hoff Kraemer received a PhD in Religious and Theological Studies from Boston University. She is an instructor in theology at Cherry Hill Seminary, a licensed massage therapist, and a practitioner of religious witchcraft. Her books include *Seeking the Mystery: An Introduction to Pagan Theologies* and *Eros and Touch from a Pagan Perspective: Divided for Love's Sake.*

Consent Culture
Radical Love and Radical Accessibility
Staśa Morgan-Appel

For many Pagans as individuals—as well as for many Pagan groups and communities—belief in the sacredness of touch is part of what makes us Pagan. Some fear that embracing a culture of consent in our communities would mean narrowing our options and opportunities for sacred touch, non-sexual and sexual. Yet the opposite can in fact be true: a culture of consent can mean expansion, rather than contraction.

Embracing a culture of consent can multiply our options for sacred touch and liberate us to explore a wider range of options for expressing love and affection. It is a path to radical accessibility and radical inclusion, which are core values for many Pagans.

Consensual touch is a way we can recognize, affirm, honor, and celebrate That-Which-Is-Sacred in ourselves and each other. Non-consensual touch deadens sacred connection. Obligatory social touch, when non-consensual, impedes sacred connection.

Obligatory Social Touch

Obligatory social touch is expected touch that is governed by conventions and unwritten rules, especially during greeting and leave-taking. In the US and the UK, we are often expected to shake hands when we are introduced to someone, especially in a more formal situation such as a professional setting; in families, young children are often expected to hug and kiss adult relatives or permit embraces from them. These rules are often unwritten. They are part of the social contract; we are expected to know them, and we expect other people to know them. Commonly-held conventions around social touch can help ease social situations. However, when someone violates those conventions, or does not seem to understand them—when they do not participate in the touch that is expected, or they engage in more or different touch than is expected—that sends a signal, sometimes subtle and sometimes more jarring, that something isn't quite right. This kind of misstep often makes people quite uncomfortable.

Replacing obligatory social touch with consent-based touch helps us to avoid missteps around unwritten social rules and even potentially opens us to deeper connection with the sacred within ourselves, other people, and the larger world.

Consent as an Access Tool

As Pagans, many of us are familiar with feeling, and factually being, unsafe in larger society. Many of us seek communities where we can feel and be safe, and many of us want to help create communities where we and other Pagans can have safety, too.

However, nearly all of us are raised and socialized in dominant culture. The same dominant culture which discriminates against us also teaches us to discriminate, often subconsciously, against members of our own and other minority groups.[1][2] Many of us are minorities in some ways (for example, as Pagans), and members of majority groups in others (for example, as white people). Consent culture can help make our Pagan communities and groups safer and more accessible for *all* of us, regardless of our status within the dominant culture.

Accessibility tools, or access tools, are tools and resources that members of minority groups may need in order to make a physical space or a community a place where we can participate fully. Access tools enable us to bring our full range of energy and abilities to a space. Some of us may be used to thinking of access around disability, primarily around mobility and sometimes hearing and vision. However, accessibility is not limited to people with disabilities. It spans all the ways people interact with each other and with the environment—through all five senses and our minds, through all five elements.

---

[1] Harvard University, "Education," Project Implicit, 18 Feb. 2013, Web. Available at https://implicit.harvard.edu/implicit/education.html.

[2] Implicit Bias & Philosophy International Research Network, "Implicit Bias & Philosophy International Research Project: Home," *Implicit Bias & Philosophy International Research Project: Home,* n.p., n.d., Web. Available at http://www.biasproject.org/.

Access needs and tools may be physical; they may be financial; they may be cognitive; they may be energy-related; they may be emotional or psychological; they may be spiritual. They encompass all the traditional Witchen elements—Earth (the physical), Air (the psychological and intellectual), Fire (intuition, the passions, and will), Water (the emotional), and Spirit (matters pertaining to the spiritual realms).

Consent is an access tool. Consent *culture* is a form of radical accessibility, and as such is an expression of radical love and radical inclusion.

Radical Accessibility

What do I mean by "radical" in this context? And how does consent, especially for non-sexual touch, widen accessibility? "Radical" has some interesting meanings, both in terms of the dictionary[3] and in terms of common usage and understanding:

+ related to, or from, something's fundamental or essential nature
+ related to, or from, something's root or its origin
+ inherent
+ unusual
+ not fitting into common patterns
+ extreme
+ reformist
+ wild
+ unbound
+ free

Some of these definitions are concerned with conserving and living out our core values. Others are concerned with reforming or bringing change to how we live our values in action. In Pagan spiritual

---

[3] "Radical," *Oxford Dictionary,* Oxford University Press, 2015. Available at http://www.oxforddictionaries.com/us/definition/american_english/ radical.

communities, we often associate "radical" with being wild or extreme, with reformation and change, and only sometimes with returning to the root, with conserving, or with focusing on what is fundamental or essential. Consent culture, radical accessibility, radical inclusion, and radical love can include both perspectives—can be about conserving and reforming; can be about being true to our roots, and also about nurturing new growth and change.

How Consent Practices Increase Accessibility

I invite you to imagine you are arriving at an annual gathering of your spiritual community, your people. This group, this event, this time, this space—this is home for you in many ways. You have known some of these people for years; others are newcomers. You may see some of these people other times and places, but these gatherings are the only times the group as a whole gets together and just gets to be its exuberant, unapologetic, Pagan self.

There might be a lot of excited, energetic, noisy, physical greetings: hugs, calls, laughter, joyful shouts. For people with different backgrounds, different experiences, and different needs, this can be quite challenging. This is where consent—stopping and asking first, no matter how many times we've thrown our arms around each other before, kissed each other on the cheek, slung an arm companionably across the other's shoulders, swept each other up in big bear hugs, slapped each other on the back—can make a huge difference in how accessible our being together is, in how possible it is for us to be together.

Different people have different boundaries around interpersonal touch, and people's needs and boundaries change over time. While some of us enjoy sharing hugs, kisses, cuddles, and more, not all of us do, and it's not safe for all of us. You and I might have had a delightful big hug last time we saw each other, but it might be not okay now. It's very easy, especially when some of us have known each other a long time, and especially in an exuberantly affectionate community, to forget that not everyone wants or can tolerate physical affection all the time.

Some people simply do not like to touch or be touched. An embrace when one of us doesn't really want to be there is not a good celebration of sacred connection; it's not sacred connection at all. If we check with each other first, we can do something else where we both feel love and joy in the experience, even exuberantly.

Some non-neurotypical people, including some people with autism, can't tolerate hugs. Some just don't like them. Some like them some of the time. Some love them. If we ask first, we can find a way to express our warmth that works for everyone in an interaction.

For people with chronic illness and/or chronic pain, the ability to participate in and to tolerate different kinds of physical touch varies. Other people can't know what will be comfortable, painful, or disabling without asking. Clasping someone's arms, hugging them, or putting an arm around their shoulders could be a wonderful experience—or it could cause someone intense pain for the rest of the day, prevent them from carrying their own tray at dinner, or make it hard for them to sleep that night. A kiss on the cheek might be lovely, or it might make someone ill, panicked, sensorily overwhelmed, or simply uncomfortable. Something that was fine yesterday might not be possible today. If we check first, we can find something that works.

For people who use mobility aids or wear orthopedic appliances—cane, walking stick, brace, cast, special shoe or boot, Z-frame, walker, crutch(es), wheelchair, sling, artificial limb, service animal, or something entirely different—there's wide variability in what kinds of touch do and don't work, and under what circumstances. If my arm is in a sling or I am using crutches and you hug me without warning, it might be painful, and I might lose my balance. If we ask first, we can share affection in a way that works for both of us.

Not all disabilities, injuries, or medical conditions are obvious; many people have "hidden" injuries or disabilities. A person with a back injury might not need a brace, or might be wearing a brace another person can't see, but an unexpected embrace might cause them pain or make their injury worse. Someone with multiple sclerosis, lupus, or arthritis might appear or sound just like everyone else, but unexpected touch might cause them pain, dizziness, or other problems.

Asking first means opening the possibility of shared touch that is accessible for all the people involved.

Some people have sensitivities to chemicals and fragrances, and others have medical conditions, including asthma and migraine, that can be triggered by fragrances or chemicals. If someone is wearing perfume, essential oil, cologne, aftershave, or another personal care product with fragrance (whether natural or artificial), or has washed their hands with scented soap, they may present a danger to people with these conditions. Being physically near or touching someone with fragrance sensitivities while wearing fragrance can trigger pain, nausea, dizziness, blurry vision, cognitive difficulty or other neurological problems, or difficulty breathing. If we check first, we can find a way to express love and affection that works and doesn't make anyone ill.

Some people with migraine disease love physical touch some of the time but can't tolerate it other times. Someone with balance difficulties might be fine if you hug them one time, but a hug might knock them over another time, even the same day. If we check first, our chances of sharing affection that is safe and enjoyable is much higher.

Checking is the first step in consent culture and in living our love and affection for each other. No matter how well we think we know it's all right, we don't assume. We ask. "No" is a perfectly acceptable answer. Sacred touch needs to work for all the people involved, or it's no longer sacred touch—regardless of the conventional rules and expectations about obligatory social touch. A community where it's the norm to check and ask before hugging or touching people is a community that is more accessible for more of its members. A culture of consent makes it more possible for more of us to participate more fully in community—expands us rather than contracts us. Consent helps make community more accessible to all of us. When we ask, we are all opened up to the possibility of more genuine physical affection.

Groups with Special Needs around Touch

People with Disabilities

For some of us, even non-sexual touch and obligatory social touch routinely carry the threat of violence and violation. People with disabilities (PWDs) regularly experience unwanted touch and the threat of unwanted touch. PWDs are constantly forced to confront society's denial that they own their own bodies and have agency for their own lives. Non-disabled people routinely violate the boundaries and the agency of people with disabilities. Another aspect of this is that many PWDs experience isolation when it comes to physical affection: non-disabled people often touch people with disabilities only in impersonal and non-consensual ways, and consensual touch between disabled and non-disabled people for the sake of affection can be rare. Some non-disabled people feel awkward about touching people with disabilities socially, or are afraid to touch PWDs—afraid of causing harm, afraid of being socially awkward, afraid of their own discomfort.

People with disabilities do not have the luxury of assuming touch is safe. When touch comes with the threat of violence and violation, it is not a clear channel for sacred connection.

LGBTQA People

Lesbian, gay, bisexual, transgender, queer, and asexual (LGBTQA) people regularly experience unwanted touch and the threat of unwanted touch. Some straight people treat LGBTQA people as a challenge. They may try to "prove" how "accepting" they are by insisting on physical contact or flirtation. Others expect LGBTQA people to prove they're "worthy" of acceptance by tolerating physical contact. Straight people have a history of explicit violence toward LGBTQA people, including assaults and beatings as well as the threat—especially for women and other gender minorities—that unwanted, non-consensual sexual contact (sexual assault and rape) can change their sexual orientation. Lesbian women routinely hear that they're not really lesbians, while bisexual women are told that they really like men better, by straight men who flagrantly disregard their agency. Some straight people worry about imagined danger to their children because they believe homophobic propaganda equating same-sex attraction with pedophilia and child rape. Others worry that the "danger" to their children is that if their children spend time with LGBTQA people, they might "decide" not to be straight or cisgender.

Lesbian, gay, bisexual, transgender, queer, and asexual people do not have the luxury of assuming touch is safe. When touch comes with the threat of violence and violation, it is not a clear channel for sacred connection.

Women and Gender Minorities

Women and gender minorities regularly experience unwanted touch and the threat of unwanted touch. They consistently face pressure to accept obligatory social touch that is non-consensual, undesired, and violates their boundaries. Non-consensual obligatory social touch is toward one end of a spectrum that also includes groping, cat-calling, pressure to participate in unwanted conversation and company, sexual assault, and other violence against women, transgender people, and gender-nonconforming people.

While cisgender[4] women face being targets of violence simply because they're women, transgender women, transgender men, and gender-nonconforming people face additional threats based on transphobia, cissexism, and sexist gender norms. In addition, many cisgender people fetishize transgender people's bodies and feel no compunction about asking transgender, intersex, and gender non-conforming people intrusive personal questions about their bodies and their medical histories or even touching them in non-consensual ways. Many white cisgender people assume, consciously or unconsciously, that transgender women, especially transgender women of color, are sex workers and are available to them sexually.

---

[4]   Someone whose gender identity is consistent with the gender assigned to them (usually at birth).

Women and other gender minorities do not have the luxury of assuming touch is safe. When touch comes with the threat of violence and violation, it is not a clear channel for sacred connection.

People of Color

Women of color experience further layers to this. White people have a history of colonizing and enslaving people of color, and many white people, consciously or unconsciously, still act as if they think they have a right to the bodies of people of color, especially those of women and gender minorities. (In the US, this is particularly evident in how white people treat African-American women's sexuality and hair.) White people often treat Black people and other people of color as sexual objects, fetishizing them and making assumptions about their bodies and their sexual availability. Even though white people are far more likely to experience violence from other white people, many white people persist in believing (and in teaching other white people to believe) racist propaganda that people of color are by nature dangerous.

People of color do not have the luxury of assuming touch is safe. When touch comes with the threat of violence and violation, it is not a clear channel for sacred connection.

Objectification and Oppression

The examples I've provided are not exhaustive. These are only some of the issues people who are members of minorities face around touch and physical contact. There are other ways touch may carry the threat of violence and violation, and people may be members of other minority groups for whom touch carries those threats. We also cannot always tell by how someone looks, sounds, or acts if they're a member of a marginalized group who experiences touch as a tool of oppression.

Objectification, violence, and violation impede sacred connection. The consistent experience of touch as one method of objectification among many, and as one threat of violence among many, means that touch is not automatically a joyful experience of sacred connection, but can instead be something very different.

Unwanted physical contact is a tool of oppression. A culture of consent, where touch is neither assumed nor an obligation, can help reclaim touch as a tool of liberation, can help transform touch from an expression of dominance or experience of domination into an affirmation of sacred connection.

Limits Create Opportunities

Being in sacred community means that touch needs to work for everyone involved. We need to check first. "No" needs to be a perfectly acceptable answer. When we come up against limits—when we do not assume obligatory social touch, when we ask and someone says "No," when we recognize ahead of time that we need to find another way to greet someone or share physical affection, when we realize something won't work for us ourselves—those limits present us with the invitation and incentive to expand our repertoire, instead of shrinking it.

There are many specific examples I have experienced and witnessed of how a culture of consent around non-sexual, social touch can broaden accessibility and our options for sacred touch, can enable us to be more faithful to our roots and at the same time grow our communities.

I remember being at the kind of gathering I invited you to imagine above when, for the first time, someone lived consent culture with me in that very clear way. A dear friend with whom I've shared many hugs arrived, flashed me an incredible grin, and asked, "I'd love to give you a hug; is that all right with you, or shall we do something else?" I was floored. But it was tremendously helpful. I was headachy and tired from travel, and my balance was wobbly. Because they'd asked, I had an opportunity to tell them what I needed. We both put down our bags, moved into each other's arms, and sank into a blissful hug.

That blissful hug was much nicer than it otherwise might have been, in no small part because we were both able to participate fully and without worry. It was lovely. I still carry the experience with me as one of delight.

While more and more groups have fragrance-free gatherings, people often have to travel through fragranced spaces to get there. Another friend said to me once, again on arriving at the same gathering, "I'd love to hug you, but I had to use the fragranced soap at the rest stop, so I'm going to stand here and wave." They waved and gave me a big smile; I waved and beamed and blew kisses back. I felt loved. They felt loved. We were delighted to see each other. I didn't wonder why they weren't hugging me, since they usually do; I didn't wonder if I'd offended them, or if they were making assumptions about hugs and my disability, or anything else. I also didn't become ill, and I didn't make anyone else ill later, either. It was a wonderful, dear, tender experience—another I still carry with me with joy.

I have another friend in my spiritual community whose dimples I have a weakness for, and who often kisses me on the cheek. It's good they ask first, so I can prepare.

Consent not only helps make community more accessible, it helps open us up to new ways of physical affection and deeper experiences of love and trust. In the communities I am part of where there is a culture of consent around non-sexual, social touch, we have less obligatory social touch and more genuine warmth and affection. We have more ways to love each other, more ways to show our love physically, and more of us can participate in them.

This has benefited all of us, not only members of our communities who are part of minority groups. Yes, consent culture helps minority people in the ways I've described, in addition to others. But it helps the rest of us, too. It removes two expectations where people often get into trouble with each other, one-on-one or in groups: the expectation of obligatory social touch, and the expectation that everyone understands the rules around social touch. It also provides us with the option of physically expressing love and affection with people we otherwise wouldn't, which again benefits us all.

Making a Place for Introverts and the Socially Awkward

I have friends who do not like physical affection, plain and simple, for any number of reasons. In the past, we've just sort of smiled at each other in greeting, sometimes enthusiastically, but also often with some discomfort. How do I let this person know I'm glad to see them in a way that doesn't make them uncomfortable, that doesn't ask them to do something they don't want to do? How do I express support or sympathy? How do they let me know they're happy we're together when they don't want to touch? In a spiritual community which lives consent, there's no strained expectation that we should embrace each other. And because we've accepted the invitation to find new ways of expressing love and affection, we can do other things—wave, blow kisses, shake hands, send air hugs, grin at each other, use words—instead of standing there awkwardly.

A culture of consent also benefits community members who have other personal preferences and personality traits—who are shy, who are introverted, who love touch and physical contact, who are extroverted, and more. Some introverts find structure, and sometimes even scripts, helpful in social situations. Shy people and introverts often find situations more accessible and enjoyable when they can choose their level of involvement and intensity of participation. This includes touch. People who appreciate physical contact are better able to connect with others who do as well, and also are not forced into the situation where they must accept touch from everyone or no one: they get to choose with whom to share touch. Extroverts similarly have less worry about wearing on introverts' and ambiverts' energy levels.

People who are comfortable with, or even enthusiastic about, non-sexual touch are not always comfortable with obligatory social touch, and they do not always wish to participate in it. A culture of consent, where community members ask each other about non-sexual social touch, frees people to choose the physical contact they genuinely wish to share without forcing them to participate in social touch they do not want. People who *are* comfortable with obligatory social touch have the reassurance that someone who is embracing them is not doing so out of a sense of obligation or having no choice, but because this is a genuine expression for them.

A culture of consent helps those of us who have trouble reading social cues to know exactly where social boundaries are. Most of us have felt socially awkward at one time or another, but for many people being socially awkward is a consistent part of social interactions. For those with social anxiety, it's even more of a challenge. Many Pagan groups, like many other spiritual and social groups, ask ourselves how we can help socially awkward people feel more welcome, and also how to handle socially awkward behaviour by our members. Embracing a culture of consent helps remove some of the most common potential pitfalls from social interactions for people who are genuinely socially awkward, especially the pitfall of unintentionally violating other people's personal boundaries around touch. When social rules are stated clearly and explicitly, they are much easier to find before tripping over them.

Identifying Predators

There is a difference between being socially awkward—violating social boundaries unintentionally, if frequently—and violating social boundaries intentionally while using the label of "socially awkward" as a cover.[5] There are people who cross such boundaries deliberately, not because they don't know where those boundaries are, but because they enjoy crossing them. These people often use the excuse of being socially awkward, when in fact they are not—they know where the boundaries are, and they deliberately choose to violate them.

Pagan communities have wrestled long and hard with how to handle people who behave this way. When a group has a culture of consent, boundaries are clear and explicit, and we gain more practice talking about them. Under these conditions, it becomes much more obvious when someone is crossing boundaries on purpose: it becomes

---

[5] In his 2014 article "Socially Awkward Isn't an Excuse," Harris O'Malley of *Paging Dr. NerdLove* has an excellent analysis of the difference between those who are genuinely socially awkward and 'creepers', people who call themselves 'socially awkward' as way to justify deliberate boundary violations. Available at http://www.doctornerdlove.com/2014/03/socially-awkward-isnt-an-excuse/.

clear that claiming not to know is in fact a cover for intentional behaviour.

The importance of addressing such behaviour has gained traction in many Pagan communities over the last few years, as we have been forced to face the realization that like many other spiritual and social communities, we have predators amongst us. When social boundaries are not clear and people are expected to participate in obligatory social touch, it is easier for predators and "creepers"[6] to get away with violating other people's personal space and with grooming them to accept abusive behaviour—and with grooming the rest of us to ignore such activity and to doubt our perceptions. In a culture of consent, when social boundaries are clear and people are not pressured to participate in contact they don't want, it is much clearer to both targets and bystanders when someone is behaving in a predatory manner. Such circumstances also make it easier for the community as a whole to let people know when their actions violate community standards and that such behaviour is not welcome, and to create policies to remove people from our communities who persist in such behaviour.[7]

Cultural Differences

There are other people in our communities who might find it difficult to assess conventions around social touch—not because they are socially awkward or flouting them on purpose, but because of differences in background and experience. These might be people from different subcultures within the same country; people from different cultures or countries entirely; people from different socio-economic or class backgrounds. Social rules around touch vary quite a

---

[6] Ibid.

[7] Stark's research has demonstrated that having anti-harassment policies in place helps reduce incidents of harassment as well as provide a framework to respond when harassment does occur, including removing offenders. See Stark 2014 and Hines 2014.

bit between different geographic regions, in both the US and the UK. The US is comprised of people from many different social and ethnic groups, and conventions around touch vary widely between them, even within the same geographic area. Both the UK and the US include a diverse range of religious groups; many Pagans come to Paganism and Pagan communities after having grown up in, and having been socialized in, other religions, with those religions' conventions or even rules regarding physical contact.

Different cultures around the world also have different conventions around social touch, and this is especially noticeable in a gathering of people from different national origins: Who shakes hands? Who cheek-kisses? One cheek or both? Who hugs? How close together or far apart do people stand? What other ways do people greet each other? Conventions around touch are not always the same for people from middle-class, upper-class, working-class, or poor-class backgrounds; people from mixed-class backgrounds, like people from mixed-ethnicity backgrounds, may be fluent in more than one set of conventions, and may greet different people differently. In a community that embraces a culture of consent, no one need feel that they are not sure whose social rules are in play when it comes to physical touch: we all ask.

A Culture of Sacred Touch

Living a culture of consent can take some adjustment. In our everyday lives, most of us do not yet live in a culture where we are expected to listen deeply to and respect our own boundaries, to ask others about theirs, and to state our own clearly. In our everyday lives, most of us do not yet live in a culture where touch, both sexual and non-sexual, is understood and honored as sacred. In our everyday lives, most of us do not yet live in a culture where it's 100% safe and celebrated to be Pagan, either.

When we create such communities, we demonstrate what is possible... by living it.

For lived experiences with consent culture, the author thanks Friends for Lesbian, Gay, Bisexual, Transgender, and Queer Concerns (FLGBTQC); Our Lady of the Earth and Sky (OLOTEAS); Roses, Too! Tradition; the Edinburgh Solstice Singers; and Love Music Community Choir.

Works Consulted

Adler, Margot. *Drawing Down the Moon: Witches, Druids, Goddess-Worshippers, and Other Pagans in America Today.* New York: Penguin, 1986. Print.

"Conference Anti-harassment/Policy." *Geek Feminism Wiki.* N.p., 23 Sept. 2014. Web. Available at http://geekfeminism.wikia.com/wiki/Conference_anti-harassment/Policy.

"Conference Anti-harassment/Policy Resources." *Geek Feminism Wiki.* N.p., 8 July 2014. Web. Available at http://geekfeminism.wikia.com/wiki/Conference_anti-harassment/Policy_resources.

Project Implicit. "Education." *Project Implicit.* Harvard University, 18 Feb. 2013. Web. Available at https://implicit.harvard.edu/implicit/education.html.

Hines, Jim C. "Nicole Stark's Survey of Harassment Policies at Fan Conventions." *The Ada Initiative.* The Ada Initiative, 17 Feb. 2014. Web. Available at https://adainitiative.org/2014/02/guest-post-nicole-starks-survey-of-harassment-policies-at-fan-conventions/.

Implicit Bias & Philosophy International Research Network. "Implicit Bias & Philosophy International Research Project: Home." *Implicit Bias & Philosophy International Research Project*: Home. N.p., n.d. Web. Available at http://www.biasproject.org/.

O'Malley, Harris. "Socially Awkward Isn't An Excuse." *Paging Dr NerdLove*. N.p., 24 Mar. 2014. Web. Available at http://www.doctornerdlove.com/2014/03/socially-awkward-isnt-an-excuse/.

Oxford Dictionary. Oxford University Press, 2015. Web. Available at http://www.oxforddictionaries.com/.

Stark, Nicole. "The Characteristics of Sexual Harassment Policies at Fan Conventions." *The Ada Initiative*. Department of Sociology, College of Sciences, University of Central Florida, 2014. Web. Available at https://docs.google.com/document/d/1BDMxrXDfMNIVQcz6HJHn8vNtidP5wwRIEKRsBnUq8So/edit.

Valiente, Doreen. "The Charge of the Goddess." *The Official Doreen Valiente Website*. The Doreen Valiente Foundation and the Centre for Pagan Studies, n.d. Web. Available at http://doreenvaliente.org/Doreen-Valiente-Doreen_Valiente_Poetry-11.php.

Valiente, Doreen. *The Rebirth of Witchcraft*. Custer, WA: Phoenix, 1989. Print.

Vaurora. "Get Your Conference Anti-harassment Policy Here!" *Geek Feminism Blog*. N.p., 30 Nov. 2010. Available at http://geekfeminism.org/2010/11/29/get-your-conference-anti-harassment-policy-here/.

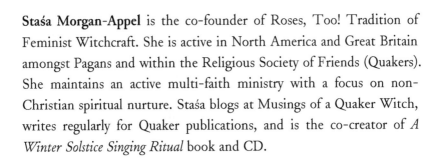

Staša Morgan-Appel is the co-founder of Roses, Too! Tradition of Feminist Witchcraft. She is active in North America and Great Britain amongst Pagans and within the Religious Society of Friends (Quakers). She maintains an active multi-faith ministry with a focus on non-Christian spiritual nurture. Staša blogs at Musings of a Quaker Witch, writes regularly for Quaker publications, and is the co-creator of *A Winter Solstice Singing Ritual* book and CD.

Wild Naked Pagans and How to Host Them

Tom Swiss

It is a powerful thing to be naked outdoors in the presence of others, especially strangers. Many Pagan/magical/spiritual festivals are clothing-optional and so provide the opportunity to explore this experience. Nudity has power because it is a violation of deep taboos in mainstream culture; therefore, empowering this exploration requires careful consideration on the part of festival organizers.

I learned this power personally on my first night at my first Pagan festival, the 1998 Free Spirit Gathering. When the sun went down, I found myself at the Fire Circle. We'd done dance and drum fire circles before in my little group, the Coven of Lovin'—much smaller circles, but I knew how this worked, and so I joined in.

It was a warm night, and FSG is a clothing optional event. Thus, there were some naked people dancing around with me. That was a first for me, but I could deal with it. I didn't want to bump up against any sweaty naked men, but I didn't want to bump up against any sweaty clothed men either. So, as long as there was plenty of space, no problem. There might have been a naked woman or two there also, but I was an adult and had seen naked women before, and it was not as big a deal as it was when I was a lad of seventeen.

So—a bit to my own surprise—I was okay with naked people dancing around with me. I just tried not to look too much. But I couldn't imagine myself ever joining them in their unclothed state. That was just too wild, too far out. Nope. Me, naked in a (sort of) public place? Not going to happen. No way.

Sure, as I got hot I took off my shirt. But as a male that was no different than going to the pool or mowing the lawn on a hot day. I was not breaking any taboos there.

But as I continued to dance, I learned three important things.

+ One: Fire is hot. When you're dancing close to it on a hot night, you want maximum cooling surface exposed for sweat evaporation.

+ Two: Fire is sacred. You want to expose as much of your skin to it as you can, to best absorb its energy.

+ Three: In this sacred space, in this time outside of time, I felt safe. I felt unconditioned. I felt free. So, after an hour or two, off came the pants.

I danced naked around a fire to the beat of the drums.

I broke one of our society's strongest taboos. The humor columnist Mike Nichols once noted, "Take off all your clothes and walk down the street waving a machete and firing an Uzi, and terrified citizens will phone the police and report, 'There's a naked person outside!'"[1]

Here's how much power there is in breaking such a rule: I used to have those dreams where I showed up at work or at school and suddenly realized, to my absolute mortification, that I was naked. But after a few years of attending clothing-optional festivals, of dancing naked around the fire or just letting myself air-dry walking back to camp from the shower, I had that dream once final time. This time, though, when I looked down while talking to someone and noticed I was naked, I said, "Oh. Anyway..." and calmly went about my dream business.

I have not had that dream since. A fear so deep it reached into my dreams has been removed from my brain. That is magic, a willed change in consciousness.

Nakedness has that power because it is wild. "Civilized" people wear clothes; the "savage," the "wild" one, goes naked. That's why nudity has been found in contemporary Paganism since its nineteenth and early twentieth-century roots. It was part of the German Lebensreform movement of the 1890s,[2] which came to be an influence

---

[1] Cooper Lawrence and Scott Baio, Cult of Celebrity: What Our Fascination with the Stars Reveals about Us (Rowman & Littlefield, 2009), 229.

[2] Gordon Kennedy, *Children of the Sun* (Ojai, California: Nivaria Press, 1998), 56.

on the American counter-culture.[3] It's in the proto-Pagan writings of Whitman: "Is not nakedness then indecent? No, not inherently. It is your thought, your sophistication, your fear, your respectability, that is indecent."[4] It's in Leland's *Aradia* ("And thus shall it be done: all shall sit down to the supper all naked, men and women"),[5] and Valiente's *Charge of the Goddess* ("as a sign that ye are really free, ye shall be naked in your rites").[6] It was used in the initiation rites of Crowley's OTO.[7]

Nudity is a powerful way to raise energy.

So I make it a point to spend a little time going around skyclad at any event I can, not so much because I need that energy myself—it's already done its thing for me—but so that I can show others that it's okay to try it. To step outside the taboo and be wild.

But from my casual observation and discussions with others, it seems like fewer people are taking advantage of this primal source of power. Some are concerned about covering up from the sun, about skin cancer and the hole in the ozone layer. Which is fine, but the sun does go down, and sunscreen will work its magic on all parts of you. More relevant is that many people just aren't comfortable being seen unclothed. But that's the point: you don't raise magical energy by doing familiar, comfortable things. There's a cliché Internet meme

---

[3] It strikes me that Lebensreform may also have been, through intermediaries, the ultimate source for Gardner's practice of naturism, but I'm just speculating.

[4] Walt Whitman, "133. A Sun-Bath—Nakedness," in *Specimen Days* (Philadelphia: David McKay, 1892). Available at http://www.bartleby.com/229/1133.html.

[5] Charles G. Leland, *Aradia: The Gospel of the Witches* (1899). Available at http://www.sacred-texts.com/pag/aradia/ara04.htm.

[6] Doreen Valiente, "The Charge of The Goddess." Available at http://www.doreenvaliente.com/Doreen-Valiente-Poetry-11.php.

[7] Israel Regardie, *The Eye in the Triangle* (Tempe: New Falcon Publications, 1993), 177.

that summarizes it well: a circle labeled "Your comfort zone" and an arrow pointing to a spot outside it, labeled "Where the magic happens."

What has startled me is that lately I've encountered some Pagans who were not just uncomfortable going skyclad themselves but were outright hostile to the idea of other Pagans doing so. One even claimed that it must surely be illegal for adults to be nude in front of children—which would be a shock for nudist camps that have served families for decades, not to mention the local Y where kids in the locker room might see me change into my swimming trunks.

It seems that nakedness is a little too wild for some contemporary Pagans.

I am not a witch, so I can't speak with any authority about the state of Witchcraft as a movement. But I found Peter Grey's 2014 essay "Rewilding Witchcraft" a worthwhile read.[8] It makes some questionable arguments—for example, the story of how the reintroduction of wolves in Yellowstone created an "ecological miracle" seems to be more myth than fact,[9] and there is no evidence for Grey's view that some inevitable nuclear catastrophe will eliminate all life on the planet for 100 million years. The "living Earth" is not "fragile": life will be here on this planet in some form even if we do our absolute worst. The question that faces us is whether we can be smart and mature enough to be part of it, or whether we'll leave the Earth to other species.

But putting aside the ecological eschatology that makes up the bulk of that essay, Grey makes a broader point about "wildness" with which I agree wholeheartedly, if I substitute the more general "Paganism" for "Witchcraft":

---

[8] Peter Grey, "Rewilding Witchcraft," *Scarlet Imprint: Journal,* 13 Jun 2014. Available at http://scarletimprint.com/2014/06/rewilding-witchcraft/ .

[9] Arthur Middleton, "Is the Wolf a Real American Hero?" *New York Times* 10 Mar 2014: A21. Available at http://www.nytimes.com/2014/03/10/opinion/is-the-wolf-a-real-american-hero.html.

I will argue that Witchcraft is quintessentially wild, ambivalent, ambiguous, queer. It is not something that can be socialised, standing as it does in that liminal space between the seen and unseen worlds. Spatially the realm of witchcraft is the hedge, the crossroads, the dreaming point where the world of men and of spirits parlay through the penetrated body of someone who is outside of the normal rules of culture....

My argument is that witchcraft became too tame...[10]

1998, the year I attended my first festival, was not that long ago. But in the years since I've seen a distinct change in the culture, a "de-wilding" and therefore a loss of power—and perhaps even a loss of purpose.

There's an idea from Joseph Campbell that has greatly influenced my thinking and my work the past few years. In his essay "The Symbol Without Meaning," Campbell points out the difference between the direct religious experience of Paleolithic, gatherer-hunter, shamanistic cultures and the mediated priestly religions of Neolithic (and later) agricultural civilizations. That Neolithic social order, Campbell says, is dissolving in the wake of the Industrial Revolution, and "what is required of us all...is much more the fearless self-sufficiency of our shamanistic inheritance than the timorous piety of the priest-guided Neolithic."[11]

In other words, we must get wild with our spirituality.

It seems to me that this is why the contemporary Pagan movement exists in the first place, a reaction to the inability of "civilized" religion to deal with the circumstances in which humanity finds itself. We are on a quest for something more direct.

Something untamed.

Something unafraid to stand naked.

---

[10] Grey, ibid.

[11] Joseph Campbell, *The Flight of the Wild Gander* (New York, N.Y: HarperPerennial, 1990), 189.

And so festival organizers are left with some important questions. How can we support people in their experiments with this power? How do we set guidelines and procedures so that people's exploration of their own boundaries does not tread on the legitimate boundaries of others?

The answers lie in creating and transmitting a supportive culture for the event, clearly communicating policies, and being prepared to resolve conflicts fairly—all matters with broader application than just the question of going unclothed.

People come to festivals with a diversity of past experience. Some have never stepped outside the boundaries of mainstream society and spirituality, while others arrive with a rich background of exploration. Therefore it is important both to explicitly set expectations and to avoid being patronizing.

New attendees are likely to first hear of an event by word of mouth (which organizers can't control) or by marketing materials (which we can). Potential attendees often then follow up through the event website. It is vital that marketing materials and the website give a clear picture of the major features of the event, including if it is clothing-optional.

Event program booklets are a time-honored way to inform attendees about festival policies, but they don't get distributed until the event is already underway. This not only makes it too late to prepare, but often attendees are distracted by all the great things going on at the event and don't take the time to read the program!

In the Internet Age we can use discussions before the event on social media and other internet forums to supplement the traditional program, as well as making the program available ahead of time on-line. If we can draw new people into discussion threads with veteran attendees, they have a chance to absorb some of the norms of the event's culture before they even arrive. Organizers can facilitate this by starting new threads on specific subjects, including the practice of going skyclad.

Event policies should spell out that nudity is not an invitation for sexual contact, and should also clearly state if there are any areas or times in which nudity is not allowed. For example, areas visible from the road may be posted as "no skyclad" zones, or if the camp has a dining hall there may be a "no shirt, no shoes, no pants, no service" rule. For those new to the practice, it is useful to state areas where nudity is allowed, but a "no bare butts on seats" hygiene rule is in effect, and people going skyclad are expected to bring a towel for seating.

It should also be made clear that photography without explicit permission of everyone in the photo is forbidden. Indeed, that photography rule should apply regardless of whether any of the subjects are skyclad, since some attendees may be "in the broom closet" or may face severe consequences if their presence at any sort of alternative culture event became widely known.[12]

Photography has become more of an issue in recent years as camera phones have become common. Ten years ago, if someone was taking a photograph, they generally used something clearly identifiable as a camera. But now, most of us carry in our pockets a phone/pocket watch/game console/two-way pager/e-book reader, and it's not clear whether someone holding such a device is checking the time, reading a text message, or taking our picture. Taking pictures and posting them on the internet has become a thoughtless habit for many people, and so repeated clear explanations of the photography policy may be necessary.

One excellent idea for dealing with unauthorized photography is demonstrated by Pagan/Steampunk/Rennie/Gothic/Geek impresario Jeff Mach. His "Geeky Kink Event" has a photo policy that assigns copyright of any photo taken without permission to the event producers and explicitly specifies their right to destroy such photos.[13]

---

[12] For a horrific example, see the case of Rachel Bevilacqua (a.k.a. "Reverend Magdalen"), who almost lost custody of her son in 2006 over her attendance at the Subgenius "X-Day". E.W. Modemac, "Reverend Magdalen," *Cast Iron Chaos,* 2010. Available at http://www.modemac.com/cgi-bin/wiki.pl/Reverend_Magdalen.

[13] Jeff Mach, "The Geeky Kink Event Rules," *The Geeky Kink Event,* 2015.

No matter how carefully event policies are drawn up and explained, however, there will be differences in interpretation and understanding. That's why it's vital to have a conflict resolution policy in place. Again, this has a broader application than establishing boundaries around nudity, but it is especially useful to have a go-to procedure when someone complains about a naked person walking through their camp. That situation is a poor time to have staff reliant on ad hoc decision making.

During my time as President of the Free Spirit Alliance, we put in place for the first time a formal conflict resolution policy for our events. It states that:

> Every person has the right to be free from threats and harassment, to have their reasonable personal boundaries respected, and to have their side given a fair hearing if they become involved in a dispute.

But also:

> Every person has the responsibility to clearly state their own boundaries, to respect the boundaries of others, to give a fair hearing to the other side if they become involved in a dispute, and to behave with due respect for their own safety and for the safety and rights of others.[14]

The policy states that we value dialogue and mediation for conflict resolution and lays out a specific procedure for finding a mediator to facilitate the process. There is a clear plan of action and delegation of responsibility. The complete policy is at the end of this chapter, and readers are welcome to use it as a model.

Pagan festivals provide an opportunity for people to step outside of their usual mainstream social structure and taboos. Going skyclad is a particularly visible and vibrant example of this, and having the

---

Available at http://thegeekykinkevent.com/rules/#photos.

[14] Free Spirit Alliance, "Conflict Resolution Policy," 2015. Available at http://www.freespiritgathering.org/conflicts.html.

appropriate policies and procedures in place to support it will also prepare the event for dealing with conflicts that can arise from less dramatic sorts of exploration. If you're ready for wild naked Pagans, you're ready for most anything

Free Spirit Alliance Conflict Resolution Policy

Perhaps the most important measure of a community is how it handles conflicts and disruptive behavior. In recognition of this, and in order to create the atmosphere of safety that is necessary for the freedom of expression and self-exploration that is the goal of our events, the Free Spirit Alliance has set forth the following policies.

Every person has the right to be free from threats and harassment, to have their reasonable personal boundaries respected, and to have their side given a fair hearing if they become involved in a dispute.

Every person has the responsibility to clearly state their own boundaries, to respect the boundaries of others, to give a fair hearing to the other side if they become involved in a dispute, and to behave with due respect for their own safety and for the safety and rights of others.

FSA strives to promote dialog and mediation for conflict resolution. Should a dispute arise, we will try to find someone mutually agreeable to the parties involved to act as a mediator. The primary responsibility for finding a such a mediator and overseeing the conflict resolution process shall rest with the Coordinator On Duty at the time, if the dispute is during an event and involves the intervention of security staff or is otherwise of an immediate nature, or the FSA President, otherwise.

During the mediation process, all parties are asked to keep in mind the rights and responsibilities outlined above.

FSA strives to create an atmosphere of freedom, subject to the requirements of safety and to the rights of others. Should a person act in a disruptive or unsafe manner, we will make a good faith effort to work with them to find a safe, peaceful, and reasonable way in which their goals can be met.

While we promote mediation and cooperation, a person whose behavior is reckless, disruptive, unlawful, or a threat to the safety or rights of others may be ejected from the event at the sole discretion of the event coordinator.

Any person ejected from an event who then displays unlawful, dangerous, or disruptive behavior at a subsequent event may be banned from future events for either a limited time or permanently. The decision on such a ban rests with the President, in consultation with the Event Coordinator(s) and Trustees.

Please remember: when reports of problems don't reach us until after the end of an event, our ability to address them is severely hampered. If you encounter a problem that you'd like us to assist in solving, we ask that you please bring it to our attention promptly. You are not bothering us by asking us to help you solve a problem; that's part of what we're here for.

Tom Swiss describes his spiritual path as "Zen Pagan Taoist Atheist Discordian," which usually baffles questioners enough to leave him alone. Over the past decade he has built a reputation as a lecturer on subjects spanning the gamut from acupressure to Zen and from self-defense to sexuality. He is an NCCAOM Diplomate in Asian Bodywork Therapy, a godan (fifth-degree black belt) in karate, a poet, a singer/songwriter, an amateur philosopher, and a professional computer geek. Tom has previously served as President of the Free Spirit Alliance. He is the author of *Why Buddha Touched the Earth* (Megalithica Books, 2013). Find out more about his wacky adventures at www.infamous.net.

Respect, Relationship and Responsibility
UU Resources for Pagan Consent Education
Zebrine Gray

I held my tiny newborn baby in my hands, filled with hopes and dreams for her future. I was still dazed from the drugs they gave me after a difficult birth, but I remember one clear thought: "I want this child to own her body and live her power. I want her to take every single level of OWL classes." My girl was not even a day old, but I was already making plans for her sex education.

OWL is an acronym for Our Whole Lives, a comprehensive sexuality education program created by a dual effort of the Unitarian Universalist (UU) Association and the United Church of Christ. The program has several levels spanning the lifespan with developmentally appropriate materials. OWL's core values are Respect, Relationship, and Responsibility. Though designed by two churches, the authors designed the curriculum series for use by any group, secular or religious. The resources offered in OWL could be incredibly useful to Pagans as individuals and as a community.

In my own childhood sex education, I learned about basic anatomy and mechanics and that sex should be saved for marriage. This did not give me the tools to manage my complex sexual development. When I discovered Paganism as a young adult, I was thrilled with the sex-positive culture. The concepts of sacred pleasure and female deity empowered me more than ever before. Yet, at some Pagan events, I did not know how to process the sexual pressures I faced as a young woman. While the rules forbade "unwanted sexual attention," I felt violated more than once, mostly because of the ambiguity from failing to say no but not really saying yes. I did not yet understand the power of consent.

By the time of my daughter's birth, I was serving a UU congregation as a professional religious educator. I learned about providing safe spaces for participants as part of my job. Nearly every UU class or group begins by creating a "covenant," or an agreement on how to be together. The most effective covenants use positive rather than negative wording. Instead of a list of "Do not do this" or "Do not do that," the challenge to choose positive wording capturing what we *will* do creates a more open sense of community. For example, instead of the words "Don't talk when someone else is talking," the group may choose to say, "Respect the words and ideas of others."

Until recently, our social standards around sex have been like a negative covenant, focusing on what people should not do. Some of these standards are part of what we call "rape culture," cultural expectations that normalize sexual exploitation and violation (for example, the idea that women should not dress provocatively if they do not want sexual attention). Even campaigns meant to prevent sexual assault focus on what is not desirable rather than what is: men are instructed not to force others sexually, and women are told not to walk alone at night or drink alcohol with people they don't know. Young people of all genders are taught that "No Means No," but that leaves a lot of gray area when it comes to maybe or even to silence. This negative context creates an expectation of violation.

Consent culture, on the other hand, focuses on the positive rather than negative and clears away ambiguities. When those who choose to engage in sexual activity are looking for an enthusiastic yes rather than trying to interpret the ambiguous maybe, there is little room for misinterpretation.

As responsible and ethical Pagans, we have the opportunity to work toward making our Pagan groups, events, and gatherings into safe spaces where consent culture is the expected norm. But how do we do that?

Unitarian Universalism and Paganism

As a non-creedal religious tradition, Unitarian Universalism embraces earth-centered spiritualities, including Paganism. According to sociologist Helen Berger, Paganism and UU have significant similarities because they both draw on multiple sources of inspiration while also stressing social justice issues and the spiritual authority of the individual.[1] Many Pagans have joined Unitarian Universalist churches, and some work in lay or professional ministry as religious educators or ministers.

In 1984, the General Assembly of UUs voted on a statement of principles and sources. This document became a type of covenant between member congregations. Rather than dictating belief or creed, the statement is intended to be an agreement about how individuals will act with one another. The statement lists the first source of UU spirituality as "Direct Experience of that transcending mystery and wonder, affirmed in all cultures, which moves us to renewal of the spirit and openness to the forces that create and uphold life."[2] This language also reflects Pagans' magical worldview, allowing for personal experience to guide spirituality and for that which is "mysterious" and "wondrous" to be explored and accepted.

In 1996, a sixth source was added: "Spiritual teachings of Earth-centered traditions which celebrate the sacred circle of life and instruct us to live in harmony with the rhythms of nature."[3] This source allows for Pagan traditions to be given the same consideration as other world religions.

As practitioners of a newer religion, Pagans are still trying to form their group identity, and there is much ambivalence about (and some outright resistance to) organizational structures. The Covenant of Unitarian Universalist Pagans (CUUPs) formed in 1987 as an independent affiliate of the Unitarian Universalist Association. The UU church provides the kind of theological openness that many Pagans are looking for, but also offers stronger organization and institutional assets. Berger believes the development of CUUPs and

---

[1] Helen A. Berger, A Community of Witches: Contemporary Neo-Paganism and Witchcraft in the United States (Columbia, SC: University of South Carolina Press, 1999), p. 116.

[2] David Bumbaugh, *Unitarian Universalism: A Narrative History* (Chicago: Meadville Lombard Press, 2000), pp. 196-197.

[3] Bumbaugh, 199.

Pagan involvement in UU churches shows how many Pagans are seeking legitimacy and consistency.[4]

Made up of individual chapters that form within UU congregations, CUUPs offers resources to individuals and groups within UU congregations. These resources include networking between Pagan-identified UUs, educational materials about Paganism, and support for Pagan-identified UU professionals. As one of the largest Pagan organizations with close to 70 continental chapters, CUUPs reaches a large number of Pagans, as well as having influence within many UU churches.[5]

Unitarian Universalism especially appeals to people looking for religious education for children. This includes Pagan families who have difficulty finding organized religious education within Pagan communities. As Berger explains, "It is a church in which they can comfortably raise their children, because it is a recognized church that their children, without negative repercussions, can acknowledge membership in at their schools, and because it allows exposure to a number of different religious traditions or inspirations. Neo-Pagan Unitarian Universalist parents feel that they are providing their children with a basis for choosing their own spiritual path."[6]

Our Whole Lives

When I began my work as a religious educator, the UU curricula impressed me, but none more than the OWL program. I trained for and facilitated OWL classes for junior high and high school youth and later for elementary ages. The program made a huge impression on me because of the values at the core of all levels of the curricula:

---

[4] Berger, 114.
[5] Covenant of Unitarian Universalist Pagans, www.cuups.org.
[6] Berger, 119.

* *Respect* – Each and every person is entitled to dignity, self-worth, and respect for his/her attitudes and beliefs about sexuality.

* *Relationships* – People of all ages, genders, races, backgrounds, income levels, physical and mental abilities, and sexual orientations must have equal value and rights. Sexual relationships should never be coercive or exploitative.

* *Responsibility* – Every person has the right to accurate information about sexuality and to have her/his questions answered. Knowledge about human sexuality is helpful, not harmful. All persons have the right and obligation to make responsible sexual choices. We need to express our sexuality in ways that enhance human wholeness and fulfillment and that express love, commitment, and joy.[7]

Each of these values contributes significantly to forming consent culture. In my observation, sexual exploitation often stems from issues of self-worth, especially for those who are being exploited. An environment of mutual respect teaches each person to respect themselves as well as others. If each of us commits to honoring the inherent worth and dignity of every other person—a principle that is central to UUs—such exploitation is unthinkable. We live in relationship to each other in an interconnected web of existence. The core value of "relationship" states that sexual relationships should not be coercive or exploitative. By insisting on responsible sexual choices that enhance human wholeness, the OWL curriculum series encourages the kind of sex-positive views that create consent culture.

These values are the implicit understanding behind the various levels of OWL, but what about the explicit lessons in the curricula?

---

[7] Elizabeth Casparian and Eva Goldfarb, *Our Whole Lives: Sexuality Education for Grades 4-6* (Unitarian Universalist Association and United Church Board for Homeland Ministries, 2000), p. 15.

Do children, youth, and adults learn about how to live in a culture where seeking consent is normal?

The youngest level curriculum, intended for students in kindergarten through first grade, introduces concepts of consent in Session 3, "Healthy Bodies, Safe Bodies." This lesson gives students the age-appropriate message that "One's body belongs to one's self." Children are taught that they do not have to accept unwanted touch, even something seemingly as innocent as a hug or kiss from their grandmother. "All people, including children, have a right to tell others not to touch their body when they don't want to be touched." Children are encouraged to learn the phrase "No! Go! Tell!" if they ever experience someone refusing to honor their boundaries. This early elementary education provides a very simple groundwork for consent culture.[8]

The OWL curriculum intended for students in grades 4-6 includes consent in Session 6, "Health and Safety." This class includes an activity where students discuss hypothetical nonconsensual situations in pairs and then as a group. Some of these situations include a swim coach mentioning a young girl's developing breasts, a girl who is kissed by a boy when she doesn't feel ready, and a boy's older brother and friends teasing him about being a virgin. Students are encouraged to think about what they would do in such situations.[9]

These elementary age OWL classes are short (8 sessions for each), and they provide an early foundation for conversations about consent. Unfortunately, they are not offered in many UU congregations. In a 2010 report, 16% reported offering K-1 and 30% reported offering 4-6.[10]

---

[8] Barbara Sprung, *Our Whole Lives: Sexuality Education for Grades K-1* (Unitarian Universalist Association and United Church Board for Homeland Ministries, 2000), pp. 20-22.

[9] Casparian and Goldfarb, pp. 67-71.

[10] All statistics found in Rev. Debra H. Haffner, *Toward a Sexually Healthy and Responsible Unitarian Universalist Association*, August 2010, p. 19. http://www.uua.org/sites/live-new.uua.org/files/documents/haffnerdebra/

OWL for grades 7-9 grades is by far the most commonly offered OWL class, as middle school is considered to be the most important age for sex education. 66% of UU congregations reported offering this level. With 27 sessions, the original (1999) curriculum includes sessions that introduce criteria for deciding whether or not to engage in sexual acts (Session 22 "Sexual Decisions"), as well as sessions on recognizing and recovering from sexual abuse (Session 25) and sexual harassment and acquaintance rape (Session 26). These sessions take a negative perspective, almost assuming that the youth in the class have already experienced some sort of sexual exploitation. Although students are again given the opportunity to discuss what they might do in a variety of hypothetical nonconsensual scenarios, the classes still seem more reactive than preventative.

The OWL high school curriculum (2000), intended for grades 10-12, includes more sessions in recognizing unhealthy relationships, power dynamics, sexual exploitation, harassment, and date rape. The curriculum also includes a workshop entitled "Between Consenting Adults" (Workshop 36). This session is the first to explicitly explore consent. Through various exercises, youth are encouraged to understand the definition of consent and determine whether or not simple scenarios are consensual. The first exercise asks the class to vote on whether someone is consenting to have sexual intercourse in various situations, including such nuanced circumstances as "makes out with you naked," "has oral sex with you," "does not say anything when you start to have sexual intercourse," and even "says yes but his/her body seems to be saying no." The second exercise includes material on drinking and consent, manipulation within dating couples (one threatening to break up if the other does not engage in sex), and even sex with a person in a position of greater power.[11] These are deep

---

sex_health_responsible.pdf.

[11] Eva Goldfarg and Elizabeth Casparian, *Our Whole Lives: Sexuality Education for Grades 10-12* (Unitarian Universalist Association and United Church Board for Homeland Ministries, 2000), pp. 227-229.

conversations, ones that would be helpful for many adults to engage in. This level of OWL is offered in only 40% of congregations and often has a lower number of participants because high school students have less time to commit to 38 workshops.

I expected to find the most useful sessions about consent in the Young Adult program (intended for ages 18-35) and Adult curricula (the only levels of OWL I have neither trained nor participated in), but I was disappointed. The Young Adult (2008) course contains one session about boundaries and a brief mention and discussion of consent in relationship to kinky sex.[12] The Adult curriculum (2000) includes no mention of consent and has brief, optional discussions of date rape and abusive relationships. Of all the OWL curricula, this is the least informative for consent culture. These two curricula are also offered the least frequently in UU congregations, with 11% offering the Adult and only 5% offering the Young Adult.

Since so much has changed since 1999, a second edition of the grade 7-9 curriculum was released in 2014. It includes Workshop 18, "Consent Education." This workshop is the most comprehensive UU resource about consent offered. It includes some of the earlier information about recognizing abusive and coercive situations, but it empowers students to do more than just discuss consent. One activity distinguishes sexual arousal from sexual consent by using the analogy of chopping onions.[13] A person may cry while chopping onions, but it does not mean the person is sad. A person may experience sexual arousal, but that does not mean they are consenting to sexual activity.

The workshop continues with an activity where students practice skills for negotiating consent. They practice requesting a fist bump and either refusing or denying the bump until every person has had the experience of all four possible positions (requesting and being

---

[12] Michael Tino, Sarah Gibb Millspaugh, and Laura Anne Stuart, *Our Whole Lives: Sexuality Education for Grades 4-6* (Unitarian Universalist Association of Congregations, 2008), p. 213.

[13] Pamela M. Wilson, *Our Whole Lives: Sexuality Education for Grades 7-9, Second Edition* (Unitarian Universalist Association, 2014), p. 289.

allowed, requesting and being denied, giving consent, or refusing consent). Another activity gives scenarios for bystanders, those who may see a nonconsensual situation and potentially intervene. The workshop concludes with the following explicit "rights and responsibilities":

> Everyone has the right to not be coerced or talked into doing something they don't want to do or feel uncomfortable doing.
> Everyone has the responsibility
>
> + Not to coerce or talk someone else into something they don't want to do or seem uncomfortable with
>
> + To look out for their own safety, including sexual safety
>
> + To look out for the safety of others, particularly if their judgment seems impaired, they're less capable of making their wishes known, or they are a member of a group that faces societal discrimination (for instance, if they fear being bullied, identify as LGBTQ and fear being targeted or outed, or are developmentally or physically incapable of giving or declining consent).[14]

By encouraging youth to pay attention to the safety of others and intervene when they see nonconsensual situations, this workshop takes consent education to a new level. The final words of the workshop, "Ongoing and enthusiastic consent matters in all sexual interactions," offer the language of consent culture rather than rape culture. "Yes! Yes! Yes!" shows enthusiastic consent, while "Maybe," "I guess," or silence indicate a lack of consent. This specific workshop gives the best resource in the Our Whole Lives curricula for creating consent culture.

---

[14] Wilson, 291-292.

Where Do We Go from Here?

I am pleased to say that my daughter participated in the K-1 OWL class last year, and she is quite confident in understanding and stating her physical boundaries and honoring those of others. But I worry a bit about her future OWL participation. I no longer work as a religious educator and have no current affiliation with a UU congregation. How will I find a way to keep my commitment to giving her these opportunities?

I will look for places that offer these programs. As a trained facilitator for elementary, middle, and high school OWL, I will volunteer my services to UU congregations and groups if I am able (though parents are not encouraged to facilitate their own child's class, especially in the later age groups). But if I am not able to offer these programs through a UU congregation, I hope to find Pagan groups who also want this sort of education for their children and youth and are willing to commit the resources to making it happen.

How could the Pagan community use these UU resources in creating consent culture? When the OWL program was first released, the Board of CUUPs adopted the program values from the OWL as their official position around issues of sexuality. However, they currently do not list this policy or any resources relating to sexual ethics on their website. CUUPs President Amy Beltaine wrote to me, "I would love to get CUUPS on record with a statement supporting consent culture. It is so important not just with rape, but with mistreatment of those with disabilities, colonizing, etc." As an organization, CUUPs hopes to offer more resources in the future.

Still, individuals and groups could be doing so much more. Every religious educator I know has challenges finding facilitators for the OWL classes. Training workshops for facilitators are expensive and take an entire weekend, and a volunteer facilitator commits not only to the training but also to a lengthy program. Smaller congregations often do not have the resources to pay for the training. Perhaps CUUPs groups could consider raising funds to send new facilitators to training, or recruiting some of their own members to be trained as facilitators. Through the training and facilitation, I learned so much about how to communicate my boundaries. At the most recent Pagan gatherings I have attended, I noticed much more emphasis on consent, and I was more confident in protecting my own needs and boundaries.

A CUUPs group may offer the OWL classes themselves and open the program to the larger Pagan community. Leaders could also incorporate some of the activities into a single workshop. I hope to use the consent workshops from the new middle school and/or the high school curricula to offer consent culture workshops for adults at Pagan events and gatherings. Unfortunately, those in our communities who tend to violate boundaries are less likely to attend such a workshop. But by educating others to be consent allies and to intervene, it helps reinforce consent culture beyond such workshops.

As Pagans, we can create a community of respect, not just in regards to sexuality but also in every other aspect of life. We can honor relationships by truly listening to one another. And we have the responsibility to make our spaces safe for children, youth, and adults. The UU Our Whole Lives resource could greatly help us in this process of creating consent culture.

Zebrine Gray, PhD, is a third-degree Wiccan priestess and a member of CUUPs. She served for ten years as a Director of Religious Education at two Unitarian Churches and edited the pamphlet "The Faith of UU Pagans" for the Unitarian Universalist Association. As a teacher of sacred dance and a scholar of ritual theatre, Zebrine has offered workshops at Pagan conferences, festivals, and gatherings throughout the country. Currently, as Artistic Director of the Imaginorium Educational Collective (www.imaginedcollective.org), she creates imaginative resources and directs events based on mythic and pop culture themes.

Self-Possession as a Pillar of Parenting
Or, modeling sovereignty in an attempt to teach said mystery to the small person who lives in my house and keeps calling me "Mama"

Nadirah Adeye

Introduction

My mother's parenting was greatly influenced by the poem "On Children" by Kahlil Gibran. She was raised by a woman whose loving "protection" often carried a tone of ownership, domination, and fear-based aggression. So when she was pregnant with me and read the book *The Prophet*, she was deeply struck by the words. Or, as Oprah would say, she had an "Ah ha!" moment.

> Your children are not your children.
> They are the sons and daughters
> of Life's longing for itself.
> They come through you but not from you,
> And though they are with you yet they belong not to you.
> You may give them your love but not your thoughts,
> For they have their own thoughts.....
> You may strive to be like them,
> but seek not to make them like you.[1]

I have heard my mother repeat, many times throughout my life, the idea that "your children come *through* you. They do not belong to you." This was a primary aspect of her personal parenting philosophy.

The influence of Gibran's poem on my mother set a great tone for me and my path of commitment to self-knowledge and self-ownership. I have had several conversations with my mother and my partner about our goals, intentions, and hopes for how we are raising our son, Torin. The vision is bold and courageous, and also completely fraught with

---

[1] Kahlil Gibran, "On Children," *The Prophet* (New York: Alfred A. Knopf, 1923) 17-18.

neuroses and "healing of family wounds." This situation is no different from that of any of my fellow parents in my family and friend communities. We want the best for our children, want them to have the best of what we can offer, and want to protect their innocence for as long as possible, while simultaneously preparing them to be courageous and confident and go out and enact positive change in the world.

In this article, I will explore the idea of self-possession or self-sovereignty and how it contributes to the development of a consent culture. I will specifically look at what it means to raise a child while honoring their sovereign nature. I will also examine what it means to parent as one who is self-possessed or strives to live from an awareness of my own sovereignty.

Before diving in, I will state that I am writing this article from my own perspective, as a cis-woman, a woman of color, an outspoken priestess, and an academic who has had the privilege of spending time and money on education, self-reflection, and personal growth. There are many ways in which my partner's views on parenting differ from my own, and I may touch on them, but I am also privileged to be the one writing this article while he only has to hash out his views between himself, me, and the kid. So, while this article is about sovereignty, self-possession and parenting, it is also specifically about mothering. Mothers are still often the greatest influencers on our kids' lives in the first years when so much of the foundation of who they are is being laid. I believe that our society is desperate for a way to incorporate more receptive, gentle and respectful practices in all areas of life, especially in the nurturing of children and their caregivers.

What does it mean to be self-possessed or sovereign? How does that relate to consent culture?

An online search of the term "self-possession" offers the following definitions: calm, confident, and in control of one's feelings; composed and/or having or showing control of one's feelings, behavior, etc.; composed; poised.

My definition of self-possession is the state of someone living in ownership of themselves. A self-possessed person is self-aware, self-knowing, tapped into a part of themselves that has a longer or more expansive view, and lives and acts from that place of alignment with their higher or Divine nature.

The blog *The Fluent Self* has an article on sovereignty that is very much in line with my thoughts on the term. The author, Havi Brooks, gives the following definitions for sovereignty:

- Being at home in your body and your life.

- Feeling what you feel.

- Respecting your capacity.

- Knowing where your edges are.

- The ability to be clear, firm, loving and unapologetic about what you stand for.

- Trusting that doing things to take care of yourself doesn't mean that anyone else is less important.

- Saying no to things that need a no, yes to things that need a yes.

- Knowing that everyone gets to be king or queen of their world.

- Knowing that the more firmly you wear your crown, the more you give permission to everyone else to wear theirs.

- Taking responsibility for your stuff.

- Remembering not to take responsibility for all the things that are not yours.[2]

---

[2] Havi Brooks, "Sovereignty 101," *The Fluent Self* 14 June 2010. Available at http://www.fluentself.com/blog/stuckification/sovereignty-101/.

I define sovereignty as the idea that one belongs first to oneself, and that each person gets to set the terms of their "belonging" to others. Each of us has the right of rulership over our own bodies and the right to expect that our yeses (and our noes) will be honored.

The definition of consent culture from the site *Only With Consent* is "a culture in which asking for consent is normalized and condoned in popular culture. It is respecting the person's response even if it isn't the response you had hoped for. We will live in a consent culture when we no longer objectify people and we value them as human beings."[3]

In my own words, consent culture makes the practice of respecting the sovereignty of others a core component of all interactions and relationships.

How does one go about raising one who is self-possessed or self-belonging? What does it mean to parent a self-possessed/sovereign child?

I had a very interesting conversation with my mother-out-law when my son was still a small baby. She was speaking on the vital importance of children being able to say no and to have their noes honored by those around them. She said that being able to say no contributes to the creation of a safe space and is also what allows one to explore and discover their yeses. I appreciated her perspective because I was already of the mindset that children should not be made to give hugs or kisses to anyone (or in any way touch or be touched) if they do not want to.

I was fortunate to be able to be home with my son as his primary caregiver for the first eighteen months of his life. I got to know him and many of his personality traits, and we developed a mother/baby bond that was very close. I practiced a modified form of attachment parenting where he got a lot of in-arms time as well as time to play by

---

[3] "Consent Culture," *Only With Consent*. Available at
http://onlywithconsent.org/blog/consent-culture.

himself in close proximity to an adult. I also had him on an extended nursing schedule, so he received a lot of nurturing, affection, and physical interaction in his first couple of years. I was very dedicated to gentle parenting practices, an easy commitment because my son was one of those easygoing trickster babies that makes one think that they are doing an excellent job at this whole parenting thing.

In line with these parenting perspectives and practices, I've been quite firm about his father and I respecting his personal bodily boundaries by communicating with him about what is going on around him and in a space. I noticed that, even as an infant, letting him know the order in which we would be doing things ("Bathe the baby, rub him down, put on your diaper, fasten your onesie, and snap your pajamas!") helped him to follow along with the process and usually kept him pretty cooperative about the entire thing. My intention has been that we support and affirm his ownership of himself and his body and that his first experience of having his boundaries crossed or disregarded not be at the hands of his parents or family.

Then toddlerhood happened and everything fell apart. His twos weren't entirely terrible, but they were a sudden and startling difference from the easygoing baby I'd become habituated to. Suddenly there were tantrums and resistance, and gentle parenting seemed like a hot pile of steaming BS. Gently suggesting or asking him to do things didn't work anymore. Telling him to do things didn't help. Sometimes, the only thing that worked was to pick him up and *make him*.

An experienced mommy helped me a lot during that phase when she said, "You have to remember that toddlers are pure want. He's not trying to be challenging, he's just a bundle of pure want and immediacy." Her tone was gentle, amused, and deeply knowing, which helped me to understand that my frustrations with his toddlerhood were no more a commentary on my parenting than his easy temperament as an infant had been.

Toddlerhood quickly taught me that we needed to show respect for his boundaries *within reason*. Also around that time, I read an article where a woman was at her wits' end because her daughter, who had previously been such an easy child, had started having tantrums since the birth of her new brother. The response from the author was that the child was requesting *more* boundaries, not fewer.

My partner and I were raised in very different households. His parents readily admit that they were permissive. As his father tends to say, his mother "raised her children wild." The method seems to have worked well for his two sisters, but less well for him. Consequently, he tends to strive for more boundaries for our son. On the other hand, I was raised in a household where there were plenty of rules and boundaries, but my brother and I were both kids who rarely sought out trouble. I've felt, at times, that we would have benefitted from fewer boundaries. (I've romanticized the free child household, and my partner longs for a household where kids have rules and follow them, period.)

So, what does it mean to raise a child who is self-sovereign or self-possessed? To be truly sovereign or in self-possession requires that one take personal responsibility. Those are burdens that need to be taken in healthy stages, with the weight of the burden (and the freedoms) increasing as the child ages.

I have a friend who is raising her son using the principles of RIE parenting (Resources for Infant Educarers), an approach founded by Magda Gerber. This style is based on respect, and it calls on parents to provide the following:

- An environment for the child that is physically safe, cognitively challenging and emotionally nurturing.

- Time for uninterrupted play.

- Freedom to explore and interact with other infants.

- Involvement of the child in all care activities to allow the child to become an active participant rather than a passive recipient.

+ Sensitive observation of the child in order to understand his or her needs.

+ Consistency, clearly defined limits and expectations to develop discipline.[4]

What I have found, in my personal experience as well as in the parenting styles of experienced mothers around me, is that what contributes to a child having a strong sense of themselves and the ability to express their boundaries is having a connection with someone who is responsive to them. They need a space to practice expressing their boundaries and receiving positive reinforcement for doing so (as well as suggestions about how to be more effective in their use of certain words or tones).

It can be disconcerting to interact with a child who is self-possessed, one who has a sense of self and who speaks out for themselves and others. As a child, I had more than one encounter with adults who liked the idea of me being "smart" but wanted me to also behave in ways that indicated submissiveness to them and their perceived authority. They wanted me to act "like a child." They did not like me making statements that challenged them and their "authority" over me as adults. (Granted, as a child who was encouraged to speak out in my family, I often mistook rudeness for honesty, and there is a difference.)

It's especially important for a child who is descended from people who were historically dehumanized and called the "slaves" of others to be raised in a home that reinforces and celebrates his sovereignty. We live in a society that is well behind the curve in respecting or honoring the sovereignty of its citizens. Anyone who comes from people who have a history of oppression (either as the oppressed or as the oppressors) would benefit from learning about what it means to live in a state of self-sovereignty. Dr. Joy DeGruy's work on Post Traumatic Slave Syndrome touches on the impact of historical wounds that

---

[4] *Resources for Infant Educarers*. Available at http://www.rie.org/.

masquerade as "culture."[5] And anyone raised in a culture or family where being "powerful" means having power over someone else is coming to a relationship with a self-possessed person at a distinct disadvantage.

I had a conversation with my partner before our son was born where I asked him, "If your son wanted to wear fairy wings or a dress, would you allow it/ be comfortable with it?" (Hint, the right answer was just supposed to be "Yes.") He surprised me with the thoughtfulness of his response, though, when he stated that while he is not comfortable with acting as though things like dresses are gender neutral (by society's standards) for a toddler, if his son were older, say twelve, and expressed a desire to wear fairy wings or a dress, he would assume that it meant his son knew something about himself and his identity, and he would respect that choice and protect his right to do so.

My perspective is that it's a good thing for children to explore and find things that they like or dislike for themselves. There are many behaviors, styles, clothes, etc. that are presented to us as being affiliated with one gender or another that are actually just things.

So much of a child's first experience of themselves is through the lens of their connection with their family, and particularly their mothers. The experience of the child is one of being merged with the mother that leads to a first pulling-away during toddlerhood.

That segues nicely into my next section: the best way for a child to learn sovereignty is to watch it in action in the adults around them.

What does it mean to mother as one who is sovereign? What does it mean to parent as one who is self-possessed or sovereign?

My perspectives here are purely my own and do not include my partner's ideas. There are ways in which he agrees with me and ways in

---

[5] Joy DeGruy Leary, *Post Traumatic Slave Syndrome: America's Legacy of Enduring Injury and Healing* (Portland, OR: Uptone Press, 2005).

which our perspectives differ, but he is a deeply private person, so I'm not placing his opinions in this space.

Sovereignty starts with self-knowledge. Parenting with sovereignty has two aspects: the way my son experiences me interacting with him, and the way he sees me modeling interactions with the world. My philosophy emphasizes the importance of self-care as well, which helps me acknowledge my needs as well as the needs of my child, family, and community.

The longer I walk this path, the more certain I am that self-knowledge is the first and most important spiritual gateway (which we will pass through repeatedly in our lifetimes). I have written about this before, and I remain convinced that Delphi's Temple of Apollo was right on the mark with this guidance. I know where my strengths are, how I can be counted on to "bring it," and I also know when I might get good marks for desire but still have plenty of room for improvement. Knowing these things makes a huge difference in the degree of respect I have for myself and in the treatment I expect from others. We often do not realize that, just as we observe others to determine their reliability, we are (sometimes only half-consciously) aware of the times when we have had our own backs or let ourselves down.

My mother has told me more than once that what gave her the courage to go out into the world and face her fears was the fact that she knew that my brother and I were watching her. Now, with my own son, I am very aware of what he sees me (and the other adults around him) modeling with their behavior. I am very aware that what our son sees us doing on a day-to-day basis will make up what he will view as "normal" for many years. He may repeat patterns in his own life that he has seen us perform—how we approach affection, loving, kissing, and connection, as well as how we handle conflict, disagreement, and moments of disharmony.

We strive to be sure that his "normal" includes a body-positive family and household, and that the milestones and rites of passage of life and the human experience are treated as exactly what they are: natural. Warning: when you raise your kids in a body-positive/sex-positive household, they're going to believe that you mean what you say—even if you're not sure exactly what you meant when you decided to do it!

Our son is already aware of and drawn to other people, and his awareness of the complexities of relationships will come in time. I hope that, from his family, he will already be familiar and comfortable with passion, with intensity, and with his body's natural desires for connection and closeness and touch. He will also know about returning to center and to balance and harmony in himself and in relationships, as well as the importance of The Sacred being the energetic buffer in the spaces between him and his partner(s).

I am also very aware of the power of my daily direct interactions with him. When I was pregnant, I received guidance that said he would be a child who needed a lot of touch. There was a period of time where I believed that I didn't like to be touched. Now, more accurately, I understand the power and the energy of touch, and I am selective about who touches me and how they touch me. This does not change what is true in our family, though. My son has a high need for touch and closeness. I want to support and nurture that in him. I also need to support and honor my own needs for space with directness and honesty. Negotiating these needs sometimes looks like my son acting out to get attention, and then us sitting together to explore what unmet needs have caused the behavior. It also sometimes looks like me explaining to him that I don't want any more kisses or hugs in a given moment, that I want some space to myself or that I don't feel like being touched. It also sometimes looks like him practicing doing the same and saying, "No, mama. I don't want any hugs or kisses right now," and that being respected.

Parenting with sovereignty also means that my job, as a mother, is to *do my own work*. My own growth, my own healing, are critical aspects of the parenting process. What I find most effective is having the *capacity* to be responsive to him and what is happening in any given moment: responding to what he needs while navigating the process of balancing his needs and my own. Mothering from a place of sovereignty means belonging to myself and seeking ways, means, and paths that suit who I am as a mother.

My perspective and intentions in parenting are also influenced by my work in mystery traditions. I want my son to have experiences that are necessary for his growth within the safe container of our home, our love, and our family and under the protection of his own guides, our ancestors, and the spirit of the family around him.

As parents, we are sovereign beings guiding another sovereign being on life's path. This kind of parenting requires being responsive to what is happening within ourselves and within our child. We live our lives, keep the lines of communication open, and do what works for as long as it works. When something stops working, we adjust as needed. As our son grows, his own opinions get stronger, and he becomes a more active contributor in this life (these lives) we are all building for ourselves and with one another.

Part of my work, and the work of all of us who strive to transform ourselves and the world, is to create a world that most of us are not actually prepared to be a part of. Walking the path of transformation requires a complex balance of living in reality and striving for what is possible. Parenting while doing that means navigating a necessary process of being honest and direct when preparing our children for the world in which we live, while also encouraging their capacity to vision a new future, live in alignment with their values, and co-create a world that works for all. For example, as a mother of a black male I encourage him to see, believe in, and then create a boundless future for himself *and* to do so with a mind that is unburdened by fears of the ugliness that are a part of America's history. However, the day will come when we will also have to have a blunt conversation with him about safety, the police, and young black men in the United States. To pretend otherwise would potentially endanger him.

Meanwhile, the world continues to shift around us at an ever-increasing pace. Social media and other technology are influencing many arenas of our lives: work, community, entertainment, romance, and even health. The sphere of potential influence on a child's life today is much wider than that of children of past generations. The blessing of this situation is that many parents have access to ideas, wisdom, and guidance from many different people. We can connect and converse with people on a global scale and find others whose perspectives on little-known or obscure issues match, challenge, or expand our own ideas. One of the most beautiful impacts of technology is its capacity to move us closer to global community and connection with others very different from ourselves.

Striving to parent a self-possessed being from a place of my own sovereignty reminds me, on a daily basis, that our lives are a co-creation and so is our world. We can look back on instances in history where there have been years of effort and action for change, and then a time comes when things are completely different. What has most helped me understand this pattern is realizing how much it has impacted my life to have been born after major decisions regarding birth control and women's right to reproductive choice and ownership over their own bodies. I simply live in a different world than the one in which my mother grew up. It doesn't mean sexism has been eradicated or that there are no more obstacles to overcome, but my world view has been shaped by access to these freedoms that created a fundamental shift in our society. The same is true of coming generations of children raised in uninterrupted connection to and ownership of themselves. They represent a tipping point in our society.

So much of the transformative path is about constantly returning to beginner's mind and to our own center. This becomes truer the more time we are "in the world." Retaining a connection to that internal spark of self-knowledge and Divine connection is the place where magick happens, and it is where we can receive great inspiration and guidance. We cannot plan or control what will emerge from a generation living from that space. We can only stay in connection with it in our own lives and guide and support our children in connecting to it in themselves.

My Sovereign Mothering Manifesto

My goal as a mother is to guide our son to adulthood while protecting and preserving his connection to himself.

◆ I honor his right to be respected.

◆ I parent the child I have, striving to respond to *him*, not my perception of what is right, wrong, or "normal."

◆ I strive to be gentle with him and with myself in this process.

◆ It is imperative that he always know that he is loved and that nothing will ever change that.

◆ Our home is a safe space for all who live there. It is not a space where he learns to be disrespected or have his boundaries disregarded.

◆ What he sees us doing is what he will think is "normal." I want his "normal" to feel like love and respect, harmony and connection, and peace and safety.

Postscript

This article has been a struggle for me to write. Recently, I've been in personal rebellion against parenting books and philosophies, because so much of parenting is about personal growth and responsiveness to the child that you have. My kid's opinions and thoughts have also gotten stronger and more individual to himself. We are all riding the waves together, as a family, with periods of harmony and moments of discord. Truly, though, this article could have just as accurately been titled, "Sovereignty Parenting is like riding a rogue wave: no matter the size of your vessel, you're not really ready for it and you're going to get soaked." There are so many differing views and perspectives to hold in the process of raising this one, solitary child. I also recognize that I have the time to explore so many of these views because I have only one child, who was born after I'd reached certain achievements in my own life.

Resources

Brooks, Havi. "Sovereignty 101." The Fluent Self blog. June 14, 2010. http://www.fluentself.com/blog/stuckification/sovereignty-101/.

DeGruy, Joy, PhD. *Post Traumatic Slave Syndrome.* Portland, OR: Uptone Press, 2005.

Gibran, Khalil. "On Children." *The Prophet.* New York: Alfred A. Knopf, 1923. 17-18.

Lansbury, Janet. "How to Be the Gentle Leader Your Child Needs." June 6, 2011. http://www.janetlansbury.com/2011/06/how-to-be-the-gentle-leader-your-child-needs/.

Stryker, Kitty. *Consent Culture: Because Safewords Are Sexy.* http://www.consentculture.com/.

Tough, Paul. *How Children Succeed: Grit, Curiosity, and the Hidden Power of Character.* New York: Mariner Books, 2013.

Tylor, Alexyss. *Power of Touch 1 & 2.* https://www.youtube.com/watch?v=PuhvNYdLNcA, https://www.youtube.com/watch?v=bJ0jyNHJB20.

Gerber, Magda. "Magda Gerber's RIE Philosophy - Basic Principles." May 1, 2012. http://www.magdagerber.org/blog/magda-gerbers-rie-philosophy-basic-principles.

Nadirah Adeye is a cis-woman, a priestess, a person of color, a proud Bay Area native and re-resident, an adoring mother of one son and a passionate partner of a magnificent god-like man (seriously, I love me some them). She has a Master's degree in Women's Spirituality, and her mission is for women (especially mothers and especially POC women) to have safe spaces to live in manners both sacred and sensual to them. Honor the Sacred, Celebrate the Sensual, and Embrace the Sustainable are her taglines. All of these identities (and their associated privileges and burdens) inform and guide her perspective.

Paganism, Children, and Consent Culture
An Interview with Sierra Black
Sarah Whedon

A note from the interviewer:

Sierra and I have known each other for a long time. We did our first ritual together in the early '90s. I learned how to parent largely by watching Sierra do it a few years ahead of me. We've taught together, priestessed together, and cared for each other's children, but this is the first time either of us has formally interviewed the other. I've edited the transcript of the interview for clarity, but also because the complete recording features the background sounds of kids and cats in a busy household. During our conversation, Sierra talked to me about developing habits of relating to children, how communities and institutions can be a part of Pagan consent culture for children, and how Pagan spirituality is connected to creating consent culture.

Being In Relationships and Communities

SARAH: When Christine first asked you to do an interview about children and Pagan consent culture, can you remember what your first reaction to that was?

SIERRA: I was just like: okay! I love Pagans! I love consent! I love children! I was excited that somebody was doing it, and I thought that you were a really great person to have that conversation with. Consent in any context is a super important topic, because it's about allowing people to live lives that are rich in agency, respect for themselves and others, and safety.

In a Pagan context in particular, consent issues are very tightly interwoven with what I believe about deity and religion, which very much involves a two-way relationship. *The gods are not these authority figures reigning over us from on high. They're among us. They're the air that we breathe and the water that we drink and the arguments that we have with our lovers and the snacks that we grow in our gardens. So our relationships with them have to be voluntary and respectful, and consent is a big part of that.* Obviously not everything about our relationship with deity is voluntary or respectful. Sometimes it snows really hard on a day you want to go to a party. But I feel like worship has to be voluntary and respectful, and that any kind of ritual and recognition of the divine in my life is something that I freely choose and my kids freely choose—if they do, which sometimes they do.

SARAH: So I hear you saying that there has to be a voluntary and consensual relationship with deity, and that is true for both adults and children. Is there a relationship between that and the ways that children and adults or children and children interact with each other?

SIERRA: Yeah. I think that's an interesting distinction, the difference between the way that adults are able to negotiate consent and the way that children are able to negotiate consent. I expect all of my kids' relationships with other children, with their peers, to be consensual and freely chosen and imbued with mutual respect. I expect pretty much all of their relationships with adults to be like that too. *I think part of raising kids in a consent culture is recognizing where authority exists, so I don't pretend to them that we're equals or that I'm not the boss of them.* The same thing is true with their teachers and the authority figures in their lives. My mom takes care of them, and as a caregiver she has some authority over them. But with the exception of caregivers, I expect them to have that peer relationship with the people they interact with. And with caregivers I expect there to be mutual respect as well; I just think it should be transparent that there is a power dimension there.

SARAH: I'm curious what you have observed or experienced of
           particular communities or institutions in Paganism, or
           outside of Paganism, or overlapping with Paganism. How
           they have been either supportive of consent culture or
           worked against consent culture? You talked about
           teachers and family members, so that also makes me think
           about schools and family structures, but I was also
           thinking about Pagan communities and social groups and
           non-profits that you're involved with.

SIERRA: When I've interacted with Pagan community structures
           with my kids—and there haven't been that many
           actually—most of them have worked really hard to create
           Pagan community around my children, but it's mostly on
           the side. They've gone to Witch Camp[1] a couple of times.
           Witch Camp is an environment that is strongly rooted in
           consensus process, really supports consent culture, and
           sets an expectation for people of all ages that they will
           respect one another's boundaries, so you don't make
           decisions for other people or force your will on other
           people. That's been a great model for me as a parent,
           especially in my early years of parenting. The informal
           Pagan community around my kids is blessed with some of
           the strongest role models I have for parenting, a bunch of
           good Pagan mamas.

           The institutions outside of Pagan community that
           my kids come into contact with are much less likely to
           support consent culture, although not uniformly. Most of
           the intentional parenting circles that I've been part of
           have had a pretty strong ethic of consent and respect for
           boundaries, like attachment parenting groups or moms'
           playgroups; we were a part of a couple of cooperative

---

[1] Witch Camps are Reclaiming Tradition's intensive retreats for the study
and practice of magic and ritual.

preschools and they really had that strong consent culture, even though they didn't call it that. Public school[2] is not a consent culture kind of institution. It's a very top down, authoritarian, punishment model, and I don't love it. My kids are really thriving there right now, though.

When Rio was at Parts and Crafts,[3] she was getting a lot of intentionality and consensus but not great consent culture, because there wasn't enough structure and/or education to frame that for the kids. The kids would kind of ride roughshod over one another, like talk over each other and push each other and get up in somebody's game and refuse to back out and, you know, it was a little bit *Lord of the Flies*. The adults were pretty great about handling it, and Rio had a great time because she is very socially skilled at navigating getting to compromises and creating consent for everyone. But some of the other kids I know who went there had a harder time navigating the social waters for themselves.

I think that Parts and Crafts has great intention about consent and imperfect execution, because the focus is so much on personal freedom. The kids really get the message that they're free to do whatever they want. *It's a nuance to understand that you're free to do whatever you want as long as it doesn't impinge on other people, and seven year-olds don't always get their heads around that quickly.* But that environment really did foster a strong sense of agency for Rio, so I'm glad that she had her time there, for sure.

Extended family is a super hard one for consent culture, for a lot of people, I think. My family has the

---

[2] Note for UK readers: a public school in the US is the equivalent of a state school in the UK.

[3] Parts and Crafts is a homeschool resource center.

complicating factor of half the kids' family being in Argentina and having a completely different cultural grounding and a completely different language, literally, for negotiating these things. That really amplifies the come-give-your-aunt-a-kiss-whether-you-want-to-or-not dynamic. I'm not well-liked by the relatives on that side of the family, I think because of that. I've been very active about protecting the kids' boundaries and insisting on a two-year-old's authority over her own body, which is not an idea they were even familiar enough with to have an opinion about, at least before they came to play with us.

On my side of the family, there've been some challenges, but I think people mostly respect me and are willing to respect my say-so about the kids. They may not get that I'm advocating for the kids' power to consent for themselves whether they want to be kissed or not, but they do understand that they can't cross my boundary about it. They might still see me in this authoritative, autocratic power over the children, but they are willing to respect the boundaries I set about letting the kids initiate touch. So the kids are still getting held in what I think of as a safe, consensual relationship, even if the great-aunt doesn't understand why that's happening.

Reflexive Consent: The Parable of the Kitten

SARAH: How does one go about pursuing or creating consent culture for children? What part of that is about choosing communities to be a part of, what part of that is about having frank conversations with children, what part of it is about modeling as an adult in the children's lives?

SIERRA: It's all those things! I'm going to tell a little anecdote about my kitten. I have a kitten, and I've noticed recently that when other people are not around and the kitten and

I are the only ones in the house, I will pick the kitten up and say, "May I pick you up, kitten?" And the kitten will go, "..." because she's a kitten. And I say, "If you make the put-me-down noise, I will put you down because in this house we always listen to each other about our boundaries." And the kitten will sit there and then eventually go "mrrrwww." And I'll put her down and say, "I'm putting you down now because you made the put-me-down noise."

Obviously the kitten is not learning any important lessons about consent here. But ten years into parenting, I so reflexively narrate the process of consent that I do it with my cats. That is at the core of teaching consent to children from infancy—and this is going back to what I said earlier about making power clear—pointing out where they have power, where they don't, how they're going to get that power, what the choices they have available to them are, and really working to back off and give them as many choices as they can while protecting their safety and providing care for them.

Taking care of hair is a good example because it can be really difficult for children. Both of my kids have been through a phase where they did not consent to having their hair washed or brushed, and I know from experience that my parents would have forcibly brushed my hair. My perhaps better—or perhaps not!—approach has been to negotiate with my kids about the choices that they have. If they want their hair to be long, then they need to either brush it themselves or let me brush it. Or we can cut it. So they may not like any of those choices, but they're being given some insight into and participation in what the choices are. It would be great if they liked one of them, and now they have grown up to the point where they do—they enjoy brushing their hair. They both have long hair that they take good care of.

Even when they were babies, if they didn't want to have their diapers changed, I'd say, okay, when you learn to use the potty then we won't have to change your diaper anymore. I give them a path towards the agency that they want. Just that constant narration of letting them know if I'm touching them and they don't want me to, it's because they put their hand on the stove or it's because they pooped in their diaper, or it's because there's some immediate health or safety concern that I'm addressing. That keeps the expectations very clear, and that fosters a sense of safety and strengthens their ability to say yes or no to what they have control over.

It's interesting—as I'm talking I'm realizing that a lot of what I'm saying about children and consent is also how trauma-aware care[4] is taught. Trauma-aware care is for people who are, as adults, relearning a sense of safety and control and relearning the ability to have agency over their own selves. Care providers do a lot of these things for them as well.

SARAH: It's making me think about some of the voiced resistance to attempts to shift adult culture around consent, specifically around sexuality. Some people have resistance to having to pause, slow down, vocalize, and explicitly say what is happening or what is desired or what is going to happen. I was thinking about that as you were describing so much vocalization around children, which I do too. But I was imagining in my head the possible resistance someone might feel—that feels weird, that feels awkward, I'm not used to saying to the baby, "Now I'm going to

---

[4] Trauma-Informed Care is an approach to mental health care that is rooted in research about the prevalence of the human experience of trauma in the wake of abuse, violence, neglect, or disaster.

change your diaper,," or "Are you ready for your diaper change?"

SIERRA: I think the thing that helps me do that most is having allies who do it too. Every time I see a friend negotiate with her toddler about putting their shoes on, it helps me be further grounded in negotiating openly and freely with my kids about putting their shoes on, which I do less of now because they're older. *Having other parents in my community who are committed to consent and teaching that value to their children is really powerful for me in helping me continue to do that. Being in community helps me be more whole in making change in the world.* The kids also help. Once you get a kid acclimatized to something, they'll remind you. They'll be like, "Mommy, this is how we do this," and "we ask before we tickle somebody," you know, they get committed to the routine.

SARAH: I've found that to be true. But now I'm imagining somebody who's reading this interview in the book, somebody who doesn't have really supportive community. I'm wondering what we can say to them.

SIERRA: The two things I would say are that it's worth making the effort to find that community. The internet is a big and glorious place full of people who like to talk to each other, and they often will open doors to local community that you may not be aware of. Of course, if you've already made that effort and you're feeling isolated and like you don't have a community, you can start to grow it, plant the seeds of it in your own house, in your own family, in your relationships with your kids—who, as we were just talking about, will remind you—and also in your relationships with other people's kids and in your adult relationships.

           If you make it a practice to always check in with your friend's child before you wipe her nose, then maybe your friend will start doing it too. Or if you make it a practice to always be transparent about negotiating consent around household chores with your partner, your kids will see that, your friends will see that, and maybe it will spread. So you can both work to find community with people who are already versed in the values you want, and also work to share those values with your existing community.

SARAH: Those both sound like helpful thoughts. We've put a whole bunch of pieces of this puzzle on the table in the last twenty-five minutes. Do you feel like there are big pieces that are missing from this conversation, or even significant small pieces?

SIERRA: The one pulling-together piece that we haven't talked about yet is the way that consent culture necessarily intersects with my spirituality. This is not to say that it necessarily intersects with all Pagan religions or communities or cultures. But for me, as someone whose background is strongly rooted in Reclaiming—and not just in Reclaiming, but in the evolving over time practice of magic and witchcraft and feminist religion that you and I have had together for many years—if I look back even at the very earliest forays into spirituality that we made, they were grounded in this belief in personal agency and freedom, as well as the responsibility to respect and cherish the safety of everyone we interact with. As misguided youth, we were never into putting demons into bottles.

SARAH: That's true!

SIERRA: For me, there are very deep roots of Paganism as the consensual religion where we are in relationship with nature and deity and community, not holding power over those things. If this is a conversation about Paganism, those things fit together and are very necessary for me.

Walking the Talk

SARAH: Can you think of particular ways that ideal is expressed through prayers or rituals or spiritual experiences?

SIERRA: The over-used and clichéd ethic of "harm none, do what you will" expresses it. The practice of inviting rather than demanding the presence of gods and elements when we cast circle expresses it. I think that casting circle heart-to-heart is a really beautiful expression of that collaborative, consensual container that we make. I have a lot of issues with Reclaiming's non-hierarchical stance, because it can disguise the machinery of power. But I also think that commitment to not formalizing power into the hands of a few is a really important expression of an ethic of consent and power-with, rather than power-over.[5]

SARAH: Maybe this is a totally unfair question... Yeah, it's a totally unfair question. I'll say it anyway and then you can say, yeah, that's an unfair question and I don't want to answer that. But the thing that's coming to mind for me is the bigger Pagan movement or communities. Reclaiming is clearly a place where you have deep roots, and it's also not necessarily representative of a lot of other expressions of Paganism. Something like the ethic of "harm none, do what you will" is also not necessarily part of everybody's Paganism, but it is maybe more widespread.

---

[5] In *Truth or Dare: Encounters with Power, Authority, and Mystery*, Starhawk described *power-over* as the power to dominate and control, and *power-with* as the power of equals working together in a group.

I want to consider how those explicitly stated beliefs or values come into practice, because I don't think they always do. Sometimes the things that we say we believe or what we value are out of alignment with how we actually act in our spiritual communities and in other places in the world. So I'm wanting to unpack how Reclaiming has—at least in some ways—successfully walked that talk. And that's not to say that Reclaiming is the only Pagan community that has successfully walked that talk, because it's absolutely not true.

SIERRA: But it's the one I have a lot of experience in.

SARAH: Right. So, how do we get to a place where we're walking the talk? And it's not just Paganism—lots of religions have a hard time linking up their actions with their stated beliefs and values.

SIERRA: I can name a couple of nitty-gritty ways in which Reclaiming walks their talk. Reclaiming does not have a centralized system of authority or power. Anyone who identifies as a Reclaiming Witch and agrees to the Principles of Unity can be a Reclaiming Witch, found a Reclaiming coven in their community, communicate with Reclaiming teachers, and study Reclaiming materials. They don't need to be hit by a magic wand by the right person at the right time, which is not to dismiss more hierarchical structures as being necessarily less consent-oriented. I don't think that that's true. You can be an Alexandrian Witch and be completely committed to consent and walk your talk on it, but it would look different. One of the ways that Reclaiming does it is by not having centralized authority.

Another way that Reclaiming does it is by teaching and priestessing in teams, so whenever you have a Reclaiming class or a big community ritual, you have at least two people who are responsible for sharing the power and responsibility of making it happen and modeling cooperation and consent.

Reclaiming intentionally design its events and teaching materials to accommodate the needs of marginalized members of the community. Those are issues Reclaiming is really sensitive to, though not perfectly so. But it really puts some intention and effort into accommodating the needs of people who are poor or physically disabled, who are in recovery from addiction, who are marginalized in other ways. Attending to the edges also strengthens the center, and that's another way that Reclaiming reflexively checks for consent in setting up events. They're really working hard to give everyone access and give everyone a voice.

SARAH: Does that include children?

SIERRA: That's a touchy subject. But increasingly it does. As the tradition matures, it is increasingly inclusive of children, and it has brought a lot of the same commitment to consent, inclusivity, and power-sharing to including children that in the past was brought to including adult members. Children are frequently on the edges in Reclaiming communities, and if people are making an effort to include them, then they're not easily at the center. But that's less and less true in my experience.

SARAH: I just want to ask one more big question. If you were to wave the biggest, best magic wand, and make the Pagan consent culture for/of/by/at children, what would that include, what would that look like?

SIERRA: It would absolutely be rooted in children's autonomy over their bodies, their minds, their feelings, and their spirit. Children growing up in Pagan consent culture would be people raised to consider their own needs in tandem with the needs of others. They would be children secure in the ability to act on their own behalf and therefore able to, in a healthy way, act on behalf of others.

It would be a model where those who hold power use it responsibly to protect the health and safety of children and other vulnerable people, and where the kids and everyone else would get to make most of their decisions most of the time. They would always be transparently aware of what decisions are being made for them and why. I think that that would foster a sense of personal power, but also social responsibility. In terms of a spiritual community, it would be one that was capable of both celebration of and support for kids.

SARAH: So mote it be.

SIERRA: So mote it be.

Sierra Black, MFA, CPS is a social work student at Smith College School for Social Work, a Peer Support Specialist for people in mental health crisis, and a volunteer rape crisis hotline counselor. Her writing on open relationships, parenting, and family life can be found at *Huffington Post, Babble, Get Rich Slowly,* and her personal blog *ChildWild.* She can often be found digging in the garden, knitting in the rocker, or casting spells in the kitchen.

Sarah Whedon, PhD is founding co-director of the Boston Doula Project, a full-spectrum doula organization; the managing editor of the Pagan Families blog at Patheos.com; the author of *Birth on the Labyrinth Path: Sacred Embodiment in the Childbearing Year*; and former Chair of the Department of Theology and Religious History at Cherry Hill Seminary. Sarah's teaching, research, and advocacy work center around topics of spirituality, feminism, and reproduction. She makes her home in the Boston area with her partner and their children.

Teaching Consent Culture
Tips and Games for Kids, Teens, and Adults
Christine Hoff Kraemer

Are you a parent, a caregiver, or a group leader of young people or adults? Do you need to teach others how to cultivate empathy and respect others' autonomy? Do you want to build consent culture in your community, but don't know where to start?

If so, this essay is for you. It is intended to give you essential information you will need to teach young people and adults about consent culture, as well as to provide some consent exercises and games. It will also cover some of the pitfalls that Pagans and others need to consider when teaching about touch- and sex-positivity.

Why Kids Need Loving Touch, and How Consent Culture Helps Them Get It

If you're a parent or a caregiver, you're probably aware that most children want a great deal of loving touch. You may not know, however, that loving touch does more than bond people together emotionally. Children, and especially infants, need pleasurable touch in order to develop biologically. Farmers, zookeepers, and other people who raise mammals have known for a long time that baby animals who are not licked and massaged by their mothers don't eliminate wastes properly and die.

Infants who don't experience loving touch die as well, though the exact mechanism is a little more mysterious than with rats or pigs. In the nineteenth century, a number of studies were conducted on urban orphanages where the rate of infant deaths from a mysterious wasting disease sometimes approached 90%. In these understaffed orphanages, although the infants were kept clean and fed, there was rarely time for the staff to pick up, hold, or play with them. Further, expert childrearing advice of the time discouraged parents from picking infants up when they cried, fearing that this treatment would "spoil" the children. Both of these factors led to the infants receiving only enough touch to take care of their obvious needs.

Researchers were stunned, then, to find that infants who were picked up and lovingly cuddled would either recover from or never develop the wasting disease. Today, hospitals and orphanages know that touch is a necessity, not a luxury, for infant care. Although the need for touch becomes somewhat less of a life-and-death issue in older children, touch deprivation is correlated with aggressive behavior in both children and adults, and touch therapy such as massage has been effective in treating disorders such as anorexia, anxiety, and depression in adolescents. (For more information on touch deprivation, see my essay "Mindful Touch as a Religious Practice," also in this volume.)

Knowing that children need loving touch, and lots of it, to develop normally, we should be disturbed by the way schools are eliminating touch opportunities outside of the immediate family—for instance, forbidding elementary school teachers to hug their students and punishing children for holding hands while in school. We all share concerns about inappropriate touch and abuse. But it's important to remember that neglect is abuse as well, and that touch deprivation causes suffering. To draw a parallel: we are certainly all concerned about our children being harmed by pesticides on fresh produce. But if we eliminate all fresh produce from our children's diet to make sure we avoid pesticides, we're not protecting their health at all, but harming it.

So how do we create opportunities for children to give and receive the loving touch that they need? We need to create cultures of consent in our communities, and that begins with education.

Consent Culture Talking Points for Children and Teens

What is consent culture? This volume explores consent culture in depth, sometimes using language that is too complex for young people to understand. When teaching young people, you will need to begin with simple language. Try adapting the following talking points for the age level(s) involved.

- When you give consent, you give your permission for an action or activity. The best kind of consent is enthusiastic consent—a clear YES! Because people are struggling so much with touch and with sexuality right now, it is especially important to get an enthusiastic "yes" when hugging or touching others.

- It's okay to change your mind about whether you want to be touched at any time. It's okay for others to change their minds too.

- In a consent culture, we believe that each person is the best judge of their own wants and needs. Each adult is in charge of their own body and mind. It is wrong to try to force someone to do anything they don't want to do, or to forcibly prevent them from doing something they DO want to do, so long as it doesn't do harm.

- Here are some examples of how consent culture looks: Don't want to try the octopus your brother ordered for lunch? That's fine. Don't want to be tickled? Then your friends don't get to hold you down and do it anyway. Want more hugs from your family and friends? Then you can ask for what you want, and they can say yes or no. Want to wear a tutu, shave your head, or paint your nails, even if people of your gender don't usually do that? Well, you can, and no one should bully you about it.

- In a consent culture, parents respect their children's right to control their own bodies as much as they can without endangering their children's health and safety or the health and safety of others.

- Children and teenagers are their parents' legal responsibility. This means that if you are below the age of eighteen, your parents give consent for you in many contexts. For example, you may not want to go to the doctor and get a shot, but your parents know what's best for your health and give consent for you.

- Adolescents under a certain age are considered too young to have sex, regardless of whether or not their parents would give permission for them. The "age of consent" varies by region. If you are under the legal age of consent in your region, it is illegal for others to have sex with you. Having sex when you are under the age of consent, even if you want to, can end up with your partner in jail. In some regions, this can happen even if both you and your partner are younger than eighteen.

These points are only a place to start. With older children and teenagers, discussions about consent may quickly find themselves in deep ethical waters.

+ What does it mean to "force" someone against their will?

+ Can persuasion be considered "force"?

+ What about relationships where forceful persuasion is desirable, like in sports where your coach pushes you hard to succeed? Does a sports coach need your consent to push you that way?

+ How is it different if a boyfriend or girlfriend pushes you?

+ What does "harm" mean?

+ Should we interfere with a friend who smokes cigarettes, since we know that smoking is harmful to their health? Or are they able to consent to smoking so long as they only harm themselves?

+ What exactly is a "health and safety situation"? When are parents obligated to intervene to protect their children's safety, even if the children do not consent? Are there times when non-parent adults are obligated to intervene? When is adult intervention *not* okay?

With luck, these talking points will create opportunities for young people, parents, and educators to have nuanced conversations about what it means to balance individual and community needs—in other words, to respect autonomy and cultivate empathy.

Basic Consent Culture Practice

How do you begin building consent culture in communities? Because we are struggling so much with issues of touch and sexuality right now, it makes sense to begin with consent to touch.

The basic practice is simple: *Ask before you touch.* Among people we don't know well, asking verbally is a good idea, i.e. "May I hug you?" In many cases, however, asking nonverbally works just as well: you can open your arms for a hug and wait for the other person to mirror the gesture before hugging them. Note that asking is only *half* of the procedure; waiting for the enthusiastic "YES!" is the other half! A non-enthusiastic "yes" is usually a "no" in disguise.

Many opportunities for teaching children about respecting the autonomy of others' bodies arise when kids play together, and we can begin to convey those values when our children are quite small. As a new parent, I've been grateful to other parents in my community for modeling how to teach consent culture for me when their kids play with my baby. "We don't force-feed babies," says one mother to her toddler as she shows him how to offer the pacifier rather than just jamming it into the baby's mouth. Another parent cautions his daughter as she hugs and bounces the baby: "Listen to the sound he's making, he's saying no, so you need to stop. Now he's smiling because you're being more gentle."

Even at very young ages, children can be taught the habit of asking for the touch they want and respecting others' boundaries. Kids who grow up believing that they have the right to control their own bodies are better-equipped to initiate respectful touch, to clearly say yes or no when touch is offered, and to interfere when they see someone else being violated.

A Consent Game for Groups of Kids

Here's a simple game that you can play with elementary-aged and older children. Not only does it teach consent and empathy, but it's a lot of fun and great for making friends! Adults should be present to model the game, make sure the rules are being followed, and ensure safety, as children playing this game can easily become rambunctious. The game can be adapted for adolescents and adults.

1) Break into pairs.
2) In each pair, one child asks his or her partner if s/he can touch them in a specific way. "Can I give you a hug?" "Can I tickle your ribs?" "Can I grab you and spin you around?"
3) If the partner wants to be touched that way, s/he says, "YES, YES, YES!" and participates in the touch.
4) If the partner does not want to be touched that way, s/he says, "No thanks!" or "Not today!"
5) If the partner refuses the touch, the child initiating the touch must do his/her best to perform the action on him/herself. This can result in some hilarious attempts at self-tickling, self-noogie-ing, etc.
6) The children switch roles. Now the second child offers a touch, and the first child can accept or decline.
7) Remind the participants that they can switch their answer from yes or no, or from no to yes, even after the touch has begun. Children may enjoy having the adults model this lesson in a silly way ("Hug! Stop! Hug! Stop!") while still driving home the importance of permission to touch.
8) Children who fail to wait for a "yes" must wait out a round before rejoining the game. (It's useful to have an extra adult to step in as a partner when a child goes out for a round.)
9) Children should switch partners every round or two. The game facilitators can also experiment with phrasing the offers of touch differently ("Can I have a hug?" "Will you tickle me?" "Will you grab me and spin me around?") or including affectionate gestures that don't include touching ("Can I blow you a kiss?"). For an additional variation, give each child a sticker or other small reward every time they complete a round while following the rules.

This game provides wonderful opportunities for discussion. How does it feel to say "No thanks," or to be told "No thanks"? How does it feel to say "YES"? What kinds of touch were really fun? Did anyone say yes to a touch that turned out not to be fun? What did they do, and what did their partner do? Did anyone say "no" and then change their mind? What was that like? What was it like for their partner?

Adults will find that, especially if played with older children or adolescents, the game provides many opportunities for children to experience both positive and difficult emotions. It may be worthwhile to stop to talk in the middle of the game: Does your partner's "no" feel like being rejected? How does it feel to say "no" back? How does it feel to say "yes" if your partner keeps saying "no"? How does it feel to say "no" if your partner keeps saying yes? Did anyone say "yes" because they were afraid of hurting a partner's feelings? Participants can use these discussions as opportunities to talk about how to respect a "no" by not taking it personally and how to find kinds of touch that both participants will find fun.

Unless the participants are already part of a group where physical, group-bonding games are played regularly, facilitators should inform the children's parents before playing this game. Note that some younger children may struggle with the rules. Children who have difficulty keeping their hands to themselves, however, may be the ones who benefit the most from learning how to explicitly ask for touch; their tendency to harass or tease others may be the only way they know how to get the contact they want.

What Consent Culture Parents Need to Know about the Sex Offenders' Registry

[Note: This information applies primarily to readers in the United States. Other countries have similar sex offender databases, but the rules and regulations around these databases may be different. Readers are advised to research their own regions' laws so as to have the most accurate information.]

Perhaps, like me, you are a parent trying to raise a kid who loves their own body and respects the bodies of others. You're teaching them about consent, you're teaching them about sovereignty, you're giving them all the best body-positive sex-education books, you're raising them in a community that's committed to consent culture. That should keep them safe, right?

Well, it certainly helps. But unless you live on an off-the-grid commune, you're still connected to mainstream Western culture, which is not particularly body- or sex-positive and which often openly supports the casual violation of people's boundaries—a reality we sometimes call *rape culture.*

As we as a society have become more aware of the frequency of sexual assault and abuse, we have created institutions to try to prevent them. Unfortunately, these institutions themselves are embedded in rape culture, which means they can do harm as well as good. The United States' national sex offender registry is one such institution.

I first became aware of problems with sex offender registries through reporter Lenore Skenazy. Skenazy is the author of *Free Range Kids,* a book and blog advocating for a return to the independent childhoods experienced by children in the 1980s and before. Skenazy attributes the new cultural norm of constant surveillance of children to a variety of factors, but she particularly highlights the American fear of sexual predators. Skenazy points out that statistically, kidnappings and sexual abuse of children by strangers is vanishingly rare; most children who are kidnapped or abused are victimized by someone they know, a friend or family member. Nevertheless, today many American children are rarely permitted outside by themselves due to "stranger danger." Those parents who do allow their children outside may find themselves targeted by Child Protective Services if a concerned (or malicious) neighbor makes a phone call.

(Even as I write, however, this situation is changing: due to a case where the Meitiv family of Silver Spring, Maryland was targeted by local authorities after their children were allowed outside alone, state-level Child Protective Services has drafted new language specifying that allowing children to play outside unsupervised does not constitute neglect unless there is evidence of harm or a substantial risk of harm.[1] Readers may want to follow www.freerangekids.com for news on recent CPS rulings on similar cases.)

As part of her advocacy for "free-range" parenting, Skenazy observed that the sex offender registry helped to feed her neighbors' fear of sexual predators. In New York, residents are able to access a map online that shows the homes of registered sex offenders in their neighborhoods. As Skenazy researched the registry, however, she began to notice that the results could be misleading—not all "sex offenders" pose any danger to children. Crimes such as visiting a prostitute or public urination can result in a person being placed on the registry, and the placement is usually permanent, with no petition process for being removed.[2]

Children or teenagers under the age of consent who touch each other may also end up on the sex offenders' registry, whether or not they consider themselves to have given consent. These situations can include curious tweens playing "doctor" and touching each other's genitals, or sexual encounters between teenagers where one or both parties has lied about being above the age of consent.

In the United States, therapists, clergy, and other professionals are "mandatory reporters" ("mandated reporters" is the term in the UK), meaning they are legally required to report cases of suspected child abuse or neglect to law enforcement or Child Protective Services. This means that if a parent seeks therapy for a child who has been abused by an adult, and who in turn abused a younger sibling, the therapist is

---

[1] "'Free-range' parents are cleared in the second of two neglect cases for letting kids aged six and 10 walk home alone," *The Daily Mail,* 22 June 2015. Available at http://www.dailymail.co.uk/news/article-3134496/Maryland-free-range-family-2nd-neglect-case-cleared.html.

[2] Tracy Clark Flory, interview with Lenore Skenazy, "Stop the sex-offender registry panic: A lot of those dots would never hurt your kids," *Salon* 26 March 2015. Available at http://www.salon.com/2015/03/26/stop_the_sex_offender_registry_panic_a_lot_of_those_dots_on_the_map_would_never_hurt_your_kids/.

legally required to report the abuse of the younger sibling. In some cases, this can result of the removal of the older child from the home, several years' incarceration in juvenile detention, and placement on the sex offenders' registry; in other cases, the child may be permitted to receive therapy in the home so long as there is no evidence that the younger sibling is in ongoing danger.[3]

It is extremely important that parents who discover sexual abuse occurring in the home seek professional help. Although it can be tempting for parents to avoid involving CPS, thinking "we can handle it ourselves," it does additional psychological damage to the victim when adults discover abuse and then fail to intervene. Additionally, if children who are engaging in sexually abusive behavior receive treatment early, it can help keep them from becoming perpetrators as adults. Children or teens who are engaging in sexual abuse have often been abuse victims themselves, and the opportunity to receive treatment can uncover this history, giving them an opportunity to heal. These benefits are worth risking a child's becoming a registered sex offender.

It is important to realize that although teaching our children good boundaries will help to prevent abuse, it will not prevent all abuse of our children, nor will it necessarily prevent children who have been abused from becoming abusers themselves. In addition to teaching children about consent, parents need to be aware of their children's sexual behaviors and be prepared to respond if abuse occurs. We want to teach our children that they have the right to govern their own bodies, but they cannot give consent for other children (or adults) to touch their genitals, nor can other children consent to being touched sexually.

Knowledge of local and state laws can help parents protect their teens. In particular, adolescents need to understand the age of consent

---

[3] "Dealing with child-on-child sex abuse not one size fits all," USA Today 7 Jan 2012. Available at http://usatoday30.usatoday.com/news/nation/story/2012-01-07/child-sex-abuse/52431616/1.

laws in their state. Parents should emphasize to their teens that they should not engage in sexual acts with partners they do not know and trust. If a teen lies about their age in order to have sex with an older teen, this fact will not protect the older teen in court—and penalties can be severe, including imprisonment, permanent placement on the sex offender registry, and being denied access to younger siblings.[4] Adolescents also need to be aware of their region's laws about child pornography. In some states, if a teenager takes nude pictures of themselves to send to a girlfriend or boyfriend, this is considered distribution of child pornography. Parents of adolescents need to help them balance their normal desires for sexual exploration with caution. The illicit pleasure of trading nude photos with a lover is not worth the risk of becoming a registered sex offender.

Overall, many of the state laws regarding sex offenders and our national sex offender registry are in need of reform. Some registered sex offenders are dangerous predators; others are children and adults who pose no danger to anyone. The sex offender registry, however, does not effectively distinguish between the two. In some states, sex offenders are subjected to dehumanizing practices that do nothing to increase public safety, such as Louisiana's requirement that sex offenders turn away trick-or-treaters and identify themselves via a sign on their homes on Halloween. These requirements can have a profound impact on offenders' families, and they apply regardless of the severity of the crime, whether the offender received treatment, or whether the crime occurred a few years or a few decades before. The public nature of the registry can also leave registered sex offenders

---

[4] Lenore Skenazy, "Another 19 y.o. Had Sex w/ Girl He Thought Was 17. Now He Cannot Be Near Anyone Under 18 — Including His Brother and Sister," *Free Range Kid,s* 8 July 2015. Available at http://www.freerangekids.com/another-19-y-o-had-sex-w-girl-he-thought-was-17-now-he-cannot-be-near-anyone-under-18-including-his-brother-and-sister/.

vulnerable to brutal assaults by those looking for a target they believe no one will defend.[5]

Building consent culture requires thoughtful, effective, and humane responses to sexual abuse and assault. In the case of juvenile sex offenders, it is clear that we are sometimes criminalizing situations that would be better served with counseling and supervision by authorities in the home. Though incarceration continues to be the right option for many perpetrators of sexual crimes, our demonizing of all people who have been labeled "sex offenders" keeps us from thinking in a complex way about these issues and helps to perpetuate rape culture.

Boundary Exercises for Teens and Adults

These exercises are intended to help people practice expressing boundaries, respecting others' boundaries, and identifying their own emotions around the process. They can be used in a youth group or affinity group, a staff or leadership training, a workshop on consent culture, or in similar contexts.

Basic

1) Break into pairs, with the facilitator either standing aside or participating, depending on whether the number of participants is even or odd.

2) Ask each person to hide one hand behind their back.

---

[5] Arielle Pardes, "Are Sex Offenders Unfairly Persecuted on Halloween?" *Vice* 30 October 2014. Available at http://www.vice.com/read/its-no-fun-to-be-a-sex-offender-on-halloween-666. Some studies have suggested that making sex offender information publicly available, rather than available only to law enforcement, may actually increase rather than decrease sex offender recidivism rates. See JJ Prescott and Jonah E. Rockoff, "Do Sex Offender Registration and Notification Laws Affect Criminal Behavior?", *Journal of Law and Economics* 54 (February 2011): 161-206.

3) On the hidden hand, signal the level of touch desired with the partner: a closed hand for no touch, one finger for a handshake, two fingers for a hug.

4) On the facilitator's cue, all participants reveal their hands. They then exchange touch (or not) based on the *lower* number. For example, if one participant reveals one finger, and the other reveals two, the partners shake hands.

5) Switch partners and repeat for several rounds. Depending on the group, the facilitator may suggest that participants experiment with requesting more or less touch than they normally would.

6) After the partners have rotated several times, stop and discuss. How does it feel to be the one revealing a higher or lower number? Did anyone experience feeling rejected or embarrassed? If we struggle not to take others' boundaries personally, how can we reframe our thinking? Did it feel unusual or enjoyable to clearly (but nonverbally) ask for touch? How is the exercise different from normal social exchanges? How can we take the lessons from this exercise into our daily lives?

Advanced

This exercise is best led by an experienced facilitator.

1) Explain the exercise and allow participants to opt out if they wish. Make it clear that participation in this exercise requires an enthusiastic "yes!"

2) As above, break into pairs.

3) In each pair, ask participants to experience the following combinations:

    a. Partner A asks for a hug, and Partner B accepts both verbally and physically;

    b. Partner B asks for a hug, and Partner A accepts both verbally and physically;

    c. Partner A asks for a hug, and Partner B politely refuses;

       d. Partner B asks for a hug, and Partner A politely refuses.

4) Briefly, stop and explore any experiences and feelings that have arisen. How does it feel to say "yes" or "no" when required to by the exercise? Even with the stilted structure of the game, participants may experience feelings of rejection or embarrassment at being told "no," or may find themselves thinking, "They must really like me!" when being told "yes." Talk about how it can be a struggle not to take others' boundaries personally. You may also want to explore how it feels to say "no" when touch is actually desired or "yes" when it isn't.

5) In each pair, ask participants to experience the following combinations:

       a. Partner A asks nonverbally for a hug (such as spreading their arms), and Partner B accepts physically;

       b. Partner B asks nonverbally for a hug, and Partner A accepts physically;

       c. Partner A asks nonverbally for a hug, and Partner B refuses with clear body language (such as shaking their head no);

       d. Partner B asks nonverbally for a hug, and Partner A refuses with clear body language.

6) Again, stop briefly and continue the discussion. How does the nonverbal communication change participants' experiences?

7) In each pair, ask participants to experience the following combinations. This part of the exercise may be challenging, and participants may need a little extra time to experiment with their body language.

       a. Partner A asks nonverbally for a hug, making movements as subtle as possible (for example, making eye contact and leaning in toward the partner), and Partner B accepts physically;

    b. Partner B asks nonverbally for a hug, making movements as subtle as possible, and Partner A accepts physically;

    c. Partner A asks nonverbally for a hug, making movements as subtle as possible, and Partner B refuses using only their eyes;

    d. Partner B asks nonverbally for a hug, making movements as subtle as possible, and Partner A refuses using only their eyes;

8) Continue the discussion. How did it feel to communicate using such constrained body language? How can we build our empathy to become more aware of the nonverbal cues people use in social situations? When body language is unclear, can we change our own body language to clarify the situation? What are some graceful ways we can switch from nonverbal to verbal communication?

9) In each pair, ask participants to experience the following combinations:

    a. Partner A asks nonverbally for a hug, and Partner B nonverbally refuses; Partner A gives the hug anyway.

    b. Partner B asks nonverbally for a hug, and Partner A nonverbally refuses; Partner B gives the hug anyway.

10) Continue the discussion. How does it feel to hug an unwilling partner? How does it feel to be hugged after refusing touch?

11) If appropriate, ask two participants to role-play a scene where a nonconsensual hug is given and the recipient tries to educate the giver about community expectations. Participants can experiment with the recipient trying different rhetorical approaches and the giver reacting in different ways: cooperatively, defensively, aggressively.

12) Continue the discussion. What approaches seemed most likely to be effective? How do we react in the face of

someone who has become defensive or aggressive? How do we differentiate an embarrassed or awkward person of goodwill from someone who is likely to violate others' boundaries again and again?

13) Return to pairs. Ask participants to make eye contact with their partners and thank them sincerely for their help with the exercise. Some pairs will spontaneously hug to shake off the nonconsensual touch; this is fine.

14) Take a short break, then bring the group together for final thoughts about the exercise. Does the exercise tell participants anything about their ordinary social interactions? If participants are part of a larger group or in leadership positions, how can they create a culture where people seek consent to touch by default and are likely to notice if boundaries are accidentally or intentionally violated?

Practicing Yes: Circle of Desire/Arms of Love Exercise for Adults

When teaching consent culture, it is easy to focus on learning to say and respect a "no." Yet our ability to say "yes" is equally important—and equally in need of practice.

I first learned this exercise in the context of a Reclaiming tradition sacred sexuality workshop led by Todd Herriott. It is designed for adults, but it could be used among a group of older teenagers with a demonstrated history of emotional maturity.

For some, openly admitting to any desire at all feels incredibly vulnerable. Facilitators should be prepared for some participants to have a strong emotional response to this exercise. The group should be able to spend adequate time with each participant and to gently transition participants who find themselves in a fragile emotional state. The exercise is best used in a group that has already established some bonds of comfort and trust.

1) Explain the exercise and allow participants to opt out if they wish. Make it clear that participation in this exercise requires an enthusiastic "yes!"

2) Divide into groups of five to seven people. Each group should contain one person who is prepared to facilitate the exercise.

3) Each person will take turns being cradled in the middle of the seated or kneeling group (the facilitator often sits at the person's head, though this is not necessary). When the person takes their place in the center, *before* the group touches them, they should let the group know how they would like to be cradled in order to feel safe and comfortable. Any areas they set as off-limits must be strictly avoided by the group (the facilitator can help to ensure these limits by gently correcting any participant who misunderstands their instructions).

4) Once the person in the middle is comfortable, the facilitator invites them to speak some of their desires. The desires can be simple or deep, so long as they are sincere. For example: "I want an avocado." "I want a partner to share my life with." "I want to be fiercely wanted by my girlfriend." It may be appropriate to be sexually explicit in groups that are exploring sexuality together; in other groups it will be quite inappropriate. The facilitator should set expectations around this aspect at the beginning of the exercise.

5) After the person being cradled speaks each desire, the group affirms that desire in the simplest way possible. For example, "I want an avocado" should be followed by the group saying in unison, "[Name] wants an avocado." Some groups will find themselves wanting to add, "[Name] *should* have an avocado" or "[Name] *will* have an avocado." These statements can feel like powerful magic, but they can lead to hurt feelings if a participant speaks a desire that the group isn't sure it can or should affirm. Facilitators should make sure the affirmations simply echo the spoken desire. The purpose is for the desire to be acknowledged and heard, nothing more.

6) Ideally, the person being cradled should be permitted to speak their desires until they feel finished. If there is a time limit on the gathering, facilitators should warn participants that they will have a certain amount of time to be in the center.

7) When the person being cradled is finished, the facilitator leads the group in an affirmation (the group should practice the words a few times before the start of the exercise). Group participants move their hands to press down gently on the person in the center, making sure to honor any touch restrictions. The group says in unison: "[Name], you are beautiful. You are worthy of your desires. You deserve pleasure in your life." Then the facilitator adds: "And if anyone has ever told you otherwise, let that weight be released from your body... now!" On "now," the group lifts their hands from the person in the center.

8) Without rushing, the group should help the person in the center to sit up and join the group to help cradle the next participant.

9) After all participants have experienced the exercise, the group should take a break, then gather to discuss and share any feelings that arose. What desires are taboo in our society? Is desire itself taboo for some people, who are expected to be acted upon rather than to act? Why is it important to building consent culture to be able to clearly articulate our desires?

Consent to Touch at Large Group Gatherings

Many social groups use hugs as standard social greetings. These greetings, however, feel invasive or inappropriate to some participants; others love them.

At large group gatherings, a chaotic social atmosphere may make clear negotiations around touch more difficult. Facilitators can use nametag labels to help establish ground rules. When participants claim their nametags, facilitators can invite them to apply a green, yellow, or red sticker: green for "Hugs are welcome," yellow for "Ask before you hug me," and red for "Please don't touch."

The stickers should be accompanied by a sheet of paper explaining their meaning, as well as reminding participants about the basics of consent, for example: consent to touch can be withdrawn at any time for any reason; a person wearing a green sticker has only invited hugs, not any other kinds of touch; etc. This "Hug Code" information sheet can also be used advertise orientation sessions or workshops that cover consent culture, safer sex, or other relevant topics.

Consent and Safer Sex

Consent education and safer sex education are a match made in heaven: they complement and reinforce each other. Unfortunately, safer sex education often includes only the logistics of STD testing and barrier use, while consent education focuses entirely on communication around desire and intent.

Whether you're talking with your own kids about safer sex or giving a Safer Sex 101 talk at a festival, emphasize that condom use should be considered the default state for new partners and for any partner with whom unprotected sex has not been specifically negotiated. Mutually deciding *not* to use a condom or other barriers is an act requiring the consent of all partners involved.

Good communication about safer sex can help to ensure that all parties engage in sex freely and enthusiastically—and that's the very definition of consent. When teaching people how to negotiate consent to sex, help them normalize the process of asking about STD status, the existence of other partners, availability for an ongoing relationship, and other factors that might influence either partner's willingness to give consent. While the failure to disclose such information does not necessarily turn otherwise consensual sex into rape, withholding important information can make a partner feel manipulated or deceived. Such behavior does not respect their sovereignty, and it lays poor groundwork for a future friendship or romantic relationship.

Conclusion

Educating young people and adults in consent culture requires nuanced thinking. We want to teach people to be touch-positive, sex-positive, self-loving, and respectful of others. Yet we are surrounded by a culture that is hysterical around issues of sexual violation: at times in denial, blaming victims for their own rapes, and at other times seeing monsters everywhere and imprisoning children for acts of mutual sexual curiosity. It is up to us to maintain sanity and protect ourselves and our families in this environment—as well as advocating for change in our wider communities. I hope that this essay will provide helpful resources for that change.

Thanks to Cat Chapin-Bishop for her comments on this essay. Some sections of this piece were previously published on the Pagan Families blog at Patheos.com.

Christine Hoff Kraemer received a PhD in Religious and Theological Studies from Boston University. She is the parent of a high-energy toddler, an instructor in theology at Cherry Hill Seminary, a licensed massage therapist, and a practitioner of religious witchcraft. Her books include *Seeking the Mystery: An Introduction to Pagan Theologies* and *Eros and Touch from a Pagan Perspective: Divided for Love's Sake.*

Asperger's Syndrome and Consent Culture
An Interview with Vinnie West, Joshua Tenpenny, and Maya Kurentz
Raven Kaldera

A note from the interviewer:

    This interview came about because Joshua and Vinnie heard that there was going to be an anthology on Pagan consent culture, and as individuals on the autistic spectrum, they asked if anyone was talking about the little-discussed and uncomfortable issue of people with impaired social skills in Pagan groups. Since the publication date of this book was looming and there wasn't time to write an article, I asked to interview them and Maya as well. I was amazed at what an intelligent bunch of Aspies—people with Asperger's Syndrome, or very high-functioning Autistic Spectrum Disorder (ASD)— had to say about consent and Pagan culture. They pointed out things that I hadn't even considered, and I'm very happy this interview happened at the last minute! Thank you all for putting yourselves out there.

RK: So, the first question is, in a putative Pagan consent culture, how do Pagan groups deal with people who—for various reasons diagnosed and undiagnosed—have social skill impairments and disabilities? This could be due to autistic spectrum disorders such as Asperger's or high-functioning autism, or brain damage from TBIs [traumatic brain injuries], or any number of other causes. Some Pagans have claimed that these folks lack empathy, and thus lack the means to navigate consent culture.

JOSHUA: A lot of people claim that ASD folks don't have empathy, but this isn't necessarily the case. There are usually other problems involved that make it look like they don't. As an example: One teacher wrote about a little boy who had ASD, and she was working with him on his social development by doing various role-plays with him. She laid out a scenario where a little girl he knew was sad because something difficult had happened to her. The teacher established that he understood that his friend was sad and asked how he would help her. He said, "I would show her my batteries! When I am sad, I look at my battery collection and feel better."

This is clearly not a failure of empathy! It's a theory-of-mind problem. Someone with ASD might have trouble understanding under what circumstances someone would be distressed, or understanding why a behavior of theirs might distress someone, or noticing that the person is distressed, or extrapolating what is an appropriate and effective way of helping. If they fail on any of these steps, it may be indistinguishable to the common observer from just being a jerk.

Another problem is that a large segment of people with autistic-spectrum issues have decided, "I am, and have always been, and will always be, a complete failure at dealing with people, so screw it. I've given up. People are always going to think I'm an asshole no matter how hard I try, because the world is unfair, so I'm not even going to try anymore."

VINNIE: There is a tendency for folks who are not used to dealing with non-neurotypical people to assume, "Well, if I were to do this thing, I'd be acting like a complete sociopath and not caring about anyone else, so this person must be feeling that way as well." But if you're going to be dealing with non-neurotypical people, you need to stop and ask yourself, "Did this person really mean to be mean and uncaring, or were they just clueless and unaware?" Ideally you can sit down with them and talk about it, and come to a clear standard of behavior. However, there are some people who will just continue to be clueless, or who lack self-control, and then you do have to set boundaries.

I'm remembering someone who came to our Pagan group who had been brain-damaged from a car accident and could not grasp that some of his behavior was inappropriate. That part of his brain had been trashed, and he just couldn't discern it. We did try to talk to him and find some way that he could control himself and understand his behavior, but he legitimately couldn't get it. So we asked him not to return, because we had to protect the community. He did say that ever since the car accident, everyone had been a jerk to him, which is really heartbreaking when you think about it. And I wish we had a way to fix that, but we don't.

JOSHUA: There does come a point when someone's behavior is so out of line, and attempts have been made to fix the problem and they are not effective, and it doesn't matter at that point where it's coming from. If you are the intervening third party in a situation where someone is being inappropriate to someone else, you do first have to deal with the person who is transgressed upon. It's one thing if someone is just being annoying, but if they're being super creepy—even without meaning to—there is a line that gets crossed where the accidental offender's feelings are not the most important, although they should be acknowledged.

I'll use a person example of when I was a stupid young Aspie kid with very poor social skills. I was at a sex club with a group of friends—so already I was in a "high-risk" atmosphere where "ordinary" conventions are loosened, people were very free with each other's bodies, and you have to sensitively figure out what's acceptable—and I touched a woman inappropriately. She was complaining about back pain because her breasts were so heavy, and so I reached out and gently "hefted" them to see what she meant by "heavy." And I said, completely innocently, "Gee, they are awfully heavy!" I honestly didn't do it with any thought of sexual gratification or to make her uncomfortable, but it was still completely unacceptable. She just stared at me, with a look of shock on her face like "I don't believe that just happened!"

My friend James, who was standing next to me, put me in a headlock and apologized to the woman. He told her that I should not be allowed out of the house without supervision, affirmed for her that this was wildly out of line, and that he would deal with me. Later, we had a sit-down about what ways it was and was not okay to casually touch someone, even in a sex-club setting. I didn't understand where the line was. My friends made sure I learned better before they took me to another sex club. But in that situation, my feelings were not on the agenda when it came to dealing with the situation in the moment.

VINNIE: That's actually a really excellent example, because the woman just stared. She didn't say no, because that's how people often react. If you'd grabbed her breasts in a creepy sexual way, she might have been able to push you away, but you were just plain weird, and it was so out of context that she didn't know how to react... and people with social skill impairment are very likely to do that sort of bizarre out-of-context violation. "Um ... why the hell did you just do that?" The example's also good because your friend stepped in, made it clear that your behavior was not okay, and got you away from the situation.

RK: At some Pagan events, because we have a sex-positive religion—and we're proud of that—there is an atmosphere of more physical "looseness" than one would see in other places. A social-skill-impaired newcomer walks in, and they don't know how to discern what's appropriate. How does a community leader deal with that?

MAYA: Sadly enough, my experiences have been that community leaders who do not automatically take the side of the offended party, one hundred percent and publicly, tend to get immediately smeared and lose group respect. We penalize leaders who try to find a balance instead of taking sides, and this means that any given community leader is going to be fighting that fear at the same time they're intervening.

VINNIE: This is a problem even for people with "normal" social skills. Someone who isn't used to nudity comes into a clothing-optional space, and thinks, "Oh, look! I can see tits! That means I can start staring at tits and commenting on tits! Maybe I can even touch some tits!" Someone with a very narrow experience of situations where nudity happens might make that cultural error and need to be corrected. But this is extra dangerous for someone who is impaired in being able to assess appropriate behavior for a new and unusual situation. Adding extra neurological challenges does not help that at all.

JOSHUA: Feeling awkward when you're social-skill impaired can make you do awkward things. I remember going to one of my first Pagan gatherings and sitting on the ground for a class, and a man in a little bitty sarong sat in a chair right across from me, only a couple of feet away. So I look up and I'm face to face with his genitalia. This had never happened to me in a nonsexual situation! First, I couldn't stop staring, because it was right there three feet from my face. Second, while I didn't say anything inappropriate, it would have been very easy to do so. In fact, it's likely that if I even opened my mouth, anything I said could have been construed as inappropriate.

MAYA: Unusual social situations, especially ones with nudity or other "taboo" activities, are a minefield for us. We don't want to offend people, but those of us with ASD usually have such a history of accidentally offending people that we can have anxiety attacks just being in situations like that. People don't realize how many resources it uses up for us to assess and gamble on our behavior.

JOSHUA: What I'd advise for a community leader—someone who has to make decisions for a group—is that unfortunately, you cannot be too generous in that regard because you risk setting up a playground for the actually malicious. If you're too willing to grant exemptions, then the rare individuals who are actually looking to get a rise out of people or make them uncomfortable will see that and they'll game it. They'll say, "Oh, look! How far can I play the 'I didn't realize' card? Oh, I'm sorry, I was just being awkward!" Which is really sad, because then it screws over the people who, for real, didn't understand.

RK: So how do you tell the difference?

MAYA: That's not easy, especially when someone who has an innocent social skill impairment is likely to get angry and defensive when confronted. Because we're people, and people sometimes get angry and defensive. There's a serious stigma around being socially clueless, and it's hard for people to admit, or face that they failed yet again.

VINNIE: Talk to them and watch their behavior. We acknowledge that it's risky—if your group culture is such that it leaves room for the clueless, the malicious will use that room to be malicious a little longer. But still, the people who are malicious will have a pattern of malicious behavior. People who purposely transgress boundaries tend to transgress small boundaries first. So if you catch someone on a small boundary transgression and tell them it's not okay, and they say, "All right, I'd better check myself from here on in," they were probably just clueless and they are highly likely to not do that particular thing again. But if they transgress again, that's a red flag.

JOSHUA: When someone asks, "Well, why is this not okay?" perhaps they don't understand why, and perhaps they want to have a debate with you about why it's not okay, possibly to deflect from the fact that they were doing something that wasn't okay! On the other hand, as a person with social skill impairments, there are a lot of actions that are deemed inappropriate, and those rules seem very stupid to me. They're not logical, and sometimes I'm rather intellectually offended by that. However, that doesn't change the fact that the society I have to live in says they're not okay. I can go around violating stupid rules all I want, and I'm still going to get arrested, or at the least ostracized. So arguing could come from either sort of person, but regardless, don't put across the idea that this is a negotiation.

VINNIE: Yes. Even if we don't have a logical explanation for why this rule is in place, you do still have to abide by it anyway. We'd like you to be able to understand, but we don't require that. We just require that you don't do it. If there are second and third offenses along the same lines, there's a very strong possibility that this is not an issue of cluelessness. There's a line between being socially inept and being an asshole.

Setting clear and unambiguous boundaries in the beginning is a good start. I've been to hot tub places and really appreciated the concise written rules on the walls— you do not touch other people, you do not comment on other people's bodies, etc. They're clear and specific, but also written in a very kind way. It's possible to set boundaries in a kind and loving way, rather than a confrontational or hostile way. You can do it gently but still do it solidly.

JOSHUA: We were at a non-Pagan event where they had bootblacks, and they had posted on the wall a long list of things that it is inappropriate to do to your bootblack. I was happy that they had the sign, but sad that they needed the sign.

RK: So would it be useful, for any given Pagan event, to have a written list of kindly written, non-confrontational, but very firm and very specific rules?

MAYA: Yes! Make them super-specific. Stupid-specific. People with impaired social skills will actually be happier to see that, because they're less likely to be set up to fail. Don't assume that everyone is able to figure out all the unspoken rules.

VINNIE: Absolutely. Yes, there will be people laughing at how specific the rules are. That's okay. It is better to have people giggling, "I can't believe someone would do that!" than have someone do that thing out of ignorance.

JOSHUA: On the other hand, I'd be careful about trying to be super-specific. I'd rather make a generous margin, and then publicly state that some people who know each other might do things that are in this gray area here. However, to be safe, if there's any question whatsoever if something is appropriate, we ask you to stay out of the gray area— because if you don't, and you make a mistake, that's going to be on you, not on the other person. This is the safe zone right here, and while you might see other people in the danger zone, don't take that as a license for you to do it as well.

For example, I have a hard time establishing a safe list of appropriate conversational topics, so I have a big list of subjects that I've flagged as inappropriate to talk about. I realize that people with good social skills can talk about many of those subjects in an appropriate way. I also realize that I often cannot. In school and in professional situations, people often assume that I'm a complete prude, when in actuality I'm a queer polyamorous trans pervert activist and educator, but I *never* talk about anything sexual in those settings. I am just never sure where the line is. Even if there was some kind of workplace policy about the appropriate level of sexual banter, I'd probably find a way to accidentally get it wrong. No level of public sexual banter is okay for Josh; it's just too risky.

VINNIE: It's important for group leaders to defend people who are doing some clueless and socially inept thing that does not actually transgress someone's boundaries. Looking stupid while dancing around a fire or going on a boring monologue about your particular fandom is not going to harm anyone. It's just annoying, and group leaders should defend someone's right to be clueless in a non-harmful way. However, cornering someone in a way that they can't get away while you monologue about your particular fandom is something else.

JOSHUA: And what constitutes cornering? I've actually got a problem with cornering people and monologuing. I've asked people who are close to me: If you see me doing that, grab me, or say something to me, because I'm not aware I'm doing it at the time. There's a good chance I will not notice the other person's uncomfortable body language, and it's incredibly humiliating to realize that I've just spent twenty minutes being "that guy." I don't want to be in that position! Please, please interrupt me!

VINNIE: Which brings up another issue. Let's say that you're a repeat cornering offender. One way to handle that is to have friends who will come up and drag you away when you're cornering someone. That's a sign of "I am willing to work with the problem and find solutions."

MAYA: Group leaders can say, "So sometimes you still end up doing this inappropriate thing. How can we address that so that you don't embarrass yourself?" If they're really enthusiastic about finding a way to address it, that's a good sign.

JOSHUA: Particularly if it's a really egregious behavior, to the point where you're seriously considering kicking them out of the group, you can say, "How would you feel about us assigning you a buddy? Someone who can hang out with you and make sure you're not doing these wildly inappropriate things." Assuming, of course, that you have someone who would be willing to do that. "Look, we're doing our best to make things safe for everyone and welcoming for you, but you've made it clear that you need closer supervision. So we're willing to go out of our way to provide you with that, but you have to go along with the program." If they are hostile about that, then you absolutely have grounds for telling them to leave.

I'm not just speaking to group leaders here; I'm also speaking to people with low social skills. If someone confronts you on that, your response should be, "My bad! I'm so sorry." If you're not exactly sure what happened, we can work that out after you apologize. Remember that they don't owe you any assistance whatsoever. They are not your parents, your therapist, or your case worker. They have no obligation to help you be a better person. So if you're offered advice or friendly supervision, don't argue—take it graciously, or leave.

VINNIE: We also need to bring up the fact that there is a certain percentage of the social-skill-impaired population who are too impaired to function well in certain kinds of Pagan groups, and not all of them are in state-run programs, either. This is especially a problem when you've got someone who is dual-diagnosis, such as social-skill-impaired plus some form of mental illness—they may not have the skills to keep their emotional issues to themselves. It's not their fault, but they may say things that would upset people, and they need special handling.

In a very direct sense, the problem of social-skill-impaired people in Pagan groups is an accessibility issue, just like wheelchair accessibility. All Pagan groups need to make the decision between accessibility and the needs of the main body of the group, and sometimes compromises may need to be made.

MAYA: In our Pagan group, one of the biggest "clash of needs" problems is between people who are social-skill-impaired and people who have trauma histories to the point where they have a lot of triggers and need very sensitive handling. Both parties may have trouble admitting to how much their disability needs special handling, or even that it is a disability at all. And they continually bump into each other, sometimes with sad and devastating results. So it's a question of whose disability gets catered to, sometimes.

JOSHUA: I think that Pagans have to accept that not every group can accommodate every disability. There are some Pagan groups—notably the small initiatory mystery traditions— where an incredibly high level of sharing and vulnerability is necessary to do that work, and emotional intimacy is expected. Someone with seriously impaired social skills is just not going to be appropriate for that type of group. They are not going to be able to navigate that tricky situation. It's like saying, "I'm sorry, but our group holds all its rituals in a little temple on a mountainside, and there's no way to get a wheelchair up there. While we would love to be able to accommodate you, our rites will always be held at this remote and inaccessible location. So we are not the appropriate group for you, and you should look for a group that meets in an accessible location." That's not unreasonable to say.

MAYA: I think that part of the problem is that Paganism in the U.S. started from Wicca, which in its most traditional form consisted of small, emotionally and energetically intimate working magical groups. I belong to a larger, less intimate congregational-type Pagan group, which can afford to be more welcoming to people with impaired social skills. I've heard Pagans in the first sort of group say disparaging things about congregational-style groups— that we're "selling out" to mainstream religion, that we aren't really Pagan (meaning not Wiccan, because the ancient cities certainly had congregations), that we aren't radical enough because we have a church choir and people who only show up on high holidays. But it's my lifeline, and I know I can have a Pagan religious experience there and restrict my level of social interaction to whatever it needs to be on that day. I think we need more of those kinds of Pagan groups, not fewer.

JOSHUA: That's true—I worked at a group home for developmentally delayed individuals who needed a lot of supervision in order to function in public, so it was our job to supervise them when they wanted to go to church... but the Baptists were just fine with having them and their caretakers at the services. It felt weird to me to know that the Baptists were more accessible in that way that any Pagan group I've ever been in. I saw the level of accommodation that was considered appropriate in that setting, and it pains me that no Pagan group is willing to provide that level of accommodation. I'd really love for my Pagan church to be able to provide something like that.

RK: So we're talking about two sorts of Pagan groups—the intimate initiatory groups and the open congregational groups. Do you notice that people with impaired social skills tend to end up in the second sort?

MAYA: Yes, because we get thrown out of the first sort.

JOSHUA: The first sort may be beyond the range of adaptation of many socially-impaired people. They would have to find one that was a really good fit for them, or where people were invested in them personally. Initiatory groups that lean more toward ceremonial magic are more structured, and often less intimate. They might be more comfortable there, although it's still a minefield of complex and emotionally charged interpersonal relationships. But spiritual groups that are more informal and personally intimate, where people want to "have a bond"... those are the hardest for us.

VINNIE: I think it's okay for initiatory mystery groups to discriminate to get the tight group they want. They can decide that they only want people of a certain ethnic background; they can decide that they only want people with a great deal of sensitivity. The more selection criteria you have overall, the less any criterion becomes obnoxious. They have that right. The group may not be what I want in my life, but it's a private group and I don't have to be around it. But a congregational-style group should be held to higher standards of accessibility.

RK: Do you have personal experience with difficult situations around socially-impaired people going well in your Pagan groups?

JOSHUA: Yes. In our group—which is a congregational-style model—we had issues with a woman in leadership who was known to have impaired social skills due to a brain injury. A member publically accused her of repeatedly pressuring him with unwanted sexual advances. The woman said she was simply flirting, and had no idea it was unwelcome, but apologized and agreed to back off.

            When he later told people that she was still making unwanted sexual advances, we assigned the woman a "buddy" during events to keep an eye on her and intervene if she was behaving inappropriately. She insisted she was falsely accused. There were a number of complicating factors, but whether we thought the accusations were true or not, our response would have been the same. If she's with her buddy, she's safe from false accusations.

            This needs to be stressed if you assign buddies: it's for the protection of both people. That's another good way to weed out the malicious from the clueless or unfairly accused: the latter should be grateful if they realize it's to protect them as well.

VINNIE: That's a good thing, because people with low social skills often can't defend themselves well from accusations. Everyone knows that they've behaved weirdly or annoyingly in other ways, so they are much more willing to believe that their inappropriate behavior would extend to physical consent issues as well. And that's only one step away from attributing malicious intent. I've seen it happen where whisper campaigns start against someone who makes people uncomfortable for reasons that don't violate anyone's consent, but they still want them gone.

MAYA: You have to balance being welcoming to people with impaired social skills with being welcoming to people who are damaged and may perceive attacks where there are none. The combination of those two in a group can be really vicious.

JOSHUA: Just last week I got a complaint from a church member who didn't like that one of our low-social-skills people was repeatedly unfriendly to him when they ran into each other casually outside of church. Not insulting or invasive, but brusque and disinterested. I explained that he shouldn't take it personally because she just isn't very friendly, especially when she is preoccupied with a task, and besides, she's not actually obligated to be his friend. That's a line you cross when you move to a congregational model—we don't all have to want to hang out with each other in order to come together and celebrate effectively as a community.

And yet, there was the complication that she had a position of authority. He had expressed interest in working in a role that would put him in a mentorship relationship with her, and was put off by her attitude. Thankfully, there was a different role he was much better suited to, because there is no way that would have gone well.

RK: What do Pagan leaders do that you feel is the opposite of effective?

MAYA: They use the words "energy" and "empathy." I've got a soapbox about those. First, energy. It's used for two different meanings in Paganism, and they're confused and unclear. One meaning is about the clues that you pick up—usually on a subconscious level, and non-neurotypical people often can't—about someone's motivations and intent. This can obviously be misinterpreted by one's own filters, so even if you're neurotypical it's not a perfect system. The other meaning is psychic—they're "putting out some kind of psychic energy." Even if you are highly psychic —and just being Pagan doesn't guarantee that, let me tell you—this is also subject to personal filters and misunderstandings. So when a Pagan leader says, "Your energy is creepy," or "We don't like your energy," or "People need to emanate good energy in here," this gives someone zero information about what they are doing that is bothering people, or how to change it. Instead, it sets up an antagonistic situation where they are being judged for not picking up some mysterious and vague clues from the stratosphere. I'd like to see Pagan leaders drop that word entirely when referring a person or their behavior. Its unclarity and unmeasurability is radically unfair.

Second, empathy. Again, Pagans have two different but frustratingly gray-area definitions. One is the ability to—again, maybe unconsciously—pick up on people's body language, tone of voice, and other cues to figure out how they are feeling. The other definition is psychic empathy—being able to pick up on how someone is feeling even if they aren't showing it with their bodies, because you have some kind of psychic gift and they aren't shielded well enough to keep you out. Not only do people confuse the two definitions, they frequently decide that they've got the second one when they've only got the first one. They convince themselves that it's psychic when it's only their ability to unconsciously pick up on physical cues. Regardless, if I fail at either of those—and as an ASD person I fail at the first all the time, and expecting the second of anyone as a matter of course is totally unfair—and you tell me that I'm not being empathic, it gives me no useful information and tells me that you're a holier-than-thou ass.

Using these words with people like me is the most unhelpful thing in the whole world. If you want my behavior to change, please explain in precise detail exactly what it is that I am doing wrong, and then give me clear and detailed examples of what you'd prefer I do instead. Write it down if it's easier for you to spell it out that way. I like things in writing; it's comforting because it's clear and not vague, and I can study it repeatedly. Talk about actions—what actions of mine are causing problems? Don't try to assume you know what I'm thinking or feeling. And if you can't articulate what you want and don't want—if you're using "energy" and "empathy" as sloppy shorthand for "There's stuff you do that pushes my triggers, but I can't actually explain it and I don't want to examine my expectations closely enough to find out," then shut the hell up and work on yourself, and stop setting me up for failure. There, soapbox done.

No, wait, actually I have one more point. On top of all this, non-neurotypical people are often very hard to read on that unconscious, intuitive level that observes bodily cues. As we are impaired in interpreting them, so we also are impaired in naturally expressing them. We might be having all sorts of emotions, but they might come across in odd ways, or not at all.

VINNIE: Yes! We might look angry or sad, but we actually aren't.

JOSHUA: For neurotypical people, a mismatch between affect and emotions will be a conscious thing. It's active deception, even if well-intentioned — "I'm really angry, but I'm trying to act chill." Someone who is psychically sensitive and picks up on the underlying emotions in a non-neurotypical person can assume the same level of deceptiveness. Even if someone has a strong amount of psychic empathy, they generally supplement that with observation of physical cues, and they can be totally thrown off by an ASD person's unusual cues, or lack of cues entirely.

As we've said, many Pagan groups don't do any kind of magical or energetic training—it's not part of their regimen. But if you're in one that does, there is an obligation on the part of the leadership to use discernment to figure out if someone is actually doing something on an energetic level or if there's something else going on.

We were at a class once at a Pagan event, and someone (one of the traumatized sorts) accused someone across the room (one of the impaired-social-skill sorts) of psychically attacking her during the class. Both were newbies. Three of the people sitting between them were experienced energy workers and reported that they hadn't noticed anything of the kind and were quite confident they would have if it was going on. It turned out to be a low blood sugar attack on the part of the first person— but if there weren't trained, discerning people around, it could have gone very badly, especially as the accused wasn't very good at eloquently defending herself.

MAYA: There's also the issue of eye contact. Many of us non-neurotypical people don't like to make eye contact. It's overstimulating, and it takes a lot out of us to make sustained eye contact for any length of time. This means that we end up looking shifty or untrustworthy. That's part of why we sometimes aren't good at eloquently defending ourselves. And if you want to talk about consent culture—what about exercises in Pagan rituals or classes where people are asked to gaze into each other's eyes? That's incredibly painful for us.

VINNIE: Eyeballs, eyeballs, eyeballs! One autistic person made a hat with all sorts of eyeballs on springs bouncing around all over it and said, "You want eye contact? Here's some eye contact!" Really, it's intense and very overwhelming for us.

JOSHUA: For me personally, I can either make eye contact with the person, or I can do anything else—like think! These are my options. Over the years I've learned to make eye-to-nose contact; I'm actually embarrassed that took me so many years to figure out, and most people don't notice that I'm actually staring at their nose. I've learned to make eye contact for those Pagan exercises, because I felt like this was a valuable skill to master, but I handle it by dropping into a light altered state. I can't do any logical processing in that state, though, or interpret anything from my surroundings, or hold a conversation.

VINNIE: Because that's where the sensory overload comes in! I can listen to you and parse out what words you are saying, or I can look in your eyes—which would you prefer? I lip-read, because I struggle with auditory processing too, which is another fun ASD issue, but at least I'm looking at their face. Eye contact means something different to someone with different neurology. It's closer to what it means to your cat. Cats look away when they like you. They'll only stare at you when they don't trust you and they are afraid you'll do something to them.

RK: So far we've focused on social-skill-impaired people as the accidental offenders in a consent culture. What happens when they are the ones whose boundaries are transgressed upon? Where are they vulnerable in this way, and how can group leaders be aware of that?

JOSHUA: Our church developed a culture where, if someone is sitting alone in a corner and not making eye contact, we leave them alone and don't run up and try to get them to be social. Non-neurotypical people of all sorts sometimes need space to de-stimulate, and bothering them during that time is the worst thing you can do. We have a lot of people in our group who require that kind of space, so we let them have it. What may seem like being welcoming to someone neurotypical actually feels violating for us. We need to be able to engage and disengage when we need to, and not have attention called to us over that.

However, this sometimes creates problems, because how are people to know whether someone could use some welcoming, or whether they need to be left alone in the moment? We've had people come to our church events and be upset because they were enacting behaviors that we interpreted as them wanting space, so we didn't engage with them, and they felt that we were being unfriendly. However, as an organization, we've decided that while we wanted to make more of an effort to welcome new guests, we are still going to err on the side of giving people space because of the number of people we've got who prefer it that way. That's not just socially-impaired people, either—many of the folks with trauma need that too.

VINNIE: Making all boundaries explicit, like we've mentioned before, is really important. Coming into my current Pagan group many years ago, that was one of the points I liked and appreciated. The social boundaries and ritual protocol in this group are very clear and explicit, and everyone knows them and can talk about them. One of the ASD people in our group even wrote them up for the website.

JOSHUA: Something I've seen in other Pagan groups is ritual leaders discussing and teaching how to encourage people to participate in rituals in ways they might initially find uncomfortable. There is an art to getting people emotionally engaged with the ritual, in order to build energy, rather than just standing there awkwardly.

Generally, this is done by starting out with activities everyone is assumed to be comfortable with, and over the course of the ritual, gradually introduce more intense modes of engagement. I know it isn't intended to be coercive. It is done in the same spirit as having "ice breakers" as social functions. But when you don't know where this is leading, it can feel coercive. It is really rare for group leaders to give everyone a rundown of all the activities that will be included, and even when there is, the language used to describe the activities can be extremely vague.

It seems like often there is an underlying assumption that it is our natural state to be willing to engage in these activities (with complete strangers) and that the only thing that would hold us back is cultural baggage that we are all better off without. So they are trying to help people grow and explore and let go of the things that hold them back from experience this wonderful thing.

This is especially problematic for people with impaired social skills. Someone neurotypical might feel a little awkward about it, or might just not be into it, but it can be nightmarish for someone non-neurotypical. (The same can apply to some people with trauma or disabilities.) When I'm at a ritual and that happens, I usually do my best to participate anyway, because I feel like I have no other option besides disrupting the ritual. Some days I am better able to do that than others. I'll generally play along as best I can, but likely I'll never come back to that group, or classes by that group leader. I wouldn't think that they're bad people, because I realize that encouraging people to sing and dance without warning is not generally considered a violation of social norms, or something that requires explicit negotiated consent, but forcing non-neurotypical people into a social minefield we aren't prepared for does not give us a satisfying spiritual experience.

MAYA: Part of navigating the social minefield is trying to discern whether it's okay for us to disrupt things or look bad by opting out. We have fewer resources to be able to figure out that uncomfortable situation, we are less likely to be able to handle unexpected awkwardness, and we are more likely to panic. You want consent culture? Create Pagan space where there is always a graceful and obvious way to sit out any religious activity, especially ones that are challenging for the non-neurotypical. At least in many mainstream churches, if you don't want to take communion, you can stay in your pew.

JOSHUA: There needs to be a socially acceptable way to say no. If there are no obvious socially acceptable ways to say no, you make the space extra unwelcoming for people with impaired social skills. I've seen this so many times in rituals—the leaders may even have said that the activity is optional, but there was (from my perspective at least) no way of really taking them up on that offer. Even in our own group, we sometimes forget to do this. But if you want to make it clear that the activity is truly optional, make it clear what the alternate option is, and actually think about how that's going to work.

Think about how it would look, at any point in the process of inviting people to participate, if someone declined. If no one in your group ever declines, think about whether it's possible that sometimes people who don't actually want to participate don't feel comfortable declining. The best way to make it clear that it's okay to decline an activity is to have someone actually model gracefully declining. If you've got rituals that are open to the public, you can ask a few long-term members to decline occasionally, even if they have no reason to. "Look, that person sat out the circle dance and it was okay! No one stared at them or asked them why they weren't participating!" If you can give people a meaningful alternative activity that doesn't require a lot of social skills or physical coordination, that helps too.

VINNIE: But if someone is feeling really socially inept and uncomfortable, they may just want to fade into the background until they are ready to come back again. Give them the option of doing nothing in a way that won't attract attention to them. Also, some of us take time to process what's going on and make a good decision. The fact that it takes me a while to decide something—I can't do it while we're having a discussion because I get overloaded, so I have to go off and think about it myself—wildly changes the nature of consent for me. Just because a group leader announces that something is going to happen and assumes that two minutes is a sufficient amount of time for people to decide on that doesn't mean two minutes will be enough for me. People who are non-neurotypical, people who have trauma, and people who have complex emotions about that activity are all going to take longer to decide. Of course, there I have to know myself and know that I can't make a good decision in two minutes, which brings us back to having a graceful way to opt out of any ritual activity.

JOSHUA: If you've got people with impaired social skills in your group, you may have to put anything requiring social engagement in the category of "to be approached carefully." You wouldn't say, "Okay, in five minutes we're all going to handle each other's genitals." You'd give people more warning, or at least more options, than that. You wouldn't put them in a position where they either had to fondle some genitals or speak up and say, "But what if I don't want to handle anyone's genitals?" You'd explicitly plan for another option. For a non-neurotypical person, singing, dancing, talking about feelings, anything that requires a specific affect or you'll be looked at weird or "ruin the energy"—these activities are nearly as serious for some of us as my genital example is for neurotypical people.

We can't anticipate everything that's ever going to be difficult for anyone, we can't plan for everything, but we can keep an open mind, and when it comes up we can add it to our list of stuff to make space for. For some people, it might be best to just email them the ritual script beforehand, because it makes them feel a lot safer. Especially since we're one of the few religions where you often risk showing up to a ritual with a group you've been to twenty times, and yet have no idea what might happen.

MAYA: Then there's the issue of touching. This isn't true for all ASD people, but many of us have a lot of trouble with being touched, because it's overstimulating and we have to brace ourselves. At the very least, if there's going to be handholding or hugging, I want to know beforehand so that I can opt out or psych myself up to enduring it. I also want a graceful way to opt out there, too.

People with impaired social skills who are okay with touch sometimes go the other direction and hug too much, or longer than people would like, because we aren't able to read them. If we see people hugging all over the place, we might assume it's socially normal here—and then inadvertently do it wrong. I've seen groups with a "huggy" culture do a quick "public service roleplay" at the beginning of their events where they demonstrate how to nonverbally ask for a hug (opening your arms with a questioning look on your face) and how to pleasantly refuse one (holding up your hands with the palms facing out, while still smiling to let the other person know it's okay, it's not about them). It's also helpful to demonstrate how long it's OK to hug—two breaths, for example, no more.

JOSHUA: My partner is a non-hugger, and he's gotten emails after events from people he wouldn't hug, and they're basically asking him, "Why don't you like me? What have I done to offend you?" It has to be okay to say no to anything. I also have a lot of rules around touching people—rules I've established for myself—which may be more stringent than those of others, because I do not want to accidentally violate people's physical boundaries. Incorporating the ability to hug strangers into those rules has taken something like ten years. It has only been very recently that I'm comfortable hugging women who I do not know, because of my fear of inadvertently doing something sexually inappropriate. So if you offer to hug me and I am not extremely confident that it won't result in you feeling violated by me, I'm going to turn down the hug. I have a zero tolerance policy for myself with failing at that, because I never want to put a woman in that position again. I think it may not occur to some people that refusing a hug might be a way of keeping both of us safe.

VINNIE: At large events, color-coded wristbands or colored stickers on badges really help us, because we don't have to negotiate and guess, we can just look at the color. Red means don't touch me ever, yellow means you can ask, green means I love hugs all the time. Okay, now I don't have to depend on skills I don't have, the answer is right there. If I decide I can't take the stimulation of touch, I'll be able to give a signal that won't require me to be in an awkward position.

MAYA: But ritual organizers at those events who are running ceremonies that involve touch need to think about what happens when five people with red stickers walk in. Do you say, "Take off your red stickers for this ritual or leave; touch is required!" Or do you figure out something else? Because if you have non-neurotypical people wearing those red stickers, it's not necessarily something we can push ourselves past without trauma.

JOSHUA: As a non-neurotypical person who thinks a lot about accessibility, I have to state that there is no way a group or teacher can account for everyone's problem. Humans are so diverse as a species, and we have so many different and individual needs, that we can't accommodate for all those needs or it would make the process of saying hello take 45 minutes. I don't mind people making certain socially-agreed-upon assumptions. What I mind is when you tell them that their assumption is incorrect, and they respond in a hostile or argumentative manner. Which can be triggered by the first person correcting them in an equally hostile manner.

I think there needs to be a cultural assumption that it's okay to make mistakes, and the ideal should be that the transgressed-upon just neutrally corrects the transgressor because it's also okay to correct someone, and then they both move on with their day and don't make a big deal out of it. If either of those—erring or correcting the error—is a huge social sin, that's where things get ten times worse. In some communities, just making the mistake is unthinkably awful. If you ever accidentally transgress these boundaries, even if they aren't made explicit and everyone just says, "You ought to have known that!," you are the worst person ever. You're an offender. That makes it more difficult for people to bring themselves to correct someone. If your only options are that you always get it right or that you're an offender, then if someone does something that makes you uncomfortable, your only options are to publicly call them an offender, or to ignore it and allow it to continue.

VINNIE: That's a hard one for ASD people to negotiate on either side of the offense. Do we call someone out and get them in trouble, when they might just have made a mistake—and we know how hard that is? Or do we shut up and let it go by? You've got to have something besides a sledgehammer to fix the problem.

MAYA: We understand how people often inadvertently break the rules, because it's probably happened to us throughout our lifetimes, and we may be more likely to shut up when we our own boundaries are violated because of that. On the other extreme, some ASD people have been told that it's okay to be upset when you feel violated, and they translate that mentally to "Every time someone upsets my easily upset neurology, I can complain and demand that they change." Which isn't going to get you anywhere but ostracized. Since we may feel "violated" by things that wouldn't bother neurotypical people, figuring out what's okay to complain about is ten times harder for us.

VINNIE: We need to do a lot of public talking about consent as a community, and in person as well as just on the Internet. If these discussions are taking place in public, and people with impaired social skills can hear them and ask questions—and not be penalized for those questions—then they might pick up a lot that will inform their future actions. There are so many things around the social norms of consent that it's assumed everyone has just picked up, and if you've got sketchy social skills you may never have picked those up.

JOSHUA: Particularly with regard to sexual behavior, because you never see that except in movies, which are appallingly bad models. We also have a terrible time understanding the social white lie and differentiating that from deception. ASD people especially would all tell the blunt truth every time if we were allowed, because navigating social white lies is another minefield for us. We can't give honest feedback, because there are complicated rules around social feedback, and we've been accused of being inconsiderate when we do it. So what's the difference between a social white lie, of allowing something uncomfortable to pass in order to let someone save face, and having one's boundaries violated? It's harder for us to figure that out than it would be for someone neurotypical.

When it comes down to it, we have to live by the rules of the society we live in, even if we have trouble understanding them. We have to accept that these are the ways people will act, and insisting they act differently is one of those rookie mistakes of the non-neurotypical that we hopefully get over by the end of our twenties... although it takes some of us a little longer, and some of us never quite make it. But the world is never going to conform to our expectations. Social rules are never going to make sense to us, just like grammar is not obligated to make sense, but deciding to only use your own idea of grammar is not going to get you anywhere. Rejecting the rules of society is just going to get you outcast from social groups.

This makes it extra difficult for us to navigate groups that are deliberately rejecting some, but not all, of the rules of society, and many Pagan groups fall into that category. Many Pagans say, "Oh, we're not going to let society tell us how to act." But from a non-neurotypical person's perspective, you *do* let society tell you how to act, all the time. You may rebel around this one thing, but if you really didn't care, why don't I ever see you walking around with rubber galoshes on your heads, licking yourselves in public? "Oh, but that's just weird. Why would I want to do that? We don't mean that." You don't see how much you conform, and pressure each other to conform, every day. But we do, because all these rules are arbitrary to us. People who actually don't let society tell them how to act are wildly inappropriate and end up transgressing people's boundaries on a regular basis. "It's a beautiful day! I don't need any clothing to keep me warm." The only reason you always wear clothing in public is because society tells you that you have to!

So I think it's important not only to talk about which social norms you are challenging, but also which ones you're not challenging, and why, especially around sexual and physical consent. Some communities imply that it's all up in the air... except when it's not, and you're supposed to know. To the non-neurotypical person, that communicates something entirely different. Pagans will talk about how they're going against social norms, but with an unspoken baseline of "...except for all these other things which all reasonable people would know are still true."

MAYA: So take our presence among you as a challenge to think more clearly and mindfully about why you have decided to do, or not do, any given thing; about what your unspoken rules really might be, and how to make them above-board; and what your assumptions are about each other. If we become this for you, instead of just annoying people who are all too often conflated with harmful people, we might all make this religion a lot more functional for everyone.

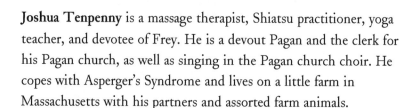

Joshua Tenpenny is a massage therapist, Shiatsu practitioner, yoga teacher, and devotee of Frey. He is a devout Pagan and the clerk for his Pagan church, as well as singing in the Pagan church choir. He copes with Asperger's Syndrome and lives on a little farm in Massachusetts with his partners and assorted farm animals.

Vinnie West is non-neurotypical, way too curious, has far too many interests and entirely too many piles of unfinished projects. She has been a Pagan since her early teens and lives in Central Massachusetts with four cats, and a rabbit.

Maya Kurentz is a radical Aspie Kemetic/Hellenic and disability activist. She lives in Arizona and loves camping in the desert.

Consent in Gardnerian Wiccan Practice

Jo Anderson, with the Triple Horse Coven

It was after 11:30 the night I got the phone call. The woman caller was interested in finding a Wiccan group for training and had been invited to join a Gardnerian coven, just an hour ago, at the local pub moot. She had been told that as part of the initiation, she would have to kiss the genitals of members of the coven and perform other sexual acts. She was told that she should not tell anyone about this invitation. She felt very uncomfortable and unsure. She asked for my advice. Was this normal practice? What should she do?

Luckily for the woman in this example, I was able to tell her that she should not participate in anything that made her feel threatened or uncomfortable in any way, and that Gardnerian Wiccan initiation at the first degree does not include sexual acts of any kind.

In a situation like this though, how many seekers for training in Gardnerian Wicca would have access to advice on such an issue? How many would go ahead, despite their misgivings, believing that there was no other way to join a coven? There is an obvious need for clarity on the issue of consent in Wiccan practise.

In this chapter, I will be talking specifically about initiatory Gardnerian Wicca, where ritual practice has a common foundation and lineage. This essay is not meant to encompass Wicca in general or eclectic Pagan paths where practices may be very different.

In the context of initiatory Gardnerian Wicca, attitudes toward hierarchy, authority, gender, sexuality, and personal boundaries vary greatly between covens. There is no real consensus among Gardnerian Wiccans on these issues, simply because each coven is an autonomous unit within the Craft, and its ethos and practices are not open to outside scrutiny. This makes issues around consent and power dynamics within the coven setting potentially very complex.

For seekers and new initiates, this situation can be particularly challenging when deciding on which group to approach for training or initiation. In the mundane world, consent is usually given in response to clear and accurate information. Given the "oath bound" nature of much of the ritual material, and perhaps more importantly, the subjective nature of religious experience, the process of training and initiation into a mystery tradition is not something anyone can consent to in full possession of the facts. Wicca is an experiential tradition, and many of those experiences are so profoundly personal that words cannot adequately describe them. It is particularly difficult to express such deeply religious experiences to a seeker or trainee who has perhaps never had such an experience themselves.

The first degree initiation and many other rituals are now widely available, having been published, and initiates are to some extent aware of the basic content. Yet to read the published text of the initiation, with no connection with the initiator or contact with a working coven, is the equivalent of going to a good restaurant only to eat the menu. It is mistaking the words on the page for the experience itself. The reality of circle working is an entirely different order of experience from the knowledge of it on the page, and it may be profoundly different from anything the new initiate has experienced before.

Candidates for initiation must necessarily enter the circle with trust in both the initiator and the ritual process, yet without knowing exactly what is about to happen to them. Accordingly, there is a potential conflict between the mystery and secrecy surrounding Wiccan initiation and circle working, and the openness and availability of information required for consensual practice, a conflict which is perhaps unavoidable on the initiatory journey to self-discovery. This being the case, the seeker can only rely on the integrity and empathy of the initiator, and their own sense of good judgement and trust in the initiating coven, when taking that step into the unknown.

Not all covens work on the foundation of close personal connections or friendships, and some do not have very much social contact at all outside of ritual. This need not make the coven any less able to provide a powerful group experience. A deep commitment to the process of magical working and to the responsibilities of Priest or Priesthood can often be enough to build a strong sense of group cohesion, and this commitment can be a perfectly valid substitute for deep personal relationships outside the circle. A coven founded on a strong sense of respect for ritual, hierarchy, and structure can feel just as safe as one founded on deep, loving, and intimate friendship, and it can function very well in a less personal and more "professional" capacity.

If the initiatory experience is to be a good and fulfilling one, however, the initiate must have built a foundation of trust and some emotional and spiritual connection with the initiator, whether that be personal, professional or both. This trust is necessary for the initiate to be open to receiving the experience of initiation and to consent to it in love and trust, rather than requiring precise information about the content and process of the ritual itself.

When the initiate consents to trust in and be open to the experience of initiation, they can reasonably expect the initiator to take on the responsibility of facilitating that experience with their best interests at heart.

How to Recognise Safe Practice

Most covens offer some sort of training before initiation, traditionally a year and a day, and some allow neophytes restricted access into the working circle. The process of training should build a relationship of trust between trainee and coven, and issues which may be of concern to the seeker, such as working skyclad (ritually nude), the role of intimate and sexual touch, and the ritual use of the scourge and cords to bind and purify, are often explained and clarified during the training period. It is perfectly reasonable for the trainee to ask about these things and to expect a clear and unambiguous answer. Levels of intimacy and physical contact vary greatly among working covens, as do attitudes to nudity and to the use of the scourge, and it may be that a particular coven's practice is not suited to every trainee. However, if a trainee is discouraged from asking questions, feels uncomfortable with the way questions are answered, or does not feel able to trust that his or her boundaries will be respected, the trainee should not consent to what for them may be an unsafe experience.

It is not always clear where personal boundaries lie, and it is the responsibility of initiate and initiator to recognise and explore those boundaries together in a way that challenges but also respects them.

This process may not be a comfortable one, but the initiate should never feel threatened or coerced. Clear delineation of personal boundaries is vital to the work of personal and spiritual growth in a group, and it is something that all coven members should be continually supported and encouraged to do.

Approaching issues of intimacy, both physical and emotional, can feel particularly unsafe for survivors of abuse, and asserting personal boundaries can be very difficult. Coven leaders may not always be sensitive to or have experience of these issues, but awareness of individual vulnerabilities is the responsibility of the coven as a whole. The empathy, personal experience, and understanding of other coven members can help to make the coven a supportive and safe environment in which to explore personal issues. The coven is not, however, a therapy group, and serious personal and mental health issues are more appropriately dealt with by professional therapists. A coven leader should always seek advice if they feel unable to deal with specific personal issues.

The foundation for coven work is the relationship between individuals, as well as the group dynamic as a whole. Building on those interpersonal connections and the collective needs and aims of the group is just as important as developing skills in ritual and magical work. Even if the coven structure is one of a more professional nature, individual Priests and Priestesses must be able to trust other coveners to perform their role competently in ritual, as well as to keep the sacred trust of oath bound material outside the circle.

Ideally, each coven develops its own social and magical framework within which a culture of openness, empathy, and personal challenge can be safely encouraged, and where personal boundaries can be respected and maintained. However, in some circumstances an established culture of trust can itself be a source of pressure to conform. It may be that coven members feel that they *should* be open to challenges to their personal boundaries, and to refuse to push against those boundaries or to feel uncomfortable with some aspects of accepted behaviour may be seen as weak, untrusting, or failing in some sense. Whilst the pressure of expectation is not overtly coercive, even the most experienced coven leader can miss the subtle effect that normative behaviour has on initiates, particularly those who are inexperienced or especially vulnerable. Coveners must remain vigilant and aware of their own and others' reactions in and out of ritual space to address and avoid the subtle pressure of conformity wherever possible.

Readiness for Initiation

It is the responsibility of the initiating coven to gauge when or if a seeker or trainee is ready for the challenges of group work, especially for the challenges that physical and emotional intimacy can bring.

Issues of consent around physical contact within ritual space are fundamental to Gardnerian Wiccan practice and are very often misunderstood or misrepresented by non-initiates. The spectrum of physical contact can range from the accidental or casual contact that can happen in any crowded space; to deliberately non-sexual touch, such as holding hands in circle dance; to sensual touch; and ultimately to intimate sexual touch. The whole spectrum of touch is possible in circle, but it is by no means necessary and is certainly not compulsory. It can only occur comfortably within clear and specific boundaries, consented to by all the individuals involved.

Skyclad working presents the first challenge to the new initiate from the moment they step into ritual space, and the impact that may have should not be underestimated. For many people, the initiation ritual will be the first experience they ever have of being in a room full of naked bodies. The boundaries of personal space; where and when it might be acceptable to look at other people's bodies, let alone touch them; and how to assimilate an experience so different from everyday cultural norms are issues that the initiate may wish to discuss and explore.

For many Wiccans, ritual nudity, far from indicating consent to unrestrained physical contact, can actually reinforce social inhibitions around avoiding casual touch. Talking openly and honestly about how it feels to be restrained by social behavioural norms within the intimate space of the circle can help to clarify where personal boundaries lie. It has been my experience that when accidentally brushing against someone else in circle, both parties will apologise and move away, more reminiscent of bumping into a stranger in the street than of a spiritual or magical encounter.

Inhibitions around casual or accidental touch may be stronger between coveners of different genders, sexualities, physical types, or ages. Even if none of these is the case, to some extent we are all challenged to overcome our social conditioning if we are to establish comfortable intimacy within the magic circle. If specific issues between individuals are not recognised or addressed, we run the risk of ignoring a fundamental discomfort between coven members that can make working together difficult and potentially disruptive. Such discomfort will certainly prevent any kind of intimacy developing.

The first step towards addressing issues of intimacy requires discussing how it feels to be in circle, to be skyclad, to negotiate personal boundaries and to recognise feelings of discomfort or uncertainty when they arise. One of the most important skills an initiate can learn is to be *present* in the moment—physically, emotionally and spiritually—so that even the subtlest change in feeling, mood, or state is recognised and consciously acknowledged. It is all too easy to dismiss, ignore, or forget a fleeting feeling of discomfort, anxiety, or even fear; to think, "It's nothing", or "I can deal with it", when in fact there may be a significant underlying issue to be addressed.

This process of feeling, recognising, expressing, discussing, and resolving issues as they arise can be very emotionally demanding and time-consuming. It requires a high level of commitment from all coven members. New initiates may not at first understand the importance of this continual processing, but it is vital for the growth of a trusting and supportive group and constitutes much of the real *work* of the coven.

The process of personal and spiritual transformation requires us to uncover that which is hidden deep within us and bring it into the light of full awareness and understanding. Issues around personal boundaries and intimacy, physical and emotional, often have resonance for the whole group and not just the individual experiencing them at any one time. Coven leaders can support open and honest discussion by encouraging an atmosphere of mutual respect and empathy. It is important that no one feels unable to express concerns when exploring issues of intimacy and personal boundaries, and new initiates will learn by example that it is safe to do so. Appropriate levels of physical contact in circle depend on these discussions. If a decision is made to explore and perhaps challenge those boundaries, the whole group must be in agreement in principle before any discussion about the practical applications is begun, particularly when new initiates are involved.

Skyclad working quickly becomes a normal experience for new initiates in circle, and at that point, the kind of natural and relaxed physical contact that might occur outside the circle begins to feel natural in circle too. Until a new initiate has experienced that transition, however, it may not be wise to challenge them further. It is vital that the process of exploring physical boundaries is slow and gradual and that each step is discussed and assimilated by the group, both individually and as a whole. Feelings of discomfort or anxiety should never be dismissed or ignored.

Exploring Intimacy

The first steps towards more intimate contact are often to welcome each covener into the circle with a kiss, to hold hands during the circle building so that physical contact is maintained, or to hug at the end of the ritual. None of these would seem unusual in a mundane context, but in a skyclad ritual they may feel very different.

It is during this initial stage of exploration that differences in gender, sexuality, physical type, or age can begin to cause discomfort. It is especially important that the individuals concerned feel able to talk about these specific issues, and that they are supported by coven leaders in doing so without judgement and with sensitivity for all concerned. It may be uncomfortable to talk about our differing responses to individual coven members, and we may worry about causing upset or offence, but if the right support is available, it is possible to discuss such issues. Those with a more inclusive ethos may find the inhibitions of others problematic or even offensive, but acceptance of differences is vital. That does not mean that prejudice and ignorance should not be challenged, quite the opposite; but if any progress is to be made, challenges must be made with kindness and empathy rather than anger and intolerance.

It may be that each covener has a different response to any one individual, and boundaries of physical contact have to be agreed upon accordingly. It is acceptable that those boundaries will be different between different individuals. If one individual is unhappy with any aspect of physical contact, then a clear boundary for them is vital and must be agreed upon and respected by the whole group. For example, it could be that a young woman, a survivor of sexual abuse, finds it difficult to have physical contact with a much older man. Safe and non-judgemental discussion of where the boundaries of physical contact lie for her is vital if she is to consent to any kind of exploration of physical touch in the group.

The first point of agreement must be that any initial exploration of physical contact in circle will not include *any* sexual touch. This must apply equally to coven members who are sexual partners outside the circle. Others may feel discomfort in the presence of inappropriate sexualised behaviour, even between partners, especially if one of the partners becomes obviously aroused.

Even within the established coven any exploration of intimacy must be openly discussed and agreed upon. Touch can be specifically restricted to non-erogenous areas of the body—for example the hands, arms and shoulders. Contact within these very clear boundaries can then be safe and potentially sensual without the threat of progressing into sexual touch. Trust and freedom of expression only result when boundaries are specific, clear, and non-negotiable, and when all concerned have given their explicit consent to the experience. This situation is very different from the first degree initiation, as discussed earlier, where the initiate cannot give fully informed consent to the ritual process. Exploration of personal boundaries should never be part of a first degree initiation.

For many coveners, one of the most basic and difficult questions around physical intimacy is "What happens if someone gets an erection in circle?" Is it discouraged, accepted, ignored, or acknowledged? Are we embarrassed, indifferent, amused, or upset?

Women's arousal may not be quite so obvious and therefore not an immediate issue for others in the ritual space, but many Priests consciously try to avoid getting aroused in circle so as not to cause other coveners discomfort. When this question is discussed, it may be appropriate to talk about how it would be if Priests did not feel obliged to avoid arousal. How might it feel to be in close proximity to someone who is obviously sexually aroused even if no sexual touch is involved? Wicca is, after all a spiritual path based on sacred sexuality and fertility, and sensual touch even of non-erogenous zones may well be arousing.

Issues such as this, and many others concerning intimacy of whatever kind, are much less problematic if coven members are able to trust that their boundaries will be respected. If it is absolutely certain that arousal will not lead to a breach of that trust, then it is far more likely that everyone will feel safe to experience their own and others' physical, emotional, and spiritual responses without fear of judgement or censure and free from the imposition of unwanted intimacy. When a coven is practised in identifying and respecting personal and individual boundaries, and where there is a culture of openness, honesty, empathy, and trust, it is possible to encompass differences in sexual orientation and gender identification and to accommodate polyamorous relationships between any number of individuals *if* personal boundaries are well defined and any issues are recognised and discussed whenever they arise.

Safe, consensual practice can transcend difference and focus on common aims. It is possible to work in circle with a non-gender specific duality of active and receptive principles, and to expand the binary focus of conventional relationships from the polarity of God and Goddess to a spectrum of aspects of deity that can encompass any number of individuals. These things are only possible, however, if all coven members are happy to explore the boundaries of conventional practice and do not feel coerced by the inclusive ethos of the group. There are, of course, exclusively same-sex and LGBT covens where diversity and difference may be more easily accepted. Seekers may feel such covens to be a safer option, given the prejudice and judgement that still exists, even within the Wiccan community. Within an inclusive coven where diversity is accepted, however, it is possible for any individual to flourish and to do so with trust in the integrity of their own physical, emotional, and spiritual boundaries.

Where coven members feel secure in the culture of consent that has been built and in the mutual respect for physical and emotional boundaries that exist within a long established group, it may be possible take the exploration of intimacy further.

Exploring Sensual Touch

In Gardnerian Wicca, the first degree initiation is not a sexual one, but established coven working does involve seasonal ritual and higher initiations that have the potential to be sexual, either symbolically or physically. The process of raising sexual energy for ritual purposes does not require any direct sexual contact between those involved, but it can, nevertheless, be highly sensual.

Sensual touch can be explored on the same basis as already described, with the full knowledge and consent of all concerned, and with the clear and honest assertion of personal boundaries. It is vital that each individual is given the space to discuss where and how they wish to be touched and to very specifically state where and how they *do not* wish to be touched. The difference between sensual and sexual touch can be a subjective one, and everyone involved *must* feel absolutely safe and sure that their stated wishes and boundaries will be respected and strictly observed. One simple vehicle for sensual touch within ritual space, for example, is to use massage oils or body paint, which can be applied as part of a symbolic Sacred Marriage or Great Rite to help raise energy.

Where clear and specific boundaries of touch have been decided, it is never a good idea to go beyond what has been agreed in the heat of the moment, even if all parties feel they could go further. In the heightened state of ritual consciousness, it is not possible to make a clear and consensual decision to change the agreed-upon boundaries. To do so may well put pressure on some coveners to go ahead with something they are not entirely comfortable with, which would amount to a breach of trust. Many factors can affect individuals' boundaries and coven leaders must be continually prepared to facilitate the discussion and negotiation of changes outside of the magical working space, so as to maintain the safety and integrity of ritual.

Sexual Initiation and the Great Rite

To me, the ethics of sexual initiation are very clear. Intimate sexual touch should *never* occur without the prior knowledge and consent of those involved, and personal physical and emotional boundaries should be respected at all times.

Traditionally, the Great Rite may be performed symbolically, known as *"in token"* or physically, known as *"in true"*. There is a potential value judgement in these terms; some initiates may give the impression that the physical act of sacred sex is preferable, and certainly more powerful than the symbolic act. This is simply not the case, and such a view should never be used to coerce an initiate to take part in ritual sex against their will.

Where the Sacred Marriage or Great Rite is to be performed *in true* it is always, in my experience, between established sexual partners, or between consenting magical working partners, where personal boundaries are already very clearly defined. It is never performed during a first degree initiation.

The Great Rite is part of the initiation at the third degree. It takes place in circle between the God and Goddess, embodied by the Priest and Priestess in a re-enactment of the unifying principle of creation. As such it is primarily a magical act. This means that a symbolic, sensual, but non-sexual rite is just as powerfully life affirming and erotic as the *"in true"* and is by no means a lesser experience.

It is important that initiates are aware that the embodiment of God and Goddess is a vital and fundamental part of the Great Rite. It is an archetypal ritual that lies at the core of Wiccan belief and practice. Magical work involving sexual touch for other purposes is simply "sex magic", which should be subject to the same respectful and consensual practices that govern any ritual.

Everything that happens in the magical circle has an effect on the mundane. The choice to enact the Great Rite *in true* can have deep implications for relationships outside the coven. The Great Rite *in true,* although a profoundly beautiful, magical experience, is nevertheless a sexual act. If it takes place between magical rather than life partners, it can have deep implications, in particular for Wiccans with monogamous life partners outside the Craft.

Some might argue that sexual contact in ritual, under the mantle of God or Goddess, doesn't count as a breach of trust with a monogamous partner outside the Craft. I disagree with this idea. The magical circle is a place of trust and a microcosm of the physical, emotional, and spiritual universe we inhabit. As such, everything that takes place there has consequences in all those spheres of our existence. Whether we choose to be honest about that is a matter of personal conscience.

Conclusion

A culture of trust, empathy, and consensual practice should extend beyond the magical circle and inform an ethical life style where there is universal respect for every individual's right to control their own body and choose their own physical, emotional, and spiritual boundaries. Though we often we cannot control what happens in mundane life, we can work to ensure that our covens are safe and trustworthy places for spiritual exploration and personal growth.

***

Jo Anderson trained as a mental health nurse before going to university as a mature student. She recently completed a research M.A. in Early Buddhist philosophy and has worked for the last fifteen years in social care for the elderly with dementia and challenging behaviour.

Jo was initiated into an Alexandrian/Gardnerian coven in Blackpool in 1991.

The Triple Horse Coven was founded in 1996 in East Yorkshire as a training group. The coven now consists mainly of experienced 2nd and 3rd degree Priests and Priestesses dedicated to creating a safe space within which to explore the boundaries of magical working and experience. This chapter is based on that exploration.

Teaching Sex Magick
Sable Aradia

I was anorexic and bulimic as a teenager. Shame about my body and my sexuality were successfully imparted to me by a combination of old-fashioned ideas from my parents, some very religious friends growing up, emotional abuse, and the fact that I was an ugly duckling. When I discovered sex—which I held out for until I was sixteen and had been with the boyfriend I loved for two years—it was magical, and it literally saved my life. I decided that if something so lovely and transcendent could exist in this world, the world couldn't be all that bad. I healed my soul and, against the odds, I left my eating disorder in remission and to this date have not had a relapse.

I quickly warmed to the sacred sexuality aspect of Wicca. A liberated and respectful attitude towards sex, and reverence of it, is a big part of what attracted me to the Craft. As a feminist, I found it personally empowering. I could not see why something as beautiful and powerful as sex should be so demonized. For me, sacred sexuality is one of the Craft's core Mysteries, driving many aspects of Craft study and theology. It's an essential part of my faith. One of the most important Works that Wiccans, "Wiccanate" Pagans, and Goddess worshippers are doing is redefining an ethical sexuality that does not involve double standards, fear, or shame.

That's the key, however: *ethical* sexuality. As a culture, we have been Christianized for so long that we no longer have any idea what an ethical sexuality free of shame or fear could look like. A couple of factors make this process especially difficult in the Pagan community. One is that our policies of secrecy and "the curse of Pagan niceness" can lead to us to becoming a haven for abusers, a problem that the Council of the Phoenix and others are trying to address.[1] Another factor is that the Pagan community includes a greater-than-average

---

[1] The Council of the Phoenix is a group designed to aid those who find themselves caught up in domestic and/or sexual abuse in the Pagan community. See https://www.facebook.com/councilofthephoenix/.

population of abuse survivors[2] (present company included). Many of us are rightly afraid of triggering events, and our attempts to avoid them sometimes lead us into potentially challenging situations. Thus, balancing the pole of protection with the pole of liberation is difficult at best.

This essay will examine a few of the issues that confront us in the practice of sacred sexuality and the teaching of sex magick. They are presented not as the final word on teaching or practicing sex magick, but rather to spark discussion and work towards possible solutions.

Youth Standards and Consent

Policies around children and youth are probably the biggest area of concern in the community right now. Many children are now second- and third-generation Pagans raised in Pagan families. How do we handle our attitudes about sex and youth? When does the difference in ages between partners make any sexual activity abuse? What age is the age of consent? When is nakedness appropriate around children?

Abuse, and especially abuse of children, is absolutely unacceptable and must be actively and vigorously opposed. Yet our inconsistent Western attitudes about children and adolescents confuse the issue of what abuse is. We recognize that children cannot properly consent, but we disagree about when childhood ends. Many of us avoid the issue by refusing to allow our children to get involved in Paganism until they are adults. But that sends the unconscious message that Paganism is something shameful to keep secret. Also, Wicca and "Wiccanate" Paganism teach that "all acts of love and pleasure are Her rituals." So why do we believe teenage sex should be avoided? Our children are confused by the mixed messages. And why do we have different standards for boys and girls? Why do some of our Pagan men still joke about getting shotguns when they have pretty daughters?

---

[2] Helen A. Berger; Evan A. Leach; Leigh S. Shaffer (2007), *Voices from the Pagan Census: A National Survey of Witches and Neo-Pagans in the United States, 1993-1995*, Columbia, SC: University of South Carolina Press.

Why shouldn't our daughters claim their sexuality as their own, and why should their fathers have any say in it at all? I think that my partner had the best Wiccan attitude about sex I had ever heard when he said to his daughter, "The only acceptable reason for you to have sex is for your pleasure, because you want to."

Is this too permissive? For some, especially those of us who have been abused, perhaps it is. But because of my own issues with sexual shaming and body shaming, I never made an effort to conceal nakedness in my house, and I raised my children in this way. I told them if they were old enough to ask the question, they were old enough to get the answer, which I dealt with as honestly and as directly as possible, given their ages and context. My children, my son and daughter both, called me to tell me when they had chosen to claim their identities as sexual beings. Both of them had an attitude of celebration; both of them viewed it as an empowering choice, and neither has any regrets about the decision. Both of them also chose to experiment with male and female lovers. My daughter is bisexual, and my son is heterosexual and engaged to a lovely young woman whom he has been with for almost five years now. I believe that for me and for them, I did the right thing. But each of us must find our own answers.

Age of Consent

I think it safe to say that we all believe that adults should not engage in sexual activity with children. As a society we view child molesters as sick, evil human beings, and some of us advocate drastic punishments for them. When, many years ago, Gavin and Yvonne Frost wrote a book[3] that advocated a Pagan sexual coming-of-age ritual, the outcry was huge and the resulting tidal waves have continued to lash the shores of Paganism ever since. Indeed, the reason we're all currently talking so much about sexual abuse is that a

---

[3] Gavin and Yvonne Frost, *The Good Witch's Bible* (1999); originally published as *The Witch's Bible* in 1972.

respected Pagan elder was recently accused of possessing child pornography, and other allegations of abuse in the community emerged as a result.

So here's the heart of the question really: when does childhood end?

Perhaps I should approach this dilemma with a less volatile example. Let's take sex out of the equation entirely. Recently in Kelowna, BC (the closest major city to me), a man was arrested for leaving his children in the car in the Wal-Mart parking lot on a very hot day. Most of us, me included, would immediately say, "What a jerk! Glad they caught him!" Now here's the catch: the boys were ten and five years old respectively. When Dad came to the car to be put in cuffs, he was with his eleven-year-old daughter who had accompanied him into the store.

I'm a parent. I can visualize this scenario pretty clearly:

Dad: "Okay, let's go in."

Older Boy: "Awww, DAAAD, I don't wanna go in the store! It's *boring!*"

Dad: "Come on, you have to go."

Older Boy: "But I don't WAAAANNNA!"

Younger Boy: "I don't wanna either." (*bottom lip comes out, signaling impending whining*)

Dad: [*with exasperated sigh*] "Fine, you stay here and look after your little brother while your sister and I go get stuff for dinner. Here's the keys. If you decide to come in, lock the doors behind you."

How many of us are asking, "And what's wrong with the ten-year-old that he was incapable of taking his brother into the store and finding Dad if he got hot or thirsty?" Thirty years ago, my ten-year-old self was considered capable of getting on a bus unescorted and travelling 300 miles from Vernon to Chilliwack with a transfer en route. Certainly taking my brother into the store if he or I got too hot was not beyond my capabilities. Yet now allowing a ten-year-old to supervise a younger sibling in a parked car is against the law, and this man is being criminally charged.

Certainly a ten-year-old is indeed a child. But our society is confused about when childhood ends. Legal age of majority for various issues varies from country to country and state to state. In my province and country (British Columbia, Canada) you can be held criminally liable at twelve, drive at sixteen, join the armed forces at seventeen, and vote and sign contracts at eighteen. You must be nineteen to drink and gamble, and twenty-one to smoke. You are considered to be legally responsible for criminal behavior six full years before you able to take legal responsibility for a contract; you can be sent to fight for your country a full year before you're allowed to help decide who runs it; and you can kill people your government tells you are enemies a full two years before you're allowed to engage in activities that might harm yourself. Oh, and apparently you should know whether or not you want to kill yourself with alcohol a full two years before you can know if you want to kill yourself with tobacco.

What is the current age of consent where you live? You have to know. When I was a teenager, the age of consent was fourteen. Now it's sixteen. So does that mean that sixteen is old enough to engage in sex magick and Great Rite? Don't worry, I sense your hesitation and I agree with you. Certainly when the Frosts thought that was okay, the community disagreed! But I also happen to have heard a story about a coming-of-age manhood ceremony for a sixteen-year-old in the early nineties. A couple of Aphrodite priestesses discussed with the men performing the ceremony whether or not they should offer a sexual initiation to the young man. The men felt that publically offering this as part of the ceremony would put social pressure on him to do something he might otherwise not wish to do, so one of the men quietly made it known to him that these women had made the offer; and the young man turned it down. Was this appropriate? A reasonable person might conclude that because the young man was of the age of consent and the offer was made in such a way as to avoid any kind of coercion, be it covert or overt, that this was perfectly fine;

but others might not agree, and I would not make such an offer myself.

Let's try a different thought experiment. In 2013, the news media reported a case where an eighteen-year-old lesbian was charged with statutory rape for her relationship with her fifteen-year-old girlfriend. In initial news coverage, the older girl was reported to have turned eighteen only recently, with the younger girl's parents taking the opportunity of her birthday to press charges and end their daughter's homosexual relationship.[4]

How do you feel about this situation? What if the eighteen-year-old girl were an eighteen-year-old boy? What if the younger partner had been the boy? How about if the older partner were transsexual? What if they engaged in a little "slap and tickle" as part of their sexual relationship? Would these circumstances change your feelings at all? This case is a great example of the grey areas, and I bet no two of us would have precisely the same opinion about what's right or wrong in this situation. Let's consider the manhood ceremony I spoke of. What if the candidate had been a girl? What if it was a priest of Eros or Pan who made the offer? How does that change your feelings?

These issues haves more wide-reaching implications. Remember our Pagan elder and the child pornography? Well, let's consider nudity at festivals. Is it okay for children to be exposed to naked adults? At what age? What if the festival is clothing-optional and your ten-year-old daughter is running around naked? What if that ten-year-old

---

[4] Life Site News, "18-year-old woman accused of statutory rape becomes homosexual icon," May 28, 2013. Available at https://www.lifesitenews.com/news/18-year-old-woman-accused-of-statutory-rape-becomes-homosexual-icon. *Editor's note: Initial media coverage of the relationship portrayed the ages of the two young women as being only three years apart; later coverage corrected the younger girl's age to fourteen and debunked the story that the two had a long-standing relationship before the older girl's eighteen birthday. Given these new facts, it seems less likely that the law was applied with specifically homophobic intent, as the older girl's parents claimed.*

watches a slightly-drunk couple necking at the fire? What if there's an Aphrodite Temple on site (a tent or building specifically allocated to sacred sex)? If such a Temple is unacceptable, should we have adult-only events or rituals as an alternative, or ban these practices entirely?

How would you feel about teenagers practicing sex magick together? How would you feel about teenagers undertaking their own sexual initiation rite with one another? If they came to you for advice on how to go about it, what would you tell them?

I would think that a group that practices sex magick or sacred sexuality would start with a firm commitment to, *at the very minimum*, obey the law (clearly not enough, but let's start there); so we aren't about to accept anyone into our practice or instruction who is not *at least* of the regional age of consent. After that, it gets grey, and we're going to have to talk about it, both among our groups and in the community at large. What happens if a fourteen-year-old comes to me and asks about sex magick? Should I put on a poker face and seek refuge in the law? ("I'm sorry, I am simply not allowed to talk to you about that at all until you turn sixteen.") And yes, that's *exactly* what I would do. Do I now have an obligation to contact the youth's parents? A recent issue that came up in our own tradition is that a fifteen-year-old girl who is practicing with her parents in one of our covens wanted to initiate to First Degree, and her High Priestess and High Priest both believe she has the necessary knowledge and maturity to do so. The tradition leaders (of which I am one), however, forbade it because our initiation rite is a traditional one; it's done skyclad and involves ritual binding, blindfolding, and a challenge at the threshold. Too much potential for that to be taken badly, whether you think a fifteen-year-old can have the maturity to truly understand it anyway (and I don't).

I have a personal policy that I will not engage in sex magick with anyone under the age of nineteen, and even then I would hesitate. I was twenty-one when I performed my first Great Rite, and I know I had the maturity then to understand it, so that would be my minimum age for that ritual; and I would have serious questions and hesitations with anyone below the age of twenty-five. Those are my personal decisions on the subject. Each of us has to find our own answers, but it is essential that we discuss these issues in community.

The Teacher/Student Relationship

I'm not going to dance around it or sugar-coat it: Wicca has a fatal flaw. Here's the dilemma: in many places in the Western world it is against professional ethics, and in some cases against the law, for a teacher to have sex with a student, or for a clergyperson to have sex with one of the congregation. It is culturally understood that people in such a position of authority might exercise undue pressure on a person who looks to them for guidance, and that a person under their authority might feel that s/he has no choice but to engage in a sexual act. But many Wiccan traditions have initiation rites that could either be perceived as having sexual elements (skyclad practice, bondage, scourging) or are undeniably sexual (Great Rite). Some Thelemic orders have similar dilemmas. And therein lies treacherous ground for those of us who are involved in such practices.

We magickal types, from the earliest shamans, have danced on the edge of cultural taboo, and many would say that this is where the power is found. By nature we question everything and find the limits. But this is a dangerous area and it requires some extra caution.

Most of us would probably say these days that our traditions don't require sexual acts for initiation; or at least, that such things are not required of our neophytes, though they may be for those of the higher degrees (and I'm definitely on board with that). I think that's how we have to handle it: we have to dance the razor's edge. And if sexuality is sacred, we must be assured of consent in order to avoid blasphemy. But for some traditional types, that idea that a symbolic, non-sexual Great Rite could come to replace the sexual Great Rite sits uneasily, and I must confess, I understand this. The Great Rite is a sacred mystery. Does a person who wishes to initiate to Third Degree actually grasp the truth of the mystery if she, he, or they is/are unwilling to engage in the Great Rite? There are still quiet traditional groups out there who would say that they do not, and would not do the initiation.

And what happens if your Craft students think they're ready for First Degree, but they don't want to do it skyclad? I have a student in this category and am currently considering my feelings on the matter. For me, the First Degree is about birth. You go into the ritual bound, blind, and naked, and you are birthed into a new life with a commitment to the path of Wicca; that's why some call initiated Wiccans the "twice-born." Your nudity symbolizes your vulnerability and rebirth. Everyone else is naked too, so you're not in a position of disadvantage and you're not a sex object. Does she understand the mystery if she's not willing to be skyclad with us? And how am I to take this when her sister covener, who was once a victim of rape, was willing to go skyclad as long as she could wear panties (which we were happy to accept)? Of course everyone has their own opinions and feelings and levels of comfort, but part of the point of initiation rituals is to challenge your comfort zone and face your fears. If my Priest and I decide not to do the initiation because of our doubts, are we placing coercive pressure on her to accept a practice she's uncomfortable with? What if we try to refer her to someone who is willing to do it without requiring skyclad practice? Does that remove any potential pressure?

To be able to dance on this razor, we need to consider our approach. What does initiation mean? What do the degrees mean? What is the nature of our relationship to our initiates?

We say that we are all Priestesses and Priests of the deities. If you truly have that understanding, then initiation rituals are acknowledging a peer, not elevating a student. From that point of view, you have successfully negated both the student-teacher relationship and the clergy-congregant relationship. But then you also have an obligation to be sure that your initiate understands that you are peers! The community at large seems to have this idea that initiations are like grades in high school. Initiating to the next degree, for many, is viewed like collecting merit badges that raise you in the hierarchy. Until I have successfully dissuaded my coveners of this notion, I must not do any sort of sexual ritual with them.

Gerald Gardner believed that the reason that Wicca was a religion of Priestesses and Priests was that it was forced underground, and that there would soon come a time in which Wicca could reveal itself, and once again there would be a priesthood and a laity. In other words, though initiated Witches are members of a priesthood, not everyone who practices Wicca is required to be a priestess or priest. From that point of view, there is no requirement for initiation, so there should be no pressure to initiate. Yet, most of those who come to me for coven training believe that initiation is something they should all be working towards. So are they really coming to the threshold of their own free will?

Here's where those who object to hierarchical traditions have a point. If you have authority, inviting those you have authority over to participate in sexual ritual could be an abuse of power. If you don't have authority, any sexual ritual is a practice among peers.

Issues of hierarchy also apply in the context of festival sex. From one point of view, a High Priest who has sex with a covener at Beltane is demonstrating clearly that he regards him or her as a peer; but he might also be abusing power if that person views him- or herself as his student.

Another possible approach to sexual ritual is to bring in outsiders who are peers to perform initiations. If you are not the teacher of the initiate, that might remove some of the ethical greyness. I know that some groups do this.

Again, there are no easy solutions for ensuring consent to sexual ritual. The uneasy compromise that my tradition is currently operating with is that none of the transgressive elements of our initiation rituals are required, but they are strongly encouraged, and those of us who can initiate have the right to choose under what circumstances we will perform initiations. If we are unwilling to do an initiation under a given condition, then we must refer the candidate to someone else in the tradition that will, provided they meet all the other requirements. Our minimum age for First Degree initiation is sixteen (preferred eighteen); our minimum age for Third Degree initiation is twenty-one (though most of us would not initiate someone so young). I don't know if that solves all the problems, but it's our best attempt to be ethical and hold true to our beliefs. Personally, I do my best to use my discernment and take each situation on a case-by-case basis.

A legally-incorporated group must be even more careful. I would say that such groups should not engage in skyclad or sexual initiations at all—certainly never as part of their official activities, anyway. And I'd say that if clergy in such organizations (like me) do so off-camera, then they should be sure that anyone they practice with is either also clergy in the organization, or not a member of that organization at all. If you're going to engage in sexual ritual, being part of a group of peers that you can consult with is advised. If the coven leaders that I spoke of earlier with the fifteen-year-old bucking for initiation had not spoken with the rest of our tradition leaders, they might have gone ahead with the rite, blissfully unaware of the risks. Witches who are part of a tradition have an advantage in this because Wicca has been around for sixty years now and they have older practitioners' experiences to draw upon; Thelema's been around for even longer than that. People who are not part of a tradition should seek out reputable figures in the community for advice. As a practical and useful side effect of this practice, a climate of transparency makes it more difficult for abuse to fester when someone *is* doing something inappropriate.

Above all, realize that no matter what, you are taking a risk when performing sexual ritual, just as driving means you are risking a car accident. Despite your best intentions, problems may arise. The law, your tradition's guidelines, and your own personal judgment are all that you can go on. Divination probably can't hurt either! One might think that it's safer to avoid the issue entirely, but if sacred sexuality is an important part of your practice and belief, you can only do your best to try to consider the consequences of your actions and do the right thing.

Freedom vs. Security

Here's an awkward topic: How do we assure that we have safety in our small, already odd communities without losing our inclusiveness?

We are hampered from dealing with this issue effectively for several reasons. One is the curse of Pagan niceness. We try to be so inclusive and "live and let live" about things that we can provide an excellent space for a predator or a mere jerk to run rampant over us. Sometimes the right and proper thing to do is to tell someone to take a hike because their garbage is not welcome here. We can be inclusive and still have healthy boundaries. "Sex-positive" does not justify being, or tolerating, a creeper.

There are two forms of coercion. One is overt, in which direct pressure is applied to encourage people to do things they might not otherwise do; and the other is covert, in which indirect social pressure shames or embarrasses people into doing things they might not otherwise do. At a sexually open event or within the confines of a coven practicing sex magick, there's a thin line to be walked here.

In my experience, the only way to be sure that there is no coercion involved is a combination of transparency in groups and individual discretion.

A group or an event that involves open sexuality needs to be up front about its purpose and intention. If you're going to hold an adult-oriented Beltane, make that very plain. Also make plain that no one is required to do anything at all that they do not wish to do. Be sure to talk to your participants in an opening speech to emphasize that just because some rules of sexuality and nudity are relaxed here, the rules of politeness and respect are not.

Another problem is overreaction. We tend to attract a lot of people with issues around sex and sexuality. As I said before, I include myself in this group. It's important for us to create a safe space; but this does not necessarily mean a hermetically sealed space devoid of situations that might make someone uncomfortable. It's unrealistic, and more than a little unfair, to expect everyone else to anticipate our issues and avoid anything that might be vaguely triggering, any more than it's fair for me to attend a gathering and expect that all meals will be cooked in a gluten-free kitchen without any milk products (though I'd hope for some gluten-free options). Nor would it be fair for my husband, with his artificial leg and mobility issues, to go camping and expect that there will be complete wheelchair accessibility to every part of the site (though again, we expect that there will be reasonable attempts at accommodation). If we accept that our emotional trauma is just another form of injury and our mental illness actually is an illness, we must take some degree of responsibility for ourselves and our difficulties, just as the community has a responsibility to try to accommodate us. "Safe space" means reasonable accommodation of a diverse group of participants, not total control and perfect safety for all.

One might ask, "But what if I see something going on that's not just uncomfortable, but actually unethical?" The curse of Pagan niceness wrongly suggests that we should put up with unethical, pushy and rude people when we shouldn't. You need to ask yourself a few questions when you see a situation you don't like. First of all, is anyone actually getting hurt? And second, is it your right to interfere? If you think that someone's behavior is inappropriate or ill-advised, you have a right to express your opinion; and if you think harm is being done, you have the right and the duty to bring it up with the organizers of the event.

Our final problem comes in when lifestyles rub up against each other's raw edges. There is no such thing as a common "Pagan sexuality." Making assumptions that we have a common ground when we include traditional monogamous heterosexual Asatruar, lesbian Goddess-worshippers, radical faeries, BTW nudist swingers, kinky goth-witch dominatrix vampires, and eclectic polyamorous Wiccanate neo-hippie family constellations (to name just a few), is not only foolish, it's counterproductive. Many of us do things that others in the community do not approve of. Here we have an awkward dynamic tension, but the solution is not in "siloing" and exclusion.

Let me tell you a parable. There was a Pagan event that I enjoyed attending for many years. Originally created as a family-friendly festival, there was also a small group who liked to have a good party (ideally, separated from the rest of the group so as not to bother them) and a certain degree of sexual license in specific locations (an Aphrodite's Temple, intended for romantic encounters and friendly trysts, and a Pan's Lair, intended for alternative sexual practice often involving groups) where children were forbidden. As part of the balance, particular areas were designated as strictly family-friendly. There was a constant tension between the needs of one group or another, and from year to year things leaned in one direction, then the other. Then the "serious crowd" got control of the event, and they strictly forbade the "party crowd" from doing their thing. So the party crowd got together and created a party event. The result? After several years, the serious crowd's event is going broke and often cannot secure enough registrations to make their festival happen; and the party event is doing well financially but has degenerated into a drunken revel with nothing more than a passing nod towards spirituality. I don't find either result desirable. Both events have lost something in the division.

A safe space means a safe space for everyone, both the sworn virgin and the sacred whore. Prudishness and sleaziness equally violate that safe space.

Auntie Sable's Practical Tips for Sexy Pagans

Getting Jiggy with the Gods

Many of us choose to worship our gods and goddesses in a sexual way. Some of us engage in the Great Rite to unite with our deities sexually. Some of us are called to become sacred prostitutes and heal with sacred sex. Some of us are godspouses; we are bonded with a particular deity, whom we may or may not unite with sexually on a regular basis, and that deity asks a great deal of us but also looks after us. And some of us are Vestal Virgins or just not interested.

Just as there are infinite variations in human sexuality, there are infinite variations in ways to relate to the Divine through sex. As long as no one is getting hurt, none of them are wrong. The Great Rite can be done in an almost infinite variety of ways, in pairs or in groups or through solitary masturbation, through whatever gender(s) or cultures as desired. I have personally drawn down the Moon to lie with the Lord in the form of a priest, drawn down the Sun to lie with the Lady in the form of a priestess, served as a *cheval* for Erzulie, and called to gods and goddesses to couple with me in the wilderness and in my bedroom, sometimes one at a time and sometimes in groups. I think there's room for all of this, and I think people who don't like that should get over themselves.

So what if you feel called to engage in sacred sex with a deity and you don't know where to start or who to ask about it?

First of all, determine if the entity you are dealing with really is a deity. Logically, if gods and goddesses can exist in forms that you can engage with sexually, other entities probably exist like that too. Ever heard of a succubus or an incubus? They're out there. So how do you know the difference? Well, the answer is, does it make you feel good, or not? Do you feel tired and drained after interacting with this spirit-being? Do you feel ashamed and guilty and unable to help yourself? Chances are, this is not a creature with your best interests in mind and you should banish it, cast it out, and ward against it.

Coupling with deities should be invigorating, empowering, and liberating. Your soul should feel rejuvenated and enlivened, even if your body is tired (Erzulie can sure wear out the mortal flesh!). It should be a transcendent, powerful, and holy experience. Just like in human relationships, it's not a relationship unless it's good for you.

So what happens, one might ask, if, say, one of the Greek deities chooses you and, just like in the myths, doesn't give you much of a choice? I would argue that rape is rape is rape, whether it's deities who do it or mortals, so drive them out anyway or seek out another deity to protect you. I believe that we are co-creators with the deities and we have the right to free will. If a deity is not benefitting your life and your soul, then that being is no better than a demon.

What if you feel called to "Aphrodite work"? Well, be practical about it. There are blogs that discuss sex work frankly and openly and give great practical advice.[5] Always practice safe sex. And always be up front with your lovers or your partners about your calling. Also, be

---

[5] Such as Maggie McNeill's "The Honest Courtesan." Available at http://maggiemcneill.wordpress.com/.

sure it's a calling, and not you trying to deal with a guilt complex, past traumas, or addictive behavior.

Finding People to Practice Sex Magick With

Finding others to work with can be challenging. First of all, how do you ask? Secondly, what if you are not interested in engaging in sex with another person in the group? What if you're in a tradition that initiates traditionally and you're ready to take your Third Degree, but you think the priest smells funny? We all have our personal sexual interests and quirks. What if most of the group is straight and you're gay? What if you just don't like big breasts and one of the women in the group has triple Es? What if you don't like another person in the group? Also, how do you avoid groups that are unethical or possibly threatening?

Ideally, in the spirit of "perfect love and perfect trust" we *should* be able to find the Divine in anyone. But in reality it just doesn't work that way. Much of the time we're not even consciously aware of why we are attracted to one person but not another. Again, I think the key is complete transparency. Just be honest. And try not to take rejection personally. One person's trash is another's treasure, remember? I like curvy women myself, so I'll probably be perfectly delighted to work with the lady with the triple E brassiere if you don't want to!

Also, I think we can take instruction from the various swinger and kink communities. First, clarify everything that is going to happen in advance. Second, ask if everyone is okay with that. In couples work, clarify with each other at each step of the way that everything is *still* okay. In groups, there should be a referee who is facilitating the organizing and communicating. Remember that anyone can change his or her mind at any time and only yes means yes; an absence of a "no" is *not* permission! Establish conditions and safe words, and never continue when someone has asked that things stop. Don't ask why and don't try to persuade them to continue; just *stop*.

Seeking others is best grown out of natural circumstances. Perhaps you will meet a group of like-minded people at the Sabbat or the Gnostic Mass. Maybe you will meet a bunch of Pagans at the local fetish club (I'd be surprised if you didn't, actually). If you allow anyone else into the group, screen your candidates carefully first. Make sure they're a good fit before you start playing together. And yes, that includes physical elements as well as personality elements; you don't want to pair the skinny chick with a guy who prefers larger ladies, and you don't want to pair the Sasquatch's cousin with the man who prefers men to be smooth. There's nothing wrong with preferring one thing to another, any more than it's wrong to prefer chocolate ice cream to vanilla; but there's no need to deride the vanilla ice cream because it isn't chocolate either.

As to finding ethical groups: interview group members. Interview other people who have had experiences with that group. Do not trust to hearsay, but be aware of a negative reputation and proceed cautiously. The Advanced Bonewits Cult Danger Evaluation Frame[6] serves especially well in this regard; don't be afraid to use it. If at any time you are unhappy, express your concerns; and if you feel you ought to, leave. Trust your gut and never do anything about which you are uncertain.

And what if you're just not interested in this sex business at all? You know what? That's cool too. Don't feel you have some obligation to get involved just because others around you do! I'll defend your right to stay out of the pool. I'll even make sure to come and hang out with you on the dock for a while.

Honesty Is a Pagan Ethic

I have run into situations in which people in monogamous relationships feel a genuine calling to engage in a spiritual sexual practice, and they feel that calling trumps the monogamous agreement in their relationship. I personally believe that the only ethical thing to do in that situation is to end the relationship.[7] If you are the person

---

[6] Originally published in Isaac Bonewits' classic book *Real Magic: An Introductory Treatise on the Basic Principles of Yellow Magic* (1972, 1979, 1989; York Beach, ME: Weiser Books). Available at http://www.neopagan.net/ABCDEF.html.

[7] I recommend Shauna Aura Knight's great blog post on this subject,

who is so conflicted, you have the obligation to inform the people you intend to practice with of the conditions of your relationship and let them make their own decisions. I have heard of people in officially monogamous relationships misleading new partners more than once, and I have myself been misled in this regard. Do not ever do that to another person.

Also, be transparent as to expectations. If you're going to call upon Pan or drum up Erzulie, people should know that things might get... interesting. Please warn them. If you're doing a fertility spell, it's only fair to alert the man you're spending the night with, since he might have to pay you child support for eighteen years. Non-consensual magick is a violation of free will, and that's not okay. And for the love of the gods, don't cast lust spells or frigidity spells on people!

Festival Advice

Some festivals are sexual. Some aren't. Some have specific places dedicated to sexual themes. Here's my advice: don't cross the line. Don't take your orgy out of the Pan's Lair if that's where such things are designated; don't bring your kids to the adult Beltane. Respect each other's boundaries.

Don't cross the line in regards to limits and boundaries either. The woman you had a casual fling with at Beltane might not want a relationship; don't take it personally and don't act like you're in one. Don't touch people without permission; even the hugging that people often do at festivals is a violation of personal space if you haven't asked, and an unwanted hug might be very triggering for someone.

Don't pressure people. Some people just aren't interested. Some people just aren't sexual at all. There's nothing wrong with that; they're just not interested. Leave them alone.

One idea that I have picked up from a sexually-themed event I have attended in my area: because of our cultural biases, it is a good

---

"Predators, Cheating, and Lying," *Shauna Aura Knight* 8 Aug 2014. Available at http://shaunaaura.wordpress.com/2014/08/08/predators-cheating-and-lying/.

idea to put the right and responsibility of proposition in the hands of women at large, mixed-gender gatherings. Rightfully or wrongfully, men are often perceived as being pushy about sex. When women have the power and the responsibility to broach the question, there's less chance that anyone will feel coerced. It helps to create a safe space.

Safe Sex Magick

I thought this issue was resolved back in the nineties, but I have recently run into situations that tell me that it bears revisiting. In the '60s and '70s, when witchcraft was sexy, people were engaging in unprotected sex all the time with multiple partners in all kinds of different situations. In the age of AIDS, this is no longer realistic, and I believe we are obligated to practice safer sex with the use of condoms and other barriers.

There are certain practices involved in sex magick that you cannot do without a great deal of preparation and planning, as well as the full, transparent consent of everyone involved. For instance, there are different magickal properties associated with commingled bodily fluids, which sometimes are used to bless talismans and sometimes consumed. I believe the only ethical way to handle magickal work with sexual fluids is complete honesty, STD testing, or even limiting things to couples or groups who are already "fluid bonded."

In group activities, there needs to be special care taken with safer sex. I would even suggest that one person be appointed as an officer to look out for such things (is the condom on properly? Did the fluids of one couple get cleaned up before they broke off to engage with others? Where was her tongue before she moved it to that spot?). Gloves and dental dams, condoms and lube need to be applied to all toys as well as body parts. Safe sex aids can be blessed and consecrated just like any other magickal tool (though I'd advise you skip the salt water).

Conclusion

I hope that if nothing else, I have sparked some thought and discussion. Be safe, be ethical, and celebrate the Divine according to your own free will—an it harm none.

Author's Note

This essay was adapted from a series of articles I wrote on teaching sex magick on the *Agora* blog at the Patheos.com Pagan channel. Some of the material was cut due to space concerns and overlap with other essays in this anthology. The original series can be found at http://www.patheos.com/blogs/agora/author/sablearadia/page/2/.

Sable Aradia (Diane Morrison) has been a traditional witch most of her life, and she is also a licensed Wiccan minister and a Third Degree initiated Wiccan priestess in the Star Sapphire tradition. A popular writer at the Patheos Pagan channel ("Between the Shadows: The Craft of a Liminal Witch") and PaganSquare ("49 Degrees: Canadian Pagan Perspectives") she makes her living doing psychic and Tarot readings, writing, and teaching workshops, and she is also a speculative fiction writer and a musician. Sable is the author of *The Witch's Eight Paths of Power: A Complete Course in Magick and Witchcraft* (Red Wheel/Weiser, 2014). She lives in Vernon, BC, Canada with her two life-partners and her furbabies in a cabin on the edge of the woods. For further information, please visit her website www.sablearadia.com.

Healing the Hungry Heart
Rituals for Furthering Touch Positivity
B. B. (Dreamer) Blank

Touch-positivity has been an essential thread in all the most important aspects of my life. As a massage therapist of over three decades, encouraging and empowering my clients in their own healing process compelled me to look beyond the "skin deep". As an activist and community leader, I found I needed to incorporate appropriate touch to facilitate better communication. As a bisexual coming of age in the '60s and '70s (and if I am honest, into the '80s, '90s and beyond), becoming sensitive to my own and other lovers' needs required constant re-evaluation of what constituted touch-positivity. Finally, as a Pagan utilizing the power of ritual, developing touch-positivity went hand-in-hand with my own recovery as an incest survivor.

Which began first, I cannot say; was it ritual to assist in recovery, or recovery that necessitated the formation of specific ritual? Regardless, as I fumbled and stumbled my way, first with my own recovery efforts, then with a counselor, then with a group, it was only when I added the element of ritual that I began to move past my injuries. Ritual enabled me to step back and see with other eyes, other perspectives besides my own. Ritual was like the Hanged Man tarot card, where I placed myself deliberately off-balance, forcing myself to examine touch issues with increased perspective and depth.

It seems many in the Pagan community have wrestled with the same demons I have. We don't really have to go very far to see how social structures—at least here in the West—attempt to pull us all into a confined and strangling pattern of touch avoidance. In the article "To Touch or Not to Touch" by psychotherapists Ofer Zur and Nola Nordmarken,[1] a breakdown of the taboos surrounding touch are brilliantly articulated. These taboos include:

---

[1] Zur, O. and Nordmarken, N. (2011). *To Touch Or Not To Touch: Exploring the Myth of Prohibition On Touch In Psychotherapy And Counseling.* Available at http://www.zurinstitute.com/ touchintherapy.html.

+ "Don't touch people of the opposite gender!" This taboo is based on a worldview that sexualizes most of all forms of touch.

+ "Don't touch same-gender friends!" This boundary is primarily based in the homophobic fears prevalent in our culture.

+ "Don't touch yourself!" This injunction stems, in part, from religious and puritanical doctrines and phobias around self-pleasure and masturbation.

+ "Don't touch strangers!" This command is based on a cultural fear of "the other," a paranoid attitude towards unfamiliar persons and those who are outsiders to one's own group.

+ "Don't touch the elderly, the sick, and the dying!" This reflects a negative attitude in American culture towards the elderly, the sick, and the dying that manifests itself by segregating them from the rest of the population. The sick and the elderly are often housed away in specialized board and care facilities, where much of the time hospital staff do not value touch as an essential part of care.

+ "Don't touch those who are of higher status!" This unspoken rule is prevalent in our culture, where it has been documented that people of higher status or power touch those of lesser status more frequently than the converse.

I would add to this list, hinted in the first point, that the inequality and double standards of touch applied by men against women, rooted in patriarchal conditioning, are a serious ongoing issue. Getting around this problem by saying men simply "shouldn't touch a woman" fails to really address the underlying cause(s) of touch abuse and further inhibits the development of consent culture.

Those of us wishing to overturn touch taboos must wrestle with challenging questions. Is being "touch-positive" the same as being "sex-positive" in consent culture? How do we effectively cultivate our touch consent needs as well as the consent needs of others? How do we navigate the tenacious and constantly shifting waters of cultural and historical change in relation to positive touch?

These questions can be very confusing even to the most astute and aware individual. As I grew up in the San Francisco region in the '60s, the prevailing climate of conformity and separation I had been raised with withered under the sunny days spent at clothing-optional beaches, the touch experiments conducted by Bernard Günter and Steve Stroud at the early Esalen Institute, and the mind-ripping breakdowns that accompanied my first guided L.S.D. trips.

Now we have, seemingly, swung far in the direction of caution due to touch abuse issues arriving front and center—and our caution is well-founded. However, in this new climate, those of us seeking a balanced approach to touch may fear being labeled as incautious or insensitive, leading us to retreat into solitude. For me, ritual has provided an expressive center, a means of empowering others and healing my own wounds that has brought back hope—both for myself and the community I serve.

I do not want to suggest that ritual, with its elements that place one between the worlds of everyday reality and the sub/unconscious mind, replaces a therapeutic approach. I like to think of ritual as one tool in my toolbox, one piece of artillery in my "Go Deeper" arsenal. Yet there is something about ritual that seems to enable breaking through layers of cultural denial and control surrounding touch. As Aidan Kelly wrote on his blog *Including Paganism*, "For me ritual is essentially about connection. I engage in ritual in order to connect with something greater than myself." The rituals presented here are offered in that context.

The following practices were developed over several decades and arise from what I learned under the tutelage of some wonderful instructors. These rituals were actually practiced both solo and in group circles, in public ceremonies and at several Pagan festival workshops. You may see elements selected from rituals initially developed by Z. Budapest, Starhawk and the Reclaiming Collective, and the Zell-Ravenhearts with the Church of All Worlds. In addition, I want to acknowledge the invaluable insights provided by Riane Eisler, Terence McKenna, and "Radical Honesty" pioneer Brad Blanton. I truly thank my teachers, Priestesses, and God Herself for the many sources, the many waters I have been blessed to draw from.

...and with that, I hereby present the rituals.

Editor's note for ritual organizers:

Touch-positive rituals can be a powerful tool in building a culture of consent. When organizing a ritual that explores touch boundaries, organizers should take care that participants are educated about consent practices, and that their expectations about what will happen in the ritual have been accurately set. Facilitators should also make it clear that participants may decline to participate or cease their participation at any time with full community support.

The Mask and the Mirror

In a cast circle, the participants enter wearing masks of their own creation, covered by see-through lace or black veils. In the process, the group can invite whatever deity or deities they feel may aid this journey. My own group chose Echo and Venus.

I suggest the "white generic" full face masks usually sold at most hobby shops because they can easily be drawn upon with a permanent marker. Before the ritual, the wearer draws, paints, or adds a set facial expression that most closely identifies how that person feels about touch contact.

As a low and soft drum beat commences, a full length mirror is placed in the direction of the West (water), situated so that the full body can be shown in its reflection.

Each participant, in turn, stands before the mirror and raises or removes their veil. As they gaze into the mirror, they hold a conversation with the reflection. They are free to comment on how the expression of the mask got there, what they like (or don't like) about that expression, and what they would like to do differently (or not) about how they view touch contact. Upon conclusion, they return to their previous position in the circle, still wearing their mask.

When the last participant has finished, the drumming stops. One at a time, the participants step into the circle's center, surrounded by the others. As they remove their mask, they speak their intention to change... or not. Respecting that person's decision, the rest of the group touches that person as invited and within their own comfort levels, being careful not to exceed the mandate. The kind of touch that the participant invites can be anything: a handshake, a caress, a body hug or beyond.

At the conclusion of the ritual, the group joins hands. The masks are laid on the main altar or in the direction of the North (earth). Participants may recite something to this effect:

"We are the Mask and the Mirror. We are the Agents of Change. Perfect Love and Trust is our Goal. We Bless Each Other with the Gift of Touch."

The circle is closed and released, or other functions can occur. I suggest a social time with refreshments to process the event.

Web of Flesh/Web of Now

This is a variation of a ritual performed for a Beltane celebration by the "Web of Oz" community near Lawrence, Kansas in 1987. Acknowledgment is extended to HPS Sue Westwind Elkins, who helped craft the core concepts for this ritual. (I say "a variation," because in the time since this ritual was enacted, the dominant gender paradigm and its traditional "balance," defined as male/female, has—thankfully!—been challenged. Feel free to adapt the ritual further for a more inclusive and open model.)

Beltane is a great time to challenge conventional negative views about touch contact. With the observation that, for our group, men were more likely to approach women and other men sexually than women were, our group came up with the idea of turning the tables, so to speak. Here's how this was accomplished:

When the Maypole dance concluded, the men who wanted to participate in the event were placed in an inner circle, facing outwards from the now-bedecked Maypole. (For your group, this might be anyone who is comfortable with the idea of the ritual and considers themselves sexually assertive—I encourage celebrating diversity here!) Each man linked arms behind them with those on their left and right. This made the use of the hands impossible. Following that, each man was also blindfolded. No peeking allowed... these actions in and of themselves elicited some interesting commentary from everyone.

When the drums commenced, the outer participants were allowed to choose from pre-written messages printed on business cards. They were allowed to take as many cards as they wanted. These messages can vary. We had one that read: *I would love to go explore in the woods with you. We owe each other the courtesy of an answer. So please say "No, thank you" or, hopefully, "Yes."*

Another read: *Let us share in the feast: I will feed you and you me. We owe each other the courtesy of an answer. So please say "No, thank you" or, hopefully, "Yes."*

Lastly, a blank card was offered for a more personal message. I will leave it up to the ritual creators to come up with differing touch variation cards.

As the music began, the outer participants danced sunwise around in a circle, feeling free to go up to any subject of the inner circle to place a card (or not) where the inner participant could retrieve it afterwards. The outer participants also tickled, caressed, or fondled the objects of their interest. The inner circle members were instructed to holler "YIKES!" as a safety word to indicate the action(s) might be going too far. In our event, we didn't hear that uttered very often!

When the outer dancers finished with their "selections," they left the outer circle. As the last participant finished, the music stopped and the inner circle was free to remove their blindfolds and detach hands.

For a pre-arranged amount of time (think of this as "speed dating Pagan style"), the inner circle members were permitted to try to track down the people from the outer circle who placed the messages. This activity can also be woven into the feast after the dance. Enjoy the (often hilarious) outcomes.

Breathe Hope

Life can be defined as a series of breaths: The first one when you are born, the last one when you die. In between the breath is creation. In between the breath is inspiration. In between the breath is revelation.

Hope rises as a bubble out of infinite possibilities, drifting in any and all directions, ready to burst at an unknown moment, born out of a breath and ending out of hope's desire to return to the unseen, the intangible... and work its magic upon us.

This ritual requires all participants to be skyclad, in itself a considerable act of trust. For me, ritual nudity is about body acceptance and equality. The most obvious thing about nudity is that the social masks we all carry are stripped off along with clothing.

The ritual also requires a massage table, enough sheets to provide fresh linen for each participant, a chalice with either almond or (even better) coconut oil, antiseptic hand wash, and towels. There should be at least five participants. When our group tried this, we had over twenty!

After casting the circle and draping the table, one participant lies on the table face down. As one body, the rest anoint their hands with oil, chanting words to the effect of "Body/Mind/Spirit: We are One." As a single entity, the hands are lowered and simply held, covering as much skin area as possible. An officiant leads the group to breathe in unison, drawing up energy from the Earth and down through the hands.

Upon the completion of seven deep breaths, the participant turns over, face up. Again, the same pattern is enacted: oil, chant, laying of hands, breath. At the conclusion of the seventh breath, the hands are slid under the person's back, supporting the neck, pelvis, and legs.

Taking a deep breath, each person lifts up the participant onto their fingertips and, again in unison, they chant, "As above, so below... We are one!" This is followed by a simple mantra such as "Om." When the energy wave peaks, the participant is lowered to the table. The hands are, once more, simply supportive. Allow for a period of silence, then signal everyone to remove their hands as one body, shaking out any excess energy and grounding. The hands are cleaned with the antiseptic, the sheet is replaced, and another participant is brought through the same experience.

Use this ritual as a basic template. The actual choice of words, chants, or mantras I leave up to the participants. Practice with different methods of raising the energy and grounding through breath. Upon completion, release the circle and serve something soothing, such as a chamomile tea. Allow time for processing the feelings, positive or negative, that the exercise produces.

This ritual resembles the Eleusinian Mysteries in that each person's experience is different and every individual interprets the energies from a unique perspective. Use it as a stepping stone to explore deeper avenues of positive touch and consent culture development.

A Guided Image Journey for Beltane

Special thanks go to priestess/musician Lady Isadora for her album *The Witching Hour,* which inspired the phrasing in this ritual. Ideally, for this rite the Maypole is already in place and the ribbons have been secured to the pole. If the ribbons are long enough, they are tied around the waists of each participant, linking their individual energies to the Maypole itself.

Participants sit on the ground, facing out, shoulder to shoulder with others to form a circle. The knees, if possible, connect. Hands are folded in the lap. Voice may be pre-recorded with music; the drum can be live or also pre-recorded.

"Close your eyes and get comfortable. Take a deep breath, exhale, and relax. Feel the drumbeat slow your heartbeat, feel the fire that is your divine spark, ignited and alive in front of you. Feel the warmth and protection of your fellow travelers seated beside you... for we will all face the Beltane Fire together."

(several drumbeats / breaths go by...)

"In your mind's eye, you step out of the night sky. The stars glow like enchanted fireflies as you move onto soft grasses, noting the scent of fragrant flowers, of your washed skin's own scent. You are now walking slowly, comfortable in your own body, happy with the way you stride. You are confident, almost tingling with excitement about this special evening."

(several drumbeats go by...)

"In the distance there is a raised hill, ringed in candlelight, illuminated with a central fire. A couple, shimmering by the flames, slowly turn to await you to join them. To your delight, it is playful Pan—that horned and randy goat of animal fertility—and his consort for the evening, the Star Goddess, tonight as Queen of Love and Pleasure. They are just as breathtaking as you imagined them to be, as voluptuous, as enticing as any fantasy lover you could imagine. They greet you each with a gentle kiss and bid you to sit with them."

(several drumbeats go by, slightly elevated... participants now clasp hands, allowing them to rest in their respective laps)

"The Star Goddess leans towards you and whispers gently: 'Great Pan and I have shared our love of *you*, Child of Human Loins. It pleases us both that you honor us with your visit here, and we bring you Beltane blessings. We desire to be with you, to share with you all the joy and bliss that is Life and the Sacred Fire that burns within you. Journey with us now, share with us your Heart's Delight."

(several drumbeats go by, elevating slowly, slightly faster...)

"You focus on the warmth of the fire, on the fragrance of flesh and remember. You remember back to a moment in your life when longing left you trembling, when the need and hunger to merge with another cried out for fulfillment. Remember that moment: See its passion expressed in a kiss, a caress, a pulling towards. Remember the smell of that lover, the sweetness of that first taste like warm honey.

Remember your breath, speeding up with your heartbeat, losing itself in the rhythm and movement of your arms, your legs, your sex.

"You look into the eyes of that lover and see all the stars of creation, all the lives you have lived and will live once more, all the blood in your loins that tells you: You are alive. You are desired. You are the Sun and Moon and Earth. You are the Tree and Stone and River."

(drums move faster, building... hands now caress the other participants' hands, as sensuous in the touch response as possible)

"You remember that you have emerged from a place of pain into light, from the darkness of the winter bones into the embrace of divine ecstasy. You remember whether it was once yet to be or a hundredfold loves in the past that each time you willingly consented, each time you chose to be a lover—be it with yourself or another—each act affirmed your Divine Essence, your fluid state of grace."

(drums moving towards crescendo.. .the hands now become firm, fingers interlaced, the palms slapping into each other simulating the act of coitus)

"You remember: with your breath drawn tight, your blood pounding hard, your pelvis shaking. *You remember Him, remember Her, remember Them, remember YOU!*"

(drums fully built up...)

"And you answer them back across the Bridge of All Space and Time."

(All chant, volume increasing: "Yes! Yes! Yes! Yes! Yes! Yessssssssss!")

(Drums recedes, beat slows down to a crawl. The hands release from the pounding palms and return to casual contact, fingertips grazing each other, lost in languishment)

"Your racing heart now slows... the dance of life is restored. Push that release of energy, that thought of release down your spine, out your base and into sacred Earth, ready to add your nourishment to her seasonal purpose."

(Drums return to original beat)

"Now Pan addresses you, saying: 'Child of Human Loins, we do thank you for your offering of remembrance... for Oh! It is good to commune in your presence."

(Goddess:) "We bring you the kiss of life, of love, of joy on this Earth."

(Goddess and God together:) "And remember always: we will be here, waiting for you, at the end of your desire."

(drums pause, begin again slowly)

"...and now you rise, relaxed and refreshed, taking a deep breath. You return how you entered before, but not before looking back over your shoulder for one last stolen glance as you see the Lord and Lady embracing, joined together and merged once more into the fire of creation. They pause, cast you a smile and resume their dance, the dance of creation of which you are part. You take another slow breath, moving your legs, arms, neck, and slowly ascend back into that starry field of night. You open your eyes now—see the flame before you. You are now ready... to join the dance."

Participants may now rise with ribbons (if attached) for the Maypole dance.

Conclusion

There are, of course, many elements other than touch-positive ritual that are needed to develop healthy consent culture. Trust is built slowly, and each of us has to determine what barriers to lower and when. Yet it is within the community created by a circle, drawn from each memory and pulled from each heart, that change occurs. May these rituals in some small way contribute.

Blessings in Her Many Names.

A true child of the Aquarian Age, **B. B. Blank** (also known as Dreamer) grew up in the heart of San Francisco's 1960s counter-cultural explosion. An initiate into the Reclaiming tradition at Starhawk's "Witch Camp" starting in the 1980s, he co-created the "Web of Oz" of Lawrence, Kansas and the first Heartland Pagan Festival while being a foot soldier in anti-war, environmental, GLBT, and pro-feminist politics. Bruce resides in Wichita, Kansas where he acts as caretaker for Ma'at's Temple, an outdoor Wicca sanctuary that hosts regular Pagan community events and produces documentaries and short film subjects under "Nature's Revenge Films." He is currently trying to adjust to being a new grandfather.

Appendices

Additional Resources

Editor's Note:

For web resources, we have given the current URL as of late 2015. Since URLs tend to change, however, we suggest doing a web search using the document's full title if you find one of these pages to be inactive.

Consent Culture

+ *PaganConsentCulture.com* Support website for this collection. Check it out for a free study guide, additional web resources, model safeguarding policies, workshop materials, and more.

+ *Yes Means Yes! Visions of Female Sexual Power & A World Without Rape.* Jaclyn Friedman and Jessica Valenti, eds. Berkeley, CA: Seal Press, 2008. Highly recommended introduction to sexual ethics and consent culture that includes perspectives from various gender identities, racial and ethnic backgrounds, and sexualities.

Model Policies

+ *Geek Feminism Wiki Conference Anti-Harassment Policy.* An example anti-harassment policy originally designed for technology conferences, but which can be easily adapted to festivals and other events. Website: http://geekfeminism.wikia.com/wiki/ Conference_anti-harassment/Policy

+ *Unitarian Universalist Association Youth – Inclusion and Safety Guidelines for Staff.* An example policy for leader-youth interaction. The "Adults in the Company of Youth" and "Adults Responsible for Youth" sections will be particularly relevant to Pagan organizers of large events. Website: http://www.uua.org/sites/live-new.uua.org/ files/documents/yaya/youth_inclusion_guidelines.pdf

- *Unitarian Universalist Association Manual: Keeping Children Safe in Congregations.* Provides information and procedures for leaders dealing with the potential presence of sex offenders in their communities. Website: http://www.uua.org/safe/children

Organizations

- *Rape, Abuse and Incest National Network (RAINN)*
  Largest anti-sexual assault organization in the USA.
  Website: https://rainn.org/

- *Rape Crisis England and Wales, Rape Crisis Scotland*
  Specialist services for women and girls who have been raped and/or experienced any other form of sexual violence at any time in their lives. Websites: http://rapecrisis.org.uk/
  http://www.rapecrisisscotland.org.uk/

- *ChildLine (UK)*
  Service for children who are in danger of physical or sexual abuse.
  Website: http://www.childline.org.uk/

Paganism 101

- Aburrow, Yvonne. "Paganism for Beginners" series. *Dowsing for Divinity* blog on the Patheos.com Pagan channel. 2015.
  Website: http://www.patheos.com/blogs/sermonsfromthemound/tag/beginners-guide/

- BBC religions. "Paganism." 2014.
  Website: http://www.bbc.co.uk/religion/religions/paganism/

- Higginbotham, Joyce & River. *Paganism: An Introduction to Earth-centered Religions.* 2002. Llewellyn Publications.

- Harvard Pluralism Project. "Paganism." *America's Many Religions.*
  2013.Website: http://pluralism.org/religion/paganism

Sample Handout: Tradition-Specific Consent Culture Class

From the Editors: This handout for a one-hour class on Wicca and Consent Culture is provided as an example. Readers are invited to adapt the text to their own tradition(s) or to use it as given.

Wicca and Consent Culture

What is consent?

+ Consent draws its moral force from the idea that individual freedom and autonomy is a basic human right. Consent cannot be given to acts that destroy that autonomy.

+ Consent must be informed, with both parties fully understanding the activities they are agreeing to perform and their risks;

+ Consent must be enthusiastic and intentional, not being used as a bargaining chip;

+ Consent must be voluntary, not compromised by the threat of force or harm;

+ Consenting individuals must be competent (not intoxicated, under extreme emotional duress, underage, etc.).

(Definition paraphrased from ethicist Morten Ebbe Juul Nielsen.)

What is consent culture?

A consent culture is one where the prevailing narrative of sex is based around enthusiastic mutual consent, rather than conquest or other objectifying narratives. Additionally, in a consent culture, consent is a concern in all social interactions. Empathy and respect for individual autonomy (bodily and otherwise) are central values.

In order for consent between individuals to be as clear and uncompromised as possible, the entire group or community must be committed to good consent practices. Good consent practices are difficult to maintain when the surrounding culture normalizes boundary violation, encourages shame about sexuality or bodies, or treats people as objects.

What aspects of Wicca support consent culture?

- The Rede: Harm none.

- The concept of Will or True Will: we respect others' sovereignty (and our own).

- All acts of love and pleasure are My rituals: pleasurable touch requires consent.

- My law is love unto all beings: we need empathy and clear communication to understand how to treat others lovingly.

How do you exchange valid consent to touch (or other activities)?

- Set clear expectations for what the activity will involve.

- Explicitly acknowledge that non-participation is appropriate and acceptable.

- Ask and accept verbally if possible, especially with people you don't know well, but also watch for nonverbal cues (throwing one's arms open for a hug = yes; dropping the eyes and turning the body away = no).

- Respect refusals; don't accuse others of prudishness or of being party poopers, and don't allow others to do so.

- If you are being asked for consent, take responsibility for getting all your questions answered.

- For taboo or highly-charged activities, avoid asking for consent from a group rather than from individuals (don't risk someone passively going along because everyone else is).

+ If you are uncomfortable, tell someone you trust as soon as possible; if you trust no one present, remove yourself from the situation immediately.

What common situations can make it difficult for individuals to give enthusiastic consent or unambiguous refusal to touch (or other activities)?

+ Social conventions: people participate because it is expected, not because it is desired.

+ Ambiguity around boundaries: people may be uncertain about what constitutes proper behavior, especially if they are new to a group.

+ Lack of experience with consent practices: people may find it embarrassing or awkward to ask verbally for consent or turn down touch if they have never done so before.

+ Lack of self-regard: people may fail to enforce boundaries because they want acceptance or attention, or struggle to assert themselves out of fear of offending others.

+ Power dynamic: people may fear loss of status in a group, rejection by an admired authority figure, or other consequences if they refuse or limit participation.

+ Abuse history: people who have been abused may find it difficult to determine whether or not they want touch or how they will feel when an activity occurs.

What kinds of situations might require good consent practices?

+ Negotiating touch (such as greeting hugs or kisses) with a new friend or new dating partner.

+ Taking on a new group member. Group leaders should be responsible for briefing the new member on group practices (in general and especially around touch), finding out if the new member has any special needs, and communicating those to the group.

- Rituals can be emotionally intense. Even having seen a ritual script, participants cannot know how a ritual will affect them in the moment. Especially for rituals that include taboo acts or subject matter (sexual imagery or acts, drugs and alcohol, nudity, dominance/submission imagery, scourging, etc.), participants should be reminded that they can seek help or withdraw at any time. Implicit social pressure and being in a trance state can influence people to remain in a ritual space that is psychologically unsafe for them. It is important to set participants' expectations as accurately as possible before the ritual begins and explicitly describe the process by which they can withdraw. Participants must understand that withdrawing is really okay and that the offer is not just a formality. (Ritual leaders might, for example, model the process of approaching a ritual leader for help or to be cut out of circle, or model stepping back from the ritual to sit to the side.)

What if a new group member is uncomfortable with standard Wiccan practices?

Getting consent shouldn't be rushed. A group member should not be pressured to engage in touch or other practices with which they feel uncomfortable. Groups should be open to accommodating members' special needs. However, if a person does not desire to become comfortable with a group's traditional practices, the group is probably not a good fit.

The Earth Religion Anti-Abuse Resolution (1988)

Editor's note: This statement was written by Morning Glory Zell. At the time of its publication in 1991, it had been formally endorsed by the Pagan Ways festival, Heartland Pagan Gathering, and Pagan Spirit Gathering, along with over one hundred Pagan organizations and individuals in positions of leadership. The copy of the statement from which the text here is drawn was part of a law enforcement handbook entitled Witchcraft, Satanism, and Occult Crime: Who's Who and What's What *(4ᵗʰ edition), distributed by* Green Egg. *The endorsements were followed by a list of Pagan therapists willing to volunteer their services to adult survivors of ritual abuse.*

The statement is reprinted by permission of Oberon Zell.

To Whom It May Concern:

Two disturbing trends that have been growing in the United States—1) that there has been a rise in violent criminal activity with Satanic ritualistic overtones, and 2) that some fundamentalist Christian groups have been spreading false and malicious statements about Witchcraft, Paganism and Earth Religions to media and law enforcement personnel attributing such crimes to Witches and Pagans—have made it necessary for the Pagan and Wiccan community to delineate our position to local, state and Federal levels of government. This Resolution was first conceived, written and presented at the Ancient Ways gathering in Northern California on May 22, 1988, and has been successively modified to incorporate input from the Pagan community. This final version now continues to be reprinted and circulated to help clarify the fact that Witches and Pagans are not Satanists and do not engage in abusive or criminal activities. Please share this information with law enforcement officials, educators and media.

The Earth Religion Anti-Abuse Resolution

We, the undersigned, as adherents of Pagan and Neo-Pagan Earth Religions, including Wicca, or Neo-Pagan Witchcraft, practice a variety of positive, life-affirming faiths that are dedicated to healing, both of ourselves and of the Earth. As such, we do not advocate or condone any acts that victimize others, including those proscribed by law. As one of our most widely-accepted precepts is the Wiccan Rede's injunction to "harm none," we absolutely condemn the practices of child abuse, sexual abuse, and any other form of abuse that does harm to the bodies, minds or spirits of individuals. We offer prayers, therapy and support for the healing of the victims of such abuses. We recognize and revere the divinity of Nature in our Mother the Earth, and we conduct our rites of worship in a manner that is ethical, compassionate and Constitutionally-protected. We neither acknowledge nor worship the Christian devil, "Satan," who is not in our Pagan pantheons. We will not tolerate slander or libel against our churches, clergy or congregations, and we are prepared to defend our civil rights with such legal action as we deem necessary and appropriate.

A Pagan Community Statement on Religious Sexual Abuse (2009)

Editor's Note: This statement and accompanying commentary is reprinted by permission of the statement facilitator, Brendan Myers. We have edited it minimally from its original electronic format.

Following the call for a universal statement of condemnation of sexual abuse, which first appeared on The Wild Hunt blog, a gathering of volunteers and I have now crafted the final version of the text. The full text appears below.

This text came about after a vigorous, productive, and at times intense three-week process. Passing through four "cycles" in which a draft of the text was subject to the criticisms and revisions of all the volunteers, we think we have achieved about as much of a consensus on this text as we are likely to get. Integrating various important considerations, such as the variety and multiplicity of moral views within Paganism's many communities, the need for grammatical and stylistic correctness, the need for moral decisiveness, and for rhetorical and exhortative strength, has not been an easy task. But together we have produced a statement of moral agreement which we are prepared to sign our names to, and stand by. We hope that you agree.

At this time, I am happy to hand the reins of leadership on this project back to Jason Pitzl-Waters, author of The Wild Hunt blog, where the project began. May I say that it has been a privilege and an honour to host this process on my forum and to work with all of you. I am confident that the public reception will be good, and that it will generate wide support in the Pagan community and beyond.

—Brendan Myers

Part 1

1. We are here: A circle of spiritual people from many traditions, groves, hearths, and circles. We are young and old, from many walks of life, and many parts of the world. We are Pagans of the modern era, Druids, Heathens, Wiccans, Witches, Shamans, practitioners of

magical lore, and many more paths besides these. We walk the paths of the sacred Earth, in the footsteps of the Goddesses and Gods of the Land, the Sea, the Sky, and the Tribe.

2. We have learned of recent incidents of sexual exploitation and abuse perpetrated by individuals claiming to be religious teachers, some of whom claimed to be members of our community. In response to these incidents, we have crafted this statement.

3. We hereby categorically reject, disavow, oppose, and repudiate any and all coerced, nonconsensual, harmful or exploitative sexual acts, especially when claimed to be part of our ways and traditions. We identify all such acts as sexual abuse, and we refuse to tolerate them in our community.

4. Many of us believe the human body is profoundly sacred. Many of us believe that the presence of the Divine dwells within in the body. We therefore find that human sexuality, and acts of love and pleasure between consenting, informed, and mature people, have great religious significance. We affirm the goodness of human sexuality, and the goodness of celebrating sexual identity.

5. Because of these beliefs, we also find that coerced, nonconsensual, harmful or exploitative sexual acts are extraordinary affronts to the Divine presence which dwells within every human body. These acts grievously harm the victim, and inflict deep wounds upon the sense of bodily identity which all of us hold so dear.

6. A sexual predator who exploits the relationship of trust that exists between teacher and seeker harms the whole religious community, and undermines the good work of the honourable teachers in our midst. Similarly, acts of sexual abuse between seekers in the same circle, whether one party is a teacher or not, also harm the whole community.

7. An accusation of sexual exploitation is a very serious matter. The accusation alone, even in the absence of evidence, can damage the reputation and the self-esteem of good people. We therefore find that a false or vindictive accusation of sexual misconduct is but another form of sexual abuse.

8. Yet we also recognize that real sexual abuse victims experience deep feelings of guilt and shame, and that they often struggle to admit that they have been abused. Their condition should not be made worse by a predisposition to doubt the validity of their claims. Nor should they be automatically counter-accused of having a vindictive intention, or of lying. We hold that anyone alleging sexual abuse should always be treated with compassion as a primary response, and that claims of sexual abuse should be handled with intelligence and concern for all.

9. We voluntarily commit ourselves to this declaration, and we encourage others to commit themselves to it, whatever their path.

Part 2

1. Our movement has many principles of moral thought, not just one singular monolithic principle. As there are many gods in the world, so there are many models of the good and worthwhile life for humankind. Some of us practice Heroic Virtue, others Classical virtue, others a Utilitarian principle such as the Wiccan Rede. There are also many among us who find that ethical principles are revealed through the intuition of a Divine presence that dwells within the human heart and mind. This presence unites us with the Earth, with each other, and with the cosmos.

2. Among our many traditions, groves, hearths, circles, and communities, there are broad areas of moral agreement. For the purpose of this statement, we (the authors and the undersigned) wish to emphasize the matter of sexual abuse. We agree to the broad and general principle that the human body is a sacred temple, a work of art, and a good home for the self and the soul. Many of us believe that the body is the dwelling-place of the Divine, and the seat of a deeply integrated web of relations which ultimately includes the whole of life on Earth. The human body is thus among the first of all things that deserve our care and respect. On this principle, the differences between our various circles tend to be only a matter of emphasis. Indeed, on this principle, we may share some moral agreement with the dominant

religious traditions of our dominant culture: the view that the body is made in the image of the Divine.

3. In our circles, the sacredness of the body, as a religious truth, leads to positive conclusions about human sexuality. Our view is that sexuality, sexual identity, sexual expression, and acts of love and pleasure, between consenting, informed, and mature people, have great religious significance. Indeed such acts can take on the significance of ritual. We hold that our sexual identities are worthy of celebration. And for many of us, an occasion of shared sexual pleasure and lovemaking is a most spiritually meaningful event: a communion with the Divine which dwells within ourselves and within each other.

4. Indeed, there are some traditions in which a sexual act is performed as part of some rituals, such as higher-level initiations. Various names designate these rituals: Hieros Gamos, the Great Marriage, or the Great Rite, to name a few. In most cases, the Great Marriage is performed "in token": for instance, a priest touches the tip of a wand or a blade to the bottom of a chalice held by a priestess. This is an ancient gesture, with precedents in the ancient cultures of the Greeks, the Romans, the Hindus, and other great civilizations of the distant past.

5. Naturally, given our perspective on the sacredness of the body, our view is that all coerced, nonconsensual, harmful or exploitative sexual acts, are seriously morally wrong. We find that sexual exploitation and violence are particularly worse than other forms of criminality, such as property offences, because sexual offences invade the body. Sexual abuse ignores the sacredness of the body, and ignores the privacy, the dignity, and the freedom of the victim to use and delight in his or her own body. It is an extraordinary affront to the Divine presence which dwells within every human body and which animates the body with goodness. It severely harms the victim, and degrades the dignity of both victim and offender. Sexual abuse also inflicts deep wounds upon the precious sense of bodily identity which all of us hold so dear. No exceptions or relativist interpretations can alter the basic moral wrongness of sexual exploitation and violence.

We identify all such acts as sexual abuse, and we refuse to tolerate them in our community.

6. Thus in our contemporary circles, the rite of the Great Marriage, if it is not performed in token, is held privately and by invitation only. The participants come in full knowledge of what they have been invited to. If there are any initiatory "surprises," they are never intended to violate the sacredness of the seeker's body. Ideally, the invitees already know, love, and trust one another. They have already given their informed consent, and retain the right to withdraw from the event without prejudice at any time. When we mix sexuality with religion, there is no space for deception or coercion. Religious sexuality is always consensual and never obligatory. No one should enter a circle with eyes covered when sexuality, sexual identity, and the sanctity of his or her own body is put to a test. This remains true even when the ritual participants are not strangers to each other. Initiatory surprises, tests, and ordeals are intended to help a seeker find the sacred within him or herself. If they threaten or invade that self, then the initiators are harming, and not helping, the seeker.

7. If someone finds a private group's practices uncomfortable, he or she is always free to find another group to join. It is wrong to hold someone back from spiritual progress or knowledge for refusing to participate in a sexual act. We are always right to doubt the sincerity, honour, and spirituality of someone who claims that a sexual act is a mandatory requirement for initiation, or for any kind of relationship with the gods, goddesses, or deities.

8. An accusation of sexual exploitation is a very serious matter. The accusation alone, even in the absence of evidence, can damage the reputation and the self-esteem of good people. We therefore find that a false or vindictive accusation of sexual misconduct is another form of sexual abuse.

9. Yet we also recognize that real sexual abuse victims experience deep feelings of guilt and shame, and that they often struggle to admit that they have been abused. Their condition should not be made worse by a predisposition doubt the validity of their claims. Nor should they be automatically counter-accused of having a vindictive

intention, or of lying. We hold that anyone alleging sexual abuse should always be treated with compassion as a primary response, and that claims of sexual abuse should be handled with intelligence and concern for all.

10. It is clear that one need not be a spiritual person to recognize the wrongness of sexual abuse. Yet we are especially outraged when the perpetrator is a leader or a teacher in a religious community. In our circles, religious teachers are held in high esteem. A seeker who approaches a teacher in search of spiritual guidance and comfort offers a special kind of trust to the teacher. Teachers and seekers often open their hearts and minds to each other, and thus they become very vulnerable. It is for this reason many of our traditions require teachers to possess not only great knowledge, but also great integrity and honour. It is also for this reason that sexual predators will pose as religious teacher: in that way, they may find more victims for their gratification. There are also some teachers who, exploiting the trust given them, become sexual predators as well.

11. Furthermore, a person who uses this relationship of trust to exploit people thus harms the whole social environment in which teaching and seeking take place. For the sexual predator's harm touches more than just the victim. It affects all the victim's friends, family members, fellow seekers in the same circle, colleagues at work, and anyone to whom the victim may turn for help. The harm of sexual abuse thus affects numerous other people who the predator may not know, nor ever meet. Moreover, sexual abuse also casts suspicion and doubt on the intentions of the honourable teachers in our midst, undermining the good work that they do.

12. Finally a sexual predator can sometimes exploit the relations of trust that grow between fellow seekers in the same tradition, hearth, or circle, even when he or she does not pose as a teacher. This kind of exploitation also harms the whole community. In all cases, we maintain our condemnation of unwanted sexual acts.

Therefore, we, the authors and signatories of this statement, commit ourselves to:

* Demonstrate by example a fully moral sexual spirituality;
* Vigorously entreat others to agree to the principles of this statement;
* Handle all accusations of sexual exploitation and misconduct with intelligence and compassion, for victims of real sexual harm, and for victims of false or vindictive accusations;
* Cooperate with the police when an incident of sexual abuse in our circles is under investigation;
* Help bring comfort, medical assistance, legal aid, and spiritual healing, to victims, as far as ability and opportunity may allow; and
* Help seekers find groups, circles, traditions, or individual teachers, whose practice involves as much or as little sexuality as the seeker feels comfortable exploring.

We voluntarily commit ourselves to this declaration, and we encourage others to commit themselves to it, whatever their path.

We remain, respectfully,

A community of Pagans.

Postscript by Brendan Myers (2014)[1]

With the revelation that the well-known Pagan musician and author Kenny Klein had confessed to possessing child pornography, a criminal offence, there's been a little bit of renewed interest in the "Community Statement on Religious Sexual Abuse" which I helped to write, back in back in 2009.

I'd like to say a few words about what happened to it.

---

[1] Originally published at
   http://www.brendanmyers.net/blog/2014/03/whatever-happened-to-the-Pagan-community-statement-on-religious-sexual-abuse/.

The version of the piece which appears on my web site[2] is the most up-to-date version that there is. No further work was done on it since that time, because *most of the various contributors and critics had lost the will to continue with it.* There was a lot of disagreement, often angry disagreement, about whether the statement went too far, or didn't go far enough, and so on. I've included below a list of the common criticisms, as I saw them on Jason Pitzl-Waters' blog, and on my own website forum (which I've since taken down, to stop the spambots from filling it with 419 scams). But there's one group of criticisms that I'd like to draw special attention to.

There were *a lot of angry voices who continued to demand the right to perform sexual acts as part of initiation ceremonies, even when the inductee would not be warned in advance about the nature of the ceremony, and even when the inductee was legally a minor.* The most common argument in favour of that position was an appeal to tradition, which is normally a fallacy of logic. Some said that initiatory surprise was an important part of the drama and the power of the ritual, and that therefore initiatory surprise had to be preserved, even when it involved a sexual act. Some also justified it by saying that if they were disallowed from performing such a ritual, that would be an unjust limitation upon their personal freedom. Some people even went so far as to claim that the utterance of any moral statement, or even ordinary moral indicator-words like "should," constitutes oppression on someone, somewhere, somehow. Even when the "should" was a condemnation of sexual abuse. Some voices really were that absolute with their rejection of all ethical propositions.

Frankly, I think a lot of these arguments are nothing more than *a kind of cover-up or a justification for a situation that can be far too easily twisted into a criminal act.* I think that no tradition, however old, can be ethically acceptable if it permits such surprises on its initiates, or keeps secrets from them about whether they would have to undergo a sexual act in their initiation. And I think that if someone seriously and

---

[2] Not currently available. The latest version of the text appears above.

truly believes that he can harm others and ignore their feelings and rights, all in the name of his personal freedom, well then he has simply not learned the first thing about ethics.

But when I raised these objections, my voice was drowned in all the shouting about the importance of initiatory surprise and craft secrecy. And I eventually gave up trying. There's no sense in debating someone who only wants to shout about how right he is and how oppressed he feels when someone raises a criticism. It's worth noting that I wasn't always the most polite debater around the table. I apologized for it back then; I do so again now. But nonetheless, the strong resistance against the statement, in the name of tradition and freedom, left me feeling disenchanted with the Pagan community. For a long time I doubted whether I should remain part of it.

But I still think the statement is important. I'd like to see it spread around, talked about, argued about, modified by different groups to suit their specific needs and priorities, and incorporated into the policies of any Pagan organization which offers teaching, or public services, or which collects money from members.

A Record of the Main Concerns and Criticisms of the Statement

(Asterisks indicate the seriousness of the concern, as indicated by the comments of others agreeing with it, or noting a similar concern.)

+ Fear of coercion into signing the statement. **

+ "Harm" undefined, and may include BDSM practices **
  (although the discussion produced reasons to keep the word 'harm' undefined).

+ Remove the word "harm" altogether. ***

+ The Wiccan Rede is "not utilitarian"; remove the word "utilitarian."

- Stronger statement that sex with children/teenagers/legal minors is wrong; that children are unable to give consent. ****
A suggested text: "We recognize all laws related to minors and sexual activity. As minors are legally unable to give consent to sexual activities, we consider all sexual actions with minors to be non-consensual, and therefore they are not to be tolerated within our community."

- Also a statement about the problems of children who witness (if not participate in) sexual acts.

- Brendan's "pet theory being passed off as universally accepted truth."

- "Vigorously entreat others to agree" may seem too evangelical, too close to proselytizing. *** A suggested alternative: "sincerely entreated to consider the principles of the statement."

- "No one should enter a circle with eyes covered when…" this line may seem to condemn common skyclad/blindfold initiations.

- Various attachments could be appended, including:

    - Definition of sexual abuse applicable to a variety of contexts, with contrasting crucial common denominators of healthy relationships (such as but not limited to sensible boundaries and the need for *consistent* boundaries).

    - Fact: sexual abuse crosses social, cultural, religious, financial, political, academic/intelligence, and other boundaries.

    - Sexual abuse rates of children.

    - A quality list of warning signs of a pedophile.

    - Sexual abuse clearly categorized as not a crime of passion or attraction but as one of power and control.

- Practical steps as to how to protect children. People need to know what to do, why to do it, and how to apply what they've learned.

  - An ongoing outlet for open dialog with which to process the above.

- What happens if a sexual predator steps up to sign the pledge?

- A firm rejection of the use of cultural or historical precedents to justify pederasty and sexual abuse generally.

- Strangeness of saying "X is bad" without committing to take action against someone who does X. Puzzlement concerning a disconnect between "X is bad" and "We should intervene to stop X from happening."

- Some Pagans believe the body is not sacred/not made in the image of the divine. ****

- A possible alternative: "Human beings contain the essence of the divine."

- The victim of a false accusation of abuse should not be conflated with a victim of actual sexual abuse. **

- Need for a brief section which defines major terms.

- Document too long, too wordy. **

- Danger of going into too much detail over various Pagan sexual practices such as certain kinds of initiation: it risks "providing fodder for those who would like to sensationalize the Pagan movement." ***

- A suggested change/addition: "We as individual Pagans of many paths (and where appropriate representing our covens, groups, clans and tribes) find sexual abuse, rape, and molestation to be immoral. We agree to act with upstanding integrity in the care of the victims, and in the prevention of future victimization."

- "Commitment to cooperate with police" doesn't go far enough. Should also include commitment to report allegations of criminal conduct to police, especially when minors are involved.

- The phrase "sexual predator" too sex-negative.

- The phrase "some of whom claimed to be members of our community" may be misleading, as some sex offenders are members of our community.

- Alternative possibility: "Recent incidents and allegations of sexual abuse in the guise of religious leadership or instruction prompted us to look carefully at our own community, its history, and its practices to assure the safety of its members and the children in their lives. This statement is our response."

- Too much extraneous info about multiple aspects of Paganism

- Section 7 is rape apologism. *****

- Only one commentator that I saw articulated a support for sec. 7 as it stands now.

- Need for a professional grammar proofreader.

- Naming various trads in the first section insufficiently inclusive: it can appear as if the trads that are named are important enough, and others are not.

- Statement claims to be speaking on behalf of everyone "with just enough weasel-words to not be lying outright."

- If timing of statement is not relevant, then reference to "recent events" can be cut. **

- Sexual abuse as claimed to be part of a Pagan ritual is not worse than sexual abuse in any other context.

- Need for acknowledgement that sex abuse is emotionally, mentally, psychologically damaging, and not just an affront to the divine.

+ Sex abuse that affects community not worse than other sex abuse.

+ Danger of allowing local laws to decide what's ethical; although that does not mean people should break laws.

+ The statement should avoid mentioning legalities altogether, and stick to the moral.

+ Various discussions about the relation between morality and the law, esp. the age which the law in various jurisdictions fixes as the age of sexual consent.

+ Statement should mention spiritual practices that do not require sexual acts; needs affirmation that sexual acts are not necessary for fulfilling practice.

+ A suggested text for that purpose: "Some of us practice a deep and meaningful spirituality and communion with the Divine without performing any sexual acts as part of our rituals. We collectively recognize this as one possible way to practice and do not judge those rituals to be better or lesser than rituals that do include sexual acts."

+ Remove the word "guilt" from the statement about the feelings of sexual abuse victims. A suggested alternative: "We recognize that sexual abuse victims experience deep feelings of self-blame and shame, and that they often struggle to admit that they have been abused."

+ Statement could give advice to people who, upon reading the statement, "suddenly realize that what they experienced in a Pagan context was indeed sexual abuse."

+ The paragraph that begins "If someone finds a private group's practices uncomfortable, he or she is always free to find another group to join" need not say anything more than that first sentence.

CPSIA information can be obtained
at www.ICGtesting.com
Printed in the USA
LVHW091312251118
598196LV00001B/318/P